CIVIL RIGHTS IN BAKERS-FIELD

HISTORIA USA
A series edited by Luis Alvarez, Carlos Blanton, and Lorrin Thomas

Also in the series

Luis Alvarez, *Chicanx Utopias: Pop Culture and the Politics of the Possible*

Felipe Hinojosa, *Apostles of Change: Latino Radical Politics, Church Occupations, and the Fight to Save the Barrio*

Patricia Silver, *Sunbelt Diaspora: Race, Class, and Latino Politics in Puerto Rican Orlando*

Cristina Salinas, *Managed Migrations: Growers, Farmworkers, and Border Enforcement in the Twentieth Century*

Perla M. Guerrero, *Nuevo South: Latinas/os, Asians, and the Remaking of Place*

CIVIL RIGHTS IN BAKERSFIELD

Segregation and Multiracial Activism in the Central Valley

OLIVER A. ROSALES

University of Texas Press   *Austin*

Copyright © 2024 by the University of Texas Press
All rights reserved
Printed in the United States of America
First edition, 2024

Chapter 2 was originally published as "Civil Rights 'beyond the Fields': African American and Mexican American Civil Rights Activism in Bakersfield, California 1947–1964" from *Civil Rights and Beyond* edited by Brian D. Behnken, Copyright © 2016 by the University of Georgia Press. By permission of the University of Georgia Press.

Chapter 5 is used with permission of Taylor & Francis Group LLC–Books, from "The Chicano Movement: Perspectives from the Twenty-First Century" by Mario T. Garcia, Copyright 2014; permission conveyed through Copyright Clearance Center, Inc.

Requests for permission to reproduce material from this work should be sent to permissions@utpress.utexas.edu.

♾ The paper used in this book meets the minimum requirements of ANSI/NISO Z39.48-1992 (R1997) (Permanence of Paper).

Library of Congress Cataloging-in-Publication Data

Names: Rosales, Oliver, author.
Title: Civil rights in Bakersfield : segregation and multiracial activism in the Central Valley / Oliver A. Rosales.
Other titles: Segregation and multiracial activism in the Central Valley | Historia USA.
Description: First edition. | Austin : University of Texas Press, 2024. | Series: Historia USA | Includes bibliographical references and index.
Identifiers: LCCN 2023038654 (print) | LCCN 2023038655 (ebook)
    ISBN 978-1-4773-2959-7 (hardcover)
    ISBN 978-1-4773-2960-3 (pdf)
    ISBN 978-1-4773-2961-0 (epub)
Subjects: LCSH: Civil rights movements—California—Bakersfield—History. | Coalitions—California—Bakersfield—History. | Activism—California—Bakersfield—History. | Minority activists—California—Bakersfield—History. | Segregation—California—Bakersfield—History. | Bakersfield (Calif.)—Social conditions—History. | BISAC: HISTORY / United States / State & Local / West (AK, CA, CO, HI, ID, MT, NV, UT, WY) | SOCIAL SCIENCE / Race & Ethnic Relations
Classification: LCC F869.B16 R67 2024 (print) | LCC F869.B16 (ebook) | DDC 323.09794/88—dc23/eng/20231214
LC record available at https://lccn.loc.gov/2023038654
LC ebook record available at https://lccn.loc.gov/2023038655

doi:10.7560/329597

CONTENTS

Introduction   1

1. "A Laboratory of Races":
   Racial Segregation in Greater Bakersfield, 1870–1950   15

2. Civic Unity:
   Mexican Americans, African Americans, and Civil Rights Activism in Bakersfield, 1947–1964   47

3. "Maximum Feasible Participation" and Opposition:
   The War on Poverty in Kern County, 1964–1967   67

4. Agrarian Chicanismo:
   Jesus "Jess" Nieto and the Chicana/o Student Movement in Bakersfield   101

5. "Hoo-ray Gonzales!":
   Civil Rights Protest and Chicana/o Politics in Bakersfield, 1968–1974   123

6. Police Violence, Fair Media, Rural Health Care, and Civil Rights Activism in Greater Bakersfield   147

7. A New Battleground for Civil Rights:
   The Desegregation of the Bakersfield City School District, 1969–1984   179

Conclusion   213

Acknowledgments   223
Notes   227
Index   269

CIVIL RIGHTS IN BAKERS-FIELD

INTRODUCTION

In the late 1970s, California state senator Walter Stiern was honored by the United Food and Commercial Workers Union (UFCW) in Bakersfield, California. During introductory remarks, union president Mel Rubin spoke glowingly of Stiern, venerating the Democrat's legislative accomplishments over the previous two decades in Sacramento's tumultuous political environment. In the moderator's view, Stiern's historical legacy was secure. After the audience's enthusiastic welcome, the legislator smiled and quipped, "Thank you for your overly generous introduction. But I must tell you that a hundred years from now only two names [from Bakersfield] will still be remembered, Buck Owens and César Chávez."[1]

This book moves beyond Senator Stiern's prediction that only two names will be remembered from the Central Valley. It also moves beyond a polarized discussion of California's rural labor and civil rights history that focuses exclusively on the legacy of the United Farm Workers (UFW).[2] This book offers a more nuanced approach to the so-called rise-and-fall narrative of the UFW by offering a narrative of civil rights history in the San Joaquin Valley that goes *beyond* the fields. While an expansive historiography of the farmworker movement has centered the San Joaquin Valley within the story of California's labor and civil rights history, activism outside farm labor within the region remains largely unexplored. Excavating stories of activism beyond the fields more accurately characterizes the history of race, politics, and civil rights activism in this important region of California and the American West.

Known as the breadbasket of the United States, greater Bakersfield is rich in social and political history. The region is the historical home to the Yokut people and has seen migrant settlement from white gold-seekers, mestizos, and generations of immigrant groups, including southern white and Black populations, Basques and Chinese, and European hopefuls. This multiracial infusion created dynamic experiences in terms of political development and the influence of a southern cultural diaspora. Located in the southern San Joaquin Valley of California's Central Valley, Bakersfield has long been the home of American Far West conservatism. The legacy of the "Okie" (agricultural worker) migration of the 1930s and 1940s shaped the political and cultural history of Bakersfield during the latter half of the twentieth century.[3] "California's political transformation . . . is rooted in a natural disaster that happened over 80 years ago—the 'Dust Bowl,'" notes political scientist Adam J. Ramey. "Social and political attitudes among both whites . . . as well as Hispanics . . . has . . . affected everyone living in the former Okie heartland, irrespective of ethnic background."[4] The particular brand of Bakersfield conservatism, notes historian Thomas R. Wellock, is anti-statist, oriented toward localism and hostile toward state and federal government.[5] This conservatism helped shape activism by African American and ethnic Mexican residents both before and after Kern County became the center of a labor and civil rights struggle in September 1965, when Filipino and Mexican farmworkers organized a strike in Delano, just north of Bakersfield.[6] Within the context of the farm labor struggle in Kern County, Black and Brown activism flourished in the urban sector.

The civil rights history of California's San Joaquin Valley is a multiracial story marked by the growth of urban racial coalitions, particularly between Mexican American, African American, and white racial liberal allies in Bakersfield. Racial segregation was normative in greater Bakersfield during the first half of the twentieth century. Migration and settlement patterns of different racial and ethnic groups, first through railroad and agribusiness and later amid the Dust Bowl and Second World War, produced a unique racial geography in the southern San Joaquin Valley. Within a context of racial segregation, the formation of racial coalitions was not a foregone conclusion. Racial coalitions championed civil rights reform in urban Bakersfield during the heyday of the farmworker movement. Multiracial activists galvanized movement within urban and rural spaces, as well as engendered opposition forces hostile toward labor and civil rights reform.

As in the farmworker movement, racial coalitions in Bakersfield proved critical for advancing civil rights reform. African American and Mexican American activists built racial coalitions with white racial liberals to challenge racism and discrimination in Bakersfield and throughout Kern County in the post–World War II era. The most important urban coalition was the Kern Council for Civic Unity (KCCU). Representing a racially diverse coalition of organizations through the 1960s and 1970s, the KCCU was at the forefront of urban civil rights reform in Bakersfield and produced local activists who advanced a variety of social justice causes. These included struggles to integrate the housing and labor markets, ensure equitable access to city services, overturn racial segregation, and challenge a variety of racially discriminatory practices in greater Bakersfield. Grassroots activists involved themselves in organizing for local democratic politics, the War on Poverty, the burgeoning Chicana/o movement, and efforts to overturn racial segregation in local schools.

Bakersfield's civil rights history is complex and marked by both success and failure. Within a long-standing history of racial segregation, racial coalition activists championed civil rights reform. The eclipsing of Bakersfield's civil rights coalitions is not a narrative that can be evaluated strictly by the course of the farmworker movement. Ultimately, a multiracial urban civil rights history of Bakersfield better contextualizes the broad scope of civil rights reform and challenges activists faced in the San Joaquin Valley.

TOWARD A CENTRAL VALLEY HISTORIOGRAPHY

The history of civil rights in the twentieth-century United States is often framed within a Black-and-white racial binary, and limited spatially into southern and northern regional narratives. Historians more recently have uncovered the role of the multiracial West in shaping the course of US civil rights history. This book focuses on the importance of Bakersfield within this developing historiography of race and civil rights, specifically through examining Bakersfield's lost history of urban civil rights activism following World War II. These lost histories of multiracial activism in Bakersfield, the challenges activists faced in community organizing, and the legacies of coalition building in this important region of California inform this book.[7]

Since the early 2010s, there has been a rise in scholarship documenting the dynamic history of California's farmworker movement.[8] New scholarship has highlighted the UFW's impact as a labor and social justice movement, the union's forging of multiracial civil rights coalitions, and assessments of the UFW's alleged decline. Scholars have intervened to counterbalance what they characterize as a tendency among earlier UFW chroniclers toward hagiography and "search for heroes," to quote historian Matt Garcia.[9] The new UFW scholarship offers a more complete and nuanced understanding of the union, its leadership, and its rank and file. The thrust of this scholarship is a welcome intervention that more fully assesses the influence of the UFW and its vast activist networks in and beyond the fields.

This scholarship, however, lacks a postwar urban civil rights history of Bakersfield and its connection to the farmworker movement. The result is an obscured historiography that evaluates the civil rights legacy of California's San Joaquin Valley strictly through the lens of the farmworker movement. To better contextualize the history of the UFW, greater focus is needed on the long and diverse history of labor and civil rights reform throughout the racial frontiers of California's rural interior, or what historian Albert Camarillo has called America's "racial borderhoods." Specifically, the racially segregated spaces of southeast Bakersfield played a key role, along with rural Kern County, in fomenting a large-scale civil rights revolution in rural California.[10]

Although the Central Valley is understudied in comparison to other parts of California, scholars have established a framework for studying it.[11] Two strands of scholarship help contextualize civil rights history in the region: one focused on horticulturalist ideology, and the other on the rise of the UFW. The former establishes a foundation, both long term and short term, for understanding grower antipathy toward farm labor unionization. It also sheds light on the Republican emergence in central California, away from a New Deal Democratic base.[12]

The migration of Okies in the late 1930s and 1940s was arguably the most significant event to shape the modern history of the southern San Joaquin Valley. This migration affected the region's culture, reflecting a neo-southern diaspora in terms of politics, ideology, and racial thinking. Wellock captured this essence, writing that "urban Californians tend to think of the valley, especially Bakersfield, in southern-gothic stereotypes. . . . [White] Bakersfield has [often] been the state's scapegoat . . . for racism, violence, and reactionary political views."[13] The Okie migration influenced the development of country music in Bakersfield, a place musicologists refer to as Nashville West.[14] James N. Gregory's examination of outward migration from the American South confirms this analysis of the "southernization" of the western United States, first proffered in his landmark study *American Exodus*. Gregory wrote of Bakersfield in 1989 that "Okie subculture survives today. . . . Visit Bakersfield or one of the surrounding towns in the southern portion of the valley. . . . These days a Hispanic population shares these communities. . . . The political climate is . . . revealing. . . . The area votes for conservatives of either party who talk tough on defense, crime, and moral issues and who stay away from minority causes like school busing or Cesar Chavez's United Farm Workers."[15]

While Okie subculture developed California's multiracial interior, the influence of agrarian capitalism and political ideology was set in motion in the late nineteenth and early twentieth centuries. German immigrants Henry Miller and Charles Lux, who formed the Miller Lux Company in 1858, transformed the Central Valley, especially Kern County. David Igler notes that these "industrial cowboys" created a pattern of economic control that shaped the physical and social environment of the region. The deep social divisions and lack of corporate environmental restraints facilitated an economic and political trajectory where "wealth and power remained with those who could engineer the landscape and temporarily elude the environmental and social consequences."[16] David Vaught examines several neighboring counties in the northern San Joaquin Valley, illustrating how California growers shaped political ideology across the region. Vaught views grower political culture through the lens of horticulturalist ideology, the grower worldview that stressed the agriculture industry's exceptionalism compared to other industries.[17] This ideology shaped growers' understanding of themselves, their land, the community, and the workers, until, eventually, this worldview was challenged by the rise of the UFW.[18] Yet, as Vaught suggests, horticulturalist ideology still dominates the political and ideological imaginations of growers and farmworkers in California's Central Valley.[19] Moreover, the evolution of this agrarian worldview helped shape race relations between white Okies, their descendants, African Americans, and ethnic Mexicans in the postwar era.

NEW FARM LABOR HISTORY

The death of César Chávez in 1993 led to public activism across the United States to name parks, streets, and cultural centers in his honor. While the public celebration of his legacy was a welcome recognition of the nation's most important Mexican American civil rights icon, Chávez's shadow eclipsed many preceding events formative to the early 1960s rise of the UFW. Labor historians have narrated a history of labor and activism in Central California that preceded the farmworker union.[20] Ernesto Galarza has documented early struggles to organize farmworkers in California's interior. Describing the significance of the organizing efforts of the National Farm Labor Union (NFLU) in the 1947–1949 DiGiorgio farm labor strike—a precursor to the 1965 Delano grape strike—Galarza notes that a "chain of [labor] locals extending north into the Central Valley was in the making. . . . The union was registering voters and manifesting a preference for liberal congressmen. Something new was being added to the social landscape of Kern County."[21] That something *new* was an expanse of community organizing, both labor organizing and non-labor-oriented mobilization. Galarza, an organizer with the NFLU, captures in his retrospective testimony the activist currents propelled by the NFLU. That union, while short lived in Kern County, affected labor and civil rights organizing beyond the late 1940s.

Although valley growers quashed farm labor organizing efforts by 1950, labor and civil rights reformers found other avenues to express their energies. The NFLU created important precedents for the coming UFW, specifically a legacy of strong anti-unionism in the fields.[22] Growers' harsh response encouraged activism away from the fields toward urban problems. In a letter in November 1950 to the national headquarters of the National Association for the Advancement of Colored People (NAACP), NAACP West Coast (WC) regional director Franklin Williams remarked on the suppression used against workers during the DiGiorgio strike: "outside of Birmingham it would be difficult to conceive of an entire public administration conspiring against organized union activity as was done in Kern County."[23] The growth of the Bakersfield NAACP was important, especially in its challenge to racial segregation and discrimination within city limits. The failed DiGiorgio strike and the activism it engendered were mostly lost to historical memory. While the NFLU's rise and fall signaled events to come in Kern County, postwar civil rights mobilization in California's interior was broader than the farm labor struggle.

UFW historiography helps clarify the larger scope of labor and civil rights reform in rural California. Beginning with the rise of the UFW in the 1960s, journalists documented the biography of César Chávez and the circumstances surrounding *la huelga* (the strike).[24] Since Chávez's death, a number of books have asserted his importance in the pantheon of US Latina/o history.[25] As scores of books emerged with a general focus on and praise of Chávez's leadership, feminist scholarship challenged the gender bias of UFW scholarship. Among the first and most cited works on UFW history is Margaret Rose's scholarship of the late 1980s and early 1990s. A Kern County native, Rose had unique access to former UFW members, and her writings are rich with oral histories about the role women played in UFW activities.[26] Chicana boycott participation, Rose argued, remained obscured because women balanced domestic responsibilities with union duties. Yet, these same UFW women "provided a new space to express a gendered resistance to the status quo based on their own lives and experiences."[27] Rose's distinctions in Chicana leadership—for example, that between Dolores Huerta and Helen Chávez—provided a complexity to Chicana feminist activism at a time when most narratives of the Chicana/o movement focused on men.[28]

The new farm labor history has focused on a myriad of issues, including the perceived leadership mismanagement of César Chávez, dissention within the union's ranks, and tensions between rank-and-file farmworkers.[29] New scholarship also addresses racial and social justice coalitions built and effected by the UFW, including relations with the African American freedom struggle, and the influence of the union on immigrant rights and other social justice movements. Another vein of research emphasizes the UFW's effect on organized religion, or the "browning" of American Christianity.[30] This scholarship as a whole affirms the role of rural California in shaping the postwar landscape of labor and civil rights history in the American West.

Miriam Pawel has led the way in declension scholarship on the UFW. In 2006, she published a series of articles in the *Los Angeles Times* focused on the legacy of the UFW. Her investigation questioned why the union did not have more of an organizing presence in California's agricultural fields, given the original mission of the UFW to unionize farmworkers.[31] Pawel's articles established a basis for two books, *The Union of Their Dreams* and *The Crusades of Cesar Chavez*. In both, she dislodges Chávez as the primary character in organizing the UFW, emphasizing the role of other crucial activists and highlighting Chávez's political and personal limitations. In her estimation, Chávez has received too much credit for the success of the union and too little blame for its demise.[32]

Other scholars have expanded the critique and scope of the UFW's historical significance and legacy. Ana Raquel Minian notes the strategic use of gender conservatism within the UFW, surrounding sexualized discourses on promiscuity, homosexuality, and birth control. She shows the effects of such gendered ideology on reinforcing state-sanctioned discrimination against farmworkers. The UFW's initial, heteronormative positions perpetuated homophobia, sexism, and institutional violence, "shut[ting] out the possibility for a more sex-positive union culture and discourse to emerge" within the union.[33] Matt Garcia chronicles the rise and fall of the grape boycott, the UFW's weapon of choice. Chávez's missteps, Garcia argues, compromised the health of the union, alienated key allies, and eventually rolled back gains made during the late 1960s and early 1970s.[34] Garcia focuses exclusively on the grassroots organizers, many both white and Jewish, who facilitated the national and international boycott of California table grapes. While many activists found ethnic nationalism and separatism empowering and appealing in the late 1960s and 1970s, the UFW by contrast renewed the possibilities of multiracial cooperation and faith in the tenets of grassroots American democratic participation.[35] Garcia's account also gives appropriate attention to the *rural* struggle for labor and civil rights in Central California—a world as deeply *southern* as the American South in terms of racial discrimination and civil rights struggle.[36] The southern San Joaquin Valley became a "nexus of power," drawing white college liberals from coastal California, as well as activists from across the country, all coming to Delano to participate in the farmworker movement and offer a meaningful challenge to growers. This book suggests that such a nexus of power was intricately connected to a broader base of civil rights reform in greater Bakersfield, beyond issues of farm labor.

Other scholars have noted the importance of racial coalitions built by the farm labor movement during the postwar civil rights era.[37] Mark Brilliant offers an important assessment of California's multiracial civil rights history and the opportunities forged and lost by racial coalitions in California's civil rights movement.[38] The Community Service Organization (CSO), where Chávez first learned his organizing skills under the tutelage of Fred Ross, shaped the contours of Mexican American civil rights reform, as would later the National Farm Workers Association (NFWA). The CSO and NFWA agendas created space for cross-racial collaboration, but also had different priorities than did African American civil rights organizations. Issues of old-age pensions and bilingual education were important civil rights issues for Mexican Americans, while desegregation in the housing market and public school system was paramount for African Americans, Brilliant notes. Varying civil rights agendas at best created divergent paths to reform among California's racial minorities, and at worst caused outright friction, animosity, and discord. Lauren Araiza offers a more cooperative interpretation of African American–Latina/o relations during the civil rights era, chronicling the important coalitions built between five African American civil rights groups (the Student Nonviolent Coordinating Committee [SNCC], NAACP, National Urban League, Southern Christian Leadership Conference [SCLC], and Black Panthers) and the UFW.[39] Araiza finds that African Americans' understandings of their relationship to economic systems of exploitation, as well as regional variations, shaped the extent of solidarity found between their organizations and the UFW. The NAACP-WC, particularly director Leonard Carter, acted as a bridge between African Americans and the UFW, whereas the national NAACP office, in New York, was silent on the matter of supporting the UFW.[40] Both Brilliant and Araiza provide a framework for understanding how African American and ethnic Mexican civil rights organizations built civil rights coalitions in greater Bakersfield.[41]

METHODS AND SOURCES

Finding a history of urban activism in Bakersfield beyond the farmworker movement is a methodological and archival challenge. Many of the most valuable archival collections are located outside the region, and those within the region are either private or located in personal paper collections not readily available to the public. This book, then, uncovers a variety of previously unexamined archival materials. The most valuable original source materials utilized in this book are the personal paper collections and local newsletters of the KCCU, as well as oral histories with former activists. These include African Americans, Mexican Americans, and white racial liberals. Archival collections are also utilized, including records of the Office of Economic Opportunity (OEO), Mexican American Legal Defense and Educational Fund (MALDEF), NAACP-WC, and CSO. Several collections within the UFW papers at Wayne State University and the Jacques Levy papers at Yale University provide informative details and historical context. Minutes from the Bakersfield City Council and Kern County Board of Supervisors are also utilized throughout the narrative, as is news coverage in the *Bakersfield Californian*. Telling the stories of activists who championed civil rights reform beyond the fields is central to this book. The untold stories of ordinary people and the ways they envisioned the work they did in pushing for reform, as well as the institutional and political responses by opponents of civil rights reform, shape the historical narrative of this book.

CIVIL RIGHTS ACTIVISM IN BAKERSFIELD'S "RACIAL BORDERHOODS"

The urban civil rights history in Bakersfield beyond the fields offers a more comprehensive understanding of California's rural struggle for civil rights. Civil rights reform in Bakersfield preceded, moved in tandem with, and was dramatically affected by both the activities of the UFW and the response by the political establishment. The struggle for civil rights in greater Bakersfield included issues beyond farm labor and ultimately gave gravitas to the idea that the UFW movement embodied a social and political revolution. Multiracial coalitions were an important factor in urban civil rights reform in Bakersfield's racial borderhoods. Historian Albert Camarillo's definition of a borderhood is apropos when explaining the position of southeast Bakersfield in the history of the city. Camarillo defines borderhoods as "urban spaces often bordered by neighborhoods of working-class or middle-class native-born whites and that were located in or near the most undesirable residential areas close to industrial plants or other workplaces where unskilled or semi-skilled work was available."[42] A marginalized and racialized laboring population has historically surrounded Bakersfield, Kern County's only major urban center. This surrounding community was central to civil rights struggles in postwar Bakersfield.

CHAPTER OVERVIEW

This book is divided into seven chapters. It begins by examining the origins of racial segregation and civil rights reform, from the late nineteenth century through the immediate years following World War II. The postwar civil rights activism in greater Bakersfield was rooted in fighting the region's deep history of racial segregation. A fuller account of the origins of racial segregation and multiracial coalitions contextualizes the growth of civil rights reform following the 1965 Delano grape strike, which was a turning point in the burgeoning Mexican American and Chicana/o civil rights movement. From there, the book examines the course of civil rights reform through the lens of the Chicana/o movement and its impact on multiracial civil rights activism in Bakersfield. Finally, the book turns to the diversity of civil rights reform beyond the fields, including the struggle against police violence, the fair media movement, the fight to expand rural health care, and the struggle to desegregate local schools.

Chapter 1, "'A Laboratory of Races': Racial Segregation in Greater Bakersfield, 1870–1950," offers an overview of the formation of racial segregation in the southern San Joaquin Valley; the connection of racial segregation to labor, employment, and settlement; and the growth of racially segregated enclaves in the region. The chronology of the chapter follows the growth of railroads, urban development, and racial segregation in greater Bakersfield since the founding of city in the 1870s. The growth of the railroad and agribusiness, along with the impacts of Dust Bowl migration and wartime industries, created a context for the nascent growth of civil rights organizing through 1950. Agricultural mobilizations for labor rights in the 1930s and 1940s affected the course of civil rights reform and opposition to labor and civil rights activism in the decades to come.

Chapter 2, "Civic Unity: Mexican Americans, African Americans, and Civil Rights Activism in Bakersfield, 1947–1964," examines the formation and growth of Mexican American and African American civil rights organizations in Bakersfield. It also explores issues of local discrimination that mobilized the formation of coalitions among Black, Brown, and white racial liberal activists. Racial composition in greater Bakersfield changed dramatically over the course of the twentieth century, especially with increasing Mexican immigration. Civil rights leaders crafted reform agendas to meet changing racial realities in greater Bakersfield. Beginning in the late 1940s, urban civil rights leaders built organizational networks influenced by the struggle in the fields. The Bakersfield branch of the NAACP, the CSO, and the KCCU were the most active postwar urban civil rights groups to emerge in Bakersfield's southeast borderhoods. Racial coalitions were by no means a natural relationship in the open spaces of California's Central Valley. The boundaries of racial alliances were permeable, porous, and contingent on circumstances. Multiracial civil rights organizations faced an opposition that benefited from long-standing traditions of racial segregation in a city and county referred to pejoratively as "Mississippi West."[43] Battles were fought over segregation in public accommodations, annexation into the city proper of the local minority community, establishment of a municipal fair employment practices commission, integration of the housing market, and institution of a city-sponsored civil rights body. The racial liberalism and civic unity that marked the first era of postwar civil rights activism in Bakersfield were challenged by an influx of federal resources during the War on Poverty, continued conservative resistance, and the rise of ethnic power movements.

Chapter 3, "'Maximum Feasible Participation' and Opposition: The War on Poverty in Kern County, 1964–1967," narrates the history of the early War on Poverty in Kern County. The influx of federal resources affected grassroots civil rights organizations in Bakersfield. Many of these organizations fought migrant poverty long before federal intervention, though the influx of federal resources expanded their work rapidly. Working out of a nondenominational, multiracial religious center called Friendship House, African American and Mexican American groups won the first antipoverty funds in Kern County for southeast Bakersfield. The politicizing of the antipoverty movement gained steam when an antipoverty grant was awarded to the NFWA in September 1965, the same month that its director, César Chávez, announced a strike against Delano growers. Kern County voters scoffed at the notion of subsidizing what they deemed an unholy alliance between radical civil rights activists and the federal government. Events climaxed in 1966, when the city of Bakersfield declared by political referendum that it would not support antipoverty programs with local tax dollars as mandated by the 1964 Economic Opportunity Act. Local conservatives thereafter consciously usurped the grassroots aspect of the antipoverty movement, specifically the federal mandate of "maximum feasible participation of the poor," by placing themselves within the bureaucratic structures of the War on Poverty program.

Chapter 4, "Agrarian Chicanismo: Jesus 'Jess' Nieto and the Chicana/o Student Movement in Bakersfield," discusses the growth of Chicana/o activism in Bakersfield. The Delano grape strike and farmworker movement galvanized civil rights activism, specifically the formation of a Chicana/o youth movement and Chicana/o studies programming at Bakersfield College. While the Chicana/o movement in Bakersfield had its roots in multiracial coalition building, the rise of ethnic nationalism altered dynamics among civil rights coalitions in Bakersfield. The creation of a Chicana/o educational curriculum and other instructional reforms at the college level was an arena of struggle in Bakersfield's urban civil rights movement. Higher education was the principal means by which the children of farmworkers achieved economic and social mobility. Educational reform was met with significant resistance from those hostile toward the idea of ethnic studies. The relationship cultivated between educational reformers and student activists was a significant part of Bakersfield's urban civil rights movement. In short, for urban Chicana/os in Bakersfield, education rights were civil rights.[44]

Chapter 5, "'Hoo-ray Gonzales!': Civil Rights Protest and Chicana/o Politics in Bakersfield, 1968–1974," focuses on the multiracial political mobilization in the election of California assemblyman Raymond Gonzales. A civil rights activist from southeast Bakersfield, Gonzales was intimately involved in many of the multiracial civil rights organizations in Bakersfield during the late 1960s and leveraged that experience to become the first Chicano elected official from Kern County in the California legislature. Composed of urban Chicana/os, African Americans, and white liberals, the Gonzales coalition marshaled the first grassroots Chicana/o political victory in Kern County with his 1972 election to the state assembly. Gonzales's campaign and time in office—a single term, 1972–1974—reveal the impact of grassroots political mobilization during the civil rights era, the fissures within civil rights coalitions, and the counterresistance on the political right toward grassroots mobilization. Gonzales's relationship with the UFW both resulted in his maiden election victory and contributed to his reelection defeat in 1974 to future Republican congressman William "Bill" Thomas. In many ways, Gonzales's election defeat marked an eclipse of grassroots racial coalition building and political activism on the liberal left within the region.[45]

Chapter 6, "Police Violence, Fair Media, Rural Health Care, and Civil Rights Activism in Greater Bakersfield," analyzes the diversity of civil rights reforms in Bakersfield beyond the fields. The UFW affected Mexican American activism well beyond the War on Poverty. Campaigns for labor rights made Mexican Americans more comfortable in their brown skin, notes historian Nancy MacLean.[46] In Kern County, a growing awareness of the importance of racial identity informed the development of Chicana/o nationalism among urban activists, which, in turn, changed the dynamics of racial coalition building among local civil rights groups. The farmworker movement united ethnic Mexicans, both urban and rural, in new ways, as well as grew alliances between African Americans and ethnic Mexicans. Struggles against police violence in southeast Bakersfield galvanized activism and created a sense of crisis for both Black and Brown activists. Holding law enforcement accountable for violence was a struggle in a law-and-order region of California with a long history of police violence toward racial minority groups. Another important struggle of urban activism was the national fair media reform movement. Bakersfield civil rights leaders produced one of the most successful campaigns of Bakersfield's civil rights era: the McGraw-Hill media concessions of 1972. Since 1969, Black and Brown activists within the civic unity movement had leveraged pressure on local and national media outlets to include minority interests in news coverage, fair labor practices, and programming. Bakersfield civil rights activists built a five-city coalition, collectively brokering the first major media concessions for Chicana/os from a national media conglomerate. The coalition capitalized on the then-recent success of fair media concessions won by African Americans and the United Church of Christ in the American South. This corporate media reform resulted in some of the earliest educational film series on Chicana/os, chronicling their long history as an indigenous American culture, and countering the more negative stereotypes of Mexican Americans that dominated the mainstream media. The chapter concludes by examining the fight to expand access to rural health care, a struggle that reveals dynamics of cooperation and conflict between Black and Brown activists during the civil rights era.

The final chapter, "A New Battleground for Civil Rights: The Desegregation of the Bakersfield City School District, 1969–1984," charts the origins of school desegregation in Bakersfield. African American and Mexican American children were historically racially isolated in the district's southeast schools. Bakersfield—one of the largest elementary school districts in California—became a new battleground for reforming racially segregated schools in 1969. In that year, civil rights organizations working with the US Department of Justice launched a multiyear investigation into de jure racially segregated schools in Bakersfield. While the effort to desegregate the Bakersfield City School District (BCSD) brought important momentum in the struggle for racial integration in Bakersfield, desegregation efforts were tempered by the creation of magnet programs during the Reagan presidential administration as a solution beyond the forced integration perceived in mandatory busing.

The conclusion reaffirms the argument that the civil rights legacy of California's Central Valley is obfuscated when we ignore the diversity of civil rights reforms within the region. Telling these diverse stories of reform helps bridge polarized historiographies that evaluate California's rural civil rights legacy strictly through the lens of the farmworker movement. The conclusion also connects the history of multiracial struggles for civil rights and social justice to more contemporary struggles in the twenty-first century, including the immigrant rights movement and struggles over historical memory. This excavation of the forgotten history of Bakersfield's urban civil rights movement holds potential lessons for civil rights and social justice organizations working on the ground today by showing the deep roots of their diverse struggles in and beyond the fields.

I | "A LABORATORY OF RACES"
Racial Segregation in Greater Bakersfield, 1870–1950

The realtor [should be] sincere and not sell to Chinese, Japanese, Negroes, Mexicans, unless it is in their section of the locality, and where they should be.
Edward Kelly, chair of the Bakersfield realty board, circa 1920s

When I first came to Bakersfield and I had an education, but I did domestic work because there wasn't anything else open for Negro people.
NAACP activist Johnie Mae Parker, circa 1971

On a Monday evening, March 7, 1949, over one hundred residents of the Sunset-Mayflower area of southeast Bakersfield attended a mass meeting. Organized by the Sunset-Mayflower Progressive Club, the meeting brought together residents to discuss the annexation of the area into Bakersfield's city limits. The area, approximately one square mile, was home to a dense concentration of Black residents. It was located less than a mile east of Union Avenue, a thoroughfare former African American Bakersfield city councilman Vernon Strong referred to as "Separation Street," demarcating Black and white Bakersfield.[1] The roots of Black migration to the tract stemmed back nearly half a century, to the cotton migrations from the American South, supplemented by continued Black settlement through the Dust Bowl era. The benefits of joining the city's municipal boundaries seemed promising. Greater municipal services, street lighting, a Black fire department, and improved sewage and sanitation services were of particular concern, given the perceived public health nuisance of Dust Bowl migrants, both Black and white, as they settled on Bakersfield's municipal periphery. The majority of club members were assuaged by arguments in favor of annexation, voting eighty-four to thirteen to push forward a citywide petition the following month.[2]

The struggle of Black residents in the Sunset-Mayflower tract to join Bakersfield's city limits became a catalyst for reform in the burgeoning post–World War II civil rights movement in Bakersfield. The fight over annexation galvanized progressive African American and ethnic Mexican residents in southeast Bakersfield. In the coming decades, the fight for better housing, working conditions, and racial equality in greater Bakersfield would build on the mobilization engendered by annexation.[3] The annexation moment is also significant for another reason, one rooted in the region's deep history of racial segregation. The fight over annexation symbolized the growth of the racial minority populations in greater Bakersfield, African American and ethnic Mexican predominately, as well as efforts to maintain racial segregation in greater Bakersfield by marginalizing people of color in the rural periphery.

The history of racial segregation in the San Joaquin Valley shaped how civil rights activism unfolded in greater Bakersfield following World War II. Deep histories of racial exclusion, racialization of immigrant groups, and social marginalization created the social context for civil rights activism after 1945. Racial segregation was shaped regionally through multiracial migration, settlement, custom, and public policy. The multiracial landscape and racial boundaries that formed across California's San Joaquin Valley were created and maintained by migration and a wide range of institutional practices. Racial boundaries across greater Bakersfield reflected a white interior within city limits, surrounded by racially excluded communities of color in the rural county periphery. Dismantling exclusionary practices and building coalitions across racially segregated communities became a focus for civil rights activists in postwar Bakersfield.

MIGRATION, SETTLEMENT, AND RACIAL FORMATION IN THE SAN JOAQUIN VALLEY

Anglo settlement played a key role in shaping economic development and race relations in Kern County beginning in the nineteenth century. "Unlike the towns, cities, and counties that stretched along the California coast from San Francisco to San Diego, most of which claimed Spanish/Mexican origins, the interior counties of the Central Valley were initially settled by Americans from other regions of the United States," writes historian Albert Camarillo.[4] Founded in the 1870s by Thomas Baker, the city of Bakersfield became the county seat of Kern following the California gold rush and the mining boom that happened in the southern San Joaquin Valley near Havilah, the original county seat. Prior to the Anglo settlement of Bakersfield, the southern San

Joaquin Valley was occupied by Penutian-speaking Indians, who had a history of resistance toward European encroachment dating back to the Spanish mission period, only to be "brought under subjection" by Anglo militia units in the 1850s.[5] Census records show that the population in Bakersfield grew from 801 residents in 1880 to 2,626 in 1890, while the county grew from 5,601 to 9,808 during the same period.[6] The city's white population was diverse in origin, including Anglo-American and European immigrant groups, white migrants from the American South, and French, Italian, German, and Basque immigrants, who developed agricultural industries and local businesses in the city and surrounding rural communities. Despite the varying origin stories of white Bakersfieldians, a common bond of white racial identity shaped race relations between these groups and the working-class residents of color who labored in the region. For nonwhite residents, access to economic and social mobility in greater Bakersfield was limited by racial segregation.

Anglo-Mexican relations in Bakersfield reflected California's racial fault lines. Local newspapers noted tensions over race and settlement from the time of the city's founding. On July 26, 1873, the *Kern County Courier* noted that "one of the first habitations erected onto the present site of Bakersfield was a small tule hut, or Mexican jacal." The presence of the structure caused discontent among white residents. "The orgies that are nightly held there are not only disgusting but hideous. We trust our city fathers will attend to this matter and cause the removal of the nuisance. . . . We suggest the passage of an ordinance consigning it to flames. No other ordinance . . . would afford the place sufficient purification."[7] Environmental historian Linda Nash notes that "boosters and their supporters often attributed ill health in the [Central] valley to bad habits rather than to the local environment. Predictably, disease among nonwhites was easily and frequently dismissed as personal rather than environmental in origin, the obvious outgrowth of their vice and unclean habits."[8] Historian Natalia Molina theorizes that various racial scripts have historically justified treatment toward immigrant groups. In this case, Mexican settlement in Bakersfield was caricatured as a public health threat defined by a culture of moral turpitude—a racial script that would affect Chinese, Mexican, and African Americans across greater Bakersfield's communities of color in the coming decades.[9]

In late nineteenth-century Bakersfield, tension existed between the desire for cheap labor and white tolerance of racialized communities. The Chinese experience in Bakersfield illustrates the role of racial scripts in shaping Anglo-nonwhite relations, as well as the history of racial segregation within the city. "Language, district or tong associations, and the sometimes-hostile outlook of neighboring Americans," helped form the bedrock of Bakersfield's Chinatown, notes Kern County historian William Harland Boyd.[10] Anglos in Bakersfield frequented services provided by Chinese workers yet condemned on moral grounds the vice culture associated with Chinese settlements. Bakersfield's Chinatown had a reputation for vice activities, including gambling and prostitution. "In February 1880 the Kern County Californian [newspaper] reported that law enforcement officers had found dingy subterranean gambling rooms, with 'devious, mysterious passages,' that reeked with filth and the odor of opium."[11] As in other Chinatowns throughout the American West, Chinese immigrants in Bakersfield made the most of being confined by racial segregation, excavating space beneath their residences to avoid having to move horizontally across municipal streets. "In 1882, an anonymous newspaper reader wrote to the editor of the [*Kern County Weekly*] *Record*, 'The Mongolians are packed in like rats, stacked away on shelves, and in underground apartments all huddling together reeking with filth, disease and rottenness.'"[12] Racial animosity toward the Chinese extended even after death. "Discrimination was codified in the bi-laws of the Bakersfield Cemetery Association when directors banned Chinese burials," notes Bakersfield historian Gilbert Gia.[13]

While anti-Chinese violence spread across California in the 1880s, many within Bakersfield cautioned residents to avoid racial violence. "In April 1891, at a time when there was strong anti-Chinese agitation in Tulare, Selma, Fresno, and other San Joaquin Valley towns, the editor of the Kern County Californian expressed the hope that there would be none against the Chinese in Bakersfield."[14] The potential effect of losing an important local Chinese labor supply within the vineyards, as well as concern over extralegal violence, tempered calls to anti-Chinese action comparative to other parts of California's Central Valley.[15] "Kern County's harvests proceeded on schedule. The town's power structure influenced the people, called-up man power and weapons, and preserved the peace. Although the *Californian* helped suppress violence, it remained steadfastly anti-Chinese. . . . Violence continued to flare in agricultural California, but at Bakersfield business continued uninterrupted."[16]

Despite the racialized views Chinese and Mexicans encountered in the San Joaquin Valley, Mexicans settled down as homesteaders and entrepreneurs of the land. A descendant of Ventura Ruiz from Sonora, Mexico, reflected in 1956 that his grandfather "homesteaded 160 acres on the north side of Panama Road, at Rio Bravo about 1865. . . . Dolores Montano on the south side did the same." The grandson Ruiz further recorded that his "grandfather in 1874 sold his Panama Ranch to J. C. Crocker, a cattleman and later agent for Miller and Lux."[17] Beyond Bakersfield, Mexicans populated the small town of Havilah, county seat from 1866 to 1872. An article in the *Visalia Delta* noted in 1866 that the suburb of Havilah was "known as Mexico from the nationality of its inhabitants."[18] In 1870, Mexicans settled in San Emidio, approximately thirty-five miles from Bakersfield, between the foothills and Buena Vista and Kern Lakes, where "crops of corn, barley, and vegetables attain[ed] high degrees of perfection."[19] Mexicans also settled seven miles south of Bakersfield by 1874, in the Panama settlement, allegedly once a destination for Mexican bandit Tiburcio Vásquez.[20]

Kern County's economic transformation to Anglo dominance mirrored similar processes playing out in California and the US-Mexico borderlands. The Miller Lux Company, one of the largest agribusiness corporations in the American West during the late nineteenth century, transformed the region's economy and set a foundation for a migrant racialized labor force within the southern San Joaquin Valley. Henry Miller and Charles Lux's company, which specialized in cattle production, "represented important facets of American conquest . . . [namely] the replacement of Mexican landowning elites by Anglo elites, the increasing influence of San Francisco over the surrounding hinterlands, and the emergence of industrial enterprises across the Far West," writes historian David Igler. "[J. C.] Crocker knew the country well. . . . He located the best swamp and desert lands in the Buena Vista Slough, cultivated relationships with the county land officials, and convinced Miller and Lux that this underdeveloped San Joaquin range could produce prime cattle for its northern ranches."[21] As Miller and Lux expanded their landholdings in the southern San Joaquin Valley, these "industrial cowboys" (to quote Igler) created a pastoral economy on a scale theretofore unseen in Central California, altering the trajectory and importance of traditional Mexican ranch labor. "In the area that is now Kern County, early *Californio* landholdings included *Rancho San Emigdio*, *Rancho El Tejon*, *Rancho Castaic*, *Rancho Los Alamos*, *Rancho Agua Caliente*, and *Rancho La Liebre*," notes anthropologist Ruben Mendoza in his photographic history of the Mexicans of Kern County.[22] Many of these ranches were gifted in the 1840s by the Mexican government to residents from San Juan Capistrano, Santa Barbara, and Los Angeles—whose land claimants were interested in growing the region's pastoral economy. Absentee landholders, in many instances, encountered difficulty. In the Rancho Castaic region, "the vaqueros [herdsmen] refused to remain . . . because of the hostility of the Indians."[23] As the Miller Lux Company developed the scale of the San Joaquin Valley's agricultural economy, traditional Mexican vaqueros declined in status, their intimate knowledge of the land less of an asset to the region's economy as migrant labor filled more "unskilled positions in the agricultural workforce."[24] Moreover, as continued Mexican immigration altered the racial landscape in the southern San Joaquin Valley, the "Spanish heritage" of the ethnic Mexican population became whitewashed in early accounts of the county's history. In one early rendering, Thelma B. Miller wrote of Spanish California's legacy in Kern: "Just South of Fourth Street on Union Avenue, Bakersfield, lives one of the oldest native white Californians; Felipe Paredes, 84 years old; a handsome man who could easily pass for fifteen to twenty years under his real age.... Sr. Paredes is not Mexican; he makes a distinction between his own race and the parvenu immigrants, the peons, from the land south of the Rio Grande. He is a Spanish Californian."[25] Other than a reference to recent arrivals, Miller's account ignores the contributions of Mexican immigrants in the settling of Bakersfield.

Wallace Smith, another early chronicler of the San Joaquin Valley, expanded the historical narrative of the region with his publication *Garden of the Sun* in 1939. Smith described the incoming Mexican population vis-à-vis the multiracial settlers of the San Joaquin Valley. "The Mexican peons . . . are usually of Indian blood and are not to be confused with the Spanish Californians of an earlier day. Under present conditions they are a necessary adjunct to a successful development of the San Joaquin Valley." Referring to the racial diversity that defined the region, Smith wrote, "the last group of people to arrive in the valley are physically indistinguishable from the aborigines. Every racial type in the world is to be found [here]. . . . A laboratory of races is found in the San Joaquin Valley."[26]

RAILROADS, SEGREGATION, AND COMMUNITY BUILDING IN GREATER BAKERSFIELD

Like large-scale agricultural development, railroads transformed the history of greater Bakersfield. Following the expansion of the Southern Pacific railroad into the San Joaquin Valley in the early 1870s, Mexican settlement expanded as *traqueros* (track workers) and other railroad workers settled near the Southern Pacific depot on Sumner Street in East Bakersfield.[27] As the late historian Jeffrey Garcílazo wrote, "Mexican workers were inextricably linked to the railroads, mining, ranching, and agriculture. But the railroad was the physical conduit in which Mexican workers found employment and transportation to virtually every section of the country."[28] Railroads transformed the San Joaquin Valley, bringing new settlers and migrants from across the United States and Mexico. As Bakersfield grew, it developed into two separate towns. Sumner (also known as Kern City), or what is referred to generally as East Bakersfield, developed around the Southern Pacific depot on Baker and Sumner Streets, while the larger town of Bakersfield, located west of Sumner, maintained distance from the depot. The location selection for the Southern Pacific depot was somewhat controversial locally. Public opinion ensued in the local press over the potential influence of Sumner on Bakersfield, and vice versa, in terms of future development.[29] Ultimately, "the Southern Pacific depot was established a mile and one-half east of Bakersfield city limits, a location described in the *Kern County Courier* as barren, uninhabited, and treeless."[30] Trains began arriving at the depot in 1874.[31] Following the establishment of the station at Sumner, "there was consolation in the removal of the 'dens of drunkenness and debauchery [and] the Mexican dance houses' to Sumner," away from white Bakersfieldians, notes Harland Boyd.[32] However, as the population grew, Sumner was incorporated into greater Bakersfield by the board of supervisors in 1889.[33]

Arturo Rosales was one such ethnic Mexican, born into a family transformed by the railroad in East Bakersfield. Born in 1909, Arturo came of age in a boxcar home just off Baker and Sumner Streets, adjacent to the Southern Pacific depot. He graduated from the Lincoln School in East Bakersfield in 1925 and then briefly attended Bakersfield High School, dropping out after his sophomore year. Many ethnic Mexican children in Bakersfield were tracked by local educational institutions into manual labor, or otherwise faced varying barriers to education, including poverty, segregation, and social marginalization. In a 1929 study of nonattendance in Bakersfield city schools, John Compton wrote: "the Mexican children rank first in 'poverty or broken home' and . . . parents were unaware of the meaning of compulsory education and child labor laws."[34] Compton's study further noted that the "Mexicans who come to Bakersfield are largely a migratory people, with a high percentage of illiteracy. They are paid a low wage for their labors, frequently spend their earnings unwisely and find themselves in mid-winter with no work available and with no funds with which to buy food or clothing."[35] Although Compton was biased in his moral judgment of the ethnic Mexican population of East Bakersfield, a dearth of archival records related to the history of Bakersfield's ethnic Mexican population in the early twentieth century makes his observations valuable, if only for their illumination of white racial stereotypes about the ethnic Mexican population. Moreover, Compton's observations echo some of the difficulties and challenges Arturo faced as an ethnic Mexican coming of age in East Bakersfield.

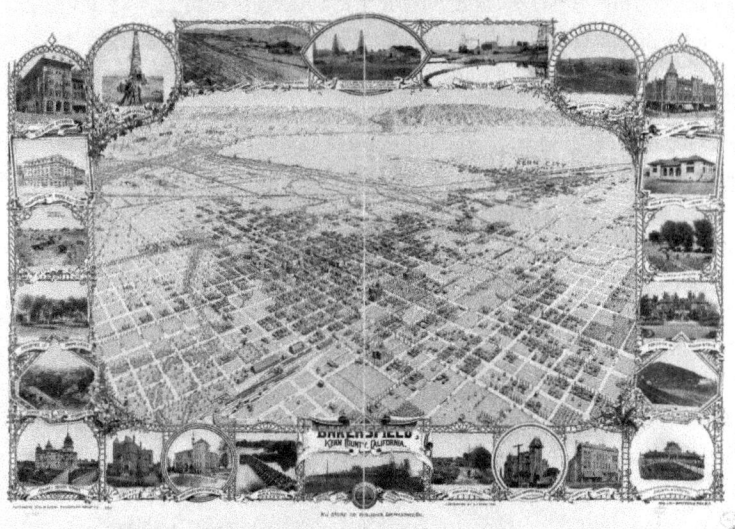

FIGURE 1.1 Bakersfield, Kern County, California, 1901. A bird's-eye view of greater Bakersfield, showing the division of Bakersfield and Kern City, which came to be known as East Bakersfield. Library of Congress, LCCN 75693087.

As the child of Mexican immigrants, Arturo faced multiple challenges in Bakersfield schools. His mother, Mariana, developed mental health problems following his brother's birth and would send Arturo and his two siblings to school with blackened faces, using soot to color their complexion. After they arrived at school, the nurse would bathe them. This was a painful memory for Arturo as he recounted later in life to his wife.[36] Arturo completed his sophomore year of high school at Kern Union High School and thereafter found employment on the Southern Pacific railroad, where his father, Hermenegildo, worked as a boilermaker. Born in Chihuahua, Mexico, in 1872, Hermenegildo came to the United States in 1881, following his father, Jose Maria Ricano Elano Rosales, who first came to the United States in 1874. In 1907, Hermenegildo married Mariana Rojo, and together they had three children, Manuela, Arturo, and Donald. Employment in the rail yards of East Bakersfield was a viable financial path for the men in Arturo's family by the time he came of age.

Aside from being home to *traqueros* and their families, East Bakersfield was home to a larger Mexican colony in Sumner, also referred to in its early years as both Kern Island and Kern City. Given the affinity of Mexican residents for their country of origin, Mexican independence was celebrated in September and Cinco de Mayo each spring. These community celebrations

FIGURE 1.2 Boilermaker Arturo Rosales (*second row, fourth from left*) stands with workers from the Southern Pacific railroad at the Santa Fe Roundhouse yard, on Truxtun Avenue near Bakersfield High School, following a union election, circa 1943. Photo courtesy of David and Irene Rosales.

were noted in local newspapers, which highlighted community leaders among the Spanish-speaking population. The Kern City Mexican club, led by president Felipe Nunez, vice president Trinidad Grijolba, secretary Pedro L. Pinuelas, and treasurer Max Nunez, was the principal group organizing East Bakersfield's events celebrating Mexican culture. Traditional street fairs with dancing, music, and cultural celebration marked the beginning of a community event and would continue in the coming decades—an opportunity for residents to celebrate their ethnic identity and presence in the city. Max Nunez, a prominent member of East Bakersfield's Mexican colony and organizer of the community's cultural celebrations, was selected as a delegate for the Republican Party, representing Sumner, in 1892.[37] Middle-class ethnic Mexicans such as Nunez represented an important growing political constituency within greater Bakersfield. The *Morning Echo* noted that the "Mexican Republicans of East Bakersfield" formed in July 1914 and registered fifty-seven people.[38]

As ethnic Mexicans settled in greater Bakersfield, community leaders and organizations developed Mexican culture and institutions. Prisciliano Gomez founded *La Cronica Mexicana*, a Spanish-language newspaper, in

Bakersfield in 1890. Mexicans in East Bakersfield established the Sociedad Juarez Mutualista Mexicana (Juarez Mexican Mutual Aid Society) in 1910.[39] The Juarez Hall served an important community need in East Bakersfield's ethnic Mexican community, offering mutual aid and fundraising opportunities for various causes, creating nostalgia for the Mexican homeland, and helping connect the younger generation born in the United States to their immigrant past.[40] Jesus Cruz (J. C.) Nava, a Protestant minister, attempted to build an interdenominational Mexican mission in Bakersfield. A reverend at the Mexican congregational church located at 517 Baker Street, Nava was involved with the September celebration of Mexican independence from 1916 to the early 1920s. Born in Chihuahua, Mexico, Nava graduated from the Colegio Internacional in Guadalajara, Mexico, migrated through El Paso, Texas, in 1907, and initially settled in Venice, California, before arriving in Bakersfield in 1910, the same year that the decade-long Mexican Revolution broke out. Nava thereafter attempted to open a school for the study of Spanish in 1913. In addition to his religious and cultural activities, Nava was a local publisher, creating the Spanish newspaper *El Centenario*.[41] Nava began publishing his paper in 1912 and was characterized by the Anglo press as "a Mexican gentleman with strong sympathies for the insurgents in Mexico."[42] Nava's ambition with his Spanish-language newspaper was "to reach the Mexican population in Kern County and give them the benefit of news from the insurrection as soon as it [was] received . . . in the American papers." The paper's transnational focus was intended to "promot[e] a sense of patriotism" among Bakersfield's *la colonia* Mexicans, encouraging them to "become good citizens of that soon to be republic."[43]

While the Mexican Revolution led middle-class ethnic Mexicans like Nava to develop Bakersfield's Mexican institutions, continued Mexican immigration and settlement developed the ethnic Mexican working-class population's experience as a racialized labor force. Many Mexican immigrants came to Bakersfield through El Paso. The Texas border city was "the premiere point of entry and destination for Mexican immigrants . . . easily accessible via the Mexican rail connection that stretched southward into Mexico," notes historian Zaragosa Vargas.[44] The growth of the railroad and displacement caused by the Mexican Revolution contributed to the growth of greater Bakersfield's ethnic Mexican population. Both African American and ethnic Mexican settlement occurred heavily in the city's unincorporated southwest rural periphery. According to the 1930 census, the population of Kern County was 82,570, while the city's population was 26,015. In Kern County, the Mexican population in 1930 was 7,109, and the Black population was 2,142. In Bakersfield, the Mexican population was 1,967, and the Black population was 868.[45] The majority of Mexican and Black residents thus lived outside Bakersfield's municipal city limits. Many of Bakersfield's ethnic Mexican residents first settled in southeast Bakersfield, outside municipal limits and adjacent to the city. "According to Father Meyers of the Guadalupe Parish, about 40 per cent of the Mexicans [in greater Bakersfield] are foreign born and from those 15 to 20 percent are naturalized citizens," notes a 1940s study of the Mexicans of East Bakersfield.[46] Our Lady of Guadalupe Catholic Church was established in 1925 on East California Avenue, in the heart of the East Bakersfield Mexican barrio. The church "served as a center for the religious, social, and ceremonial gatherings of the local Mexican American community" during the 1920s and subsequent decades.[47]

One such first-generation Mexican immigrant to Bakersfield was Ignacia "Nancy" Romero.[48] She was born in El Paso in 1917, to parents Caterino Romero and Guadalupe Salas, who had come to El Paso two years earlier. After Caterino died in 1920, Guadalupe relocated with her young children to Bakersfield in the early 1920s. Nancy, as a child, worked at the restaurant El Parian, which was owned by her stepfather, Jose Flores, and located near Bakersfield's Chinatown. These early years were the most stable during her childhood, and Nancy recalled often working at the restaurant cleaning tables and eating pancakes before the school day began. Unfortunately, the restaurant burned down on June 1, 1928, and the family never recovered from the financial loss. The family soon moved to Delano to find cheaper residency and work. Jose Flores never recovered from the loss and died shortly after the restaurant was destroyed. Nancy's mother, Guadalupe, passed away the following year. Prior to her death and at the height of the Great Depression, Guadalupe consented to the marriage of her fifteen-year-old daughter. Nancy married twenty-six-year-old Rafael Martinez and thereafter gave birth to the first of three girls, Mary, followed by Nelly and Dolores. The family lived with Rafael's father a half mile southeast of the Southern Pacific depot, at 920 Dolores Street. Rafael passed away in 1939 in San Francisco at the age of thirty-two, after suffering a kidney ailment. Nancy soon moved out of her father-in-law's home after he became controlling of her behavior. As a widow with three daughters, Nancy moved a mile south, to 216 Kincaid Street, where a family friend built a small house for $200.[49] Adjacent to her new home lived Don Rosales, brother of Arturo, the latter of whom Nancy would soon meet and marry. The two would have five children of their own in the coming years.

SOUTHERN INFLUENCE AND RACIAL THINKING

The migration of white southerners shaped race relations and segregation in the San Joaquin Valley. "No place in California is more Southern than Kern County," writes historian Michael Eissinger. "Not only does Kern County reflect southern cultural food and music, but also the long-standing traditions of Jim Crow and other manifestations of Southern culture."[50] While the Okie exodus of the 1930s grew a southern diaspora across the United States, including in Kern County, earlier waves of southern migration affected the region and shaped racial thinking.[51] Historian Albert Camarillo, while serving as a historical consultant for the Mexican American Legal Defense and Educational Fund (MALDEF) in the 2018 *Luna v. County of Kern* case, argued in federal court the importance of white southern migration from the US South in shaping the history of race relations and racial thinking in the San Joaquin Valley:

> In many of California's Central Valley towns, including those in Kern County, . . . the color line was maintained and reinforced over time. This can partly be explained by two factors: 1) the over-representation of residents who migrated from former Confederate and border states in the late 1800s and early twentieth century (many of whom became local community leaders and politicians) and who carried with them to California attitudes about white supremacy that exacerbated race relations; [and] 2) the development of agricultural economies bifurcated by race and class relations on a white/non-white axis, not only in the work place but in social and residential settings as well.[52]

Camarillo's testimony regarding Kern's deep history of racial segregation and discrimination proved valuable in the courtroom, with the judge finding the county guilty of racial gerrymandering and of using a "rigged political system to exploit Latinos for decades."[53]

The development of oil within the region triggered white migration and the growth of racial violence. As the oil industry developed in Kern County, the industry "only hired whites to work their oilfields thereby creating segregated communities with few women, and no minorities. . . . In Kern County, the Klan made major inroads in Bakersfield (and surrounding Oildale), in Tehachapi, at Kern River, and in Taft," Eissinger notes.[54] Camarillo in his legal testimony reiterated that "it is no surprise that the resurgence of the Ku Klux Klan in the 1920s found receptivity in Bakersfield, [in] Taft, and in

Fresno. Klan membership in these chapters surged as other chapters of the KKK sprouted throughout the Valley (for example, between 15 percent and 16 percent of the Klan members in Bakersfield and in Taft were born in the South)."[55] Tarea Hall Pittman, a longtime civil rights activist and National Association for the Advancement of Colored People (NAACP) worker from Bakersfield, reflected on her family's collective memory of racial violence, given their late nineteenth-century roots in Bakersfield. "People were very cruel to Mexicans. My mother said she would be so frightened because sometimes she'd go out and she'd look up in a tree and a Mexican would be hanging there. Oh, they just hanged Mexicans at will. They had no rights. They were very cruel to Mexicans during these early days," Pittman recalled.[56]

The rise of the Ku Klux Klan in Kern County, while wedded to ideas of white supremacy and the lost cause, included a broader emphasis on Christian morality rather than strictly racial considerations. Historian Alicia E. Rodriquez notes that the rise of the Klan in Kern County in the 1920s was more about "enforcing morality and prohibition" rather than responding to "ethnic menaces." The overwhelming whiteness of Kern County's demographics in the early 1920s provides important context for understanding the Klan in Kern. "In 1920 the county's population stood at nearly 55,000. Slightly more than a third (just under 19,000) lived in Bakersfield. . . . Taft, the center of oil production in the county's West Side, was home to 3,317 inhabitants, with more scattered among farming, ranching, and oil communities. Blacks made up only .09 percent of Kern County's population, with American Indians, Chinese, and Japanese together comprising 2 percent. Foreign-born whites, a category which would have included 1,856 foreign-born Mexicans, comprised just under 14 percent of the population, 2 percent below the national average," Rodriquez records.[57] Thus, there was only minimal "ethnic menacing" going on in Kern. Rodriquez further notes that "though Kern County did experience its share of vigilante violence in the oil fields, it did not have a noteworthy tradition of violence resulting in lynchings, though people of color were disproportionately the victims in those cases."[58] One account of note was the lynching of Antonio Maron, Francisco Encinas, Miguel Elias, Fermin Eideo, and Bessena Ruiz in Bakersfield in 1877. The group was taken from a jail by a mob of a hundred people and executed for theft. Mexicans in Bakersfield at the time suspected that the group was targeted because of their race. Local newspapers affirmed, however, that the men would have been executed had they been white and claimed that they were targeted not because of their racial class but because of the crime.[59]

In the early 1920s, the activities of the Ku Klux Klan were investigated by a grand jury and district attorney. A growing backlash against Klan activity in Kern County helped thwart the Klan's growth there. Some public officials nevertheless openly supported the Klan. Kern County Board of Supervisors member Stanley Abel openly supported the Klan, yet survived a recall campaign. Other local politicians across the county who were associated with the Klan's activities did not.[60] The Klan's demise in Kern County did influence the racial trajectories of the valley. The Klan suffered significant levels of public condemnation following the 1920s grand jury investigation, while the broader public, "however sympathetic the latter might have been to the ideology and values that the Klan officially professed," never publicly accepted its brand of racial politics.[61] Nevertheless, commitment to white racial supremacy and segregation continued. "The Klansmen were the most extreme representatives of white supremacist ideologies that took growth in Valley towns, but . . . also reflected dominant racial attitudes that reinforced antipathy of many whites toward racial minority groups in Kern and adjoining counties," noted Camarillo in his testimony against racial gerrymandering in Kern.[62]

FARM LABOR AND RACIALIZATION

As the Mexican working-class population increased in the San Joaquin Valley through migration, so too did practices of racial segregation and discrimination. In Kern County, the racialization of Mexican immigrants and their descendants was shaped largely by experiences with farm labor. "The history of race and labor relations in Kern County and throughout the Central Valley is inseparable. From the 1930s to the 1950s, multiethnic and multiracial farm labor unions organized strikes for higher wages and better working conditions against large farm operators, only to be met by violence and suppression of their fledging labor organizations," notes Camarillo.[63] Agricultural labor during this era also affected settlement patterns among the Mexicans of the San Joaquin Valley. Many Mexican immigrants and members of other migrant ethnic groups lived in farm labor camps, while others surrounded Bakersfield's city limits in racially segregated enclaves. Across the San Joaquin Valley, "the pattern of agricultural work had helped create two separate, although sometimes touching, Mexican communities. One was the community of workers on the west side, where Mexicans lived in labor camps. . . . The other was the Mexican community that lived in towns, mostly on the east side, where barrios developed in the towns of Visalia, Fresno, Bakersfield, Tulare, and Delano," writes historian Devra Weber.[64] The racial bifurcation of the valley created segregated spaces that had long legacies on the valley floor.

Anthropologist Walter Goldschmidt, in a 1947 study of three agricultural communities in the San Joaquin Valley (Arvin, Dinuba, and Wasco), critiqued the effect of large-scale agribusiness on the civic life and democratic participation of the valley's rural communities. "Social ties are not close, invidious social distinctions are maintained without reference to personal qualities. . . . The ties which bind individuals living in this area are subservient to the ties of social classes and cliques which are at all times dominant."[65] The "substantial colonies of Mexicans and Negroes" on the periphery of the three small valley towns that Goldschmidt examined experienced "urbanized social relationships," where social relations followed the "pattern of the city."[66] Like the Depression-era photography of Dorothea Lange, Goldschmidt's research offered a powerful critique of the consequences of large-scale agribusiness and its effects on those who worked the land. Explaining his research in 1972, Goldschmidt reflected "that the industrialized farming that characterizes the San Joaquin Valley resulted in an urbanized rural life."[67]

Goldschmidt's research advanced empirically the issues highlighted in texts like Carey McWilliams's *Factories in the Field* and John Steinbeck's literary account of the migrant Joad family in *The Grapes of Wrath*. These two books, both published in 1939, brought national attention to the plight of migrant farmworkers in the San Joaquin Valley. Patterns of large-scale landholding, a desire for cheap labor, and racially segregated labor forces defined life in the San Joaquin Valley's small rural towns. Goldschmidt referred to the resulting social division as the "nuclear group" and "the outsiders." In the case of Wasco, just northwest of Bakersfield, "the nuclear group is that body which grew up with Wasco and inherited the institutions of the community—that body to which Wasco belongs. The outsiders are those who have arrived somewhat later to serve as agricultural laborers." He continued, "two minority groups developed an internal unity which resulted in their having communities of their own. The 'Mexican colony' and the 'n——r town' still exist as separate entities."[68] Goldschmidt's landmark study—and his thesis that "industrial agriculture is corrosive to the civic and economic life of rural communities"—received significant backlash from the agricultural industry and its supporters. "No other single piece of research in the valley was as virulently contested over a longer period of time. Powerful interests relentlessly weighed in to hinder, obscure, censor, and suppress its findings," note Daniel J. O'Connell and Scott J. Peters in their study of scholars and the fight against industrial agribusiness in California.[69]

Organized agricultural labor across racial lines represented a threat to the status quo of racial segregation in the San Joaquin Valley. As migrant workers

FIGURE 1.3 "Street meeting at night in Mexican town outside of Shafter, California. Organizer for United Cannery Agricultural Packing and Allied Workers of America (Congress of Industrial Organizations–CIO) talks to mixed crowd. The strike failed," reads the caption of this 1938 Dorothea Lange photograph. Library of Congress, LCCN 2017770938.

flooded into the valley, especially during the 1930s, efforts to organize farmworkers gained significant traction among organizers, as well as opposition forces from agribusiness. The 1933 cotton strike in the San Joaquin Valley, the largest labor strike in California agricultural history (and one of the largest in US agricultural history), demonstrated the significance of the rural struggle for labor rights among both labor organizers and agribusiness. The strike involved twenty thousand workers across multiple valley counties over six weeks.[70] For labor organizers, the notion of promoting solidarity among a multiracial farm labor population was appealing and drew strength from the history of the people. Historian Devra Weber notes that "a transnational perspective elucidates Mexicans' experience in social conflicts that dramatically shaped their responses in the cotton fields," becoming a "basis for later cooperation between progressive Anglos and Mexicans in California's agricultural fields."[71] Ethnic Mexican experience with interracial and class-based coalitions during the era of the Mexican Revolution provided an important ideological foundation for interethnic alliances between ethnic Mexican and Anglo farmworkers in the 1930s and 1940s. Moreover, the latter multiracial alliances between ethnic Mexican, Black, and white farmworkers in the San Joaquin Valley would themselves underpin cross-racial alliances a generation later, in the era of the United Farm Workers (UFW).

Of course, given the division of Mexican settlement in the San Joaquin Valley between farmworker communities, including labor camps, on the west side and the more urban-peripheral segregated Mexicans on the valley's east side towns, creating solidarity among ethnic Mexicans in support of labor strikes was no easy task. Not all ethnic Mexicans in Kern County favored views aligned with labor organizers. The Comisión Honorífica Mexicana (Mexican Honorary Commission), Bakersfield chapter—one of the more active fraternal organizations among ethnic Mexicans in Bakersfield, with

FIGURE 1.4 "Camp talent provides music for dancing at Shafter camp for migrants. Halloween party, Shafter, California," reads the caption of this 1938 Dorothea Lange photograph. Library of Congress, LCCN 2017770942.

its established connections to the Mexican consulate—opposed calls for a strike in the cotton fields in the spring of 1934.[72] At the about the same time that the Comisión Honorífica was announcing its opposition to a strike in the upcoming harvest season, the secretary for the Cannery and Agricultural Workers Industrial Union was arrested just north of Bakersfield, in Tulare County, for a minor traffic infraction. Newspaper accounts noted that plans for "guerrilla picket lines and [a] war on workers in the field" were obtained by law enforcement from the vehicle.[73] The local news press sensationalized the arrest as evidence of a vast communist conspiracy among labor organizers in the valley. Lillie Ruth Ann Counts Dunn, who became involved in the cotton strikes near Pixley and Tulare in the 1930s, recalled: "we were called Communists but the whole town didn't even know what Communism was."[74] The politicization and red-baiting associated with a proposed general strike in the fields and perceived threat of violence tempered the possibilities of broader solidarity among ethnic Mexicans in greater Bakersfield. The fragility of solidarity illustrates interethnic differences among the valley's ethnic Mexican population, including geographic differences between rural and urban identities, as well as the successful red-baiting tactics of agribusiness to polarize the issue of supporting farmworkers.

Aside from the mobilization engendered by the agricultural strikes of the 1930s, one of the most significant outcomes of the era was the rise of "farm fascism" in Central California. This organized opposition within agricultural industries to collective bargaining and interethnic racial coalitions helped blunt the struggle for higher wages, better working conditions, and unionization. The Associated Farmers (AF) embodied organized response to farm labor organizing in the San Joaquin Valley. "The AF was perhaps the most virulent and notorious right-wing group in American history, with the possible exception of the Ku Klux Klan," write scholars Nelson A. Pichardo Almanzar and Brian W. Kulik.[75] The need for grower activism was highlighted by the agricultural strikes of the 1930s. The AF organized at both the state and county level and had the ambition to organize nationally but was ultimately thwarted by the LaFollette Commission's investigations in the late 1930s and 1940s.[76] The organizational drive by the Cannery and Agriculture Workers Industrial Union also encouraged growers to countermobilize against labor organizing. Grower organizing tempered the effectiveness of labor organizing in the valley's multiracial agricultural labor force while, at the same time, creating an organizing infrastructure on the right that would mobilize again in the 1960s with the rise of the UFW.

The growth of government labor camps exposed the dreadful conditions of migrant workers, as well as showing the importance of the state in subsidizing living and working conditions in the fields. The latter became the literary inspiration for John Steinbeck's *The Grapes of Wrath*, published first as *The Harvest Gypsies*, where the Joad family finds salvation in a government-run camp after being run off of a company housing unit. The expansion of the federal government's labor camps brought interesting characters to the San Joaquin Valley. Photographer Dorothea Lange spent time traveling rural America and documenting the plight of migrant farmworkers, including in the San Joaquin Valley. In 1939, Fred Ross, future mentor to César Chávez and Dolores Huerta, was "promoted to manage the Arvin Migratory Labor Camp."[77] During the second half of the 1930s, Kern County's population had jumped by 60 percent, triggering a backlash against Okie migrants, who were seen as a public nuisance and potential public health risk. While the migrant camp, which had previously been under the leadership of Tom Collins, was somewhat glorified in Steinbeck's novel, it was in shambles by the time Ross arrived. Under Ross's leadership, the Arvin camp became a magnet for labor organizers, attracting organizers from the United Cannery, Agricultural, Packing, and Allied Workers of America (UCAPAWA), an organization interested in mobilizing "unskilled" field workers, ignored by mainstream labor organizations such as the American Federation of Labor (AFL). In October 1939, UCAPAWA launched a strike in Kern County, calling for $1.25 wage rate. Growers, however, were able to break the strike in two weeks with replacement workers.[78] "The 1939 strike was . . . the last notable conflict of the 1930s, a tumultuous decade that saw more than 127,000 California farmworkers engage in at least 140 strikes," notes Ross biographer Gabriel Thompson.[79]

BLACK, BROWN, AND RURAL

African American laborers began to be recruited to Kern County in earnest by landowners and cotton growers in the 1880s. Historian Michael Eissinger writes that "by 1881, several . . . planters experimented with cotton production in Kern County, however, labor issues continued to plague farmers who planted this labor-intensive crop."[80] The changing nature of US immigration policy was a constant concern for those seeking to maintain a steady labor force in California agriculture. "F. W. Ownbey, on behalf of . . . Kern County planters, traveled to the South to recruit . . . blacks, specifically to replace Chinese workers in the fields." And while the "initial cotton experiment failed . . . many of these early black families . . . participated in the development of Central California."[81] The creation of Black settlements across the San Joaquin Valley was an important part of African American settlement in the American West, particularly in light of the rural-to-rural migration patterns (in comparison to the rural-to-urban migrations typical of Los Angeles or Oakland).[82] Many Black families established deep roots in communities such as the Sunset-Mayflower tract, southeast of Bakersfield and outside city limits. One of southeast Bakersfield's most important Black female activists, Johnie Mae Parker, reflected on her own migration to southeast Bakersfield from Texas: "When I first came to Bakersfield and I had an education, but I did domestic work because there wasn't anything else open for Negro people. And I picked some cotton. All of my family have. . . . We will do any kind of work . . . as long as we are making an honest living."[83] As Parker recalled, Black people in southeast Bakersfield mobilized in response to poor living conditions. "The Mayflower community . . . it was very crude. It had outdoor privies. It had tents for houses and it had discarded street cars and box cars for houses. And there were no playgrounds and no public facilities for the people who were migrating from the South by the thousands."[84] Beyond southeast Bakersfield, there were also small but established Black settlements in Wasco and Delano, as well as north through the San Joaquin Valley.[85]

Allensworth is an especially important Black settlement in the story of racial segregation and Black settlement in the San Joaquin Valley. Founded in 1908 by Black US Army colonel Allen Allensworth, the onetime flourishing Black colony represented the freedom dreams of African Americans in the post-Reconstruction era, but also helped shape the development of other Black communities in the San Joaquin Valley. The story of Allensworth sheds light on the vision of self-improvement many Black migrants brought with them as they settled in the San Joaquin Valley. Historian Lynn M. Hudson notes that "Allensworth became a sanctuary for black Californians, but only

FIGURE 1.5 "Sunset District, East Bakersfield, Kern County, California. High school students from the Negro shacktowns," reads this caption of a 1940 Dorothea Lange photograph. National Archives, NAID 521669.

briefly. What was meant to be a place of belonging was, for some, a mirage.... Allensworth offered many [Black] migrants a second chance, a final migration to a town that promised to live up to the dream."[86] For two decades, Allensworth served as an important mecca for African American settlement and freedom struggle in the American Far West. The dream of building an independent Black town based on agriculture attracted African Americans from across the United States. Southern California and Pasadena served as recruiting grounds for Black Californians to come to Allensworth.[87] The promise of a second chance in California was important for Black migrants who experienced racial exclusion and lack of opportunity in Southern California, Oakland, and San Diego. In many Black colonization efforts throughout the West, motivation also "rested largely on the search for a refuge from lynch law and the dependency of sharecropping in the South."[88]

Black men played a key role in shaping the freedom dreams of the Allensworth colony. Joshua Singleton, son of Benjamin "Pap" Singleton, progenitor of the Kansas Exoduster movement, moved to Allensworth in 1910 and "became a central figure in the politics and social life of the westernmost

FIGURE 1.6 "Bakersfield, Kern County, California. Housing for Negroes in a new district on the edge of town. A rapidly growing community of colored people, mostly from Texas, some from Oklahoma. Rent of this house without plumbing twelve dollars per month," reads this caption of a 1939 Dorothea Lange photograph. Library of Congress, LCCN 2017771444.

all black town."[89] Colonel Allensworth's reputation as a leading "race man" and high-ranking Black military officer created a celebrity around him when he moved to Los Angeles and helped leverage his reputation in the founding of the all-Black town.[90] The establishment of Allensworth developed the politics of Black uplift in the San Joaquin Valley. Hudson describes the political leanings of the town's founder: "Allen Allensworth's embrace of black nationalism is hardly surprising given his predilection for colonization. Whereas the tendency has been to exaggerate the distance between figures like Washington, Du Bois, and Garvey, a figure like Allensworth borrowed from the philosophies of all three."[91] In 1921, an Allensworth branch of the NAACP was formed. Additionally, "by the mid-1920s, they had established an Allensworth chapter of the United Negro Improvement Association [sic] (UNIA)."[92]

Allensworth was also transformational for Black women in an age of gendered limitations. Women in Allensworth, aside from helping run businesses and growing food, served in a variety of other capacities, including attending to people's medical needs. "Most doctors in nearby towns refused to take black patients unless the patient was employed by a white rancher."[93] Allensworth lived on in the experiences of Black women and their families in the San Joaquin Valley, long after the town's decline.[94] Josephine Triplett, whose grandparents lived in the town between 1909 and 1918, reflected on her family legacy. "My granddaddy, named William Henry Bud Hall, and [his wife] Elizabeth Hall left their home on South H and Pacheco in Bakersfield (which the family had occupied since 1885) to come and live in Allensworth to follow the dream.... They were among the first families to come to Allensworth and had thirteen children."[95] According to Josie, her grandparents always considered Allensworth to be their hometown and thought that the town offered the children the "best chance to succeed and have a good life." "My grandfather was a person people called a race man.... These were men that were leaders and took initiative to see that things got done.... People [would] ask him about political things.... He would tell you the person to watch, which white men you could trust, which white man you couldn't trust, and which black would go and tell everything you did.... He stood up for people's rights. That's what a race man does.... My family enjoyed living in Allensworth, they hated coming back to Bakersfield under the conditions that they did, but they survived."[96]

The dream of sustainable living in an all-Black town failed to materialize because of the interdependence of Allensworth with the local, regional, and state economy—making the town dependent on interactions with white society.[97] Despite the efforts of Allensworth settlers to escape Jim Crow, "racial segregation and discrimination played a part in every era of the town's history from its founding to its slow decline."[98] The obstacles Black residents in Allensworth experienced over access to water and transportation via the railroad made the town's sustainability nearly impossible. As Delores Nason McBroome notes, Allensworth "illustrates the difficulties blacks encountered in agriculture in California at a time when it was increasingly becoming an industrial enterprise, requiring substantial capital and a hired labor force."[99]

Despite the difficulties Allensworth encountered in its attempt to establish a flourishing Black rural enterprise, the migration of Black families to the area positively affected surrounding communities by offering an alternative life for Black people in an era of racial segregation and exclusion. Although Allensworth's population by 1930 was in decline, the Black population in Tulare County increased "from 190 people in 1910 to 819 by 1930."[100] Kern County also experienced a rise in its Black population following Allensworth's decline. "The Depression decade marked the beginning of a bonafide black community in such counties as Kern where the population nearly doubled by 1939 and in cities such as Tulare where the proportion of blacks rose dramatically from 2.7 percent in 1929 to 5.2 percent in 1939," notes historian Peter LaChapelle.[101] As Black migrants settled in Kern County in the years following Allensworth's decline, they experienced racial hardships and segregation but continued to build Black community in greater Bakersfield. Susie Bell Nichols-Brothers, born in 1914 in Clay County, Mississippi, moved to

Bakersfield in 1942. There, her family "found colored people living in California just as bad as they were living in Oklahoma."[102] Roberta Nichols-Allen, born in 1908 in Seminole, Oklahoma, moved to Bakersfield in 1946. She recalled of that year, "I became the first in my race to become employed as a registered nurse at Kern General Hospital in Bakersfield, California. When I went to Kern General Hospital . . . to apply for a job, I was told by the operator at the information desk that the hospital did not hire colored nurses. . . . I broke the barrier."[103]

South of Allensworth, on the western side of Kern County, another rural town with a multiracial farm labor force emerged at the turn of the century. In Buttonwillow, a company town founded by the Miller Lux Company at the dawn of the twentieth century, agricultural migrants settled into a social environment segmented by a racialized labor force that was exploited by employers to drive down the price of labor. Historian David Igler notes of the Miller Lux Company that "to fill its constantly changing labor needs, the firm employed migrant, low-wage workers and divided them along racial and ethnic lines. Mexican Americans and Mexican, Italian, Portuguese, and Chinese immigrants each occupied distinct spheres of the unskilled labor force."[104] As Black migrants settled into Kern County's agricultural labor force in growing numbers during the 1930s, they settled into a racialized labor force and socially segregated landscape. African American Dust Bowl–era migrant Robert Williams recalled seeing a No Colored Trade sign in a café window along the Bakersfield-McKittrick Highway, the main roadway traveling east and west between Buttonwillow and Bakersfield.[105]

Buttonwillow's Black population experienced a segregated landscape in the small rural town. Black resident Christina McClanahan recalled, "the neighborhood I lived in was a black settlement. There was nothing in it but blacks in Buttonwillow. It was not part of the town. It was away from the town and we were out there in two and a half acre parcels. We only had contact with whites when we went to wherever they were."[106] Living in areas disconnected from the town meant a lack of infrastructure. "When we moved to Buttonwillow we had no electricity or gas or running water. So, we had an outhouse and a slop jar. That was the toilet." In Buttonwillow, many agricultural workers lived in company housing. "Each farmer had his own housing on his own farm. Now they're furnished by the government. . . . Then each farmer had his own little rural houses that people who worked for him lived in," McClanahan recalled.[107] Her son Brent McClanahan recalled his parents sharing difficult memories of the family's experience with racism. Reflecting on his father's experience working for the Kern County sheriff and post office, Brent remembered: "Dad faced a lot of racism. He kept it from us, but he faced a lot of it on all his jobs."[108] After leaving Buttonwillow, Christina McClanahan faced similar barriers in Kern County. "I could not attend the Kern County Trade School. Negro students were not allowed to enroll," she recalled. Christina ultimately headed to Los Angeles to attend Henrietta's Beauty School.[109]

Ethnic Mexican families that worked in western Kern County's agribusiness faced similar hardships to African Americans. Such was the experience of Buttonwillow resident Irene Ramos and her family. The Ramos family faced a racialized migrant life. Born to parents Jesse Cortes and Tomás Ramos in 1951, Irene grew up in a housing unit provided by Parsons Ranch in Buttonwillow. With their town located about thirty miles west of Bakersfield, many Buttonwillow residents often made the journey to Bakersfield to go shopping, or—in the case of the McClanahan family and other Black residents—to attend Cain Memorial African Methodist Episcopal (AME) Church in East Bakersfield. Yet, despite Buttonwillow's proximity to Bakersfield, Irene and four of her five siblings were born in Upland, located near Ontario in Southern California, a two-and-a-half-hour drive from Buttonwillow. Irene's mother, Jesse, was born in Pomona, California, and grew up in a migrant agricultural family working in the Southern California citrus industry. Despite living so close to Bakersfield, Jesse felt more comfortable with the medical services provided in Upland than with those in rural Kern County.[110] Irene recalled, "She had a negative experience with a hospital. She never talked about it much, but I believe it dealt with her first, failed pregnancy." Jesse's husband, Tomás Ramos, worked as a bookkeeper for the rancher and was provided with company housing. "I remember the place where I grew up was small, one or two rooms, with a community shower and toilet room attached to the labor camp for multiple families. Later, Parsons, the rancher, arranged for my father to have a house built on the ranch. My parents lived there for many years before moving into the main area of Buttonwillow," Irene recalled.[111]

RACE AND HOUSING SEGREGATION

Racial segregation in greater Bakersfield was most dramatically reflected where people lived. As Bakersfield developed as the county's largest city, white settlement within city limits was maintained by residential segregation and restrictive housing policies adopted at the local level. Racial separation in the housing market became a selling point for real estate agents and was popularized in California after 1900. Developed first in east San Francisco

Bay and Los Angeles, racially restrictive housing covenants grew in popularity among American real estate agents and soon spread across the United States, including to Bakersfield.[112] While the conflict in the agricultural fields was triggered by migration and new arrivals, it "was symptomatic of much broader patterns of racial animosity and systematic forms of discrimination and segregation that developed in the towns and cities of . . . [Kern] county. . . . Segregation based on the color line relegated most Mexican Americans and African Americans in towns such as Bakersfield and Delano to separate public schools, public and private facilities, and neighborhoods restricted by race," notes Albert Camarillo.[113]

As Bakersfield experienced dramatic growth in its population in the early decades of the twentieth century, racial segregation in the housing market was pronounced. Edward Kelly, chair of the Bakersfield realty board, noted in a survey on race relations in the late 1920s that racial segregation in Bakersfield was maintained through subdivision restrictions.[114] The survey, "conducted by the California Real Estate Association at the request of a Stanford economics professor," posed the following questions on race and housing: "Are there segregated sections in your locality based on the Color Line? If so, which races are affected?" Kelly replied, "Negroes, Chinese, Japanese, Mexicans or any others not of Caucasian race."[115] When asked how the problem of racial segregation could best be solved by real estate interests, Kelly replied: "for the realtor to be sincere and not sell to Chinese, Japanese, Negroes, Mexicans, unless it is in their section of the locality, and where they should be."[116] Sincerity here, Kelly defined, was commitment toward maintaining neighborhood racial division. The Hillcrest tract, located in the northeast part of the city, for example, enacted a restrictive covenant in 1939 to ensure that "no part of said realty shall ever at any time be used or occupied or be permitted to be used or occupied by any persons not of the White or Caucasian race, excepting such as are employed as servants upon said realty by the owners or tenants of said realty actually residing there."[117] Racially restrictive covenants in a growing Bakersfield ensured that new housing tract developments would maintain white property ownership and keep people of color in their place on the city's rural unincorporated periphery.

Bakersfield's real estate agents played a key role in shaping the vision of Bakersfield as a white city where people of color knew their place. While Bakersfield's newest residential housing tracts were racially segregated, Kelly noted that "older residential [and] business districts [should] circulate [a] petition restricting their property, not otherwise restricted."[118] The affirmation of racial boundaries by the realty board was critical for maintaining racial segregation. This division was especially important given the increased number of Black southerners and Mexican immigrants who came to Kern County as part of the Dust Bowl exodus, drawn to the San Joaquin Valley by employment opportunities associated with farm labor and military mobilization in the late 1930s and 1940s. In Oildale, immediately north of Bakersfield's municipal city limits, "the North of the River Association went on record [in 1941] to restrict the population to members of the Caucasian race."[119] Oildale would maintain its white racial community identity and its reputation as a place of potential hostility toward Black people and racial minorities for several decades.[120] Such racially divisive tactics in housing helped maintain racial segregation in greater Bakersfield and created opportunities for white people to accumulate wealth and equity, while simultaneously marginalizing people of color in the rural periphery and denying them similar opportunities for economic and social mobility.

The population growth experienced throughout greater Bakersfield and Kern County during the Dust Bowl era reinforced racial boundaries in the coming decades. Many Dust Bowl migrants settled in the San Joaquin Valley's small rural towns and labor camps, as well as in southeast Bakersfield, in an area known as "Little Okie." This area, located outside city limits, was adjacent to African American and ethnic Mexican settlements in the southeast. White laborers augmented the region's multiracial agricultural labor force during the first half of the twentieth century. Recalling the early years of Joseph DiGiorgio's farming conglomerate, Edgar Combs, a grower in the Arvin area, recalled: "He brought in a lot of Mexicans and he had a Mexican camp there. I don't know whether they went down and hired them in Mexico and brought them back or if they just came here themselves, but I remember he had a Mexican camp."[121]

The relegation of people of color to the margins of greater Bakersfield, be it through labor market segregation or racially restrictive housing tracts, tempered economic opportunities for African Americans and ethnic Mexicans. Even after California implemented fair housing legislation at the state level, racial segregation within the housing market persisted. The problem was acute for African Americans in greater Bakersfield. "Union Avenue was the dividing line.... It was very, very difficult to find a home that could be sold to blacks if it was west of Union Avenue," recalled Vernon Strong, who arrived in Bakersfield in 1946. "There were places that had 'No Colored' signs on them."[122] Most Black residents were left to purchase homes in the southeast part of the city, outside city limits. Donato Cruz notes that "when suburbanization became visible in postwar Bakersfield, with the expansion of housing, minorities were still buying homes on contract.... The reality ... resulted in [African Americans] attempting to purchase homes under the agreement and conditions of a real estate broker," particularly within the southeast, where the majority of the Black population lived.[123] The precarity of Black homeownership in southeast Bakersfield reenforced the color line there, an issue that would later become a battleground in the fight for civil rights.

North of Bakersfield, in Delano, author John Dunne observed similar patterns of racial segregation in the mid-1960s, when he traveled there to chronicle the burgeoning farmworker movement:

> Today the population of Delano is approximately 14,000 and it is split almost evenly between the "Anglos," who live east of the freeway, and the Mexicans, the Filipinos, and the few Negroes who live west of Highway 99.... The East Side is somnolent and well-kept and no different from any one of a dozen other Valley towns. Most of Delano's businesses are located here.... Highway 99 is a social as well as a geographical line of demarcation between the two Delanos. It is not just that the skins of the people on the West Side are darker. The bungalows are shabbier and the cars are older. Occasionally a drainage ditch is exposed, and there are more potholes in the streets. ... It was in this area that Delano's once flourishing red-light district was located.[124]

The history of racial segregation in Delano, aptly described by Dunne, catalyzed the burgeoning farmworker movement in the early 1960s. Franciscan priest Mark Day captured this racial geography of Delano in 1971, writing, "Delano is separated physically as well as racially by the Southern Pacific Railroad."[125]

The experiences of people of color within Kern County's segregated landscape are embedded in the oral traditions of communities of color. One African American who participated in the Civilian Conservation Corps in the Depression era recalled his visit to Taft, just southwest of Bakersfield: "A few of us blacks and a number of whites were returning to camp and decided to stop in Taft. As we entered the city a sign read 'Read n——r and run; if you can't read—run anyway. N——r don't let the sun go down on you in Taft.'"[126] The normative segregation in places like Taft during the first half of the twentieth century illustrates how the color line was maintained regionally through various formal and informal policies and manners. "Juanita Price, one of the few black Oklahomans to come west during the 1930s," notes historian James N. Gregory, "recall[ed] some of the violence in the Bakersfield area." He quotes her: "When the White Southerners came here a lot of them got whippings from black people.... The blacks had a little hostility in them when they came out to California[;] they thought the situation was different so they could just whip a white fella and forget it." "'Tex's Bar,' an Okie hangout in Bakersfield, prominently displayed a 'NO N——RS' sign on the door. When a black man walked in one day, the owner tried to throw him out. The would-be customer then pulled a knife and 'cut him up real bad,'" Price recalled.[127] African American and ethnic Mexican residents also experienced hostility from law enforcement. Kern County sheriff John Loustalot noted at a public intercultural meeting in 1945 that "some of his men were prejudiced" and that "Mexicans and Negroes were picked up for minor infractions," compared to white residents.[128]

RACE, SEGREGATION, AND SCHOOLS IN GREATER BAKERSFIELD

Schools also reflected Bakersfield's segregated reality, beginning in the late nineteenth century. Racial groups' experiences varied depending on time and circumstance. While the 1896 *Plessy v. Ferguson* decision codified the separate but equal doctrine in American institutions, Californians prided themselves to an extent on drawing distinctions between the West and southern states in terms of race relations. Bakersfield historian Gilbert Gia notes that over time, "the climate of Bakersfield schools . . . changed since 1896 when the town bragged about its pupil diversity. . . . 'There are in our public schools side-by-side, students of American, English, Irish, Scotch, Swedish, French, Italian, Portuguese, Spanish, German, Greek, Colored, Chinese and Japanese descent, and various intermingled races, yet all live in peace and harmony,'" read the *Bakersfield Californian* in 1896.[129] By 1910, however, forty Chinese students were enrolled in the new Hawthorne School, which included a special class for Chinese pupils not performing at grade level.[130] In this case, language deficiency was the justification for separating out Chinese children by race.

Ethnic Mexicans also experienced racially segregated schools in greater Bakersfield. The uptick in Mexican immigration following the Mexican Revolution of 1910 expanded Bakersfield's Mexican population. In 1921, the *Morning Echo* noted that "the number of [Mexican] children attending Edison school is so great" that school officials were pondering whether to add a teacher for Mexican children within the "Mexican colony of Edison."[131] As ethnic Mexicans pushed north through El Paso and onward to cities throughout the Midwest, all the way to Chicago, cities near rail lines like Bakersfield expanded their ethnic Mexican population. Incorporating Mexicans into local institutions proved challenging. "Bakersfield teachers and administrators are prejudiced in varying degrees toward Mexican students before they ever see them," John King noted in his 1940s study of the Mexicans of East Bakersfield.[132]

African American and ethnic Mexican student experiences in the rural periphery of greater Bakersfield were also affected by racial segregation and racialization. African American Dust Bowl migrant Christina McClanahan recalled encountering racialized views in Buttonwillow's public schools. "I remember a woman who came to our class from fifth grade from Iowa. We were all in the classroom when she arrived and she walked in and said, 'I've never had any n——rs in my class before.' If she decided to pick somebody to do something she'd say, 'Eeny, meeny, miney, mo, catch a n——r,' and she pointed, 'a n——r by his toes.' She did it. What are you going to do?"[133] Buttonwillow was a feeder community to Shafter High School, located northeast of the small company town. White Bakersfield Okie migrant Vivian Leah Barnes Kirschenmann recalled: "The schools weren't as mixed [then]. We had a few Spanish children in school. When I graduated in 1940, we had only one colored person in the class and the two Spanish [kids]. . . . We had what we called a Mexican colony. I think they had their own school. They didn't mix so much."[134]

Segregated enclaves of African American and ethnic Mexican residents blanketed portions of southeast Bakersfield by 1950. School enrollment data reflects the segregated patterns of settlement. "The Lincoln school contain[ed] two tenth of one percent of the majority group [white], 73.9 percent of the Negroes, and 34.8 percent of the Mexicans. . . . The Lincoln [school] is the most concentrated for both the Mexican and Negro minorities. . . . In a district formed by Lincoln, Fremont, and McKinley, 90.5 percent of the Negro enrollment is found," noted King in the 1940s.[135] Clearly, the Bakersfield City School District designed school boundary lines reflective of the segregated living patterns of the African American and ethnic Mexican populations of East Bakersfield. "The dramatic lines of segregation for the Mexican are not as apparent as they are for the Negro. . . . Mexicans have at least a degree of freedom of movement if economic circumstances permit. However, this mobility does not exist for the Negroes," King argued.[136] Despite the possibility of greater mobility within the school system, Bakersfield schools had a legacy of poor educational outcomes for ethnic Mexican children. In a study of retardation in Bakersfield schools in the 1920s, one author opined, "If it were not for the foreign element . . . we would have a much better showing. . . . Here the Mexicans . . . are very much retarded."[137]

The marginalization of African Americans and ethnic Mexicans within the San Joaquin Valley was embedded into everyday exclusionary practices associated with racial segregation. An African American school counselor at the Lincoln School, Mrs. Jarrett (as she's referred to in a 1952 study of race relations in Bakersfield), who coordinated many activities for Bakersfield's Black community, noted being discriminated against after stopping in Wasco for lunch after a teachers' association meeting in Delano. "The women were refused service," the study notes, while being "requested to retire to a shed" to take lunch. Jarrett also recalled an incident when Marian Anderson, the noted Black opera singer, was denied lodging in Bakersfield.[138] While Jarrett obviously did her job well and prided herself on teaching Black students in Bakersfield, her experience is contextualized by "the rumor that Lincoln School was used to some extent by the administration as a disciplinary school for teachers," given its concentration of Black students.[139] The legacy of the Lincoln School as a symbol of racial segregation persisted in the coming decades, when ending segregation at the Lincoln School became part of the fight to desegregate Bakersfield city schools.

In the years after World War II, segregation in Bakersfield began to be challenged in new ways. Students played a role in the early struggle against segregation. A high-profile incident involving discriminatory signs occurred early in 1950 across from Bakersfield High School. By this time, the city and county had experienced a large influx of residents, Black migrants included, although many African Americans continued to settle in areas outside municipal limits. The Elbo-In, a meal stand close to the high school, was advised by students and staff to not hang any restrictive signs prior to opening. Nevertheless, the owners displayed a sign that read "no colored trade solicited." Various campus clubs voted to boycott the establishment. The "colored students" were not allowed into the meal stand's student clubroom. A group of these students tore down the signs and replaced them with ones that read "colored trade wanted." The event was noted in the Bakersfield High School newspaper to have "rocked the campus" and entire city.[140] The incident showed a generational difference at the school as well. Back in October 1915, seniors at Kern Union High School (later renamed Bakersfield High School) had dressed as Klansmen in celebration of the film *The Birth of a Nation*, which had debuted earlier that year.[141]

The Elbo-In incident marked a new era of growing activism among young people and civil rights groups. "Practically every club on campus boycott[ed] the snack bar," read the campus newspaper following the incident.[142] In an editorial to the campus newspaper, Letha Brooks opined that "the Negroes in this school are students as well as the white students, and a person putting in a stand near here should expect colored trade. . . . Should this person come into this area and make trouble for the school by putting up such a sign as this?"¹⁴³ A few weeks after the incident at the Elbo-In, the Bakersfield City Council passed an ordinance banning discriminatory signs at cafés and business establishments. Following the city council's resolution, H. H. Collins, president of the Bakersfield branch of the NAACP, organized pressure on the Kern County Board of Supervisors to pass a similar measure countywide.¹⁴⁴

CONCLUSION

Given the size and influence of the student body at Bakersfield High School, the Elbo-In event marked a turning point in the history of racial segregation in Bakersfield. After 1950, a burgeoning civil rights movement led by racial liberals challenged racial segregation in greater Bakersfield. The removal of Jim Crow signs became a catalyst for and symbol of the growing tide of multiracial organizing for civil rights reform that would sweep Bakersfield. The postwar civil rights movement in Bakersfield challenged racial segregation in the southern San Joaquin Valley by promoting common ground and solidarity among the region's racial minority groups: the city's marginalized southeast communities of African American and ethnic Mexican residents, as well as residents of surrounding rural peripheries associated with the farmworker movement. Subsequent chapters offer a more complete narrative account of the diversity of civil rights reform in greater Bakersfield, the multiracial coalitions that sustained civil rights activism, and the complex challenges of trying to overturn long-standing racial segregation and inequality within the southern San Joaquin Valley.

2 | CIVIC UNITY

Mexican Americans, African Americans, and Civil Rights Activism in Bakersfield, 1947–1964

In all of my experience as an NAACP worker throughout the deep South I have never seen conditions as dreadful, unsanitary and depressing as those under which thousands of Negro migrant workers have to live on the outskirts of Bakersfield.
NAACP West Coast regional director Franklin Williams, 1950

[Bakersfield] remains probably one of the most racist cities in California.
Marshall Ganz, 2023

Between World War II and the mid-1960s, urban multiracial coalitions championed civil rights reform in Bakersfield. Mexican Americans, African Americans, and white liberals forged coalitions rooted in farm labor, fair housing, and the struggle to establish a municipal Fair Employment Practices Committee (FEPC). White liberal activists worked as cultural brokers between Black and Brown communities in confronting an institutional conservatism complicit in the city's long-standing history of racial segregation. White liberal involvement in Bakersfield's early civil rights struggle was key to building racial coalitions in southeast Bakersfield's racially segregated corridor. The Bakersfield branch of the National Association for the Advancement of Colored People (NAACP) and the predominately Mexican American Community Service Organization (CSO) worked in concert with the Kern Council for Civic Unity (KCCU) to address civil rights issues in the racially divided city. These coalitions battled anti-statist and racially conservative opponents, which were hostile toward civil rights reform at both the city and county levels.

To propel the goals of racial integration and civil rights, progressive community leaders worked with the Bakersfield City Council to form the Intergroup Relations Board (IRB) in 1963. Local activists believed that the formation of the IRB—which was charged with advising the city government on civil rights and race relations—marked a triumph of racial liberalism. The IRB's mandate to work collaboratively with local government, however, proved difficult to implement. Resistance of local officials to this community body prevented the board from becoming effective in the realm of civil rights. Multiracial collaboration with local government proved largely unfeasible in Bakersfield and Kern County.

Although organized conservative resistance toward political, social, and economic reform stymied civil rights enforcement, the emergence of the KCCU in the immediate post–World War II years and its subsequent resurgence through the later fair housing and FEPC movements were significant developments in Bakersfield's urban grassroots civil rights history. The civic unity movement in Bakersfield drew on the larger efforts of the California Federation for Civic Unity (CFCU), an important, albeit short-lived, multiracial civil rights organization founded in the late 1940s. Although the CFCU ultimately suffered disarray as a statewide organization, due in part to what historian Mark Brilliant calls California's "multiple streams" of civil rights efforts, multiracial civic unity activists were key in sustaining Bakersfield's urban civil rights movement long after the CFCU declined statewide.[1] Unfortunately, the early Bakersfield movement suffered a leadership vacuum when its founder, Rabbi Sanford Rosen, migrated north to San Mateo, California. Bakersfield's civic unity movement nevertheless survived the anticommunist politics of the 1950s and reemerged to champion civil rights reform a decade later.

The course of the civic unity movement highlights the successes and limits of multiracial coalition building in Bakersfield, as well as the racial liberal politics that defined multiracial coalition building in California's interior during this time. When the civic unity movement rematerialized in 1963, it did so in direct opposition to the politics of the IRB and that group's ineffectiveness in pressing civil rights enforcement and reform. Black and Brown civic unity activists, brought together in part by their white liberal allies, posited a more direct form of civil rights protest. Their efforts, while not always successful, are important examples of Black and Brown unity during the civil rights era. Black organizations and activists especially drove urban civil rights reform efforts in the late 1950s and early 1960s in Bakersfield. Mexican American organizations also joined these causes. Organizational conflicts between the IRB, the KCCU, and the Bakersfield City Council, however, as well as an ideological challenge mounted by Black and Chicana/o Power movements regarding the tenets of racial liberalism, would alter the course of civil rights reform in Kern County after 1965.

EARLY ACTIVISM

Improving the living conditions of farmworkers helped advance coalition building for civil rights reformers in the late 1940s. Between 1947 and 1949, the National Farm Labor Union (NFLU) carried on a strike and secondary boycott against the DiGiorgio Fruit Corporation. An offshoot of the Southern Tenant Farmers Union (STFU), the NFLU committed to organizing farmworkers in the rural outskirts of southeast Bakersfield because of the sheer poverty of surrounding towns like Lamont, Weedpatch, and Arvin.[2] Reflecting on race relations in the DiGiorgio strike, organizer and scholar-activist Ernesto Galarza recalled that Local 218, affiliate of the American Federation of Labor (AFL), successfully gathered white Okies, Black people, and Mexicans "all into a common effort across color lines," despite the fact that DiGiorgio segregated its labor force.[3] While the DiGiorgio strike lasted for thirty months and helped generate a spirit of multiracial solidarity across Kern County, a series of factors contributed to the strike's failure. Strikebreakers, congressional pressure, and libel suits against the AFL and its NFLU affiliate for publishing the short film *Poverty in the Valley of Plenty* (1948) forced farm labor organizers to reconsider their strategies.[4]

The strike helped put the San Joaquin Valley on the radar for national civil rights organizations. Writing to the national NAACP offices in New York City in 1950, the West Coast regional director, Franklin Williams, commented, "in all of my experience as an NAACP worker throughout the deep South I have never seen conditions as dreadful, unsanitary and depressing as those under which thousands of Negro migrant workers have to live on the outskirts of Bakersfield."[5] The Kern County farmworker population in the late 1940s was, however, multiracial and included African American migrants from Texas, Arkansas, and Oklahoma as well as white people, Mexican Americans, and Mexican nationals. The area's poverty had been the subject of Dorothea Lange's photography a decade prior, when she documented the conditions faced by migrant families, including Black and Brown families, who came to California in search of agricultural work. Assessing the segregated communities outside Bakersfield's city limits, Williams continued, "there are hundreds of ramshackle temporary dwellings without light or sanitation whatsoever, the people having to use pit toilets, the odors from which are readily recognizable for miles away."⁶ Such poor living conditions were synonymous with migrant labor camps and settlements. In August and September 1950, state inspectors from the Division of Housing in the Department of Industrial Relations surveyed housing conditions for agricultural workers in the San Joaquin Valley. Of the seven counties surveyed in California's Central Valley, Kern County had the highest estimated number of labor camps (375) and ranked near the bottom for the number of annual inspections (85).⁷

In light of the national attention brought to the alarming conditions of rural poverty and migration faced in Kern County, Bakersfield's civic unity movement articulated a multiracial approach as a means of solving the social and economic problems of the region's poor. The first target area for reform was the old Sunset-Mayflower tract. Originally a rural Black colony, the Sunset-Mayflower district developed at the dawn of the twentieth century as a space for Black farmworker families.⁸ During the first half of the twentieth century, migrant farmworkers continued to settle in and around this unincorporated section of southeast Bakersfield. What united the Black and Brown communities—and, for a time, the white Okie residents—was rural poverty. Efforts to improve relations between the more affluent residents of Bakersfield's urban core and the rural periphery of Bakersfield was challenging, but the city's civic unity movement helped bridge this gap.

Rabbi Sanford Rosen's efforts to promote civic unity in Bakersfield helped propel a spirit of multiracial unity in a segregated city. Ordained in 1947 at the young age of twenty-seven after studying at the Hebrew Union College–Jewish Institute of Religion in Cincinnati, Ohio, Rosen moved that same year to Bakersfield with his wife. There, he and 120 families established a reformed Jewish congregation, the Temple Beth El in northeast Bakersfield.⁹ Rosen's racial liberalism, which he embraced through his religiosity, was matched by that of the leadership of Bakersfield's Ministerial Union, an organization composed of Jews, Black ministers from southeast Bakersfield, and white evangelical Protestants. In a sermon delivered to Temple Beth El parishioners in the winter of 1948, Rosen stressed the importance of action and leadership in enacting true and meaningful democracy in Bakersfield. Recalling his attendance at a CFCU meeting in Asilomar, Rosen said, "there we met . . . men and women who have not yet shown themselves in Bakersfield. . . . Men and women of courage who have decided that glib talk is cheap when it comes to offering equality to racial and religious minorities."¹⁰ Speaking to Bakersfield's progressive Jewish community, Rabbi Rosen challenged his congregation to take action by noting that that CFCU's racially diverse members included "Jews, Protestants, Catholics, Negroes, Mexicans, and Chinese—some personally attacked and mistreated." Racial liberals and progressives in Bakersfield, Rosen reasoned, needed to "clean up the hypocrisy that speaks of equal rights, but does nothing about it."[11]

Racial segregation throughout greater Bakersfield posed a challenge for coalition building. In a January 1950 CFCU board of directors meeting, Rabbi Rosen highlighted the difficulties of organizing a Bakersfield council for civic unity. Rosen noted to the statewide organization that "the serious cases of segregation and discrimination in Bakersfield . . . [and the] organized opposition the Council [had] to meet" hindered the forming of an effective unity branch in Bakersfield.[12] Much of the resistance Rosen highlighted to the board came back to the problem of racial segregation in southeast Bakersfield and the fact that civil rights reformers were encountering stiff resistance by local government. And while Rosen proved critical in energizing the early civic unity movement in Bakersfield, he would depart for the San Francisco Bay Area in 1951, creating a leadership vacuum within the local civic unity movement that ultimately would not be filled until years later. Rosen would, however, continue cultivating his passion for civil rights and social justice causes, eventually marching with Dr. Martin Luther King Jr. in Selma, Alabama, in 1965 and fighting alongside César Chávez during the Delano grape strike that same year.[13]

In early 1950, the Greater Bakersfield Ministerial Association pressured the Bakersfield City Council to adopt an antidiscrimination ordinance, making it a misdemeanor to "display discriminatory signs in restaurants and businesses."[14] The city council's law, known officially as Ordinance 860, was approved on February 14, 1950. It stated that places of public accommodation in Bakersfield known to have signs excluding racial groups from such accommodations had to remove those signs.[15] In an effort led by ministers Lynn Wood and John Whiteneck Jr. and Bakersfield NAACP secretary Clara Howard, the ministerial alliance and the NAACP then successfully lobbied the Kern County Board of Supervisors to follow the city council's lead in early March 1950, instituting legislation to remove racially discriminatory signs. Despite the efforts of civil rights leaders to enforce municipal and countywide anti-segregation measures, the legacy of "sundown" towns persisted in the county outside Bakersfield, particularly in Taft (just south of Bakersfield) and Oildale (directly north of the city limits). While the idea of opening places of public accommodation to all persons regardless of race gained the approval of the municipal government and was generally viewed favorably as an indicator of social difference from the Jim Crow South, other matters of racial integration proved more divisive.

The contentious issue of expanded public housing in southeast Bakersfield mobilized urban civil rights activists. In March 1953, a heated local political battle surfaced over the issue of subsidized public housing in the Sunset-Mayflower district, the predominantly African American and Mexican American area of the city that earlier in the year had been annexed into the city's metropolitan limits. The contest centered on a local initiative known as Measure 4, which would expand city services into the racialized southeastern area of the city. This rezoning ordinance was designed to expedite a contract between the city of Bakersfield and the Kern Housing Authority to construct a public housing project at Owens Street and East California Avenue, just east of California Avenue Park (later renamed Martin Luther King Jr. Park).[16] A citizens committee emerged to challenge Measure 4 in early 1953. In newspaper advertisements, the committee urged taxpayers to vote against Measure 4, arguing that its passage would ultimately mean a higher financial outlay for "ALL KINDS OF PUBLIC SERVICES FOR THEM . . . schools, police, and fire protection, etc."[17] Such public denunciations of the initiative clearly indicated to white Bakersfield voters the connection between the allocation of local tax dollars and racially segregated spaces.

The Sunset-Mayflower Improvement Committee sponsored Measure 4, appealing to pragmatic concerns and a sense of civic unity to assist the poor. On March 24, 1953, however, Measure 4 for the Oro Vista Housing Project was defeated. Even so, the referendum's failure did not negate the legal mandate of the contract between the city of Bakersfield and the Kern Housing Authority. Construction of the Oro Vista Housing Project therefore pressed forward, albeit without broad public support. The opposition to Measure 4 would not be the last time Bakersfield's conservative base utilized the ballot box to oppose state-subsidized efforts to improve living and working conditions for Bakersfield's poor residents of color.

THE COMMUNITY SERVICE ORGANIZATION

In mid-1950s Bakersfield, opposition to subsidized housing projects was rooted in anticommunist politics and hostility toward migrant labor settlements. Anticommunism, moreover, provided local politicians with useful language to appeal to Cold War conservatives and civil rights reformers, particularly Mexican Americans. In Bakersfield, many Mexican American groups, such as the CSO, promoted the virtues of American citizenship and the rights associated with participatory democracy. In greater Bakersfield, amid a rising tide of Mexican immigration through the Bracero Program, the CSO championed the rights of the more permanent Mexican American population of southeast Bakersfield and throughout the more rural areas of Kern County. Voter registration, citizenship classes, and provision of information to the impoverished Spanish-speaking residents of southeast Bakersfield consumed much of the Bakersfield CSO's attention through the 1950s and early 1960s.

Established in Los Angeles in the late 1940s, the CSO organized active chapters throughout California. The Bakersfield chapter was established by César Chávez and other key Mexican American activists. The Bakersfield CSO, like many branches, was a family affair. The Govea family, including Juan, Margaret, and their young daughter Jessica (who later became a key organizer in the United Farm Workers [UFW]), was particularly important to the local CSO. Margaret Govea, following the death of her daughter from breast cancer in 2005, recalled, "My daughter Jessica was at one time president of the junior CSO. . . . They had . . . quite a few projects . . . [including] voter registration. . . . They were bird dogs" (activists too young to legally register voters).[18] The Bakersfield CSO chapter's emphasis on citizenship for the Spanish-speaking population of the city met resistance locally. The Kern County clerk's office was particularly slow in deputizing Spanish-speaking applicants for the CSO's voter registration drives. Referring to county clerk Vera Gibson, CSO organizer Fred Ross wrote to his fellow organizer César Chávez that "Gibson has never investigated Deputies like she is investigating the Spanish speaking applicants. . . . [It] is absolutely insulting to the Spanish speaking population and outright racial discrimination."[19] Later, the UFW used similar techniques of door-to-door organizing in the Central Valley. The CSO's tactics proved influential in community organizing in the following decade in the farmworker movement.

Though nonpartisan, the Bakersfield CSO worked closely with Democratic congressman Harlan Hagen, whose anticommunist credentials reflected the political sentiments of his Central Valley constituents. In March 1954 Hagen proposed legislation in Congress to outlaw the Communist Party in the United States.[20] Hagen's alliance with the Bakersfield CSO was evident in matters concerning immigration. The congressman worked diligently during the first six months of 1955 to prevent the Immigration and Naturalization Service (INS) from closing its Bakersfield office. The office was scheduled to be closed in July of that year because of budget cuts. Hagen's effort to keep the branch open was a response to local support, including from members of the city and county government, and an especially effective letter-writing campaign from the CSO. As labor and civil rights scholars have noted, the "alien" or "wetback" labor problem of the 1950s became a rallying cry for Mexican American civil rights leaders. Ernesto Galarza, who spent a significant amount of time as a labor organizer in California's Central Valley, pressed for the deportation of "wetback" labor. Such positions, however, "reflected . . . pro-union rather than anti-immigrant politics."[21] The tension between Mexican American citizens and undocumented laborers, as illustrated by the conflict over the closure of the INS center, continued well into the Delano grape strike (1965–1970) and the subsequent activism of the UFW.

At the time, however, the CSO's concern over the closure of the INS center was focused on advancing citizenship rights and civil rights for greater Bakersfield's Mexican American population. "The problems confronting the 'applicant for citizenship' are numerous and continuous in nature," wrote CSO members Justina and Daniel Arias to Congressman Hagen. "Unless we maintain the local immigration office, we shall have a huge increase in . . . alien labor problems. Many laws will be violated and enforcement of immigration laws will be down. The cost of return transportation of aliens will be imposed on the local law enforcement agencies and . . . paid by the taxpayers."[22] CSO members also referenced the practical implications of the office closure for Kern County law enforcement. Writing to Hagen, José R. Burciaga argued that "our local law enforcement officers have enough to do without having to check every Mexican they believe might be illegally residing here in Bakersfield."[23] Stronger anti-immigrant sentiments, too, were part of the rhetoric deployed against closing the immigration office—although not by members of the CSO. Jack White of the Kern County Labor Council wrote to the INS head that "illegal entrants create a serious problem in the realm of law enforcement through increased narcotics traffic; increased illegitimate children which become the responsibility of the county; and the spread of social diseases which cause an added load on the Health Department."[24]

The CSO's arguments against closing the immigration office, by contrast, stressed the potential lack of access to services for Mexican residents in Kern County and Bakersfield. Many Mexican residents aspired to become American citizens or were already in the process of doing so. Writing to Congressman Hagen, Bakersfield CSO president Henry Martinez opined, "a better reason for maintaining the Immigration office in Bakersfield . . . cannot be had as was observed by School Officials . . . on June 3rd, 1955 at the Potomac School Auditorium. Approximately one hundred and ninety-six persons received Certificates of Completion for attending Citizenship classes formed by the CSO and sponsored by the Adult Education Evening Program."[25] Despite the stronger strains of anti-immigrant sentiments expressed by Kern County's labor movement, the Bakersfield CSO was committed to its Spanish-speaking constituents and noncitizen population. The chapter was instrumental in garnering support for the noncitizen pension bill in 1961 and sent a large delegation to Sacramento to witness Governor Pat Brown sign legislation guaranteeing pension rights to persons over the age of sixty-five, regardless of citizenship status.[26]

GROWING CALLS FOR CIVIC UNITY

While African American and Mexican American coalitions had begun to form around farmworkers' rights and housing, the municipal FEPC movement in Bakersfield aroused the most important cross-racial activism of the period. Following World War II, California cities began adopting municipal FEPC ordinances, intended to prevent racial discrimination in employment or job training. The Earl Warren gubernatorial administration, however, resisted signing a state FEPC civil rights law. In May 1949, the Richmond City Council passed the first fair employment practices ordinance. Over the next decade, other cities followed suit, until 1959, when California finally adopted a statewide FEPC law under Democratic governor Pat Brown.[27]

In 1957, Bakersfield attempted to model its ordinance on what other California cities were doing. Bakersfield mayor Frank Sullivan visited Oakland with Bakersfield African American city councilman Henry Collins to study job laws in preparation for the creation of Bakersfield's municipal FEPC law.[28] The struggle to implement a municipal FEPC ordinance in Los Angeles also influenced the strategies adopted by Bakersfield civil rights leaders.[29] In fact, despite the failure of the Los Angeles civil rights coalition to pass a municipal FEPC law in the late 1940s, Bakersfield civil rights leaders adopted a version of the Los Angeles plan. The multiracial and organizational diversity of the FEPC movement between 1949 and 1959 illustrates the dynamics of multiracial coalition building and multiethnic civil rights activism in California.

Despite these cooperative efforts, the FEPC movement initially provoked a good deal of controversy. The West Coast (WC) office of the NAACP had pressed for FEPC legislation as the organization's most "paramount concern" in light of potential job losses in postwar California.[30] But other civil rights groups pushing for reforms chafed under the leadership and attitudes of the state's NAACP officers. Moreover, while a municipal FEPC ordinance was enacted in Bakersfield in September 1957, implementing the reform proved problematic. Specifically, an "enforced gag rule" for complaints registered with the local commission was controversial. Section 6 of Ordinance 1146, as Bakersfield's municipal FEPC law was known, described the duties of the commission in this regard: "it shall constitute malfeasance . . . for any

Commissioner to divulge or reveal to any person . . . evidence obtained in any proceedings."[31] The *Bakersfield Californian* came out publicly against the FEPC ordinance because of this "secrecy clause." "The ordinance includes provisions for secrecy that would damage seriously the public welfare," noted one editorial. While the *Californian*'s editorial staff sympathized with the goal of preventing discrimination and promoting equal employment opportunities, the secrecy clause obscured issues that the local press deemed public information. Defenders of the FEPC ordinance countered, noting that the law "provides for open court hearings in the event [closed] arbitration was unsuccessful."[32]

Local civil rights leaders lauded the passage of the Bakersfield FEPC law, despite the controversy over the gag rule. Assessing the legacy of the FEPC movement, historian Zaragosa Vargas has remarked, "FEPC laws in the southwestern states were defeated or narrowly passed, [but] were put on the agenda by a labor and civil rights coalition that mobilized community support on an enormous scale, anticipating the mass action efforts of the 1960s civil rights movements."[33] In Bakersfield, such a carryover effect was evident. The fair housing and antipoverty movements of the mid- to late 1960s were rooted in coalitions formed to create a meaningful municipal FEPC law in Bakersfield during the 1950s.

Racial integration in Bakersfield's housing market became a reality in the late 1950s and early 1960s. On August 9, 1960, for example, an African American family moved into the Hillcrest area of northeastern Bakersfield, a white and affluent community near the Bakersfield Country Club. But the new residents were not welcome. They kept a journal of the events and subsequently published their account anonymously in the city's only liberal periodical, *California Crossroads*. Among other things, repeated racist telephone calls forced the family to disconnect their phone service the first week in their new home. Airing their grievances to the *Crossroads* readership, the Black couple wrote, "We have not enjoyed one single moment in the beautiful house we bought. It is no pleasure to leave work tired at the end of the day and be called names and be looked down on by people who judge themselves to be better than you because they belong to a different ethnic group."[34]

An interest in maintaining the racial integrity of Bakersfield's metropolitan city limits was clearly on display during this public episode. One anonymous response to what *Crossroads* called the "colored man's journal" was submitted by a white female neighbor from the Hillcrest area. She claimed her opinion as "generally the same as a large majority of the neighbors living in the immediate vicinity." In blunt reply to the journal, the woman claimed that "I am not afraid to say that I do not want to live in a Negro neighborhood.

This is not because of prejudice, but because of my own personal experience, which is too personal to relate here. Since the Negro moved in, we have been literally a guinea-pig neighborhood with car after car of Negroes driving by to see the conquest.... I would like very much to know what this negro is trying to prove.... If it is Christian to live where one cannot be friends with his neighbors, where one has caused considerable mental anguish [and] ... physical pain ... then this Negro gentleman is indeed the greatest Christian in Bakersfield."[35] The anonymous woman's comments reflect the self-interested investment of white Bakersfieldians in maintaining a racially segregated housing market. A Mrs. Edna Buster wrote to Congressman Hagen in September 1962, inquiring of the Democrat, "I trust you are proud of Mississippi Governor Ross Barnett in staunchly fighting the usurpation of Miss.' State Rights.... This is a deadly serious fight the Mississippi Governor is making for *all* of the US.... California's laws could just as easily be ... next.... I pray you take of [sic] the cudgel along with Governor Barnett in defending our FREEDOMS."[36] A member of the Bakersfield chapter of the Daughters of the American Revolution, Buster saw no issue in supporting Mississippi governor Barnett's defense of racial segregation in Mississippi and pressed the congressman to take similar measures to protect racial segregation in Bakersfield.[37]

The struggle over fair housing in the early 1960s led to the second coming of the civic unity movement in Bakersfield. In the fall of 1960, Bakersfield's racially progressive religious community struck an alliance with its Southern California neighbors, borrowing some of the progressive strategies used by Los Angeles–based activists. On October 11, 1960, George Thomas of the Los Angeles Human Relations Council attended a large meeting at the Bakersfield Police Department auditorium, sponsored by the Bakersfield Council of Churches. Thomas discussed the potential of implementing a strategic plan used in Pasadena to promote open housing in Bakersfield.[38]

The rebirth of the civic unity movement was central to multiracial activism and coalition building. One early attempt at 1960s multiracial civic unity was the Intergroup Relations Board, the advisory group formed in July 1963 by the Bakersfield City Council. The IRB's mandate was to advise the city council in all matters related to "promoting harmonious racial relations" within the city limits of Bakersfield.[39] Resolution 47-63 noted that as of that year there was "no organization [in Bakersfield] enjoying official status nor representative of the entire community, having the promotion of interracial, religious, and ethnic harmony and progress as its primary purpose."[40] Although the IRB may have been the city council's effort to temper and control civil rights protesting, African American and Mexican American civil rights leaders expressed faith that the IRB could become a meaningful civil rights body. After the struggle to establish a municipal FEPC ordinance in Bakersfield, the IRB seemed like a logical step to Black, Brown, and white civil rights activists. And while some activists were skeptical of working with the local government on civil rights matters, the vast majority of Black and Brown residents were enthusiastic and hopeful about the IRB. In a 1963 field report, however, an NAACP-WC officer criticized the fact that civil rights efforts in Bakersfield were being carried out under the banner of the IRB and not the local NAACP. "Some of the things that are being done, are not being done in the name of the NAACP. The local NAACP branch and the Black churches organized about 1,200–1,400 people to attend a city council meeting where the human relations board was formed. It was apparently never included into the community dialogue that the NAACP branch was instrumental in this achievement."[41]

The bureaucratic structure of the IRB illustrates the problems civil rights leaders faced when working on enforcement issues with local government. Resolution 47-63 stated that each of the seven city council members had the "absolute right" to appoint one IRB member. The mayor appointed the remaining two IRB members, for a total of nine board members. The IRB was granted the responsibility of listening to community complaints of racial discrimination and advising the city council on appropriate action for redress. Complaints of discrimination were to be kept confidential and not made available to the public. The latter proviso was a source of complaint for civic unity–affiliated board members and the racial minority leadership, similar to criticisms years before about the "gag order" enforced through the municipal FEPC ordinance.

The most important aspect of the IRB was that it had both official city sanction and grassroots support from African Americans and Mexican Americans. Two key African American leaders who helped form the IRB were a prominent local attorney, Gabriel Solomon, and the Reverend Julius Brooks. Solomon served as the legal representative for the Bakersfield NAACP, and Brooks was an NAACP activist and the pastor of Cain Memorial African Methodist Episcopal (AME) Church in East Bakersfield, one of the area's oldest and largest Black churches. Brooks was appointed to be the IRB chair. Despite feeling some skepticism, Brooks took his position seriously. His role as IRB chair superseded in many ways his participation in the Bakersfield NAACP. The local NAACP was in disarray in the early 1960s. In a letter to former Bakersfield resident Tarea Hall Pittman, then serving in the NAACP's regional office in San Francisco, Bakersfield NAACP officer G. E. Stevens wrote that "for three years now this branch has operated in a cellar and will continue in a cellar.... If you are in any ways concerned as to why other organizations have taken it upon themselves to carry the civil rights ball ... the answer is ... the present administration."[42] Unfortunately, the original IRB resolution was vague, particularly regarding the group's exact functions. Brooks expressed confusion in August 1964, petitioning the city council to "write a resolution stating the purpose, powers, and functions of the board."[43] This political dilemma led to the eventual collapse of the IRB and the development of the KCCU.

KERN COUNCIL FOR CIVIC UNITY

The fundamental difference between the IRB and the KCCU was the inclination of civic unity activists toward direct action. In its short life, the IRB was perpetually stymied by conservative resistance on the city council and by a lack of organizational clarity. Integrating Bakersfield's housing market would require direct action, according to civic unity activists.

The passage of the Rumford Fair Housing Act in 1963 brought hope to civil rights activists that California's segregated cities might finally be liberated from the racial covenants that had prohibited people of color from moving into all-white neighborhoods for decades. But one year later, the passage of Proposition 14 overturned Rumford, halting efforts to end racial covenants in the California housing market until 1967, when the state supreme court ruled Proposition 14 unconstitutional. In Bakersfield, civil rights leaders mobilized against Proposition 14 during the 1964 campaign season. According to an early KCCU recruitment flyer, the ad hoc "No on 14" committee "developed a great sense of *espirit* [sic] and despite the overturning of the Rumford Act, decided to hold the committee together by forming the KCCU."[44] Founding KCCU members included a Bakersfield College faculty member, Duane Belcher; the local NAACP chair, Art Shaw; and a War on Poverty activist and teacher, Mel Brown. A consortium of urban civil rights organizations and activists (including the NAACP, the CSO, the National Farm Workers Association [NFWA], and antipoverty workers), the KCCU emphasized civic unity and racial liberalism rather than endorsing a narrow agenda defined by an alliance with a national civil rights organization or a particular racial group.

The KCCU had a broad agenda. Beyond housing, the KCCU worked to improve "education, employment, and [cross-racial] communication."[45] After 1965 the group worked diligently to assist African Americans and Mexican Americans and bring attention to key social, political, and economic issues.

One early KCCU effort included a photo publicity project of Bakersfield's southeastern ghettos and barrios, since Bakersfield's white residents seldom approached these communities. The previous year, a handful of housing tracts in southeastern Bakersfield had become the proposed site for implementing antipoverty programs, and KCCU chair Belcher held public forums to highlight the poverty in the area.[46] Despite the legal limbo of the Rumford Act's mandate to partially end racial discrimination in the housing market, KCCU members implemented a voluntary, good-neighbor fair housing program, requesting that homeowners and real estate agents sign nondiscrimination pacts for sales and property rentals. This program foreshadowed later efforts by KCCU members to force fair housing among resistant local real estate agents, after Proposition 14 was overturned in 1967.[47]

In March 1965, the KCCU organized a large peaceful protest in the name of civic unity and racial harmony in Bakersfield. Like many other civil rights activists throughout the United States, the organizers were influenced by events occurring in the South. The protest was described as "a combined civil rights demonstration and memorial for the Unitarian clergyman James Reeb slain in Selma, Alabama."[48] A multiracial crowd of nearly three thousand people marched from Cain Memorial AME Church to the Kern Civic Center in downtown Bakersfield. The speaking roster indicated a connection between the southern civil rights movement and Bakersfield. The Reverend Ralph Click of the Church of the Brethren spoke passionately about the day's march and its connection to Selma: "The freedom of both black and white is at stake. This is true of areas outside the South. I know there were people afraid to join us today; they were afraid to be seen here. They might lose their job, or their status in the community or their friends. . . . We are met here today for freedom for Selma and Bakersfield."[49]

Other community leaders in attendance included IRB members and antipoverty activists. Sylvia Ganz, who was appointed to the IRB in 1965, addressed the crowd: "Our destiny and the destiny of the children [are] inseparably bound up with the people [and] will determine the meaning of democracy for all of us."[50] For Ganz, this notion rang especially true. Her son Marshall was at the time a Harvard senior on academic leave working with the Student Nonviolent Coordinating Committee (SNCC) in Mississippi. Soon, Marshall Ganz returned home to Bakersfield "with Mississippi eyes" and joined the struggle in the agricultural fields, working full time as an organizer for the newly founded NFWA under the leadership of César Chávez.[51] An ethos of civic unity and racial harmony characterized the speeches made that day at the KCCU rally, and racial liberalism was at the core of civil rights leadership in Bakersfield through 1965.

The beginning of 1966, however, tested the limits of racial liberalism in Bakersfield. In January, the White Citizens' Council initiated a public campaign to develop its local chapter in order to counter civil rights activism occurring in both the agricultural fields of Kern County and the city of Bakersfield. White supremacy had a long history in the county. In 1922, a Kern County grand jury had returned its first partial report on an investigation of the local Ku Klux Klan. This was the first such investigation in the United States, and the grand jury found that over four hundred Klan members resided in the county.[52] As the decades wore on, white supremacy manifested itself in somewhat more discreet and subtler organizations, like the John Birch Society and White Citizens' Councils. Founded in Mississippi following the *Brown v. Board of Education* decision in 1954, Citizens' Councils spread rapidly throughout the southern states, espousing a rhetoric of "state's rights and racial integrity."[53] The effectiveness of the IRB and the KCCU was tested when the White Citizens' Council made public inroads in establishing a grassroots challenge to racial liberalism in Bakersfield.

Cooperative action among Black, Brown, and white liberal activists was clearly seen in the opposition to the White Citizens' Council. On January 18, 1966, the White Citizens' Council held a meeting in downtown Bakersfield to publicize the group's activities and distribute racist literature. African American, Mexican American, and white civil rights activists protested the meeting. About thirty to forty community demonstrators disrupted the Citizens' Council meeting at the El Tejon Hotel, after a "broken water pipe" had forced the Citizens' Council to relocate from a previously booked downtown conference center. After the demonstrators had delayed the meeting for two hours, the Los Angeles White Citizens' Council field director, Frank Bain, phoned the Bakersfield city police, informing them that the protesters were disrupting a private meeting. The protesters in turn claimed that the Citizens' Council had invited any interested community members to attend the meeting and that the demonstrators had become upset when they were not made welcome.[54]

As local folks protested the Citizens' Council gathering, the demonstrators called the newspapers to document what was happening. Speaking to reporters, Bain said, "Kern County was in need of a group that could speak for the majority white citizens.... The White Citizens' Council ... opposed ... federal intervention in local affairs, especially education."[55] The civil rights protesters were blunter. Marshall Ganz, fresh from his work in Mississippi with the SNCC, told reporters that the "Citizens Council was a secret Deep South organization made up of racists."[56] Direct action against the expansion of the White Citizens' Council was the type of activism KCCU members embraced, especially compared to the more passive responses offered by the overly bureaucratic IRB.

On January 21, 1966, the IRB reported to the city council that the board should officially investigate what had happened between the civil rights protesters and the White Citizens' Council just days prior. Julius Brooks, the IRB chair, was one of two board members especially concerned with the presence of the Citizens' Council in the city. According to his testimony and that of others, the White Citizens' Council had confronted the Community Action Program (CAP) Committee earlier that year and sought out information about antipoverty programs and Black members who had initiated the antipoverty movement two years earlier.[57] African American activist Art Shaw reported at the city council meeting that the White Citizens' Council was very "selective" at the El Tejon Hotel and did not give any of the group's literature to African American or Mexican American civil rights activists, who sought the information in the hotel lobby. Shaw reported that the principal view of the White Citizens' Council "promote[d] separation of the races, . . . [and] school segregation . . . [was its] primary target."[58] City councilman Richard Stiern interrogated Shaw, questioning whether the IRB was investigating other segregationist groups, such as the Black Muslims (i.e., Nation of Islam).[59] Stiern's thinking epitomized that of the larger Bakersfield community of voters. James Armstrong of the Bakersfield Forum for American Opinion publicly accused antipoverty activist Mel Brown, Reverend Brooks, and other civil rights "agitators" of being "behind the White Citizens' Council and the Muslims [sic] . . . attempt[s] to trigger another Watts in Bakersfield."[60] Hyperbolic claims regarding left-wing minority conspiracies surfaced noticeably during these years, especially as the Delano grape strike garnered national attention.

Brooks urged city council members to send an official letter condemning the presence of the White Citizens' Council and its disruptive and mean-spirited activities in Bakersfield. But after a heated debate, the council members decided not to issue a letter condemning the Citizens' Council.[61] They instead agreed to send the group a copy of Resolution 47-63, the resolution that had produced the IRB and articulated the goals (if not the functions) of the board. The only city council member to support the IRB's position to publicly condemn the Citizens' Council was African American councilman Del Rucker, a longtime funeral home proprietor and the only racial minority member of the city council. Representing the First Ward, in southeastern Bakersfield, Rucker made a motion to have the city council officially take a stand and condemn the White Citizens' Council, reiterating that the group was "disturbing racial harmony." Rucker's motion died for lack of a second.[62] Other city council members, particularly Bill Park and Dennis Hosking, disagreed with the Citizens' Council's message, but stressed that it was not within the legal right of the city council to condemn the presence of any group.

African Americans and Mexican Americans nevertheless continued to bombard the city council in protest over the White Citizens' Council. On January 31, 1966, Reverend Brooks again addressed the city council, this time speaking for forty-five minutes. He addressed the city council's failure to directly rebuke the comments made the previous week by a White Citizens' Council field representative. Brooks declared that the Citizens' Council preached "hate and segregation" and said that as the IRB chair and a concerned citizen and taxpayer, he felt it was the moral duty of the city council to officially condemn the group's presence in Bakersfield. Responding to Brooks, Councilman Park stated that he agreed but was not sure "why all the minority people were there" that night in the city council chambers. Once again, the chamber was filled to capacity with Bakersfield's African American and Mexican American residents. Park told Brooks and the audience that the "city council had taken a stand against the White Citizens' Council" by sending the group a copy of Resolution 47-63, which stated the official goals of the IRB.[63] Park did not understand why the "minority people" were in attendance, since action had already been taken.

Park's confusion about the large racial minority presence that night in the chamber illustrates the ideological division in Bakersfield over the politics of civil rights. Civil rights activists and community leaders expressed an ethos of racial liberalism, petitioning the city council for redress for the actions and presence of the White Citizens' Council in Bakersfield. African Americans and Mexican Americans hoped that if they demonstrated how the ideas and presence of the Citizens' Council promoted racial disharmony and segregation, the city council would respond favorably. The majority of the city council countered, however, that as the city's official governing body, it had done everything within its legal authority to remedy the community disturbance by sending the letter reiterating the goals of the IRB to the Citizens' Council. City council members asserted that the city government had no legal right to tell the Citizens' Council that the organization could not assemble peacefully in Bakersfield.

The city council's unwillingness to condemn the Citizens' Council ultimately helped sever the limited alliance between multiracial civil rights groups and the local government. Indeed, the anti-statist logic the city council demonstrated in the debate over the White Citizens' Council, coupled with the city's simultaneous legislative drive to oppose the funding of antipoverty programs with local tax dollars, indicated the city's inaction to end poverty and segregation. The city council's willingness to use the power of the government to oppose civil rights was contingent on circumstances rather than being based on political principles. In brief, the city council discriminatingly used the powers of local government to champion conservatism and would continue to do so to stymie the liberal, federally funded War on Poverty.

The conflict between the IRB and the city council over the White Citizens' Council also led to reforms by the city council to quash civil rights protest in its meetings. The city council voted to limit the public forum aspect of the meetings shortly after it sent the Citizens' Council a copy of Resolution 47-63. The large presence of "minority people" at the city council meetings had become a source of contention between the city council and minority residents, and the city council passed a resolution to "regulate the procedure by which citizens could address the council."[64] The state attorney general approved. According to the attorney general's office, the Bakersfield City Council was perfectly within its legal rights to regulate the manner in which the public addressed the body (and to use police power to do so). This new procedural rule for public meetings further strained the relationship between the city council and the city's African American and Mexican American citizens, silencing what had been the principal forum for urban civil rights protest in Bakersfield.

CONCLUSION

The civil rights mobilization engendered by the civic unity, FEPC, and human relations commission movements encapsulated racial liberalism in Bakersfield. Nondiscrimination and equal opportunity were core tenets of racial liberal thinking in California.[65] Racial liberals opposed both de jure and de facto racial segregation, as well as the economic, political, and social disparities between the city's and county's white residents and their Black and Brown neighbors. Although well intended, the racial liberalism that defined these multiracial coalition movements waned with the rise of ethnic power movements. Following the national attention brought to the SNCC and the Black Power movement in Los Angeles and Oakland, civic unity coalitions struggled to come to terms with the implications of Black and Brown Power. With even greater local impact, the UFW built a strong coalition of civil rights activists, especially among African American leaders in Oakland, concerning the union's boycott against grapes.[66]

Encouraged by the farmworker movement's challenge to Bakersfield racial conservatism, urban Chicana/o activists would soon take on a primary role in the KCCU, eventually eclipsing the well-intentioned white activists who had defined the earlier years of the civic unity movement and brokered organizational relations between Black and Brown activists. Ethnic power movements subsequently alienated many white racial liberals, as well as some Black and Brown civil rights activists of earlier generations. The older generations' efforts to build multiracial coalitions in southeastern Bakersfield seemed contrary to the idea of ethnic separatism posited by Chicana/o and Black Power activists. Last and perhaps most importantly, increased Mexican migration to Kern County bolstered the position of Chicana/o civil rights leaders, who moved to the center of an ideological battle over race relations and the future of civil rights reform in the lower San Joaquin Valley.

The various Black and Brown civil rights activisms, demonstrated by efforts to work both cooperatively and outside the bounds of local government, were significant in establishing Bakersfield's urban civil rights movement. Black and Brown activists, rooted in racially segregated communities, found common ground in the movements addressed in this chapter. While known more broadly for its brand of anti-statist conservatism in the second half of the twentieth century, Bakersfield witnessed a vibrant and multiracial challenge to both political marginalization and racial segregation. Such activism played a critical and foundational role in extending the scope and impact of both labor and civil rights reform in the American Far West. That multiracial activism, as well as antagonists to this movement, would find new energy under Lyndon B. Johnson's War on Poverty programs.

3 | "MAXIMUM FEASIBLE PARTICIPATION" AND OPPOSITION

The War on Poverty in Kern County, 1964–1967

> We are appalled by the amount of poverty in your congressional district. The gap keeps increasing. [T]he rate of unemployment in the Ghetto is over 3 times the average for the City of Bakersfield. . . . There is over 30 times as much unemployment . . . as in typical middle-class tracts. The average income in some parts of southeast Bakersfield is less than $2,000 per year compared to an average of $7,500. In terms of income, housing, education, and employment the plight of the migrant worker is even worse than that of our urban peer.
>
> *Letter from Henry Fuller of the Kern Council for Civic Unity to Congressman Harlan Hagen, October 1965*

This chapter expands the multiracial narrative of civil rights history in California's Central Valley by examining the early years of the War on Poverty in Kern County. The history of the antipoverty movement illuminates the intersection of neo-southern political conservatism and civil rights reform in California's interior.[1] Anti-statist conservatism, defined by the persistence of localism and hostility toward federal intervention into local politics, was connected to racial politics in the southern San Joaquin Valley. The farmworker and subsequent Chicana/o Power movements represent foundational political and social challenges to racial segregation and discrimination in Central California after 1965—fundamentally shaping civil rights reform thereafter. The California conservative ascendency associated with Ronald Reagan's 1966 gubernatorial victory was mobilized in opposition to the civil rights coalitions built in part by the 1965 Delano grape strike.[2]

Kern County has historically been one of California's most poverty-stricken rural areas. Southeast Bakersfield was home to thousands of African American and Mexican migrant cotton workers, who settled there in the late 1930s and 1940s.[3] Antipoverty leaders in rural California enthusiastically joined the larger civil rights movement for economic and social justice, symbolized by Lyndon B. Johnson's War on Poverty. Historians have reassessed scholarship that dismissed the federal effort as a dismal failure, noting the intricate connections between community action agencies of the War on Poverty and broader movements for cultural, economic, political, and gender empowerment.[4] To dismiss the Johnson administration's economic policy as a failure is to obscure the hundreds of stories at the grassroots level where African American and Mexican American communities were empowered to enact civil rights reform in a localized context.[5] This chapter shows that the early War on Poverty in Kern County brought together white, African American, and Mexican American civil rights leaders in a common public policy cause. Resistance from anti-statist conservatives and interracial power struggles over implementation and supervision of poverty programs, ultimately, however, challenged multiracial coalition building, with consequences for civil rights activist groups.

A racially diverse leadership took varying positions on antipoverty programs. Multiracial activists, legal and nonlegal residents, migrants and established residents all staked a claim in the political dialogue surrounding antipoverty programs. Activist organizations such as the Kern Council for Civic Unity (KCCU), the Mexican American Community Service Organization (CSO), the Negro Ministerial Alliance, and the National Association for the Advancement of Colored People (NAACP), as well as members of the Bakersfield College faculty, joined together to initiate War on Poverty programs. Antipoverty foes included the Bakersfield and Delano City Councils, the local chambers of commerce, members of the Kern County Board of Supervisors, and, as the 1966 ballot revealed, a strong majority of Bakersfield's registered voters. The fact that Kern County's antipoverty movement was propelled from the bottom up is also important. Bakersfield was unlike other American cities such as Philadelphia or Chicago, where the mayor's office and city council actively sought antipoverty monies for political gain. Kern County's antipoverty movement originated with community groups that sought federal assistance to improve local communities that had been marginalized for decades by city politics and racial segregation.

The political ramifications of the antipoverty movement in Kern County were dramatic. Liberal reformers and civil rights activists faced an especially virulent strand of what the historian Thomas R. Wellock called anti-statist conservatism in local government and political culture.[6] The antipoverty movement in Kern County became politically controversial when César Chávez and the National Farm Workers Association (NFWA) were awarded a $287,000 federal grant in September 1965, part of a $6.3 million, eight-state allocation for state and nonprofit agencies working on migrant issues in the War on Poverty.[7] The reaction, mobilization, and outrage of conservatives over the NFWA grant stymied the early antipoverty movement. An angry conservative voting bloc, primed for 1966, opposed antipoverty programs and elected Republican legislators hostile toward the expansion of the so-called welfare state and the federal subsidizing of civil rights. Conservatives fought the NFWA's grape strike, launched in September 1965, and sought to ensure that the NFWA (later the United Farm Workers [UFW]) would never receive any antipoverty funds. Building an opposition to the NFWA and the idea of state-sponsored radicalism, conservatives also pushed against African Americans, Mexican Americans, and antipoverty programs in southeast Bakersfield. Despite the differences between rural farmworkers and Bakersfield's southeast residents, a mutual struggle to fight poverty through federal intervention was forged in the fires of anti-statist political reaction to civil rights.

The southeast Bakersfield antipoverty alliance faced a legal referendum on the November 1966 ballot, where a majority of Bakersfield voters decided not to support antipoverty programs with local tax dollars. Federal regulations stipulated that local resources within the poverty grant area match 10 percent of the federal dollars allocated. Bakersfield was unique in its reputation as a city where local government opposed accepting antipoverty dollars, rather than treating them as an influx of funds flexible enough for political gain.[8] Notably, since Bakersfield's referendum had little legal impact, antipoverty programs nevertheless came to fruition. The symbolism of legal populism, however, was far more important to conservatives. The referendum mobilized the conservative base and marked the beginning of a protracted struggle by conservatives to undermine the antipoverty movement in Kern County and limit its impact on civil rights. Conservatives ignored the structural inequalities caused by deindustrialization and capital flight, preferring instead to focus politically on individual moral deficiencies among the poor.[9] Deindustrialization, unlike in Detroit or other Rust Belt areas, was not the cause of poverty in Kern County. The lingering reality of what Carey McWilliams called "factories in the fields" and the omnipresent need for migrant labor made poverty and Kern County synonymous and seemingly perpetually linked.[10]

THE POLITICS OF POVERTY IN KERN COUNTY

Rising poverty in the 1960s was the impetus for federal intervention to alleviate unemployment and poverty in America. The 1960 census painted a devastating portrait of this problem, affirmed for a wide reading audience in Michael Harrington's 1962 study *The Other America: Poverty in the United States*.[11] Poverty in California's rural interior had a similar effect as in other US regions, but the causes differed. In Kern County, poverty resulted from rural migration to places where agricultural laboring families, their descendants, and others managed to eke out an existence outside city limits. Civic unity leaders used data from the 1960 census to present their case for fighting poverty through federal intervention, as illustrated in the 1965 letter to Democratic congressman Harlan Hagen that appears as this chapter's epigraph.

The War on Poverty began in earnest with the passage of the 1964 Economic Opportunity Act. Community action programs and agencies formed shortly thereafter across the United States, in response to federal Community Action Program (CAP) legislation. "On October 3, 1964, six weeks after Johnson signed the Economic Opportunity Act, Congress appropriated $800 million to launch OEO [the Office of Economic Opportunity], including $300 million for community action [programs]," writes historian Allen J. Matusow. Numerous community organizations submitted grant applications to win federal funds. By June 1965, 415 community action agencies were already in existence; a year later, they numbered more than 1,000.[12] Bakersfield was one of the community actions programs nationally to gain federal assistance by 1965. Describing the War on Poverty as "a new genesis" in the long history of antipoverty work in southeast Bakersfield, civil rights activist Johnie Mae Parker recognized that the 1964 Economic Opportunity Act was linked to earlier efforts to fight poverty. "'Something old, yet something new' was the 'Equal Opportunity Act,'" she mused. "A resumption of previous experiences of volunteer community groups to wage war against poverty, a battle to be regenerated and fortified by means of federal funds," Parker recalled.[13]

The resistance of the Bakersfield City Council toward implementing antipoverty programs was a unique political gesture in the heyday of American liberalism. Matusow describes the tendency of municipal government toward implementing antipoverty monies as follows: "the bulk of CAP's money went to the 100 or so biggest cities.... The mayors of these cities were guided by their own convenient conceptions of what community action should be. To many, antipoverty was merely a new mechanism to provide an expanded flow of conventional services to restless (i.e., black) neighborhoods, with city hall garnering the credit."[14] This scenario was not the case in Bakersfield. The restless areas of the city were multiracial, and white liberals actively built racial coalitions with African Americans and Mexican Americans to pressure a resistant city hall to support antipoverty programs.

A coalition of African American and Mexican American civic and religious organizations spearheaded Kern County's antipoverty movement. In February 1965 at St. John Missionary Baptist Church in southeast Bakersfield, ministers and leaders from several African American churches and organizations met seeking information about how they could assist in activating antipoverty programs, marshal resources for action, and carry the "good news" back to their parishioners.[15] The Reverend Anand Prasad, a migrant minister and director of the Friendship House Community Center, explained to attendees the main tenets of the Economic Opportunity Act. A steering committee was formed, and the following week 150 southeast Bakersfield residents founded the Target Community Citizens Anti-Poverty Council (or Target Area Poverty, TAP). According to federal documents, TAP was a "private non-profit corporation, incorporated in 1965. It had a representative council, consisting of nine community organizations and ten neighborhood councils. The TAP Board of Directors was the governing and policy-making body of the council [and] consisted of two representatives from each member organization. . . . Total [TAP] membership consisted of thirty-nine [directors]."[16] TAP's basic organizational principle was to undertake all necessary steps to find ways and means to eliminate poverty, inform fellow citizens of programs and services, seek support and cooperation from local officials, and encourage self-help efforts within and among target area residents.[17]

Dolores Huerta, cofounder of the NFWA, was somewhat skeptical of the Bakersfield TAP board, specifically Anand Prasad. In a letter to OEO official Ruth Graves, she questioned whether Prasad wanted the NFWA to succeed in its own antipoverty programs for rural Kern and Tulare Counties. After meeting with Prasad and discussing the two organizations' programs, Huerta reasoned that Prasad believed that if the NFWA was successful in its program, the OEO might award future grants to the NFWA, not TAP. Huerta reiterated to Graves that despite her skepticism, there was enough poverty in Kern County and the southern Central Valley for both agencies to work together.[18] The exchange also highlights the geographic differences between TAP's programming in southeast Bakersfield and the more rural-oriented programs outlined by the NFWA.

The geographic target area for TAP covered most of southeast Bakersfield within and beyond the city's metropolitan boundaries. The area housed

30,411 persons of Mexican and "Negro" origin, according to the 1960 census.[19] On August 16, 1965, an opening reception was held at the Friendship House at 2424 Cottonwood Road, celebrating the first antipoverty funds in Kern County to be awarded to TAP. Twenty-five-year-old African American teacher and Sunset-Mayflower resident Melvin (Mel) Brown was appointed the agency's first project director. Born in 1941, Brown moved as a child with his parents from Arkansas to southeast Bakersfield in 1946. He earned his college degree in 1963 from Sacramento State College and taught later that year at Casa Loma Elementary School in southeast Bakersfield. Brown led the TAP program until he was drafted into military service in 1966.[20]

TAP accomplished much within its first year. The program placed 355 people in new jobs between September 1965 and October 1966, taught English literacy classes to the foreign born, provided food and clothing to nearly 300 families, assisted over 200 people in registering for Medicare, and helped impoverished area residents obtain legal representation and medical services.[21] A coalition of African American and Mexican American urban activists led TAP's community outreach. When TAP held its opening ceremonies at the Friendship House, representatives from the most active Mexican American and African American organizations attended: L. S. Barraza of the CSO, Art Shaw of the NAACP, Juan Govea of the Comisión Honorífica Mexicana (Mexican Honorary Commission), Charles Stevens of the Sunset-Mayflower Progressive Club, Felix Ramirez of the Mexican American Political Association (MAPA), Kenneth Gatewood of the International Longshore and Warehouse Union, Salene Stevens of the National Council of Negro Women, and Willie Delouth of the Community Council of Carversville and Crystal Heights.[22] Collectively, these individuals represented key leadership organizations active within southeast Bakersfield's Black and Brown neighborhoods.

The CSO was Kern County's prominent Mexican American civic organization and was intricately connected with civil rights movements in Bakersfield and the state.[23] On October 3, 1966, the CSO acquired office space at 1206 Baker Street, once the hub of the old railroad town, Kern Island (or Sumner), which came to be known as East Bakersfield.[24] Many CSO programs operated from this location. Having a central gathering place for area residents to learn of available public services was important for the CSO's success.[25] The CSO targeted the Spanish-speaking residents of southeast Bakersfield as beneficiaries of poverty programs. One TAP worker, reflecting on the importance of the CSO, noted at the time that "the newly set up CSO service center . . . will do much for the Spanish-speaking folk in the target area and bring to them, across a language barrier, not only information about community services, but the confidence to use them."²⁶

The CSO also provided a training program for neighborhood workers that proved vital for effective community organizing. The target area was divided into twelve neighborhood councils, with at least one worker assigned to each. Suitable buildings within each neighborhood were donated by local landlords or rented by TAP to meet the required 10 percent local matching funds stipulated by the OEO. Each target area housed predominantly Mexican American and African American residents, with segregated racial enclaves therein. Area 9, for example, was represented by La Loma council and had a population that was 98 percent Hispanic. Neighborhood TAP workers Carlos Bañales and Jesse Boyar were both active in the antipoverty movement. In subsequent years, each participated in several civil rights efforts: Bañales through CSO, and Boyar in efforts to desegregate the Bakersfield City School District (BCSD). The antipoverty movement taught this area's cadre the importance of community organizing in mobilizing for civil rights struggles.

TAP neighborhood workers witnessed firsthand the poverty in southeast Bakersfield. The homes of aged and former migrant workers blighted the area, reminiscent of the poverty encountered by Dust Bowl Okie migrants in the 1930s. Neighborhood workers were outraged when, in March 1966, the Bakersfield City Council and Kern County Community Action Program Committee stalled the implementation of antipoverty programs. Disagreements among CAP Committee members and obstructionist tactics practiced by local Republicans put antipoverty programs in jeopardy. TAP workers wrote to the CAP Committee, stating, "we are deeply concerned with the tragic fact that $1.5 million in federal funds earmarked for Kern County is in jeopardy unless prompt and direct action is taken by the local CAP Committee to implement the 'Economic Opportunity Act' of 1964. . . . This Act has granted millions born in hopeless deprivation the chance of a new start in life through public works, private incentive and Anti-Poverty Programs."²⁷ The city government's lack of support for antipoverty programs was amplified by the city council's weak position on condemning the expansion of the White Citizens' Council in Bakersfield. Bakersfield's racial minority communities, as a result, suspected the motives of the city's governing board.

The Sunset-Mayflower community was soon up in arms over the city council's failure to support antipoverty programs. Census tract 22, which encompassed the entire Sunset-Mayflower community, was nearly 100 percent African American and Mexican American in its makeup. Mexican

Americans surrounded the tract in neighboring *colonias* or "island communities," beyond city limits. The construction of the boundaries of the city was a contested issue in the early 1950s, when the Sunset-Mayflower tract was annexed to the city against opposition from the city's mostly white residents. By the time African American and Mexican American civil rights leaders moved into the city's political realm and gained funding for community development through the Economic Opportunity Act, southeast Bakersfield civil rights activists had maintained a contentious relationship with the larger white community for over a decade, centered on the issue of racial segregation.

Conservative opposition to antipoverty programs ensued shortly after the War on Poverty began. Patty Newman, a California conservative author in the 1960s (later a staunch opponent of the UFW), described the War on Poverty as "bombs of cash" that the Johnson administration dropped across the country, with no apparent logic or need, other than to secure Democratic voters.[28] Within a few short years, the dollar amount spent on the War on Poverty was curtailed by the war in Vietnam, but also by conservative political pressure and public reaction to race riots in Watts, Harlem, and Detroit. Conservatives mobilized to preserve law and order in the public sphere and argued that antipoverty programs rewarded immoral behavior and would never solve the root causes of poverty.[29] The threat of racial violence was a reality during the early years of the antipoverty program in Bakersfield. In May 1966, four days of racial violence plagued the Lakeview-Cottonwood district in southeast Bakersfield. The cause of the violence was discussed by the Bakersfield City Council. Minutes indicate that the city council's lack of endorsement for antipoverty programs was a principal cause of the youth rebellion and the increased law enforcement presence in southeast Bakersfield.[30] The presence of police forces and curfews, in turn, marked the area as a racial hot spot with potential for violence. Activists argued that antipoverty programs were critical to tempering the racial animosity brewing in southeast Bakersfield.[31]

As in other areas of the United States, a political contest over the OEO mandate of "maximum feasible participation" of the poor became a dividing line between liberal activists and conservatives, affecting how poverty programs were structured and administered in Kern County. The federal thinking was that if the poor participated in ending poverty, such programs were likely to be more successful than a top-down implementation strategy. No one, liberal or conservative, challenged the moral aim of ending poverty. Disagreement centered on the root causes of poverty and the question of how to solve them. War on Poverty opponents reasoned that earlier migrants had endured worse conditions yet quietly assimilated into American culture—affirmed by Okie migrants' successful economic mobility upward during and after World War II. Other Bakersfield conservatives, conversely, sought to use the bureaucracy of the War on Poverty to limit the power of so-called radicals and communists, whom they insisted had infiltrated the ranks of federal, state, and local government. Attacks on the antipoverty program became part of a broader war by conservatives on what they viewed as irresponsible federal intervention in defiance of local control. When local conservatives supported the antipoverty movement, it was only through the highly polarized and ineffective Kern County CAP Committee, which was limited by the oppositional tactics practiced by conservatives on the board itself.

SUBSIDIZING CIVIL RIGHTS

The political turmoil wrought by Kern County's antipoverty movement exploded when César Chávez and the NFWA were awarded an antipoverty grant in early autumn 1965, around the same time the Delano grape strike began. The grant unleashed a torrent of political protest from local conservatives. Recounting the beginnings of the Delano strike, journalist Miriam Pawel writes, "In the summer of 1965 rumblings of unrest broke the monotony of another season in the Delano fields. . . . Rumors of an impending strike spread. . . . On the morning of September 8, the Mexicans found out when they showed up for work that the Filipinos had refused to leave their camps. . . . The strike had arrived in Delano."[32] Opponents of the strike roared that an NFWA antipoverty grant effectively subsidized a union bent on destroying the economic lifeblood of Kern County—agriculture. Their arguments centered on the idea that Chávez was not qualified to administer taxpayer funds, despite the fact that the NFWA had been vetted just like any other grant recipient. The NFWA grant called for a farmworker "education" project, which in turn prompted the conservatives' questioning of Chávez's qualifications. Conservatives believed that the antipoverty movement would become a vehicle for union and communist indoctrination clothed in the liberal guise of "maximum feasible participation" of the poor. The kind of education the NFWA would offer, conservatives argued, would misuse taxpayer dollars, especially if that education undermined the social and economic relations between growers and docile migrant workers that had been cultivated by Kern growers for decades.

The backlash against the NFWA facilitated a shift in local politics, specifically within the Democratic Party and among the growing Republican opposition toward liberalism. Incumbent Democratic congressman Harlan Hagen lost his reelection campaign in 1966 to his Republican challenger, former Olympic gold medalist Bob Mathias, as a result of the politicization of the War on Poverty. A member of the California State Assembly from 1949 to 1952, Hagen represented Kern County in the US Congress from 1953 to 1967, on behalf of the fourteenth congressional district (1953–1963) and then the reapportioned eighteenth congressional district (1963–1967).[33] Hagen's loss to Mathias illustrates how opposition to the War on Poverty channeled the animosity of anti-statist conservatives into political action. The controversy over the NFWA grant mobilized Republican voters eager to vent their resentment toward the grape strike, liberalism, civil rights, and the War on Poverty's perceived irresponsible use of taxpayer dollars. In this political tumult, Hagen struggled to save his career between 1965 and 1966. Having first supported the NFWA grant, he abruptly shifted position after the grape strike began. His change of heart outraged NFWA supporters, as well as African Americans and Mexican Americans loyal to the Democratic Party in Kern County. Hagen was seen as a "grower-bought" congressman who abandoned principle for political expediency.

NFWA leadership had been in contact with OEO officials about applying for antipoverty funds since 1964. In spring 1965, the NFWA submitted its grant application to the OEO. Within a few short months, the NFWA was awarded $287,000 (about half the amount requested) to fund its migrant education project. After the grape strike was announced in September, Delano residents organized a massive campaign to pressure Congressman Hagen and the local political power structure to investigate whether the NFWA was the appropriate agency to administer an antipoverty program. Opponents argued that there were more appropriate local agencies to administer the project. The antipoverty movement, as a result, became a means for union opponents to mobilize in response to workers on strike.

The NFWA believed that increased federal resources to fight rural poverty were crucial to positively affect the lives of farmworkers. According to the NFWA grant proposal, a practical migrant self-help program would educate Spanish-speaking seasonal migrant farmworkers in basic skills. The program aimed to teach workers money management and civic participation, and to provide migrant workers with information about available public and private services.[34] The OEO issued a public press announcement on October 5, 1965, regarding the NFWA grant. "Migrant workers in Kern, Kings, and Tulare counties, California, will learn citizenship and money management in a self-help education project," read the OEO press release. "Thirty-one members of the migrant population will be employed in the program. Seasonal farm workers will conduct classes in their homes on citizenship rights and responsibilities, function and services of public agencies, and ways to upgrade educational levels.... Migrant families will learn about money management, including consumer education, family budgeting, management and use of credit unions," declared Robert Sargent Shriver, OEO director.[35]

An uproar ensued over various aspects of the proposed programming and the question of which agency should best serve as fiscal sponsor. The credit union aspect of the grant was noteworthy from Washington's perspective. The NFWA had received national recognition for its previous success in establishing a consumer credit program for farmworkers and had accumulated nearly $30,000 in assets.[36] In accordance with the OEO's mandate that the poor assist where possible in alleviating rural and urban poverty, the NFWA encouraged migrant workers to help themselves through responsible consumerism, echoing in part earlier twentieth-century Americanization reform movements among new immigrants.[37] Some Delano residents opposed the NFWA grant and claimed that union radicals were in charge of the project. Educating farmworkers, opponents reasoned, was best facilitated through the Delano school system.

Despite local protest, the language and rhetoric of the NFWA grant were hardly controversial. The proposal called for enhancing "the education of the predominantly Spanish-speaking seasonal and migratory farm workers of California's southern San Joaquin Valley so that they may better cope with the various problems they face as a result of their low economic and social status."[38] The project was divided into three components: the self-help citizenship education, the service program education, and an automotive school. The self-help citizenship unit promoted farmworker awareness of and participation in the antipoverty program and assisted farmworkers in becoming active citizens with a greater voice in their own destinies, helping them enjoy "the rights and benefits which have been largely denied them because of their isolation from society."[39] The service program was designed to help migrants avoid "victimiz[ation] by unscrupulous loan sharks, and teach [farmworkers] to manage . . . incomes so as to meet basic family needs," while the automotive school would "instruct workers in auto repair, provide low-cost facilities for . . . supervised repair, . . . and aid in securing a driver's license."[40] Farmworkers, the proposal stressed, spent a large part of their earnings on transportation. The automotive school would potentially relieve the constant concern of farmworkers about transportation to and from the workplace.

Congressman Hagen clearly supported the NFWA project before the grape strike began. Hagen expressed his support to NFWA cofounder Dolores Huerta on July 14, 1965. "Be assured of my continued interest in this proposed project. If I can assist further in any way, please let me know," the congressman wrote to Huerta.[41] Hagen, in fact, had helped facilitate the OEO's knowledge of the NFWA grant application. In correspondence with Gillis W. Long of Washington's OEO office, Hagen wrote, "it is my understanding that an application has been filed with the Office of Economic Opportunity by Mrs. Dolores Huerta . . . for assistance in the establishment of a migrant farm workers project under Title III. . . . I am advised that the project contemplates educational programs in citizenship, money management and automobile repair. My purpose in writing is to express my interest in this matter and to respectfully urge that it be given every consideration."[42] On May 25, 1965, Hagen reminded Huerta that he had contacted the appropriate OEO officials in Washington, urging their approval.[43] When the NFWA announced its Delano strike in September, opposition mobilized to change the congressman's position. The result alienated his Mexican American Democratic voting base, with whom he had previously worked on a number of issues important to the CSO and NFWA.

After the strike was launched, Delano's governing body quickly organized in protest against the NFWA. The all-Anglo Delano City Council unanimously passed Resolution 1965-81 in early October 1965, stating its emphatic opposition to the antipoverty grant.[44] The resolution stated that "Cesar Chavez does not merit the trust of the City Council with regard to the administration of the grant" and that the Kern County CAP Committee and Delano High School Adult Education Program were the more appropriate agencies to administer the program. The city council questioned the OEO's decision and the oversight ability of the NFWA to properly use such a large amount of taxpayer funds.[45] The council requested that the OEO launch an investigation into the merits of the NFWA as an OEO grant recipient. Delano's Democratic mayor, Clifford F. Loader, contacted Republican senator Thomas H. Kuchel, urging him to pressure OEO officials to investigate the NFWA.[46] The Delano City Council resolution marked the beginning of an organized campaign by Kern County officials to oppose the antipoverty movement.

In response to political pressure, Senator Kuchel contacted Director Shriver. "I personally question the advisability of proceeding with this project and believe the experience and competence of the sponsors should be carefully investigated without delay. . . . The scope of the announced activity . . . seems . . . of marginal merit. . . . Responsible public bodies and officials . . . have registered objections. . . . No established agency experienced in social and educational endeavors was enlisted to take part in the suggested training program," the senator wrote to the OEO director.[47] Despite a telegram César

Chávez sent to Senator Kuchel affirming that the grant funds would not be used until the strike was over, Kuchel and Hagen pressured OEO officials to reverse their decision.[48] Hagen urged the OEO to abide by the resolution passed by the Delano City Council declaring Chávez untrustworthy of stewarding public funds. OEO deputy director Bernard Boutin assured the Delano city clerk that the OEO would hold the grant until the labor dispute was settled. Boutin rejected the Delano City Council's suggestion, however, that the Kern County CAP Committee was a more appropriate agency to receive the grant, since the Economic Opportunity Act enshrined the idea of "maximum feasible participation" of the poor.[49] From the federal perspective, the NFWA was an ideal agent, given the grassroots orientation of the farmworker movement.

Growers enlisted legal representatives to challenge the NFWA funding. In a letter to Boutin, attorney Ivan G. McDaniel expressed his opposition on the basis that the grant ultimately encouraged unionization among farmworkers. McDaniel claimed that the NFWA portrayed farmwork as undesirable—a detriment to growers' need for a cheap and expendable farm labor supply. "The tendency of the program is to downgrade and disparage farm work. . . . One of the purposes of your program is to slyly propagandize these workers and make them readily susceptible to union organization activities. We believe this to be an improper use of public funds. You can use all the generalities you can think of to justify this approach, but in fact and in actuality it is a union support approach," McDaniel wrote.[50] McDaniel's opposition to farmworker unionization was well known by 1966. OEO directors referred to him as the most "union busting attorney," referencing his representation in decades past of the Agricultural Producers Labor Committee and the North Whittier Heights Citrus Association before the National Labor Relations Board, part of the fight to prevent the extension of New Deal labor legislation to the agricultural sector.[51] A staunch defender of the Bracero Program, McDaniel also criticized the repeal of the law that had guaranteed contract labor with Mexico between 1942 and 1964.[52]

OEO offices in Washington assured opponents that the NFWA would be accountable in administering the grant.[53] OEO officials addressed the backlash in Delano in terms of the potential ramifications for the national antipoverty movement. They informed Director Shriver that "shortly before the NFWA application reached the final stages at OEO, Chávez asked a representative . . . to make sure the grant was not announced until the strike was over. . . . Unfortunately, this message was lost in the shuffle. . . . An informal agreement was arranged between OEO, the NFWA, and the local CAA [Community Action Agency] . . . to hold up the release of funds until the strike is over. But there is no real legal basis for withholding the funds should Chavez change his mind."⁵⁴ The OEO memo continued, explaining that "attacks on the NFWA are largely symptomatic of the feelings of the extremely local conservative power structure, to the effect that only they can spend money wisely and represent people in need. Any suggestion that the NFWA, composed entirely of migratory workers, is not a 'representative' group, is patently absurd."⁵⁵ Other correspondence between OEO officials highlighted concern over the potential political fallout and structural ramifications of the OEO funding a striking labor organization. OEO officer John Daum wrote his colleague Ed May in September 1965, "as far as involvement of the poor goes, this is a great program, but we could get cut to pieces on administrative structure. The growers are going to hate this program. They don't like people who tell migrants what their rights are and how to demand them."⁵⁶

While OEO officials expressed support for the NFWA, they were also concerned about potential backlash against antipoverty programs due to the grower opposition toward the Delano strike. OEO officials noted Hagen's about-face, specifically observing that the congressman had sent a letter to President Johnson protesting the NFWA grant even though he initially supported it, even arranging for Dolores Huerta to visit OEO officials in Washington. Other California congressional representatives, including Democrats Phillip Burton and Edward Roybal, affirmed their support for the NFWA grant.⁵⁷ OEO officials in turn did not buy the claim that Chávez was neither respected by locals nor competent to administer federal funds. Chávez's work as the CSO's California director had been recognized by the California State Senate in April 1961 and by California State Assembly resolution the following month, OEO officials noted internally.⁵⁸ Both resolutions had commended the CSO for its assistance to California residents of Mexican heritage and for the organization's "promotion of the harmonious integration of . . . Spanish-speaking people into all areas of community life through education, youth welfare programs, non-partisan efforts to register voters, citizenship classes . . . , [and] co-operation with . . . health, education and recreation agencies."⁵⁹ Indeed, the CSO, Chávez, and the NFWA were at the forefront of grassroots community organizing in the southern San Joaquin Valley, despite efforts to portray Chávez and the farmworker movement as fiscally incompetent "outsiders."

When the NFWA joined Filipinos on strike in September 1965, the strike exacerbated tensions over the implementation of the antipoverty funds—especially since the NFWA had not spent any antipoverty funds at the time that the Delano City Council passed its resolution opposing the

NWFA's grant award. The NFWA was outraged at growers, the city council, and Congressman Hagen for pressuring OEO officials to suspend the grant. Chávez accused the Delano City Council of character defamation over the charge that he did not merit the trust of local government. "The powerful growers of Kern and Tulare Counties, with their political allies, have thrown up tremendous barriers to halt the [grape] strike. They . . . forced the Sheriff's office to arrest us for talking out loud. . . . This grant was the first made in California to a grass-roots, poverty level, organization. Economic Opportunity legislation guarantees maximum involvement of the poor," Chávez told supporters.[60] Grower resistance to the strike and antipoverty movement were one and the same in the eyes of union supporters. The political power structure of the Central Valley, however, clearly discerned a difference between the two—arguing that fighting poverty was worthwhile, but not at the expense of subsidizing the NFWA and its strike activities.

Delano taxpayers seized on the language of the NFWA grant to challenge the qualifications of the recipients to educate farmworkers. Like the Delano City Council in its resolution, opponents argued that several other so-called responsible organizations were more appropriate outfits to educate migrant workers. Critics were convinced that the NFWA would use public dollars to propagandize the poor. Delano superintendent of schools Frank E. Dyer wrote to Congressman Hagen in October 1965, summarizing the position of area schools:

> Delano High School represents an investment by the people of this area . . . of approximately five million dollars in . . . facilities alone. . . . We have operated a well-organized and useful adult education program . . . which includes classes in fundamentals of English for Foreign Born, citizenship, homemaking, parent education, business education and industrial arts. . . . The obvious implications of the grant to Cesar Chavez and the National Farm Workers Association is that the existing schools either cannot or will not provide needed educational programs and that specifically trained "teachers" selected by and from the Association are more competent than trained professionals. . . . I cannot over-emphasize the strength of my professional protest and of my profound dismay at this most incredible blunder.[61]

In the eyes of Delano educators, the OEO had squandered taxpayer money. Unqualified teachers could not perform their duties proficiently, and far more qualified educators stood ready to uplift the migrant population. The NFWA grant would never solve the root causes of poverty, since the grant failed to utilize existing educational institutions that would endure after poverty funds had dried up. While Dyer's logic persuaded Congressman Hagen, the superintendent failed to consider the extent to which farmworker populations were marginalized from Delano's mainstream institutions, including local schools.

Association with the NFWA grant following the grape strike was politically explosive. In a letter, Mayor Loader alerted Congressman Hagen to what the Delano mayor saw as dubious reporting by local media:

> The *Fresno Bee* . . . said that you had helped arrange this grant and . . . that I had helped. I categorically denied any association whatsoever with Mr. Chavez and advised the newspaper that . . . such a grant . . . was not in the best interest of solving the problems of our area. Mr. Chavez is not a respected or responsible citizen of our community. He does not have the support of the responsible Mexican American people of Delano. He has never been active in any part of the Democratic party in this area. . . . His principal activity has been one of an opportunist that has attempted to capitalize on the strike of Filipino farm workers. This strike has been unsuccessful and poorly executed. . . . The city . . . has a great reputation of equality among all classes and races. . . . Our wages for farm workers and the conditions are the best in America.[62]

Loader's distancing from the NFWA illustrates the political polarization engendered by the grape strike. Loader may not have opposed the antipoverty movement philosophically, but he realized the challenge the NFWA posed politically in a community dominated by agribusiness. The mayor's plea highlights as well a not-so-subtle effort to identify "responsible Mexican Americans"—in this case, Mexican Americans opposed to the NFWA.

Filipino residents Mr. and Mrs. Alejandro Fetalvero were typical among Delano nonwhite residents who expressed outrage to Congressman Hagen. "It is hard to believe Chávez can even be eligible [sic] let alone the recipient [sic] of a government grant to completely destroy us. We have tried hard to be a credit to the community and be decent law abiding citizens so it is hard for us to understand."[63] Other citizens organized protests against the NFWA grant. Citizens for Facts from Delano formed in early 1966, mostly by women concerned over César Chávez as a recipient of a War on Poverty grant.[64] The organization lobbed a number of criticisms, ranging from denying that a racial problem existed in Delano to denying that workers wanted union representation, to questioning the radical political affiliations of NFWA leadership. Through opposition to the NFWA, an intense localism reinforced hostility toward the presence of so-called outsiders. Local residents affirmed that they, not the federal government, knew what was best for the region.

Mexican Americans also expressed skepticism toward the NFWA. Mrs. Joe Luque of the Delano CSO chapter wrote an editorial in the *Fresno Bee* on November 2, 1965, denouncing the NFWA and other "agitating groups" that claimed to be "friends of the poor."[65] According to the editorial, several Mexican American organizations, mostly from the Porterville area (a small farming town just north of Bakersfield, on the border between Kern and Tulare Counties), supported the CSO position; these organizations included MAPA, the Comisión Honorífica Mexicana, and the Sociedad Progresista Mexicana. Shortly after Luque's editorial, Eduardo Quevedo, then state president of MAPA, issued a letter to the NFWA disavowing MAPA's role in this condemnation: "as far as this office knows there is no such Porterville Chapter of this organization . . . [and] no chapter of MAPA anywhere in the State can take a position contrary to the State Executive Board."[66] Luque's editorial alleged that "the true facts about the Mexican race" in California's Central Valley needed to be known and that "agitation from outside individuals should be stopped immediately for the betterment of the Mexican people."[67] The Delano CSO chapter continued its protest against the NFWA in a general letter to all California MAPA and CSO chapters. The letter condemned "the mis-use of the Mexican flag in the picket lines," as "introducing 'nationalism' . . . and [being] . . . completely alien to the cause of the Mexican-American in California. . . . The newly introduced 'movimiento' which we are being asked to back is causing a breakdown of the established respected channels that our leaders have built with great care, patience, and resourcefulness throughout the progress-conscious communities of our State."[68] Statements such as these from Luque and other people of color in and around Delano offered critical support to claims made by growers and Delano's political establishment that Chávez did not enjoy the trust or respect of local Mexican Americans.

The Kern County Board of Supervisors also opposed the NFWA grant. Supervisor Vance A. Webb wrote to Director Shriver at the OEO, pleading, "a program of this magnitude should, at the very least, have been brought to the attention of [the] local CAP Committee. . . . In view of local interest in the anti-poverty programs, it is believed important that local people be assured of the purposes and intent of the organizations and individuals responsible for administration of this program."[69] Webb's position reiterated the idea that

CAP was the more appropriate agency to administer antipoverty grants and that CAP would never have approved the NFWA as a recipient, given its reputation. The federal government, according to Webb, had circumvented local institutions and political judgment in granting funds to the NFWA. The local CAP board thereafter became the institutional means to stymie the potential radicalism of "maximum feasible participation." While the poor saw the antipoverty program as a vehicle for civil rights, Kern County's political establishment used the structure of the OEO to limit grassroots organizing.

The alliance between the local political establishment and business interests grew as growers became outraged that the government had funded the NFWA. The Delano Chamber of Commerce joined its city council and passed a resolution opposing the NFWA antipoverty grant, condemning "the intrusion of outsiders in a strictly local matter."[70] The chamber's resolution argued that a less controversial organization should administer the grant—once again naming the CAP Committee of Kern or the Delano High School Adult Education Program.[71] As the grape strike dragged into 1966, protests against the NFWA continued to mount. Kern County supervisor David S. Fairbairn asserted to California Democratic congressman John J. McFall that Chávez was "bent on destroying the existing socioeconomic structure of American society through his announced [labor] revolution."[72]

The Council of California Growers also orchestrated protest against the NFWA. "The propriety of granting more than a quarter of a million dollars to a union at the very time it is engaged in a dispute with employers is open to question.... It appears to be at least endorsement of one party, if not direct financial support," read one organizational newsletter.[73] Grape grower Stephen Pavich represented the typical view of Delano growers. In a letter to Congressman Hagen, he wrote, "I don't believe any act or legislation has upset me as much.... This man is not qualified for this job.... His handling ... [of] money doesn't seem to me morally right. He will use this money to further his personal aims.... I feel if this goes thru there will be ... repercussions and ... noises from around this area the likes of which haven't been heard in many a moon. I hope you take this letter into consideration."[74]

The Kern County Farm Bureau echoed Pavich's sentiments. In an October 1965 letter to Shriver, the Farm Bureau advised:

> Your zeal in attempting to increase the opportunities to our Mexican-American citizens should be commended. However, your desire to by-pass established local government and responsible civic groups in this matter is very suspect. Most citizens of Kern County

have never heard of the National Farm Workers Association, and consequently can have no confidence that it is capable of administering anything, much less a quarter of a million dollars of public money.... We are ... amazed ... at the audacity of your bureau to believe that we would be so overwhelmed by your judgment and wisdom to know exactly how to attain your goals in our own backyard.[75]

The Kern County Farm Bureau pressured Hagen to encourage the OEO to suspend the grant. "As our elected officials, you must develop a plan and strategy to stop such out pouring of public funds, without due consultation with locally elected officials. Such funds must be administered in connection with local government [so] proper accounting can be made.... Stop this original grant," the Farm Bureau stressed to Hagen.[76]

On the other side, various segments of the American labor and anti-poverty movement supported the NFWA and pressured politicians and the OEO not to side with growers. Paul Perlin of the International Longshore and Warehouse Union argued to Senator Kuchel that "powerful and sinister forces of special interests among anti-union agricultural employers are trying to block Anti-Poverty funds initially earmarked for the National Farm Workers' Association.... The move on the part of a few wealthy growers and their representatives to deprive the hard-working, poverty stricken farm workers of essential funds for education, housing, and jobs is one of the cruelest and [most] vindictive actions conceivable."[77] The Tulare CAP also disagreed with Hagen's political flip-flop. The Tulare county CAP chair suggested that an alternative advisory board could be formed to administer the NFWA grant, but that such a proposal would prove "gratuitous since the OEO itself ha[d] many operational safeguards to guarantee the fiscal integrity of ... program[s].... The project is a solid, well-conceived proposal [and] ... will be a success or failure depending upon the participation and administration of the farm workers.... Cesar Chavez ... is an intelligent, highly able person, strong-willed and hard working. I daresay, much of the criticism of him stems from the fact that the growers recognize his ability as an adversary," the chair opined.[78]

Doug Adair, son of a prominent American historian and NFWA volunteer, voiced his opinion that the OEO should maintain the grant. Adair wrote to Democratic congressman Adam Clayton Powell, the first African American to serve in Congress from New York, alerting him of the situation in Delano:

You have a reputation for defending minority rights, and . . . have . . . defended the rights of the poor. . . . Since September we have been involved in a huge strike in the grapes around Delano. . . . We feel that the best way to fight poverty in rural America is to organize farm workers and get higher wages. As a supplementary effort to help Mexican-Americans, the F.W.A. applied some months ago for a Poverty Program grant for education in citizenship, in English, in money-management, and in various other self-help programs. . . . But the big growers and Anglo power structure raised such a howl that the funds were cancelled within 36 hours. The all-Anglo Delano city council and various growers imply that the F.W.A. is Communist (an absurd charge, though a typical libelous charge), and that as Mexicans we are unfit educationally, morally, spiritually, and politically to administer such a program. They don't want any program that they don't control. They demand that all programs be run by and for the power structure. And the big growers got congressman Harlan Hagen of Bakersfield to demand that the program be cancelled. . . . We were disgusted that political pressure could make the administration back down so quickly. If this is typical of the poverty program, how can it ever help the Negroes in the South and in the big cities, or the Puerto Ricans in New York, or the Mexicans in California and Texas? . . . I am appealing to you since Hagan is a grower-owned spokesman who has betrayed us.[79]

Other NFWA supporters chided Congressman Hagen's hypocrisy for initially supporting the NFWA and then questioning the integrity of the organization. One Student Nonviolent Coordinating Committee (SNCC) press release commented, "Democratic Congressman Harlan Hagen worried about the possibility that money might be used as a union weapon against the growers. In pretending great impartiality, Hagen neglected to worry about the growers using their federal subsidies as an anti-union weapon against the workers."[80] The SNCC further noted that many farms and ranches in the Delano area received federal subsidies through water projects. "If Hagen were really consistent he would also call [for] suspension of the Friant-Kern water deliveries to struck ranches until it can be determined if the growers are using any of their federal subsidies as a union busting weapon against the workers," the SNCC rationalized.[81]

The KCCU also protested Hagen's vacillating support for the NFWA grant. A leading civil rights racial coalition in Bakersfield, the KCCU was intimately involved with initiating the antipoverty movement in Kern

County. KCCU chairman Henry Fuller wrote to Hagen, "many of our members are actively involved in the Bakersfield T.A.P. self-help project (one of our directors is the TAP director) and we feel that we are fairly well-informed about the plans of the Farm Workers Association. Their plan is in many ways similar to the one already in operation in Bakersfield. The novel aspect of the NFWA grant is that it has been made to a union. Nevertheless, the plan is sound.... Our area has had only limited success in attracting poverty funds. ... We feel that the NFWA grant is vital."[82] KCCU support for the NFWA was key, since, as Fuller stated, TAP was then the only organization in Kern County actually utilizing poverty funds.

The KCCU argued that there was enough poverty in the San Joaquin Valley to occupy multiple organizations. Mel Brown, Bakersfield TAP director and KCCU member, wrote to Hagen to protest statements the congressman had made in the *Bakersfield Californian*, questioning the overall intent of the antipoverty programs. "The position that you took came as a big disappointment to us, not that we whole-heartedly endorsed the National Farm Workers Association Project, we too found fault with it, but to make strongly critical statements of the OEO and question the integrity of local poor people does great harm and injury to the sincere efforts of poor people everywhere," Brown said.[83] He reminded Hagen that southeast Bakersfield residents were staunch Democrats and worked in a variety of capacities to support Democratic initiatives and register voters. Hagen's public statements undermined the Democratic loyalty Brown and others had helped build in southeast Bakersfield's Black and Brown community. "Poor people take it as an affront to them personally," Brown wrote. "To strongly question the integrity of poor people anywhere, question[s] the integrity of poor people everywhere.... Reassure the 31,000 poor people who reside here in [southeast] Bakersfield that you are a friend and not an enemy," he warned the congressman.[84]

Hagen was concerned that his constituents with ties to agribusiness would abandon the Democratic Party because of his partisan affiliation with the War on Poverty. Hagen wrote to William G. Phillips, an OEO congressional relations officer, that "bitterness ... has arisen because of the strike and the inappropriateness of the NFWA as an OEO grantee."[85] The congressman as a result red-baited Chávez as a communist in order to boost his own anticommunist credentials and divert attention away from the fact that he had actively supported the OEO grant before the strike. "Mr. Chavez['s] ... activities ... at various college campuses ... have resulted in [the] appearance on the picket line ... of individuals from various groups, including members of SNCC, CORE [the Congress of Racial Equality], and even

Dubois Clubs. . . . This latter organization has been publicly identified as a Communist Front. . . . The subject of this grant is one of the most disturbing political phenomena in my area from the standpoint of my re-election and the re-election of Democrats running for statewide office who must to some extent depend upon voters in my Congressional District," the congressman informed Phillips.[86]

The NFWA antipoverty grant controversy continued through 1966. With growers and the NFWA locked in a labor dispute, the idea that taxpayer dollars might potentially prolong the strike guaranteed that the OEO dispute would continue. Growers saw the strike as a brief interruption in an otherwise long history of peaceful community relations between growers and farmworkers, free of federal intervention and civil rights agitation. The NFWA's opponents whitewashed race relations in the valley, particularly in the city of Delano. Stanley E. Willis, president of the Kern County Farm Bureau, pressed Congressman Hagen on this point. "The NFWA . . . created discord and otherwise provide[d] irritation to a community composed of persons of all ethnic backgrounds. These citizens heretofore lived in peace and tranquility," Willis wrote to Hagen.[87] The Farm Bureau president's comments failed to acknowledge Delano's history of racial segregation and existing poverty lines that clearly delineated between east and west Delano.[88]

The 1966 *Congressional Record* verifies Hagen's futile attempt to capitalize on the controversy over the NFWA grant for his reelection campaign. Hagen pressed for grower-friendly policies during congressional debates over how migrant funds within the War on Poverty would be distributed in future grants. Hagen specifically questioned Title III, part B, of the migrant labor section of the Economic Opportunity Act. He cautioned his congressional colleagues that the language of the migrant labor section of the Economic Opportunity Act offered leeway for controversial grantees to deliberately misuse government funds. Under this section, state and local officials had no veto power over programs approved by the OEO. This lack of local control was part of what concerned Delano growers. The call to revise the legal specifics of how the OEO related to grassroots recipient organizations foreshadows the way that the antipoverty movement was later streamlined under California governor Ronald Reagan. Creating a more top-down administrative structure within the OEO, better controlling the potential radicalism and politicization of the poor, became imperative for War on Poverty opponents. "I have a grant in my area that involved this problem of potential organizing activities under the guise of education," Hagen lamented.[89] Facing a tough reelection campaign, he urged that the NFWA grant be rescinded, since the money was not being spent as the strike continued through 1966. Any scenario where the NFWA would have access to government funds meant political death for Hagen. He made clear to valley residents that he remained vigilant in opposition to the NFWA as his reelection campaign began.

Hagen recognized this political challenge for the Democratic Party in Central California. In a letter to OEO director Shriver in early 1966, Hagen forecast the political consequences for the overall War on Poverty of continuing the NFWA grant. The NFWA, the congressman told Shriver, was prepared to "sabotage the political prospects of myself and Governor [Edmund] Brown. . . . It is imperative that the OEO grant to the N.F.W.A. be killed forever. If it is not, I may decide to relinquish the field to my announced Republican opponent who will then most certainly win the election or, if I run, I will have an almost impossible hurdle to election by reason of the OEO grant. . . . If this grant is not cancelled, I cannot afford to vote for any continuation of the poverty programs."[90] Hagen made clear that the 1966 election would place conservative opposition to antipoverty programs firmly on the ballot. Kern County residents would use the ballot to voice their disapproval not only of antipoverty programs, but of the larger civil rights movement within and beyond the agricultural fields of Kern County.

The politicization of the antipoverty movement placed Hagen in a difficult position, with his agribusiness allies on one side and grassroots Mexican American and African American groups on the other. Hagen painted Chávez to OEO officials as a political and social radical who promoted revolutionary fervor, and declared the NFWA a failure. The strike had, in Hagen's estimation, flopped—and Chávez, the NFWA, and outside agitators did not represent the genuine views of Delano's racially diverse citizenry.[91] Hagen sought proof after making such allegations publicly. He contacted Donald T. Appell in early March 1966, hoping that the House Un-American Activities Committee representative could help him find information about the role of communists and other extreme elements within the NFWA strike. Hagen informed Appell that he desperately needed the information by the following week.[92] He sent the same request letter to David Bowers of the FBI.[93] The incumbent congressman needed to back claims against Chávez made by his constituents in Delano, who were inundating his office with telegrams affirming that Chávez and the NFWA were communist revolutionaries.[94] Despite the fact that no hard evidence was ever produced, Chávez as a perceived communist threat became a palpable political truth among Kern County conservatives.

Hagen expressed political hostility toward the broader civil rights movement in an effort to distance himself from his earlier associations with the NFWA. He informed OEO officers that "Chavez . . . has attempted to convert . . . [the grape strike] into a civil rights struggle to the delight of the [Marxist-Leninist newspaper] Peoples World and other elements of the Communist press and the various groups which exist on our college campuses in California."[95] Hagen further noted his disdain for the Spanish language and the foreign element of the strike. "The strike itself is virtually conducted in a foreign language with use of the word 'huelga' instead of strike. . . . [The] publication of a bulletin printed in Spanish and English with the title 'El Malcriado' and wide use of wood blocks from Diego Rivera and other Mexican revolutionaries, all evidenced the foreign element," the congressman complained.[96] Such subversive and anti-American views on the part of the farmworker movement, Hagen determined, were the primary reasons why the NFWA was not an appropriate organization to receive taxpayer funding.

Despite his effort to save his congressional seat, the fissure within the Democratic Party over the antipoverty movement exposed Hagen's seat to opportunistic Republicans. Olympic track star Bob Mathias unseated Hagen in the eighteenth congressional district in 1966. Mathias criticized Hagen before a luncheon audience of the California Republican Assembly over the incumbent's position on ending the Bracero Program, declaring Hagen clearly a "part of the extreme left wing of the Democratic Party in the House of Representatives."[97]

MAXIMUM FEASIBLE OPPOSITION

Within this context of localized protest in Bakersfield over the War on Poverty, local civil rights activists addressed the Bakersfield City Council during the public comment portion of regular meetings, calling for the city council to postpone a referendum scheduled for the November ballot. Since early 1966, Bakersfield's antipoverty coalition had pressured the city council to support antipoverty programs with local tax dollars so as to ensure that time-sensitive appropriation of federal funds would not be jeopardized. Civil rights leaders hoped to receive cooperation from local government to make antipoverty programs work successfully. Kern County had been awarded over $1 million for antipoverty programs in 1965, a significant amount of money for community development in the poverty-stricken southeast Bakersfield. The city's antipoverty coalition hoped to prevent the loss of any federal funds due to local political inertia.

A struggle over economic civil rights ensued between the antipoverty coalition and the city council, centered on the implementation and control of the War on Poverty in Bakersfield. As mandated by the Economic

Opportunity Act, local matching funds in the amount of 10 percent were required to secure federal funding. The Bakersfield City Council was reluctant to provide financial support for programs developed by TAP. Rather than committing taxpayer dollars to antipoverty programs, Republican city council members suggested placing a referendum initiative on the November 1966 ballot to poll Bakersfield voters directly as to whether they wanted to use local tax dollars to support local antipoverty programs. Civil rights activists stressed that support for the referendum caused tremendous divisiveness throughout Bakersfield and was being interpreted in racial terms. The referendum was antithetical to the values of the KCCU, as well as the city council–sponsored IRB. Both the IRB and the KCCU argued against the referendum in a mutual call for civic unity.

The last few months of 1966 had proven divisive in greater Bakersfield. The farmworker movement had brought national and international attention to the plight of poor people and race relations in California's San Joaquin Valley. Kern County and Bakersfield were polarized, divided into camps of union and grower supporters.[98] The migratory labor subcommittee of the US Senate Labor Committee had held hearings on farm labor in March of that year, some thirty miles north of Bakersfield in Delano. At that meeting, Senator Robert Kennedy had chided city and county law enforcement officers for their claims that preemptive arrests were needed of picketers who supported the grape boycott.[99] And beginning early in 1966, several African American leaders had made regular appearances before the city council (most often with hundreds of minority community residents in attendance) to plea for the city's support in allocating matching funds for federally approved antipoverty programs in southeast Bakersfield.

Republican city councilman Richard Stiern (brother of Democrat Walter Stiern, longtime California state senator for Kern County) defended the proposed antipoverty referendum. Stiern argued that there was nothing "undemocratic" about letting taxpayers vote on whether to use tax dollars to support the War on Poverty. Mayor Russell Karlen declared publicly that "the best way to fight poverty in the city was to attract jobs and not fund antipoverty programs."[100] The community antipoverty coalition was convinced that the city council's lack of enthusiasm for the War on Poverty would stall the implementation of antipoverty programs and injure economic advancement for the city's most underserved and vulnerable populations.

The 1966 antipoverty referendum epitomized the struggle between anti-statism and racial liberalism in greater Bakersfield. The city council chamber was the physical site of protest where grassroots urban civil rights activists made their voices heard to Bakersfield's political establishment. The anti-statist politics expressed by the city council were evident throughout 1966. Members of the city council made clear to African American and Mexican American civil rights leaders that local tax dollars would not be spent to improve living conditions for "minority people" at the expense of taxpayers. Only under a direct mandate from local voters would the city council expend local dollars for antipoverty programs, not because of federal or state mandates brought on by the War on Poverty. Grassroots civil rights activists argued that local government had a duty to respond to its citizens, despite the ideological or minority position they advocated.

Much of this local struggle hinged on the legality of the antipoverty referendum itself. The legal implications proved contentious among local attorneys charged with investigating the potential repercussions of the ballot results. Kern County counsel Ralph Jordan and Bakersfield city attorney Kenneth Hoagland differed in their interpretation of the referendum's legality. Hoagland proclaimed that the referendum was perfectly within the legal mandate of the city's legislative prerogative, while Jordan claimed that the referendum wasted taxpayer funds and lacked a legal mandate.[101]

TAP director Mel Brown condemned the city council for not moving quickly to help TAP raise the matching funds to secure federal dollars. Debate between TAP leadership and the city council in March 1966 revealed the governing body's reluctance to commit tax dollars to antipoverty programs prior to the referendum. Local government had neglected supporting sidewalks, parks, sewers, and sanitation services in southeast Bakersfield. Many TAP area residents were convinced that the city was not committed to improving living and working conditions in this community. A misunderstanding between TAP and the city council centered on the merits of the long-term commitment of local tax dollars, beyond the 10 percent mandated by antipoverty administrators. Richard Stiern stated that the director of the San Francisco antipoverty office had told him personally that the federal government planned to shift the local requirement from 10 to 50 percent by 1967. TAP director Mel Brown disputed Stiern's claim, saying that he had heard of no such anticipated change and had attended the same meeting with the San Francisco antipoverty director at Bakersfield College. Brown later appeared on local television, chastising Stiern for "backstabbing and double-crossing" TAP members by first alleging support for antipoverty programs and then expressing skepticism about the long-term tax commitment.[102]

The local CAP Committee became a major obstructionist block to antipoverty programs. Director Howard Roland resigned in March 1966, after serving only three months in that role (Roland was first recruited and hired by CAP in January of that year). Although charged with administering all antipoverty programs in Kern County, the CAP Committee had suffered a lack of leadership and coordination since its inception in 1965. Tensions between grassroots civil rights activists and CAP's right-wing Republican members triggered Roland's resignation. He then criticized local Republicans and their minimal interest in making the War on Poverty work.

Roland claimed that some CAP Committee members were obstructing antipoverty programs for political reasons. He called this right-wing contingent "rover boys," referencing the popular early twentieth-century novel series of the same name, about adolescent boys who consistently found trouble, acted mischievously, and proved boorish and cliquish.[103] Obstructionist Republicans were particularly offensive to Roland. He declared that they occupied a faction of the CAP Committee and used parliamentary procedure to alter, slow, and block the implementation of poverty programs—effectively nullifying what had already been approved by the OEO. "I wouldn't remain on this job if it paid $25,000 a year," Roland told the CAP Committee upon his resignation.[104] "There seems to be a block on this committee and it works beautifully. Some people on the committee don't seem to be sympathetic to the anti-poverty program but feel they should act as watchdogs of the taxpayers' money.... I don't see how we can get off the ground in time to serve the people who should be involved in projects.... If you keep going around in circles with parliamentary blocks, I can't see any success for CAP," Roland protested.[105] His testimony validated claims made by African Americans and Mexican Americans regarding the obstructionist practices of Republicans in local government.

The anti-statist political bloc on the CAP Committee included Thomas Curran, John Holt, Bakersfield city councilman Bill Park, and Kern County supervisor David S. Fairbairn. The CAP Committee consisted of thirty-two members, ten of whom represented the poor. Park was a key staffer for Olympian turned congressman Bob Mathias. The right-wing propaganda drummed up by Park effectively mobilized Bakersfield and Kern County voters against the War on Poverty and the Democratic Party, helping Mathias win election in 1966. Indeed, Park cut his political teeth as a city councilman and would grow his influence in the California Republican Party in the coming decades.[106]

Following Roland's resignation, civil rights leaders called for the resignation of CAP Committee members who resisted implementing War on Poverty programs. "You who cannot work within the framework of the program because of your philosophical beliefs should resign," said local NAACP chair and KCCU member Art Shaw. "I doubt that the entire CAP membership is concerned about the impoverished. Those who are not should be replaced—there are more than enough persons qualified for CAP membership in the target area," added Mel Brown.[107] TAP executive secretary Anand Prasad called for a reorganization of the CAP Committee. Prasad even suggested that target area residents ought to consider raising the 10 percent matching funds, since TAP had encountered so much resistance in the local government. Brown did not agree with Prasad and hoped that TAP, the CAP Committee, the city council, and the board of supervisors could work together to provide matching funds, rather than funds needing to be raised within the target area independently. In an effort to temper Republican fears of long-term commitments to the welfare state, Shaw told the CAP Committee that "the vast majority of the poor are not interested in extensions of a paternal welfare program."[108]

Despite opposition from CAP Committee members, several antipoverty projects were approved in 1966. By May of that year, a total of $492,577 had been allocated for TAP antipoverty projects. This included the establishment of seven study centers/libraries, a recreation program, renewal and expansion of the neighborhood self-help project, and a transportation project. The TAP self-help project had been in operation for a year by the time the CAP Committee approved the renewal application. The library project was designed to provide area children with study centers where they could work with academic tutors. In-kind contributions came from the Kern County Library and the Kern County Union High School District, in the amount of $11,812.[109] The transportation project provided free busing for residents who could not afford commuting costs to and from work.

The KCCU was also awarded antipoverty funds in 1966. Project JUMP, which was funded $88,130, offered job training for young adults in the target area between the ages of eighteen and twenty-two. A number of local organizations, businesses, attorneys, medical groups, and construction companies agreed to participate in the KCCU program. The broad-based and middle-class orientation of KCCU's membership provided critical job training experience for participating youth. The training program was divided into two classes of thirty, one in fall and one in spring. The program mandated forty-eight hours of work per week for twenty-one weeks. It targeted at-risk youth who might otherwise not have had many work opportunities outside of farm labor employment.

Conservatives opposed the CAP Committee's allocation of $138,228 toward a recreation project in the poverty area. Bill Park argued that the CAP Committee was procedurally out of line, given that the city council had not yet voted on in-kind contributions for a recreation project. Included in the local 10 percent contribution toward the recreation plan were the services of the city recreation director (ten hours a month at $6.47 hourly) and the use of the Jefferson Street and California Avenue park swimming pools, each facility located within the target area. Use of high school facilities was also included as an in-kind contribution. Park opposed all these "matching funds."

Following Roland's resignation, John Tallman was appointed as the permanent CAP Committee director in June 1966.[110] Controversy between TAP and the CAP Committee centered on the idea of which group would control area antipoverty programs: the grass roots (Shaw and Prasad) or a centralized administration (Tallman and the CAP Committee). The TAP council wanted Anand Prasad for the position of CAP Committee director and believed him well qualified, given that he had helped initiate the War on Poverty through his activities with the Friendship House. The CAP Committee set out a requirement, at the encouragement of Bill Park, that the director position had to be occupied by a US citizen. Art Shaw and others believed this requirement to be a direct effort to prevent Prasad from chairing the CAP Committee, although Park denied that this was the case.[111] Born near Delhi, India, the Presbyterian minister Prasad had emigrated from India in 1937, eventually arriving in Bakersfield in early 1962. He would head the Friendship House until March 1966, when he became TAP's executive secretary.[112] Park also clashed with Del Rucker, the only African American city council member (and representative of the southeast city ward). One week after the CAP Committee approved nearly $500,000 in antipoverty programs, Park told the city council that the programs "won't solve poverty problems in East and South Bakersfield . . . [and] 30 or 40 years from now there will be little to show for the funds spent on antipoverty programs." Rucker countered this claim, asserting that the city council was equally resistant toward earlier civil rights efforts and should not repeat the same mistakes made years prior.[113]

The debate over the legality of the 1966 November referendum reflected the city council's anti-statist impulse. County counsel Ralph Jordan concluded that the referendum was outside the legislative functions of the city council, since implementation of antipoverty programs was administrative, not legislative, in nature. He argued that the city council could only execute established legislative policy. "I . . . conclude that the proposition concerning County participation in the Economic Opportunity Act of 1964 does not involve a legislative function and would merely elicit an advisory note from the County electorate. It is a general rule that public funds should not be expended merely for an advisory vote where the proposition is not subject to referendum," Jordan opined.[114] Jordan's opinion indicated indirectly, then, that the referendum was about galvanizing the political right, regardless of its legality or cost to taxpayers.

The fact that the city council placed the referendum on the November ballot against the recommendation of the county counsel outraged civil rights leaders in southeast Bakersfield. Residents of the poverty area distributed a signature sheet following the city council's endorsement of the referendum. Some 3,000 signatures were gathered throughout the city poverty area asking the city council to support antipoverty youth programs through in-kind services. Residents were especially upset over Richard Stiern's insult to the "at least one-third of his ward that live[d] in the poverty area by saying that his people do not know anything about the War on Poverty."[115] OEO regional director Ray King cautioned Bakersfield residents not to resort to violence in protest of the referendum, but encouraged efforts to gain support of a broad voting populace for antipoverty programs.[116] King's statement was based naively on the premise that Bakersfield residents would actually vote to approve funding for poverty-stricken areas. The controversy surrounding the NFWA grant proved this possibility unlikely.

The NAACP West Coast (WC) and state antipoverty administrators monitored the Bakersfield referendum closely. Virna Canson, who would serve as NAACP-WC director from 1974 to 1988, was in 1966 a community action representative with the OEO in Sacramento.[117] On June 17 of that year, she wrote to Leonard Carter, then serving as NAACP-WC regional director, to ask for financial support. Canson pleaded with Carter that the NAACP needed to redirect some of its limited resources including legal support to the "seriousness of a situation existing in Kern County and its relationship to the concerns and goals of civil rights."[118] Carter contacted Art Shaw of the Bakersfield NAACP and KCCU a week later. Carter requested that Shaw send as much information to the regional office as possible, as well as contact information for Mel Brown, described by NAACP officials as the one on the "firing line" in Bakersfield's city hall.[119] Both the regional NAACP and Sacramento antipoverty administration offices were cognizant that the antipoverty movement was an extension of civil rights and that the 1966 Bakersfield referendum could affect the success of the entire antipoverty movement.

The referendum reflected the anti-statist position of the majority of city council members. Part of the resolution focused on the potential percentage increase local government would be responsible for assuming in 1967, from 10 percent to 50 percent and ultimately 100 percent responsibility.[120] At city hall, TAP representatives spoke vehemently against these misconstrued facts, which misled voters. The resolution's language reflected the long-standing animosity of white voters toward their poor and darker-skinned neighbors in southeast Bakersfield, whom they were averse to subsidizing. The resolution stated, "the target area under consideration in the recreation program presented encompasses certain unincorporated, as well as, municipal areas."[121] Such language, crafted by the city council, resonated with Bakersfield's majority white citizens, who had resisted the financial implications of annexing African American and Mexican American enclaves into the city limits years before. Local civil right leaders also understood the implications of the referendum. "The question is not city participation [in the antipoverty programs] but control of both [the] administration and project selection," Shaw wrote to NAACP-WC regional director Leonard Carter.[122] Since African Americans and Mexican Americans had initiated antipoverty programs in Kern County, control over antipoverty programs became a dividing line between TAP and the majority white city council. In light of the controversy over the NFWA grant, the Republican majority capitalized on the backlash against the grape strike by conflating antipoverty programs with the broader civil rights movement. Moreover, in early June 1966, city attorney Kenneth Hoagland argued that the referendum was perfectly within the legal and legislative functions of the city council because of power granted to localities in implementing the Economic Opportunity Act.[123]

On November 8, 1966, by a three-to-one margin, Bakersfield citizens voted against supporting antipoverty programs. Local antipoverty programs nevertheless continued to be funded in the city following the vote. TAP aggressively assumed responsibility for securing financial support for antipoverty programs to match federal funds. Grassroots activists, moreover, continued to encounter stubborn resistance from the CAP Committee and state officials interested in centralizing power within antipoverty programs.

CONCLUSION

Kern County CAP Committee director John Tallman initiated a request for the Sacramento OEO office to evaluate the TAP and CSO agencies charged with implementing antipoverty programs in Kern County. The evaluator sent in 1967 to assess the programs was Sal España. España was charged with finding out whether the CSO and TAP were "qualified" to implement antipoverty initiatives in Kern County. Given the tense relationship between the CAP Committee and grassroots civil rights leadership, Tallman's request for the state to evaluate how the antipoverty movement was implemented served as a basis to condemn the grassroots aspect of the antipoverty movement as unorganized and inefficient, ultimately promoting dependency among the poor. With such criticism rendered, the CAP Committee could streamline and centralize power within itself, eliminating the grassroots aspect of the antipoverty movement. Doing so was predicated on demonstrating that grassroots activism and "the maximum participation of the poor" were misguided and irrational policies.

After outlining specific programs implemented by the CSO and TAP, España reviewed the service-oriented details of the CSO, noting that the "service type function [of the CSO] . . . would be much more meaningful if married to programs which would assist the disadvantaged in becoming more self-sufficient."[124] Since the CSO and TAP implemented programs separately, España found little "community participation" in either of their offerings. Community organizers were frequently portrayed as leaches on the government. TAP staff centers were "overstaffed and unwieldy," España wrote. The TAP board blamed others for its failure and did not fully understand the OEO mandate to solve the root causes of poverty, the report concluded.[125]

España's findings were in line ideologically with the new Reagan gubernatorial administration's attempt to restructure the state OEO office in Sacramento. CAP Committees, of course, did not have sufficient means to fully solve the root causes of poverty.[126] España concluded in his review that he had "found no organizations as disorganized as the TAP council in Kern" and stated that "there were many other programs throughout the Valley that were functioning properly."[127] "Anand Prasad is one of the most controversial figures leading OEO programs in the San Joaquin Valley," España declared. Prasad reminded opponents, however, that TAP member organizations had existed long before the War on Poverty and had fought without federal support for the rights and dignity of southeast Bakersfield's Black and Brown communities. España ended his report by recommending that TAP be entirely revamped or have its funding fully cut off.

Art Shaw informed OEO officials of the problems TAP had with John Tallman's attempt to control Bakersfield's antipoverty movement. In a letter to OEO migrant analyst Gene De la Torre, Shaw noted that Tallman had complained to OEO officials that Shaw, as a TAP official, lacked the formal education and necessary experience in social welfare problems to perform his duties effectively. Shaw told the OEO that Tallman was unable to gain community support after assuming leadership within the CAP Committee, noting that several members had resigned following his appointment. "I am sure that you and everyone in Washington is well aware that this community has not been very receptive to the War on Poverty but while the community has resisted Anti-Poverty efforts it has found John Tallman even less bearable,"

Shaw lamented.[128] As administering the War on Poverty continued in Kern, dismantling the grassroots aspect of the antipoverty movement by delegating authority away from TAP, the CSO, and the neighborhood councils—the grassroots organizations that had initiated the War on Poverty three years prior—became the de facto position of local government.

Anti-statist opposition toward the antipoverty movement continued well into the Reagan gubernatorial years of 1967 to 1975. The end result pitted Mexican Americans and African Americans against each other in competition for financial resources in the rural welfare state, much to the political benefit of anti-statist Republicans. The following chapter examines the emergence of the Chicana/o civil rights movement in the context of multiracial civil rights activism in greater Bakersfield. In many ways, the limits of the antipoverty movement encouraged civil rights activists to push for civil rights reforms in other venues.

4 | AGRARIAN CHICANISMO
Jesus "Jess" Nieto and the Chicana/o Student Movement in Bakersfield

There will be a dramatic increase in the Chicano population in local, regional, and national areas of the country. This will have a tremendous impact on Chicano enrollments at all levels of education. It is evident the overall changes in higher education are inevitable. Bakersfield College will have to change dramatically in order to serve this "new" population. The College will have to integrate new faculty, administration, and staff sensitive and equipped to service this new population. In short, institutional change is not only inevitable but necessary.

Jesus Gilberto Nieto, 1974

The focus of this chapter is on the urban Chicana/o movement in greater Bakersfield. California's Central Valley was in many ways ground zero for *el movimiento*. According to historian and literary scholar George Mariscal, *el movimiento* was a "diffuse movement cross-cut by regional, gender, and class issues; . . . a mass mobilization dedicated to a wide range of internationalism, from electoral politics to institutional reform and even armed insurrection."[1] The farmworker movement of the 1960s, or *la huelga* (the strike), in the fields of Kern County empowered Chicanas and Chicanos politically throughout the American Southwest. The farmworker movement was in many ways the heart and soul of the Chicana/o civil rights movement. From 1965 to 1970, César Chávez led a five-year national and international boycott of grapes, effectively catapulting him into the leadership of the larger Mexican American civil rights movement. In 1970, the United Farm Workers (UFW) signed the first meaningful farmworker contract, with Giumarra Vineyards, ending the tumultuous grape strike. Historian Lorena Oropeza writes that "La Huelga . . . became impossible to separate from what people, within the movement and beyond it, were beginning to call La Causa, the wider aspirations of Mexican Americans for recognition, respect, and fair treatment [in civil rights].... It is little wonder that the farm workers' struggle became identified in the public mind with a broader impulse toward institutional reform on the part of all Mexican Americans."[2] In Bakersfield, the farmworker movement propelled urban Chicana/os to fight for civil rights both in solidarity with farmworkers and also beyond the agricultural fields.

This chapter offers the first scholarly analysis and narrative history of the urban Chicana/o civil rights movement in greater Bakersfield. While the farmworker movement is critical for understanding the course of civil rights history in California's Central Valley, a multifaceted, multiracial, urban civil rights history paralleled the struggle for civil rights in the fields. Perhaps the most critical facet of the Chicana/o urban civil rights movement in Bakersfield occurred in higher education. The Chicana/o student movement shaped the Chicana/o civil rights movement in Bakersfield and left an indelible institutional legacy in California's Central Valley. The Chicana/o civil rights struggle diverged from the strategies and ideological impulses of the racial liberal coalitions of the late 1950s and early 1960s.

The reform of higher education through the introduction of a Chicana/o studies curriculum further shifted Mexican American civil rights reform from earlier traditions of racial liberal alliances that had been formed with African Americans and white liberals through the civic unity movement. Chicana/os did not abandon their alliances with African Americans and white liberals, but the cultural renaissance engendered by the Chicana/o movement became paramount. Chicana/o civil rights leaders altered the trajectory and ideological agenda of racial liberalism in Kern County. This chapter offers a more complete account of urban and rural civil rights history in greater Bakersfield during the Chicana/o movement period.

THE CHICANA/O MOVEMENT AND HIGHER EDUCATION IN BAKERSFIELD

Higher education reform in Kern County was an important institutional legacy of the Chicana/o movement. Higher education was a major vehicle for facilitating social movements, especially during the late 1960s and early 1970s. The development of ethnic or minority studies—curriculum geared toward African Americans, Mexican Americans (Chicana/os), Native Americans, Asian Americans, and women—was fought for vigorously by social and political activists, who sought to transform the traditionally exclusive, Anglo, male-oriented curriculum in both two-year and four-year colleges and universities. As Chicano historian Michael Soldatenko notes, "The social sciences and humanities privileged empirical and realist methods to ascertain the fundamental laws that operate in nature and society.... As the American university system flourished, [it] ... created a particular knowledge whose purpose was social control and empire building."[3] The events that took place at Bakersfield College in the late 1960s and 1970s underscore Soldatenko's insight regarding the intellectual insurrection Chicana/o studies represented to mainstream academic curricula.

Much of this chapter evaluates the contributions of Dr. Jesus "Jess" Gilberto Nieto in implementing a Chicana/o studies curriculum in greater Bakersfield. A two-year institution founded in 1913 in the southernmost part of California's San Joaquin Valley, Bakersfield College was in this era the oldest continuously serving two-year college in California and the flagship campus in the Kern Community College District, geographically one of the largest community college districts in the United States. Nieto established the first Chicana/o studies curriculum in Bakersfield, developed a Chicano Cultural Center, and spearheaded other programs and initiatives to expand bicultural awareness and international education between the United States and Mexico. His efforts occurred within a larger civil rights discourse where the demand for Chicana/o studies was connected to other social justice issues in both the city and the county. Implementing Chicana/o studies was a cornerstone of *el movimiento*. In short, education rights were civil rights. The politicization of Chicana/o students at Bakersfield College both facilitated and resulted from Nieto's institutional reforms. For example, the first real grassroots Chicana/o political victory in Kern County, the election of Democrat Raymond "Ray" Gonzales to the California State Assembly in 1972, was, in part, an outcome of Chicana/o youth mobilization.

The development of Chicana/o studies at Bakersfield College and civil rights reform in Bakersfield were reciprocal. Both educational reform and Chicana/o civil rights fed off each other. Historian Ignacio M. García has suggested that the 1960s and 1970s were a period when Chicana/os developed a "militant ethos" that helped the collective community of Mexican Americans "combat racism, discrimination, poverty, and segregation, and to define itself politically and historically."[4] In Kern County, Mexican Americans during the 1960s and 1970s were politicized by the war in Vietnam and the farmworker struggle, but also by lesser known civil rights struggles to implement fair media practices, curb police violence, and desegregate the Bakersfield City School District (BCSD).

The community college played a major role in the education of Chicana/os. The community college (then junior college) was the primary site of entry into higher education for Chicana/os, rather than the larger four-year or senior institutions of California and beyond. Community college enrollment by Hispanic students was larger than in the California State University (CSU) and University of California (UC) systems. The number of students flocking to the college campus dramatically increased enrollments around the nation following World War II. Federal programs, most notably the GI Bill, made attending college financially feasible for veterans and nontraditional students. Ethnic minorities were among these nontraditional students, who entered college in unprecedented numbers, especially in the 1960s and 1970s. According to a California legislative report in 1972 on Chicana/os and public higher education, in 1967 Chicana/os represented only 2 percent and 3 percent of the student populations at UC and CSC schools, respectively, and roughly 8 percent in the community college system.[5] Historian Marisol Moreno writes that "in addition to providing a voice for their barrios, Chicana/o student activists pressured state colleges and universities to act and expand on the 1960 Master Plan of Higher Education's mandate to service all segments of California communities . . . yield[ing] significant institutional and cultural changes, which included the creation of Chicana/o Studies departments and curricula."[6] Chicana/o historians continue to explore Chicana/o student activism within California community colleges, adding important regional and activist perspectives to the movement.[7]

Chicana/o activists mobilized and refashioned higher education in accordance with the state Master Plan and the vision of Chicana/o studies articulated in UC Santa Barbara's 1969 manifesto for Chicana/o studies—*El Plan de Santa Bárbara*.[8] Composed by a group of about one hundred student and faculty activists, *El Plan* formulated a strategy for solving the problems Chicana/os faced in higher education and the community at large. *El Plan* was paramount for Chicana/os in higher education throughout the American Southwest, as it set a blueprint for budding student activists to follow and expand on. The terms *Chicano* and *chicanismo* were defined, and the objective of the policy to be enacted at the university was eloquently stated: "at this moment we do not come to work for the university, but to demand that the university work for our people."[9] In short, *El Plan* was a collection of ideas regarding the aspirations of Chicana/os in higher education, guided by a common experience of marginalization in the traditional academic community. Yet, no specific plan regarding the development of Chicana/o studies was articulated.[10] "At best *El Plan de Santa Bárbara* offered a guideline on how to institutionalize Chicano Studies in higher education. In no way did the conference participants intend for *El Plan* to be the final word on Chicano Studies and student activism," notes Moreno.[11] Nevertheless, for young and enthusiastic Chicana/os interested in changing the higher education curriculum, *El Plan* became a blueprint. Such were the materials that guided a young Jess Nieto in his reform efforts at Bakersfield College.

JESS NIETO AND THE CHICANA/O STUDENT MOVEMENT IN BAKERSFIELD

Jesus "Jess" Gilberto Nieto was born in Deming, New Mexico, in 1947 to a bracero father and a native New Mexican mother. After spending his first few years in the United States, Nieto relocated with his family to Juárez, Mexico. Nieto's first years of school were at the Emiliano Zapata Primaria school. After a few months, his family chose to move north to El Paso, Texas, where they lived until Nieto was eleven years old. From there, his family migrated west to Bakersfield for agricultural work.

The southern San Joaquin Valley would be the final destination for the Nieto family and the site of Nieto's educational and activist maturation. After attending Bakersfield High School and Bakersfield College, Nieto transferred to CSU Long Beach in the late 1960s. As an undergraduate, Nieto heard of the student gathering at Santa Barbara and became interested in the activities and development of Chicana/o education at his campus. To his astonishment, Nieto discovered that one of his former professors at Bakersfield College, Ray Gonzales, was teaching in Chicana/o studies at CSU Long Beach. Nieto took two of his classes during his senior year. Recalling those days, Nieto said, "I went on to Long Beach, and in my last year, Ray Gonzales was there. He was going to teach in the Chicana/o studies/Mexican American program. He was finishing a doctoral program in Latin American studies at USC [University of Southern California], and I was just flabbergasted that he was there on the West Coast."[12]

His former Bakersfield College professor influenced him tremendously. "There weren't very many people that I came across, but [Ray] was one I remember very vividly. I took a bunch of courses in literature, and his courses were the first ones. Ray Gonzales was the guy that opened those intellectual doors for me to explore," Nieto remembered.[13] Gonzales's classes exposed Nieto to the intercultural dimensions of Chicana/o history and culture. Gonzales, too, recalls Nieto and his wife taking his class.

> The Mexican American family [course] was the one Jess and his wife were in. We had no textbook or anything. So I decided we would make up our own book. I divided the class into five groups . . . and we [were] going to find out everything about Mexican Americans in the education system. Categories [created] were . . . the Mexican American diet, interracial marriage, etc. . . . I remember the Mexican American diet, [telling students] you're going to . . . call people up in the phonebook at random and ask them, what are you eating for dinner tonight? We invented the classes.[14]

At Long Beach, Nieto gained valuable curricular experience and built on his early exposure to Chicana/o and Latina/o literature and history. He witnessed firsthand the fight for curriculum relevant to the experiences and backgrounds of Chicana/os. Nieto shortly thereafter would be called on to replicate his experiences at CSU Long Beach in Bakersfield, where student and campus activists were putting political pressure on the college administration to create a Chicana/o studies curriculum.

After completing his undergraduate education, Nieto received a fellowship in Latin American studies at UC Los Angeles (UCLA). During this time, federal dollars were allocated to develop Latin American studies programs at the graduate level; consequently, students from top universities, such as Yale, Harvard, and Stanford, enrolled in these programs.[15] Although the degree in Latin American studies was a two-year program, Nieto was very focused and earned his master's degree in one year, one of two people to do so at UCLA in 1971. At the same time, Nieto was drafted for military service, but failed his physical examination due to a hearing disability. Regarding the ongoing war in Vietnam, Nieto held a strong antiwar position for various moral, political, and personal reasons, most notably, the fact that his brother had been critically injured in the Korean War. Recalling this family history, Nieto stated:

> I was about three years old when my brother came back from Korea in December 1950. For the next fifteen to eighteen years of my life I kept seeing my brother in a wheelchair in the VA Hospital in Long Beach, and so this had an incredible impact where I saw a lot of young guys in the paraplegic or quadriplegic ward, the spinal injury section. . . . I didn't understand the complexities of war or the politics, the only thing I understood [was] that my brother and a lot of other young Chicanos had been severely injured and wounded in the war. . . . My desire and interest in going to Long Beach . . . was motivated because my brother was there at the VA Hospital.[16]

His family's military history in Korea later influenced Nieto's reform efforts in the community college curriculum, which politicized Chicana/o students at Bakersfield College against the war in Vietnam.

Nieto received a telephone call from Teresa Gaona, United Mexican Students (UMS) chair at Bakersfield College, asking him to think about teaching at Bakersfield. Chicana/o students at Bakersfield College had become politically active in the late 1960s and early 1970s.[17] Remembering the circumstances that radicalized many students at Bakersfield College, Nieto stated:

> Conditions were most severe in Kern County and the Central Valley. You had primarily what some would disparagingly call "a redneck community" that control[led] politics, the economy, the social life. This is also where the farmworker movement got started. It was in an area of severe economic problems for farmworkers. I remember reading about the various revolutions of Central America, Cuba, [and] Mexico. I learned a few conceptual ideas about organizing and certainly the impact that students could have. There were a number of veteran students who had been in the armed forces, and they came back and had very specific ideas about what they needed to do, and you couldn't shut them up, nothing was going to quiet them. There were sons and daughters of farmworkers who had been politicized, who had been out in the fields of agriculture organizing, talking proudly about who they were and what they were doing. So I was naive enough to believe that they could make a difference. And I think that they did. Students who came to classes had already seen their parents actively involved in the *huelga*, in the boycott, in the UFW struggle. I was motivated because I wasn't much older than students myself, I was twenty-three. I was a lot younger than a lot of students.[18]

Along with Chicanas/os throughout California, minority students at Bakersfield College created an educational experience relevant to their own academic and cultural interests. In Bakersfield, creating a vibrant Chicana/o studies curriculum was an extension of the Chicana/o civil rights movement. Burns Finlinson, then president of Bakersfield College, provided initial support for classes in Chicana/o studies, as well as for the recruitment of Nieto. "Finlinson wanted to establish classes because of student interest. [He] himself was a professor of history and understood interdisciplinary classes; however, he claimed ignorance about specific classes termed Chicano studies. He gave me tremendous leeway in creating and implementing new classes and subsequent materials required for Chicano studies," Nieto recalled.[19]

Nieto's first year at Bakersfield College, 1971–1972, mirrored the tumultuous nature of activism on American college campuses. His initiatives for broadening the narrow education offered at Bakersfield College encountered significant resistance from powerful faculty forces within the college academic community. Given the blank slate that Bakersfield represented in developing Chicana/o studies, Nieto established relationships with other progressive educational activists in the early 1970s. During the fall of 1971, he attended a conference to discuss the formation of the tribal college D-Q (or Deganawidah-Quetzalcoatl University).[20] Recalling that period, Nieto reflected: "I remember I attended in the fall of 1971 a conference near Davis. Native Americans and Chicanos took over an air force base, and they wanted to develop D-Q. . . . Talk about radicals. This was interesting as hell."[21] For Nieto, the meeting epitomized radical ethnic studies activism. Nieto felt a strong sense of assurance regarding the alignment of his activities at Bakersfield College with ethnic studies movements across California. This solidarity with progressive student movements statewide propelled Nieto's sense of determination for curricular change.

In January 1972, at the start of his last semester as Bakersfield College president, Finlinson observed that "along with the size of the college increasing, there has also been a significant effort in the developing of ethnic studies."[22] His remarks showed that the idea of minority studies was on the college agenda. In the summer of 1971, as a new hire, Nieto taught courses in American history for Bakersfield College. The subsequent fall, he taught regular semester-length classes in history and served in the counseling department. Nieto was thereafter given the charge by Finlinson to initiate Chicana/o studies classes.[23]

Significantly, in the fall of 1971, Nieto also developed the Chicano Information Center (CIC) at Bakersfield College. The center was established to serve the needs of all Chicana/os on campus, as well as to provide services to the student community at large. The establishment of the CIC encountered resistance from an unsuccessful campaign to halt the takeover of a room in the Student Activities office in Campus Center 4. The opposition's argument was based on funding. The Associated Students of Bakersfield College (ASBC) gathered funds from student body card sales, so if the CIC was to be located in this office, then it was to be funded by the student body. The Bakersfield College UMS cited its membership numbers at over seven hundred persons in the academic community.[24] Opponents therefore feared that the large presence of Chicana/os that would be affiliated with the CIC would lead to a cultural bias dominating student politics, which, subsequently, occurred. Utilizing the widely read school newspaper, the *Renegade Rip*, UMS began a weekly column to report the issues affecting Chicana/o students and their larger community. In a December 1971 article titled "La Raza," the college community was formally introduced to the political ideology of the Chicana/o *movimiento* and the concept of La Raza—the latter an ideological attempt to find a common history and experience of oppression among a colonized ethnic Mexican people across the American Southwest.[25]

By 1974, the small-scale CIC would become the Chicano Cultural Center (CCC), which facilitated counseling and other services for Chicana/o (and all other) students at Bakersfield College. Nieto's push for progressive counseling was, at the time, appreciated by students for the variety of services offered, particularly information geared toward draft counseling to avoid service in the Vietnam War. Nieto's draft counseling service was made available to all students but was primarily utilized by Chicana/o students. The purpose of draft counseling was to expand a student's knowledge regarding alternative options to military service. Options included undertaking community service and registering oneself as a conscientious objector. Many members of the campus and community felt that what Nieto was doing was un-American. Georgia Johnson, who hosted a local radio program, publicly called Nieto a communist.[26] Nieto, however, found support among members of the Kern County Selective Service Board, as well as various college administrators who felt he was a valuable resource as a link to a significant yet underrepresented group of students.[27] Recalling the institutional significance of the CIC and CCC, Nieto noted that the center "was facilitated by the idea of having draft counselors but at the same time the majority of the students being served were Chicanos. In order to institutionalize the idea of providing services on a long-term basis, the idea was . . . let's diffuse the criticism that this is . . . a MEChA [Movimiento Estudiantil Chicano de Aztlán, Chicano Student Movement of Aztlán] clubhouse, instead this is a program that serves not only all Chicano students, but all non-Chicanos who want to learn about this area."[28]

Beyond the issue of the military draft, the UFW movement politicized the Bakersfield College campus in the early 1970s. Students actively supported the boycott of lettuce at this time. When growers signed contracts with the Teamsters Union in 1973, "Chavez and the UFW redirected the grape boycott staff to a campaign against nonunion lettuce and vegetables."[29] The Bakersfield College MEChA chapter decided to boycott the school's dining commons because it carried nonunion lettuce in far less proportion than it carried Teamsters' lettuce. Instead of patronizing the cafeteria, MEChA set up picket lines outside the cafeteria and gave away free food as an alternative.[30] The free food was funded by MEChA and the Alvarez brothers, local Mexican American siblings who owned a successful supermarket in East Bakersfield. Recalling their cooperation, MEChA student activist Duane Goff mused, "I barely got the whole story [about the lettuce boycott] out of my mouth, and Maurice Alvarez was providing us free food."[31]

The administration's response was to balance the concerns of students who supported each union. "We have asked our suppliers to give us as close to 50-50 (from both unions). We've guaranteed MEChA that neither union would receive above 75% and never below 25%," said Jack Hernandez, then dean of students and assistant to college president John Collins.[32] President Collins was sensitive to the needs of Chicana/o students, especially given his previous experience at Moorpark College in Ventura County, where he had dealt with Chicana/o student activists, MEChA, and student support for the grape boycott. Historian Frank P. Barajas notes that the Mexican American Political Association (MAPA) of Ventura County "saluted President Collins at its annual banquet for doing more for the Chicano than anyone else."[33] Collins brought with him lessons learned in Ventura County when he took up the presidency at Bakersfield, and he remained a stalwart supporter of Jess Nieto and Chicana/o students.

Student response to MEChA's boycott was mixed. A cafeteria worker noted that the boycott officially began on a Wednesday, which turned out to be an "extra busy day" with increased sales of salads and lettuce.[34] However, the cafeteria ultimately lost business. After over a month of the boycott, an incidence of violence broke out between Mexican and Anglo students that resulted in damaged property. During the same period, a sulfur gas container was thrown into the cafeteria by an anonymous party. Recalling negotiations with the administration over the lettuce boycott, Duane Goff stated: "there was very little tension, students either supported us or they didn't. . . . It was completely nonviolent, other than one time where those white kids threw a tantrum and broke a window. . . . We had some white kids come by and make smart comments, but we learned to ignore idiots."[35] After weeks of pressure, the administration agreed to carry only UFW lettuce. MEChA students also supported the UFW in their boycotts in Delano and Safeway stores.

Despite opposition to the farmworker movement on campus, the Chicana/o studies curriculum development manifested in multiple ways. For Chicana/o students, the issues of the farmworkers and the reform of education were closely interrelated. Nieto proposed instituting a new graduation requirement for all students, requiring a course in cross-cultural awareness: Chicana/o studies, Black studies, Native American studies, Asian studies, or women's studies. The proposal was mired in controversy in 1973 and nearly led to Nieto's censure by the Academic Senate. A substantial portion of both the faculty and the conservative community in Bakersfield was outraged at the idea of incorporating an ethnic studies requirement into the curriculum.

An instructor of history, Tom Davis, led the opposition to the cross-cultural awareness requirement at Bakersfield College. Davis called for

FIGURES 4.1–4.2 "Chicana and Chicano students in Bakersfield College's MEChA club, marching in support of the campus boycott of nonunion lettuce in 1973. Photos courtesy of Janet Florez.

Nieto's censure, alleging unprofessional conduct during a public meeting on the cross-cultural requirement. Representatives of the college had been invited to meet with community members to discuss the requirement proposal. The meeting took place at a local elementary school with a large Hispanic student population. At the time, Nieto was involved with a coalition that was engaged in legal battles over school segregation in the BCSD. To Nieto, the cross-cultural requirement was connected to the larger battle to desegregate Bakersfield city schools. Although Professor Davis had attended the event as a representative of the college (alongside Dr. Frank Wattron, associate dean of instruction), he had believed his role at the meeting to be as audience, not participant. When both representatives were asked to speak at the meeting, "Davis expressed his utter and complete surprise at being invited to speak, stating that he expected to be a part of the audience."[36] At this point, Nieto asserted that the college representatives had been informed that they would be part of the panel discussion. Nieto apologized for any misunderstanding. Nevertheless, a determined community delivered to the college representatives an honest yet stern tongue-lashing on the need for a cross-cultural education requirement for Bakersfield College graduates.

The atmosphere at the meeting offended Professor Davis. He alleged that Nieto "sandbagged" the college representatives, exposing them to the ire of an angry community. Dr. Gus García, a member of the community group Chicanos Unidos for Progress and a founding faculty member of California State College, Bakersfield, sent a formidable letter to the Bakersfield

College graduation requirements committee, dispelling Davis's allegation in a thorough recounting of the meeting. García wrote: "the discussion could no more be described as 'an interrogation' (Mr. Davis' words) than might a television panel discussion, such as *Meet the Press* or *Face the Nation*." Garcia challenged Davis's indictment of the meeting, since "either BC representative could have chosen to leave. By remaining, they elected to, in a real sense, face the community."[37]

Radio conservative talk show host Georgia Johnson also protested Nieto's cross-cultural awareness graduation requirement. She argued that if a cultural awareness credit was to be added, students should be able to fulfill it through German, Lithuanian, Swedish, Jewish, or any other desired course, not just the ones that Nieto had proposed. After being reviewed by the Academic Senate, Nieto's proposal for the cross-cultural awareness requirement was rejected. New college president John Collins, however, overruled this rejection.[38] Collins thus quickly established himself as a college administrator supportive of the Chicana/o student movement at Bakersfield, just as he had in his previous appointment as Moorpark College's founding president.[39]

Nieto's reform efforts garnered mixed reaction from his colleagues. A faculty evaluation by Professor Gaylen Lewis in 1973 summarized Nieto's position as both employee and Chicana/o movement activist. Lewis wrote:

> [Jess Nieto] is an example of a "new" teacher, i.e., one who refuses to indoctrinate "truths" primarily designed to reinforce the status quo but one who suggests "alternatives," thus acting as an agent of the future. As the Director of Chicano Studies, Jess Nieto can continue to be involved . . . but he is running the risk of compromising his position and his function by becoming a part of the establishment. As an administrator sincerely interested in his program, he increases his chances of mis-perceiving reality. Detached objectivity is challenged by the duties/responsibilities of the organization. Lulacs, though maybe only unintentionally, often stand in the way of achieving Aztlán.[40]

Nieto attempted to balance his role as both an academic and a Chicano activist. For a young nontenured instructor, the task was daunting. Nieto recalled the opposition he encountered in expanding general education at Bakersfield College:

> Professor Davis felt I overstepped my boundaries as a young nontenured professor in formulating requirements for graduation. Yet,

until I offered the proposal for a cross-cultural requirement, the college . . . ignored the representation of minority groups in the college's general education curriculum. . . . The [opposition also] had to do with my effort to establish a Department of Chicano Studies. I brought up the issue, and I remember [Dean] Frank Wattron [saying], "I've gone to bat for you, we have established a program, in two years it is incredible. I am not going to go to the mat for you on the establishment of a department." I'll never forget those words. . . . There wasn't any faculty that would support me. The students I felt would be there, [but] the administration was not going to support me; so basically, it would be just the students and Jess.[41]

The debate over the cross-cultural requirement epitomizes the resistance activists encountered from those who perceived Chicana/o studies to be too radical a departure from the status quo in higher education. If not for the administrative leadership of President Collins, Nieto's reforms would have been quashed by the Academic Senate, despite widespread student support.

Chicana/o students in the early 1970s at Bakersfield College mobilized support for Nieto's reforms and the UFW by participating in the boycott, as well as by becoming involved with campus politics and programming. The annual Semana de la Raza (Week of the People) in early May was a campus highlight for Chicana and Chicano students. On May 3, 1973, Rodolfo "Corky" Gonzales spoke to an audience in the campus outdoor theater. MEChA student activist Janet Florez introduced the leading Chicano nationalist thinker as the week's culminating event. "What the hell do you care about what Anglos think of you? We should be worried about how we see ourselves. . . . We are the most disorganized people in the world—anywhere in Atzlan, *Chicanos son hermanos* [Chicanos are brothers]. Recognize the network and that nationalism is our form of organization."[42] For Chicana and Chicano students at Bakersfield College in the early 1970s, partaking in the "organization and nationalism" that Corky spoke of meant supporting the curricular reforms Nieto pushed as one of the few full-time Chicana/o faculty members on campus.

With minimal support from the administration, Nieto proposed the formation of both the CCC and a Department of Chicano Studies in 1974. While the center and Chicana/o studies courses were approved by the college administration, departmental status was denied due to the lack of Academic Senate and administrative support. Even so, Nieto's efforts at institutionalizing Chicana/o studies on campus meant that, as Professor Rudy Acuña of CSU Northridge noted, Bakersfield College had the reputation for being at the forefront of the Chicana/o activist movement.[43] "I have an obligation to support the struggle . . . but the students here in the San Joaquin Valley have more of an obligation because this is your home ground. This is where your roots are. This is where the battle is going to be won or lost," Acuña told the students assembled in May 1974 for the annual Semana de la Raza series.[44] Nieto was effective in developing a robust Chicana/o studies curriculum at Bakersfield College. Between 1971 and 1980, the Chicano Studies Program offered a variety of courses in the following areas: history, philosophy, art, music, theater, anthropology, psychology, women's studies, sociology, foreign languages, and literature. Additionally, these courses were cross-referenced with other departments and were made available at the university transfer level. Each course was degree applicable and easily met the requirements for a Chicano Studies Certificate, the latter being especially valuable for those wishing to increase their effectiveness in dealing with a burgeoning Hispanic population.[45]

By 1976, the CCC and the Chicano Studies Program boasted a bountiful services center and course offerings. The center's published bulletin termed the CCC "one of the leading models of the Chicano presence in higher education in the United States."[46] The CCC offered services and programs that included Cinco de Mayo Week, academic advising, community relations, international study and travel, eighteen academic courses, a Chicano Studies Certificate, bilingual/bicultural teacher training, and a research archive on Mexican and Chicana/o cultural heritage. Additionally, the center published a monthly newsletter, *Noticias de la Raza*, that included political, social, academic and literary reviews, and articles. At the same time, seven full-time faculty carried a portion of their teaching load in Chicana/o studies, and four adjunct faculty carried the remaining balance of the teaching assignments. Only Nieto was assigned full time to this program, a feature that eventually kept the CCC and the Chicano Studies Program from gaining equal fiscal footing with other academic and student services programs. Although the center and academic program were supported by institutional funding, efforts to expand these programs were administratively gridlocked and found little support for the hiring of additional staffing in Chicana/o studies.

DELANO, CHICANISMO, AND INTERNATIONAL EDUCATION

Nieto's interest in Latin American studies reaped financial rewards and internationalized community college education in greater Bakersfield. Nieto's incorporation of Chicana/o nationalism in the higher education curriculum was inextricably connected to the heritage of Mexico and Latin America. Nieto developed an international program at the community college level, sprung from events that transpired in 1973 at the annual meeting of the American Association of Community and Junior Colleges in Washington, DC. As an invited speaker to the conference, Nieto addressed the audience about the international dimension of Chicana/o studies in relation to Latin America. At the time, Nieto was completing a doctoral program in education at USC, where one of his instructors, Dr. John Carpenter, was director of the Title IX ethnic studies programs.[47] With the support of Carpenter and Jorge Manuel Pérez Ponce (director of the Office of International Programs of the American Association of Community and Junior Colleges), Nieto was invited to the conference and learned about Title IX heritage funding. Nieto in turn applied for a Title IX grant to begin internationalizing Chicana/o studies at Bakersfield College. With the $70,000 he received, Project MEChICA (Materiales para Estudios Chicanos Interculturales de América, Materials for Intercultural Chicano Studies of America) developed curriculum materials for elementary, secondary, and higher education levels at a time when resources were scarce. The program's aims were interinstitutional and international. Instruction was in Spanish and English. The bilingual aspect was important, since the federal funding had been geared toward English-only programs.[48] Nieto's proposal was a significant achievement in advancing international education in Kern County's parochial communities, especially given that of the over one thousand applications, the MEChICA project was awarded one of only forty-two grants across the nation (only three of these in California).[49] It was one of only two projects, moreover, that dealt exclusively with Chicana/o studies curriculum development.[50]

Mexican officials were excited at the prospect of working with the United States in curriculum development. The MEChICA project offered Mexico an opportunity to showcase to the United States the excellence of its own higher education system. Individual members of La Secretaría de Educación Pública (the Secretariat of Public Education) expressed concern for the treatment of Chicana/os within the educational system of the United States. Several Mexican education officials expressed their views of US higher education when MEChICA was being established: "Debemos ayudar a nuestros paisanos, los Chicanos" (We must help our fellow countrymen, the Chicanos).[51] In several letters of correspondence to Nieto, Mexican officials (including Oaxaca governor Miguel Zárate Aquino) praised Project MEChICA for its attempt to improve relations between the United States and Mexico.[52] Nieto argued that MEChICA would mend the educational system, which had failed to create intellectual environments that prepared students for intercultural awareness,

FIGURE 4.3 Jess Nieto (*center*) with Dolores Huerta and César Chávez, mid-1970s. Photo courtesy of Peggy Nieto.

interaction, competence, and functionality.[53] The college community reacted with both excitement and dismay to Project MEChICA. Ultimately, the college did not see the inherent benefits of an international effort. Project MEChICA ended with the drying up of Title IX support.

In the fall semester of 1977, Nieto was appointed dean of the Delano Center, a KCCD satellite campus some thirty miles north of Bakersfield.[54] The town of Delano had garnered national and international attention in the late 1960s and early 1970s as UFW headquarters. When Nieto arrived in Delano, racial and political divisiveness was evident. Nieto's sympathy toward the UFW was well known in Kern County. His appointment to the Delano administrative post raised eyebrows among the county's conservative grower community. Two weeks before Nieto officially began his job at Delano, two residents who supported his appointment, Esther Mansano and Bernice Bonillas, visited him. They informed him that a local committee had been formed to get rid of him. "The ex-mayor of Delano, the vice president of the local Bank of America, and some members of the Delano College Center's foundation" were all against Nieto's leadership of the Delano Center. "They do not want to see a Mexican, a Chicano with your background of activism be the dean there," Nieto recalled being told.[55] At one point, Nieto feared for his safety. Nieto remembered the harassment he had faced:

> I would leave the center at night. The first semester a police car would invariably follow me out of town and would turn on their bright lights behind me. As I got to the freeway, they would veer off. This went on for a while. One time I had gone in to check enrollments in Wasco and Shafter and I got back around 8:30. One of these local police guys pulled me over in front of the center with the bright lights and the sirens, and he said, "Can I see your driver's license?" I gave it to him, and he said, "You were speeding." I

was going maybe seven miles per hour, and he gave me a ticket for
going thirty-five and I was seething.... Someone in the Office of
Civil Rights in San Francisco had [been] read[ing] local newspapers, particularly in the rural areas, and [my] name ke[pt] coming
up and [they] wanted to find out what is going on.... So I called
the Office of Civil Rights.... They went and talked to the chief of
police. It was clearly an effort to try and harass me and make me
uncomfortable.[56]

Nieto's troubles, however, remained even after the Office of Civil Rights stepped in. The anti-union grower community in Delano was enthusiastic about getting Nieto removed from the Delano Center. Nieto recalled:

I discovered that they came up with a new tactic. If they couldn't
do that more overt approach they would infiltrate the system; they
asked [Edward] Simonsen, who was the chancellor, that they wanted
to become a part of my evaluation process.... So I got Father Ray
Tintle, the parish priest of Guadalupe, and he got five hundred
people to be a part of my committee and asked me as part of the
strategy, "why don't you do the sermons for every Mass for the next
several weeks?" And I did. I would talk about education, working for
the community, Chicanismo disguised in a nice way. And everyone
who was Catholic and lived on the west side knew Jess Nieto.[57]

Nieto's encounters with law enforcement in Delano served as a catalyst for his work in protesting police harassment with the Minority Coalition of Kern County in early 1978. The *Delano Record* reported in January of that year that four people were arrested and hospitalized after a fight broke out with police officers. Two young men were injured, but what alarmed local residents were the injuries sustained by Florentino and Gennie Vásquez, the parents of one of the young men involved in the altercation. Gennie Vásquez suffered a lower back contusion after being struck in the front. In February, the Minority Coalition reported to the Delano City Council that the city government needed to deal not only with reconciliation for the unjustified and excessive use of police force in the case, but also with the larger issue of police-community relations.[58]

Nieto was not alone in spearheading criticism of the Delano Police Department's treatment of Chicana/os. In his report to the city council, Nieto noted that without provocation or publicity, over 150 people had attended local Minority Coalition meetings in an effort to voice their own experiences of police harassment. Nieto's use of his position of authority as a college administrator gave legitimacy to popular Chicana/o protest against the Delano Police Department. The city council and the police department denied all charges of harassment. Over two years later, at other city council meetings, another citizens' group protested police harassment and reminded the council of Nieto's previous report. Local government, however, made no significant effort to resolve citizen complaints against police brutality.[59]

Despite local opposition to his appointment, Nieto's longtime commitment to Chicana/o studies and international education did not diminish. As the founder of the CCC and Chicano Studies Program at Bakersfield College, Nieto sharpened his understanding of the educational needs of the Chicana/o community and continued his efforts in Delano. Delano's farming community was majority ethnic Mexican, with some white and Filipino residents. What Nieto encountered was a town that, though overwhelmingly ethnic Mexican in population, suffered from a major communication gap between its largely white conservative growers and its mostly poor ethnic Mexican population.[60] Nieto worked to reconcile this disjuncture through education reform. His role was more than that of dean of the local college center; it was a leadership position that highlighted the cultural capital of the people.

Nieto's efforts to broaden the curriculum in Delano steered toward internationalizing the community college education experience. He accomplished this through a number of innovations and contacts he had built through his years at Bakersfield College. Jorge Pérez Ponce, director of El Congreso Nacional de Asuntos Colegiales (the National Congress of Collegiate Affairs) in Washington, DC, was an active supporter of Nieto's work in Bakersfield and Delano. Ponce reaffirmed the viability of Nieto's international agenda by stressing the populist nature of the community college and the fact that community colleges were the most readily available higher education venues for Mexican Americans to attend.[61] Nieto organized activities for Delano students that stressed the rich diversity and achievements of Chicana/o and Latina/o heritage and culture. The internationally renowned musical group Los Folkloristas—which performed in Spanish, Portuguese, and indigenous American languages—performed for young Chicana/o students and the public at various venues in Kern County throughout the 1970s.[62] The *Delano Record* reported Nieto as the liaison with Los Folkloristas, whose renown was a source of national and racial pride for Chicana/os.[63] The musicians were cognizant of the social message of their music, which articulated the hopes and dreams of *la raza*, their people. In Mexico, Los Folkloristas' reputation for political activism was well recognized. At one point, President

Luis Echeverría (1970–1976) of Mexico invited the group to play in the national auditorium after an attempt was made by conservative elements to keep the group from performing there.[64] In short, the annual performances by Los Folkloristas in Kern County broadened the cultural horizons of the Delano community and Kern County Chicana/os through the international and intercultural lens Nieto brought to his administrative post.

Los Folkloristas also agreed to provide the musical soundtrack to a documentary series tentatively titled *Heritage of Aztlán*, a film project Nieto originated that won a $30,000 grant from the National Endowment for the Humanities in 1976. The planned fifteen-part series was intended to echo the popularity and thought-provoking nature of the 1977 miniseries *Roots* (concerning the African American community), but it ultimately never gained the institutional funding it sought from both the United States and Mexico. Nieto pivoted from this plan, working in conjunction with Bakersfield College media specialist Al Noriega to produce two documentaries that were aired on Bakersfield and Los Angeles television dealing with the history of Mexican civilization.[65] Although this project did not approach the scope of his ambitious initial proposal, Nieto's efforts to bring the history and development of Chicana/o nationalism to the masses of all racial backgrounds were a meaningful step in debunking the notion that Chicana/o nationalism and racial identity were separatist and dangerous. Nieto's promotion of Chicana/o media and cultural productions illustrates the range of ways he manifested his political ideology and worldview. His push for international education at the community college level reflected an effort to create institutional space that centered the cultural, racial, and ethnic significance of the Latina/o population in the American Southwest. Moreover, despite the fact that the film series was never fully produced, Nieto gained public support for the project from educational scholars and numerous state government officials, as well as Mexican officials, all of whom wrote letters of support for Nieto's National Endowment for the Humanities proposal.[66] Even César Chávez was excited about the project, assuming of course that Nieto "retain[ed] contractual control of the project in order to assure that the portion documenting the history of the United Farm Workers [would] be presented from the point of view of the farm workers."[67]

Nieto also facilitated institutional relations between the KCCD and Mexico via his participation in the League for Innovation in the Community College. In the fall of 1980, Nieto, with support from US ambassador to Mexico Julian Nava and both the US and Mexican presidential administrations, proposed an initiative for a "new partnership between private enterprise in the United States of America and the Republic of Mexico."[68]

FIGURE 4.4 Jess Nieto (*in glasses*) with Al Noriega, mid-1970s. Photo courtesy of Peggy Nieto and the Bakersfield College Archives.

Known as the Gemini Proposal, it called for "a new way by which Mexican sales of petroleum to certain US firms would provide additional and significant benefits to Mexico, thus setting an example for a new partnership between American importers and the people of Mexico." The proposal called for the use of Mexican and US oil revenues to fund a binational university that would produce graduates to improve relations between the two countries. US-Mexico trade relations were particularly tense at the time, given the recent discovery of petroleum reserves in Mexico and the late 1970s energy crisis in the United States. Contextualizing the US-Mexico trade environment, Ambassador Nava wrote that one of his primary goals as ambassador was to "make public American disappointment that President López Portillo had at the last minute changed his mind and decided that Mexico would not join the General Agreement on Trade and Tariffs [*sic*], or GATT."[69] The GATT initiative (1947–1995) regulated international trade for the benefit of all trading nations rather than individual members. Nieto's proposal to allocate a percentage of newly refined petroleum funds from US companies to building Mexican infrastructure could have served as an important bridge to better trade relations between the two nations, but it was ultimately complicated by international relations outside his control.

Nieto's Gemini Proposal built on his existing work with international exchange programs at the community college level. Immediately prior to the Gemini Proposal, in September 1980, Nieto had worked with the League for Innovation in the Community College to provide specialized technical training to Mexican students in the American community college system.[70] In this effort, Nieto had made significant inroads into working with Mexican government officials, particularly through the National Council for Science and Technology (Consejo Nacional de Ciencia y Tecnología, CONACYT); this organization would later endorse Nieto's idea of a binational university

FIGURE 4.5 Bakersfield College student activists Debbie Rivera (Beadle) and Duane Goff outside a Bakersfield College MEChA meeting, mid-1970s. Photo courtesy of Peggy Nieto and the Bakersfield College Archives.

funded by petroleum reserves. Nieto's Gemini Proposal was contingent, however, on a friendly US administration that shared his vision of improving US-Mexican relations by aiding Mexico's infrastructural development. No such support was found with the election of Ronald Reagan in 1980. The change to a Republican administration undermined efforts of binational collaboration. Julian Nava was replaced in early 1981 by former actor John Gavin (a Latino), who soon caused controversy in Mexico because "he had lent his name to publicize a Mexican brandy."[71] With the replacement of Nava, the proposal for a binational university between the United States and Mexico lost support. Publicly, Ambassador Nava reported to the Mexican press that regardless of the change in administrations, the United States would continue to work for the mutual benefit of both nations.[72] Both Nava and Nieto knew, however, that the election results in fall 1980 meant that all hope for a binational university would be lost.[73]

CONCLUSION

The course of Chicana/o civil rights activism in Bakersfield during the heyday of the farmworker movement was an important part of greater Bakersfield's civil rights history. Higher education reform was an important expression of Chicana/o activism. The implementation of Chicana/o studies programs shifted how Mexican Americans viewed themselves and their history. Institutional reforms in higher education also altered how the larger public viewed the place of Mexican Americans in Bakersfield. Nieto's educational reforms at Bakersfield College proved long lasting, even after ethnic studies underwent significant cutbacks in college and university budgets in subsequent decades. In the early 1980s, Jess retired from Bakersfield College to pursue a career in the burgeoning field of Hispanic marketing. He continued to keep his hand in educational initiatives through the founding of his nonprofit foundation Heritage of America, however, and he remained active in civil rights and social justice struggles, both in Bakersfield and in Latin America.[74] In 2017, Jess passed away in Bakersfield at the age of sixty-nine.[75]

The question of the place of Mexican Americans in Bakersfield was brought to bear by the gravity of the farmworker movement. Chicana/o student activists and educators fought for reforms that offered a cultural space for Mexican Americans to identify with an indigenous past and build transnational relationships. Such a reimagining was important in Kern County, where relations between citizens and noncitizens have a history of tension.[76] Moreover, the mobilization of young Chicana/os and *el movimiento* would shape local politics in Kern County in the early 1970s and beyond.

5 | "HOO-RAY GONZALES!"
Civil Rights Protest and Chicana/o
Politics in Bakersfield, 1968–1974

The 30th Assembly District is a typically gerrymandered legislative district. With most of east Bakersfield and cities like Arvin, Lamont, Delano, Shafter, Wasco, McFarland, the population is both heavily Latino and Democratic. Kern County is 47.1 percent Latino, a plurality in the county. Clearly, the 30th District needs dramatic voter registration drives, citizenship efforts and political education in the broadest sense. The candidates should have a sense of missionary zeal, which would lead them to hit the streets in efforts to get people, especially Latinos, to become registered voters so that they can determine their own political destinies.
Raymond Gonzales, La Voz de Kern, 2010

All those people who've been snickering at us shall take another look. . . . It's now fashionable to talk about the encroachment of government on people's lives: we in Kern County have been saying it and voting it all along. I think we'll get stronger as the resentment against government rise[s]. . . . Kern County will become typical of representative government and politics. There is nothing peculiar or backward about Kern County or its politics. We're the future.
William "Bill" Thomas, 1978

Mexican Americans, African Americans, and their white liberal allies mobilized politically throughout the civil rights struggles of the late 1960s and early 1970s in greater Bakersfield. African Americans and Mexican Americans voiced their political and social concerns and agitated against the local anti-statist conservative body politic—embodied in the Bakersfield City Council's majority vote. Both Mexican Americans and African Americans continued a post–World War II tradition of grassroots political engagement in greater Bakersfield that would reap political rewards in 1972.

The "politics of the fields" during the tumultuous 1970s were marked by support for, or condemnation of, the United Farm Workers (UFW). The Delano grape strike and boycott (1965–1970) and opposition to police brutality helped unify the political thinking of African Americans and Mexican Americans in Bakersfield. The farmworker movement tangentially generated protest against police brutality and support for federally subsidized rural health care. Each social cause mobilized the political left and right in Bakersfield in the late 1960s and early 1970s. The political left, composed of urban Chicana/os, African Americans, and white liberals marshaled the first grassroots Chicana/o political victory in Kern County in 1972, with the election of Raymond "Ray" Gonzales to the California State Assembly. Gonzales's brief tenure in the California Assembly (1972–1974) sheds light on the changing nature of politics, civil rights, and racial coalition building in greater Bakersfield during the Chicana/o movement era. His relationship with the UFW contributed to both his maiden election victory and his reelection defeat in 1974 to local Republican Bill Thomas. Gonzales's defeat also marked a regional eclipse of grassroots racial coalition building and political activism on the liberal left.

THE POLITICS OF THE FIELD: CIVIL RIGHTS DURING THE DELANO GRAPE STRIKE

Between 1965 and 1970 the UFW waged an epic farm labor strike, including a secondary boycott against Delano area grape growers. The farm labor struggle, while national and international in scope, had an intense and vilifying local aspect in Kern County. In 1968 the Bakersfield City Council took action to officially oppose the grape strike. Urban civil rights groups mobilized in response, backing the UFW. Support for the UFW intersected increasingly with civil rights reforms in venues outside the farm labor movement.

On September 16, 1968, the third anniversary of the announcement of the Delano grape strike, the Bakersfield City Council passed by a five-to-two margin Resolution 87-68. Officially entitled "A Resolution of the City Council of the City of Bakersfield Regarding Labor-Management Disputes Outside of the Jurisdiction of Member Municipalities of the National League of Cities," the resolution positioned the city council in clear opposition to the UFW grape boycott. The resolution called for political pressure on the National League of Cities to prevent elected, as well as nonelected, municipal officials from entering "into labor-management disputes which involve areas outside their jurisdiction, so that economic and irrevocable injury to another municipality is prevented."[1] Bakersfield City Council members demanded that other US municipalities forego politicizing Kern County's three-year farm labor dispute, effectively limiting the financial losses to Kern County growers. César Chávez acknowledged local government resistance to the boycott before the US House Committee on Education and Labor in October 1969. "We have experienced things that we never dreamed we would be confronted with when we began the strike. These small communities are so well knit and the grower influence is so predominant that when we struck in Delano, we not only had the growers against us, but we had the other public bodies like the city council, the board of supervisors, the high school and elementary school districts, passing resolutions and propaganda against the strike and against the union. . . . The community wanted to destroy us as soon as possible," Chávez testified.[2] As historian Devra Weber notes, valley towns in Central California had been transformed economically by agrarian capitalism since the 1920s. The valley towns that Chávez organized through the grape strike and boycott were marked historically by a social milieu of migrant workers and growers who embraced a style of "quasi–welfare capitalism" designed to control agricultural workers.[3]

Throughout 1968, the Delano grape boycott underwent significant tactical changes. That spring, Chávez engaged in a hunger strike to call attention to the importance of maintaining nonviolence in the farm labor struggle. Violence on both sides of the dispute had escalated. Chávez was summoned to the Kern County courthouse in downtown Bakersfield that year to answer questions about violence in the fields. UFW organizers Marshall Ganz and LeRoy Chatfield seized the court appearance as an opportunity to take over the public space, turning the area outside the courthouse into a peaceful mass demonstration supportive of the Delano grape boycott. The goal was to convert the Kern County courthouse "into a cathedral," Ganz later recalled.[4] The UFW also sent representatives across the United States and abroad to key consumer markets to bolster support for a secondary boycott against California grapes. Among these representatives was a young Jessica Govea, whose parents had been active in founding the Bakersfield Community Service Organization (CSO).[5]

Even though Delano was outside the municipal jurisdiction of Bakersfield, the city council felt compelled to issue an anti-union resolution. UFW opponents reasoned that the permanent unionization of farmworkers, a likely outcome if the grape boycott succeeded, spelled financial ruin for Kern

County agribusiness. African Americans mobilized in support of farmworkers and against the city council's resolution, demonstrating racial solidarity with Mexican Americans. This racial alliance was part of a longer tradition of mutual support in terms of labor and civil rights activism between the region's two most predominant racial minority groups.[6] External support for the Delano grape strike remained a contentious issue in local politics through 1969. Tensions heightened when African American Los Angeles city councilman and mayoral candidate Tom Bradley publicly endorsed the Delano grape boycott at a UFW convention in East Los Angeles. The Bakersfield City Council passed a resolution condemning Bradley's endorsement and affirmed that "this Council does not inten[d] to tell Councilman Bradley how to take care of a special situation in Watts. . . . It is important for this Council and the Board of Supervisors and all the people to stand together in opposition to outside influence bent upon courses of action that could be disastrous to all."[7]

Upset at the city council's perceived attack on a rising African American leader, the Bakersfield branch of the National Association for the Advancement of Colored People (NAACP) argued that local African Americans supported the grape boycott because, in addition to being an issue concerning minority groups, it was "also a moral issue." Local NAACP officials argued that the city council had unfairly and in open bias sided with growers and that its antiboycott resolution "had an ulterior racial motive. . . . If Mr. Bradley had not been a black man, the resolution would not have been offered."[8] Such support from African Americans advanced racial solidarity with Mexican Americans in the struggle for labor and civil rights. By supporting the UFW, African American activists followed the mandate from the regional and national NAACP leadership, such as West Coast (WC) regional director Leonard Carter. The latter had been at the forefront of the NAACP-WC's efforts to encourage the national NAACP body to support the UFW. At the fifty-eighth annual NAACP convention, held in Boston in July 1967, the NAACP offered its first official resolution in support of the UFW. Local NAACP support reflected larger regional support from African Americans for the UFW, including from the Black Panthers of the San Francisco Bay Area.[9] Moreover, the local NAACP and African American activism were integral factors in the budding political activism of Ray Gonzales's 1972 campaign for the California Assembly, which brought together African Americans and ethnic Mexicans in the quest for greater political power and representation in Bakersfield.

"HOO-RAY GONZALES!"

Within a context of rural and urban multiracial civil rights reform—marked by continued support for the UFW, protests against police brutality, the expansion of the rural welfare state, and continued anti-statist opposition to civil rights—Mexican Americans, African Americans, and their white liberal allies mobilized behind local liberal Chicana/o civil rights leader and educator Ray Gonzales in his campaign for political office. Gonzales's political approach was complex, ahead of its time, and emblematic of the efforts of the liberal left in Kern County in the early 1970s.[10] He was the first Latino assemblyman elected in a majority white conservative city and county. At the time, only 8 percent of registered voters in his district were Latina/o, meaning that Gonzales was elected by a majority white vote.[11]

Gonzales built his public career as an educator and civil rights leader. Having begun his teaching career at Bakersfield College, he completed a doctorate at the University of Southern California (USC) in Latin American studies and joined the founding faculty at California State College, Bakersfield. Later he served as a founding faculty member of the Chicano Studies Program at California State University (CSU), Long Beach. In addition to his educational career, he was an integral part of the civic unity movement and helped broker the McGraw-Hill media concessions in late 1971—a landmark in the history of Chicana/o media reform. His 1972 campaign agenda for the state assembly included the following political platform: (1) make the tax structure fair, (2) meet changing needs in education, (3) reach full employment, (4) ensure the survival of the family farm, (5) obtain the same benefits for farm employees that industrial workers enjoyed, (6) stop the pollution of the natural environment, and (7) fill the so-called generation gap with trust and reason.[12]

A staunch Democrat, Gonzales declared on his campaign flier that "many people believe there is very little difference between the two major [political] parties." As a corrective, Gonzales suggested that "there is a great deal of difference between the party of Franklin Roosevelt, Harry Truman, and John Kennedy on the one hand and that of Herbert Hoover, Dwight Eisenhower, and Richard Nixon on the other. The . . . fundamental difference is that the Democratic Party feels that it is the duty of government to protect the interest[s] of individual citizens, while the Republican Party feels that it must protect the interests of big business."[13] Gonzales's criticism of Republicans gained grassroots support for the Democratic Party in an age of growing

FIGURE 5.1 Ray Gonzales (*left*) with his staff member Steve Barber, mid-1970s. Photo courtesy of Steve Barber.

political cynicism and third-party politics, especially among Chicana/os, as evidenced by the rise of La Raza Unida Party.[14] Gonzales stressed to Kern County voters that loyalty to the Democratic Party and its principles benefited all citizens, including Chicana/os.

Given Gonzales's Democratic partisanship, his candidacy seemed like a long shot in conservative Bakersfield. "The State Democratic Party and leadership of the Assembly did not support me when I ran," Gonzales recalled. "They could not see a liberal Chicano Democrat winning against a three-term Republican incumbent."[15] Despite the state party leadership's unenthusiastic response, Gonzales, a highly educated, articulate, and devoted community activist, made inroads into a white politically conservative district. Historically, the region had a reputation for an independent voting record, notes historian James N. Gregory.[16] Recalling his early assembly campaign, Gonzales reflected that California senator Alan Cranston, a Democrat, "spoke for me. He rarely supported anybody in the [Democratic] primary, but he supported me because of a friend we had in common, Fleming Atha. I was a long shot for the state assembly, but he supported me."[17] Atha was active on the California Democratic Council (CDC) and helped organize that group's annual meeting in Bakersfield in February 1966.[18] (When the CDC met in Bakersfield, UFW activists and their urban allies picketed Governor Pat Brown outside the convention, foreshadowing the next month's march to Sacramento and its emphasis on pressuring the Democratic governor to support the striking farmworkers of Delano.) Atha and Gonzales were also colleagues for several years in the Kern Council for Civic Unity (KCCU). After Gonzales won his election, he established working relationships with California Democratic heavyweights like US senators Cranston and John Tunney, as well as labor leader Jack Henning (executive secretary-treasurer of the American Federation of Labor and Congress of Industrial Organizations [AFL-CIO])—all of which unsettled Kern County's Republican establishment.

FIGURE 5.2 Steve Barber (*left*) with Bakersfield civil rights activist Ralph Anthony, mid-1970s. Photo courtesy of Steve Barber.

Grassroots mobilization provided a base for Gonzales's assembly election. Bakersfield College Chicano student activist and Vietnam War veteran Duane Goff helped lead registration of new voters. "I think we registered about 1,100 new Democratic voters," Goff recalled. "I had just finished the semester . . . and wasn't receiving my GI Bill during the summer. Ray called me up and asked me to work for his campaign, so I said sure."[19] Steve Barber, a resident from Taft—a majority white town with a long racist history just southwest of Bakersfield—was put in charge of Gonzales's political campaign.[20] "My campaign office was on the street corner of Kentucky and Baker in East Bakersfield. Steve walked into the office one day. He was unemployed and recently graduated from college. [He] had read an article about me being active in the ACLU [American Civil Liberties Union], [so] he started volunteering on the campaign. He was one major reason I won. He became my campaign manager and worked for one year for no pay," Gonzales remembered.[21] Once Gonzales was elected, Barber served as his full-time field representative in the assembly district. His tireless efforts and political savvy enabled Gonzales to get the most out of a shoestring campaign budget, including the $85 per month rented office space in Old Town Kern (East Bakersfield). "The Democratic Central Committee had no affinity for a fifth-generation Mexican American running for the assembly. . . . We were a grassroots salt-and-pepper campaign. We had to raise our own money," Barber recalled.[22]

Gonzales's assembly campaign emphasized partisan differences between Democrats and Republicans, particularly over the issue of campaign financing. White liberals, African Americans, and Chicana/o Democrats opposed the alliance of big business with the Republican Party.[23] Running a multiracial campaign in the civic unity tradition, Gonzales appealed to Mexican American voters by launching his campaign in the Lamont-Arvin area (a Latina/o enclave), where over six hundred people attended a rally commemorating his bid for the Twenty-Eighth Assembly District seat.[24] Gonzales professed multiracial ideals to the reporters who covered his campaign. "If I'm a crusader, I'm a crusader for human needs. Many are Chicano needs, many are black needs, and many are women needs—but almost always they are Anglo needs as well," he told reporters.[25] Gonzales's public campaign financing was grassroots in character. Rather than relying on large financial donors to fill his election coffers, as many area Republicans had done before him, Gonzales relied on grassroots contributions.

Such support from below propelled Gonzales to win the primary election, helping him defeat Democratic city councilman Bob Whittemore in June 1972 by a margin of just eighty-seven votes. The primary race was close, but Gonzales's organizing activities in eastern Kern County (the high desert area) turned the voting tide in both the primary and the later general election. After Gonzales had defeated Whittemore, Republican incumbent Kent Stacey targeted his Democratic opponent. Gonzales faced a potentially insurmountable conservative opponent in Stacey, who was bankrolled by the Republican establishment. Republicans cast Gonzales as a liberal radical and political outsider. Gonzales acknowledged his liberalism on civil rights, but denied allegations that he was a far-left liberal. "I'm not that liberal. . . . I guess because I once studied for the priesthood that I'm kind of a Puritan but I'm considered a liberal because of my involvement with civil rights," he told reporters.[26] Such a moderate tone was an effective political statement in a community as religiously cultured as Kern County, yet it also indicated Gonzales's missionary zeal concerning issues of social justice.[27]

Gonzales's connection to the Chicana/o youth vote was vital to his election. Young Chicana/os brought energy to his campaign, regardless of his political inexperience and lack of large financial supporters. At Bakersfield College, the annual student-led Semana de la Raza festival created a sense of community among young Chicana/os, both on campus and in the larger community. As part of the 1972 celebrations, guest speakers included Dr. Octavio Romano, professor at the University of California (UC), Berkeley, and editor of Quinto Sol publications; Margaret Govea, CSO activist and mother of UFW organizer Jessica Govea; and assembly candidate Dr. Ray Gonzales. Gonzales's participation reveals the scope of the Chicana/o youth movement's interests in union rights, higher education, political empowerment, and reform—all under the banner of Chicana/o civil rights. Beyond showcasing the ethnic pride associated with the possibility of electing Kern County's first Latino legislator, the event brought Chicana/o youth activists face-to-face with the electoral process, upholding a central goal of the Chicana/o Power movement. Accepting an invitation to speak at the Semana de la Raza festival connected Gonzales with his former campus, and also gained him support from the youth vote.[28] Gonzales's youth vote campaign even utilized the energies of those not yet old enough to cast a ballot, enlisting them in door-to-door campaigning. Further gaining support from young Chicana/os, Gonzales, a former Marine, spoke out against the Bakersfield City Council's use of its public platform to express support for President Richard Nixon's escalation of the war in Vietnam in 1972. His position was thus in line with larger sentiments of the Chicana/o youth movement, specifically its opposition to the Vietnam War.[29]

The *Bakersfield Californian* endorsed Gonzales for office one week before the general election, a key factor in his victory over the Republican incumbent. The editorial endorsement described Stacey as lacking an impressive legislative record. Gonzales was characterized, on the other hand, as an ethnic minority figure who had overcome numerous obstacles to attain his position as a college professor, demonstrating that he was more than qualified for public office. Prior to Stacey's defeat, however, the Republican machine in Bakersfield attempted to smear Gonzales as a puppet of California's Democratic Party. Fleming Atha, a longtime Anglo Democrat from Bakersfield and treasurer of the Gonzales campaign for the Twenty-Eighth Assembly District, challenged a statement made by Republican Bakersfield city councilman Richard Stiern. The councilman suggested publicly that the Gonzales campaign had received $100,000 from the state assembly's Democratic Caucus Committee. Atha countered that this figure was grossly inflated, noting that the committee to elect Ray Gonzales had received only $500 from the state caucus, with this money earmarked to help register voters. Atha further charged that big money corporate interests had bankrolled Richard Stiern's right-wing candidates, not Gonzales.

Atha's criticism of the collusion between monied interests and the political right proved a rallying point for Gonzales as a freshman politician in the California Assembly. Once in office Gonzales embraced open transparency and proffered a strong critique of the influence of money in politics.[30] Such outspoken criticism of Sacramento's political culture did not win Gonzales new friends among business interests and legislators, but his position highlighted the role that grassroots organization had held in his election. A principled politician, Gonzales was beholden not to special interests, but to the people. Once in office, he earned a reputation as a political maverick, controlled neither by agribusiness nor by the UFW—a unique position for a Chicano Democrat in California in the early 1970s.[31] As historians have shown, UFW and agribusiness loyalties shaped political alliances in California politics after 1965 in unique ways.[32]

Gonzales's rise as a Chicano Democrat generated both ire and hope by his unseating of an incumbent Republican. The fact that he came from the Central Valley signaled a larger ascendancy of Chicana/o political power, or so it seemed to many political observers at the time. Gonzales "arrived here [in Sacramento] with more advanced notice than most of the others [a reference to the fifteen new assembly members] and got a lukewarm reception from many of his new colleagues," the *Los Angeles Times* reported.[33] Gonzales would become either the state assembly's new "golden boy" or a political pariah. Gonzales opposed accepting gifts from lobbyists, a practice that, in his mind, revealed a character shortcoming among numerous Sacramento politicians. In addition to opposing lobbyist contributions, Gonzales spoke out against the use of profanity on the assembly floor and made his opposition to these practices known in Sacramento and his home district. These unpopular positions made political waves for the neophyte Chicano assemblyman from Bakersfield. According to one journalist, Gonzales "shocked the legislative establishment" by sending $600 back to a lobbyist with a "No thank you" note attached, showing reporters and colleagues his political gravitas on the issue of influence peddling among state capitol lobbyists.[34]

Revising the California state tax code was one of Gonzales's first efforts to follow through on campaign promises once in office. He challenged tax loops that benefited growers and large landholders.[35] Reforming the tax code appealed to urban and rural Chicana/os, especially those swayed by political rhetoric critical of agriculture elites who benefited from public policies at the expense of the poor. Criticism of the Williamson Act commanded Gonzales's attention. This legislation, known as the California Land Conservation Act, was authored by Kern County Democratic assemblyman John Williamson in 1965. It gave tax breaks to large landowners who contracted with the government to keep land as open space and thereby prevent suburban sprawl. Williamson Act supporters and industry sympathizers argued that growers and large landowners needed large tax breaks in order to keep agrarian (nonurban) land productive and financially competitive. The Williamson Act rationalized that "farmland under contract [would] . . . be assessed on the basis of its actual income rather than on the market value."[36] Kern County landowners signed up in droves, commanding 1.4 million acres out of a statewide allocation of 11 million acres. The state was obliged under this legislation to compensate counties for the loss of tax revenues, but it did not acknowledge its financial commitment to counties until the early 1970s.[37] Gonzales criticized the Williamson Act on the basis that the law lowered potential tax revenues for Kern County. Of all California counties at the time, Kern County had the most land benefiting from lower taxes under this legislation.

To the chagrin of the Kern County Board of Supervisors, Gonzales claimed before "the Assembly Select Committee on Open Space Lands that the law annually cost the county $10 million in lost revenue."[38] Gonzales opposed the Williamson Act as part of his campaign mandate to create a fairer and more balanced tax code that improved public expenditures on areas like education. Gonzales argued that "in Los Angeles County where 'urban sprawl' is a fact and measures should be taken to deter this force, the Williamson Act has not been implemented at all. In Kern County where there is little fear of 'urban sprawl,' the law has been enacted to the fullest, if not abused."[39] Corporate greed under the Williamson Act limited available financial resources for public education, Gonzales pressed. The largest recipients of tax breaks under the Williamson Act included "Tenneco West, Tejon Ranch Company, [and] Buena Vista Ranch," all large-scale companies that collectively illustrated to the Chicano legislator from East Bakersfield that the Williamson Act in its present form was "a sham and a fraud."[40] Such political posturing, particularly the notion that agribusiness benefited disproportionately under a corporate welfare state, appealed to liberal Democrats. That agribusiness did benefit in such circumstances explains, in part, the shift of the valley's population away from its New Deal Democrat origins to a Republican majority. Politics and activism of the civil rights era bred a countervailing rightward shift in Kern County politics, particularly concerning the defense of agricultural subsidies.

African Americans and Mexican Americans found unity on other fronts during Gonzales's assembly tenure. In February 1974, tempers flared over the naming of the Holloway-Gonzales Library in Bakersfield's impoverished southeast corridor. The controversy represented an opportunity for civic agreement between Chicana/os and African Americans, as is evidenced by the selection of namesakes (Raymond Gonzales and Ruth B. Love-Holloway) for the new library. Fifth District supervisor John Mitchell opposed naming the library after Gonzales and Love-Holloway, despite wide support for naming the library in honor of the two prominent racial minority educators.[41] Mitchell especially raised minority ire by asking publicly at a board meeting, "Who are Holloway and Gonzales?" Many argued that the supervisor's commentary was disrespectful. Dr. Love-Holloway was a native southeast Bakersfield resident and, at the time, the director of the national

Right to Read program, in addition to being a former Oakland School District superintendent. Dr. Raymond Gonzales was also an area resident, as well as the incumbent state assemblyman for the district and the only member of the California Assembly with a doctorate. Gonzales had also recently been appointed by Speaker Leo McCarthy as chair of the Assembly Education Committee, the first freshman ever appointed to the position.[42] "It is comforting to know that I have such high quality representation to my [local] government," read one particularly sarcastic *Bakersfield Californian* letter to the editor, following Mitchell's comments.[43] The controversy over the naming of the Holloway-Gonzales Library was especially partisan since Gonzales was up for reelection that year, and local Republicans were committed to ousting the Chicano incumbent.[44]

GONZALES AND THE DIVISIVE POLITICS OF FARM LABOR LEGISLATION

Maintaining a political base that reflected a united constituency proved more difficult for Gonzales during his reelection campaign, particularly as African American and Mexican American racial solidarity encountered new challenges. For local African American leaders in Bakersfield, supporting Gonzales's reelection in 1974 came with more hesitation compared to 1972. Bakersfield attorney Gabe Solomon, who had been a stalwart supporter and collaborator with Gonzales going back to KCCU activism in the 1960s, had previously been key to courting local Black support, as well as building statewide alliances. Having attended Hastings Law School with California assemblyman Willie Brown, Solomon worked with other local Black leaders to organize the Negro Political Action Association of California's convening in Bakersfield in 1966 with local Chicana/o leaders. Willie Brown biographer James Richardson notes that the Bakersfield "meeting grew an often rocky alliance between black and brown politicians."[45] In 1974, when Assemblyman Brown was running for Speaker of the state assembly against Leo McCarthy, Solomon was instrumental in coordinating a visit by Brown to Bakersfield to court votes from Gonzales and other members of the Chicano political caucus. After delivering a stirring speech to local Black leaders in Bakersfield at a dinner organized by Solomon and the Gonzales reelection campaign, Brown was convinced that Gonzales would still vote for McCarthy, which he did; McCarthy won.[46] "It was like a stone wall with the Black community [early in the reelection campaign. Gathering local Black support after Brown's visit to Bakersfield] was too little too late," remembered Steve Barber.[47]

In addition, opponents seized on political opportunities opened by the fracturing of coalitions amid Gonzales's 1974 reelection campaign. No more clearly was this political precariousness demonstrated than in controversy within the California Assembly's Chicano political caucus regarding farmworker legislation backed by the UFW in 1974. The Southern California members of the Chicano caucus were not as electorally affected in their home districts as Gonzales was by his support for UFW-backed legislation. Furthermore, the civic unity that had characterized Gonzales's 1972 campaign, with solid alliances among Chicana/os, African Americans, and white liberals, was not replicated to the same degree in 1974. Part of this political fracturing within the Democratic base was due to controversy over Gonzales's position on farm labor legislation, as well as the racial politics put forth successfully by Republicans in 1974.

The emergence of five Chicano California assemblymen in 1972 had marked an ascendancy of Chicana/o political power in Sacramento. Chicana/o voters mobilized that year to defeat Proposition 22 (Prop 22), which "lost overwhelmingly, 58 percent to 42 percent," notes Miriam Pawel.[48] That campaign helped contribute to the election of Ray Gonzales, Joseph Montoya, and Richard Alatorre to the California Assembly—increasing the percentage of Mexican Americans in the assembly by 150 percent.[49] The grower-sponsored Prop 22 called for banning secondary boycotts by labor unions. It was a direct attack on the UFW and its use of the secondary boycott, given the union's exclusion from the National Labor Relations Act (NLRA) (which prohibits secondary boycotts but excludes agricultural workers from its purview). Labor scholar and activist Randy Shaw notes that "Proposition 22 . . . include[ed] the standard provisions forbidding boycotts and strikes and add[ed] . . . extreme provisions . . . barring farm worker unions from bargaining on work rules."[50] Gonzales opposed the proposition on the grounds that he would champion rights for farmworkers that paralleled labor rights enjoyed by industrial workers.[51] Indeed, having to toe a thin political line that addressed all his constituents, from growers to farmworkers and everyone in between, proved an insurmountable challenge for the freshman Chicano legislator from Bakersfield.

The working relationship of the UFW to the Chicano political caucus was paramount to the future of Chicana/o politics in Los Angeles and Southern California. In his speeches, Alatorre, who championed UFW-sponsored farm labor legislation in the assembly, frequently invoked *la causa* when reviewing the progress Mexican Americans had made as a racial group since World War II.[52] Representing Los Angeles, Alatorre was free from the hostility Gonzales faced as a Kern County legislative representative and thus able to take a more pro-labor stance. Gonzales's Central Valley constituency was more racially divided across white, Latina/o, and African American populations than were the constituencies of his Chicano caucus colleagues. When the UFW levied pressure on the Chicano caucus to support UFW-sponsored legislation, this position was more politically feasible for Los Angeles and Southern California caucus members than it was for Gonzales, given their greater proportion of Latina/o voters and distance from ground zero of *la huelga*. Steve Barber, Gonzales's campaign manager, remembered attending a meeting with Chávez at UFW headquarters, arranged by Democratic strategist Fleming Atha, prior to the November 1972 election. "We don't want you to do anything, no endorsements, no comments, our race doesn't exist, ... we are not of interest to you. [Chávez] said 'done,'" Barber recalled.[53] Despite Gonzales's affinity for the UFW and his background in civil rights, assuming political office would require Gonzales to appear strongly a political independent to Kern voters.

While Gonzales, once in office, would soon land in a confrontation with the UFW over farm labor legislation, early in his term he articulated publicly the historical significance of farmworkers to California agriculture. In a 1973 *Sacramento Bee* editorial, Gonzales opined that "one segment in the history of California agriculture that traditionally has been overlooked has been the farm labor force. It is this failure of recognition which has led to many of the agricultural disputes that have plagued the industry in the past."[54] Such recognition of farmworkers from both an academic and political perspective was significant, especially as Gonzales clamored for a farm labor bill in Sacramento that same year. His argument before the voting public and his legislative colleagues rested on the idea that farmworkers had built the legacy of California's agricultural success for over a century. Gonzales reasoned that this alone should have prompted the legislature to broker a reasonable bill to end the conflict in the fields. In 1973, rather than renewing a majority of UFW contracts, growers instead signed "sweetheart contracts" with the Teamsters Union, creating fierce competition between the UFW and Teamsters over the future unionization of farmworkers and fostering contempt for supporters of UFW boycotts.

Gonzales's tensions with organized labor were visible soon after he took office, when he experienced discord from some segments of Kern County's labor movement. In January 1973, only weeks after Gonzales was sworn in, Mel Rubin, president of the Kern, Inyo, and Mono Counties Central Labor Council (CLC-AFL-CIO), pressed Gonzales to fulfill his campaign promises to the labor movement. Rubin specifically wanted Gonzales to appoint two labor members (of the five Gonzales could appoint) to the state

Democratic Central Committee—and he provided Gonzales with a list of possible names. Gonzales informed Rubin that he wanted to diversify his appointments to include Black, Latina/o, female, and youth representatives. Gonzales preferred to select from a list of names submitted to him by the general Kern County labor council. Rubin interpreted this move as the Chicano politician working to fragment organized labor. "Mel was just trying to let me know who was boss," Gonzales later mused.[55]

The potential to pass farm labor legislation influenced Gonzales's political positioning as both an assembly candidate and a freshman on the assembly. For Chicanos running for state assembly, the UFW held major influence on their political rhetoric—but Gonzales had to be careful, given the conservative nature of Kern County politics. If Gonzales was to have a future as a Democratic legislator in Kern County, he needed to have the support of the UFW, but also appear not entirely beholden to the demands of the predominantly Mexican American labor union. In a letter to Gonzales written in August 1972 during the assembly campaign season, Los Angeles assembly candidate and future Chicano caucus member Art Torres informed Gonzales that he supported the UFW and the AFL-CIO in their opposition to federal regulation of farmworkers parallel to "the National Labor Relations Act, as amended by Taft-Hartley."[56] If farmworkers were brought under the NLRA, then the secondary boycott, the UFW's principal weapon against growers, would become illegal under labor law. Torres visited Gonzales's campaign headquarters in Bakersfield to discuss potential farm labor legislation. At the meeting, Gonzales stressed the nature of Kern County politics to the Los Angeles candidate. Following their meeting, Gonzales would write to Torres, "You realize of course that running a political campaign in conservative Kern County is difficult to begin with for any candidate, and more so for a liberal minority candidate."[57] While Torres ultimately viewed support for UFW-sponsored legislation as a litmus test for Chicano candidates, albeit with little political fallout for himself, Gonzales was hesitant to show unbridled support for any farm labor bill that did not address the issue of the secondary boycott; doing so would alienate a major segment of his Kern County constituents.

Among Gonzales's other key constituents, however, was César Chávez. Weeks after Gonzales's election victory, the assemblyman contacted Chávez to discuss his relationship with the UFW. Explaining his reasoning for comments made regarding the ongoing UFW lettuce boycott, Gonzales wrote, "I had to make a choice as to either being a leader in the boycott drive or an effective legislator in Sacramento. I do not feel that the two things are compatible here in Kern County. I am sure you know that the boycott will not be won in our area; it will be won out-of-county perhaps even out-of-state. To the residents of this county this is an emotional issue. I prefer to deal in realities."[58] Such brash statements from Gonzales won him no favors at UFW headquarters. UFW officials drafted a response. "Consider the precepts which formed a major part of your campaign," a UFW staffer wrote to the assemblyman. The UFW then encouraged Gonzales to bring a lettuce boycott resolution before the California legislature.[59] Gonzales declined.

Despite early grumblings to the UFW that he would be an independent Democrat in the assembly, Gonzales tried to submit legislation in 1973 to solve the farm labor problem that existed in his district. In drafting the legislation, Gonzales walked a fine line between supporting farmworkers and trying to appear an impartial public servant supportive of labor rights. "Our most immediate priority is to put an end to the violence in the fields. . . . Only when men and women meet together as brothers and sisters with a commitment to solving mutual problems through rational deliberations and just compromises can true progress be made," Gonzales declared to his supporters.[60] Local journalists in Bakersfield kept pressure on Gonzales to push a farm labor bill representative of all his constituents in Bakersfield and Kern County. "Possibly the single most important vote in the eyes of Kern County residents couldn't be cast this year because the legislature . . . failed again to bring the issue of farm labor legislation to the floor of either house," wrote Bakersfield journalist Mary K. Shell.[61] With political pressure at home to solve the farm labor crisis, Gonzales wrote to Chávez in July 1973 to propose a temporary solution while legislation pended deliberation in the assembly. "Much has been said by many about the necessity and propriety of holding elections as the only reasonable means to settle the current conflict. Yet no one has stepped forward to initiate any action toward this end. . . . I am willing to establish a panel of persons . . . for the purpose of holding elections to determine which union a particular grower's employees sought to represent them. . . . This proposal would be a one-time only measure."[62] Gonzales's proposal, however, gained no traction with the UFW. The union focused on mobilizing other members of the Chicano political caucus and the California Assembly toward support of a farm labor bill in terms set by the union. Gonzales recalled telling Chávez that "no union can do that [the secondary boycott]. I told César you don't need the law to do that, just do it. They didn't care about me. César had one issue and the union was it."[63] The lack of support for Gonzales's reelection campaign from the UFW hindered the incumbent Democrat's grassroots support that had helped elect him in 1972. Gonzales's position on the farm labor bill resembled, especially to young Chicano and Chicana voters, calls from the Kern County Farm Bureau to bring farmworkers under the NLRA—its key provision of course outlawing the secondary boycott, the UFW's principal weapon to fight growers.[64]

Conflict continued to emerge between Richard Alatorre, César Chávez, and Ray Gonzales over the crafting of farm labor legislation in 1974. The center of the conflict was Alatorre's sponsorship of Assembly Bill 3370 (AB 3370). Gonzales proposed amendments to Alatorre's bill that, in his estimation, would have made the measure more palatable to Kern County voters. Gonzales recalled, "I knew the bill [AB 3370] was not going anywhere, but as a show of my commitment to the cause of the workers, I wanted to vote for it. But I had a problem with it which was the use of the secondary boycott. That is why I offered my amendment. I figured if I could get my amendment in, I would vote for the bill, even if it cost me."[65] As written, AB 3370 set up a three-person commission to supervise elections and also allowed secondary boycotts, recognitional strikes, and challenges to existing contracts—all provisions UFW staffers knew opponents would find uncompromising and too far reaching. The main point of debate between Gonzales and the Chicano political caucus was the possibility of secondary boycotts by a union that had lost a certification election (Gonzales wanted to exclude this possibility; the caucus wanted to allow for it).[66] This issue was a concern for the UFW since the Teamsters Union was competing with UFW organizers in the fields—often using violent tactics to intimidate workers into not supporting the UFW boycott and strike. Giving up the boycott to legislation was not an option for the UFW. Chávez was worried that potential farm labor legislation would ban the secondary boycott, despite reassurance from UFW attorney Jerry Cohen that passage of a bill so favorable to the union was unlikely. The UFW leader in fact only supported farm labor legislation as a compromise with the United Auto Workers, which had made a $1.7 million donation to the UFW.[67] In 1974, the UFW further embraced the larger tenets of the American labor movement, echoing its anti-immigrant position through a "Campaign against Illegals." Chávez argued that this campaign was "more important than the strike, second only to the boycott."[68]

Although the UFW pushed AB 3370 in Sacramento, union organizers did not expect it to ever become law. Their aim was to pressure a state constitutional amendment in 1976 that would be "far more preferable to a law that [potentially] could be eroded by future legislators."[69] Nevertheless, as AB 3370 became a major political campaign issue in 1974, legislators in Sacramento threatened "to water-down the measure on the Assembly floor."[70] Gonzales was chief among Democratic legislators who argued that AB 3370 should contain an amendment prohibiting secondary boycotts, identical to the secondary boycott provision contained under the NLRA—thus keeping his campaign promise to make farmworker rights parallel to New Deal–era protective legislation for industrial workers. To Chávez and UFW attorneys, however, "any potential farm labor bill had to preserve the farmworkers' right to secondary boycotts. Setting up picket lines in front of grocery store chains that sold boycotted products . . . was the union's truly effective tool against growers who refused to negotiate contracts."[71] The union was thus positioned directly against the Chicano assembly candidate many of its local supporters had supported in 1972, even if without a direct endorsement from Chávez.

The UFW and Alatorre announced that they would drop sponsorship of AB 3370 if Gonzales's amendment against the secondary boycott was included. Later in the legislative session, when AB 3370 was called for a vote, many Democrats who had initially supported Gonzales's amendment changed positions. Confounded by what was suddenly happening on the assembly floor, Gonzales was soon told by his Democratic colleague and San Francisco Bay Area assemblyman Dan Boatwright, who sat directly in front of him, "Ray, Jack Henning called me and said that if I supported your amendment, he would cut off my labor money. What should I do, Ray?" In reply, Gonzales told him, "Dan, just save your ass!"[72] To Gonzales, the political posturing of Alatorre and other Democrats critical of amending AB 3370 showed that ultimately they were interested not in enacting "secret ballot" elections for farmworkers, but rather in maintaining their own political "clout" in California's agricultural fields and assembly districts, particularly since there was no expectation that AB 3370 would ever pass. "[The farm labor bill] was all tied up with gubernatorial politics and union power," Gonzales lamented. "No one was really concerned about the needs of farmworkers"— or, in Gonzales's case, in helping maintain the incumbent Chicano Democrat's chance for reelection.[73]

The *Bakersfield Californian* condemned César Chávez, the UFW, and the assembly's handling of AB 3370. The *Californian* portrayed Gonzales favorably, noting that he had voted against AB 3370 because his amendments were not included in the final draft voted on by the legislature. Legislators "succumbed to extremely heavy lobbying. . . . Supporters of this bill were not the least bit interested in the farm worker," Gonzales told reporters.[74] The assemblyman's political fortunes hinged on his ability to convince voters that he was championing farm labor legislation that would solve sooner, rather than later, Kern County's agricultural labor crisis.

Despite Gonzales's efforts to pass farm labor legislation respecting of his diverse constituents, his position on farm labor legislation became a valuable campaign issue for his 1974 Republican opponent, Bill Thomas. "Bill Thomas speaks *YOUR* kind of government!" read one Republican campaign

FIGURE 5.3 Ray Gonzales campaigning in 1974. Photo courtesy of Emily Gonzales.

advertisement.[75] Portraying Gonzales as a far-left supporter of labor and civil rights, the Republican challenger favored farmworker legislation that was friendly to growers, particularly legislation that would prevent a labor strike at harvest time. Thomas argued further that Gonzales had failed to spearhead grower interests in the state assembly.[76] As the political mean season heated up in June 1974, two major issues defined the Republican campaign against Gonzales: (1) Gonzales's moral conscience vote against the death penalty in 1973 (Gonzales was an ardent Catholic and onetime seminarian), and (2) Gonzales's alleged silence on farm labor legislation, particularly the outlawing of secondary boycotts. At the time of his candidacy for state assembly, Thomas was a political science professor at Bakersfield College and Gonzales's former colleague. Recalling a growing bitterness between Thomas and himself over the Republican's political tactics, Gonzales lamented,

> Bill Thomas and I were friends.... Our wives exchanged maternity clothes. We played handball. We were hired in the same year [at Bakersfield College]. He was a Republican but always considered himself a moderate. He ... looked down on the Bakersfield/Kern County Republicans as yokels. He was smarter than they were. He supported me when I ran the first time [and] gave me a contribution under the table. We were neighbors [and] wanted to come up with a busing plan that would be acceptable, because federal law had come in and school districts were resisting. Thomas came up with a busing plan and gave it to us [the KCCU], but told us not to put his name on it. He did not want to be identified with it because he had become a member of the Republican Central Committee. Thomas was not a racist or a bigot, but there were Republicans who were. I was getting ready to run for reelection, and he was telling me, "You're in good shape and we can't get anyone to run against you, you're too

strong." He was going to run against Walter Stiern in the state Senate. Ken Maddy and the Republican leadership in the assembly got in contact with him [and] told him if he ran against Stiern he was on his own. But if he ran against me, they would bankroll him. Steve Barber called me and told me Bill Thomas filed. I called Thomas and I asked him, What's going on? He told me the story, [and] then he said, "I guess I never realized how ambitious I really [am]." He tells me we can run a classic campaign, two college professors, talk to the issues, and keep it high level. I told him, "Bill, I'm the incumbent, a strong incumbent, you said so yourself. I know that in order for you to beat me, you have to come at me with a claw hammer. How can I look at you and say you're my friend and we're running for the same office? And if you're willing to do that, how can I say this is my friend Bill?" I never talked to him again after that.[77]

Thomas soon abandoned his friendship with Gonzales in pursuit of a more polarized political campaign against the incumbent Democrat. "The time to begin the dialogue is now. . . . Gonzales has been conspicuously quiet as to where he stands on farm labor issues vital to the people of Kern County," Thomas remarked publicly.[78] Gonzales responded to Thomas's challenge. The incumbent Democrat encouraged a debate to occur later in the election cycle as he was busy in Sacramento maintaining his voting record. Gonzales's commitment to legislative purposes, however, left the public forum open to local Republicans, who used the opportunity to control the political dialogue. Gonzales's multiracial base, moreover, had splintered by late 1973 over farm labor legislation. Competition between African Americans and Mexican Americans over federally subsidized rural health-care dollars, in addition to Gonzales's controversial conscience vote against the death penalty (Kern County's law-and-order voters overwhelmingly supported capital punishment), further undermined his reelection campaign. Reflecting on Ray Gonzales and Kern County's support for the death penalty, longtime state senator Walter Stiern remarked in an oral history: "The fact that a minority could get elected out of Kern County at the time was surprising to me, in the first place. But he went up there [to Sacramento] with the idea that he was going to teach the people of Kern County a lesson. They were not going to vote against capital punishment. . . . He was there two years and he was out. They dumped him so fast in Kern County he didn't know what hit him."[79] Thomas took political advantage of these weaknesses. "Thomas's campaign was very racial. He ran pictures of me with [César] Chávez, and his ads would say 'elect one of us,'" Gonzales later recalled of his Republican opponent's strategy.[80] Thomas's challenge to his former friend and colleague would be remembered as "a move that established Thomas' reputation for ruthlessness and arrogance," as *Bakersfield Californian* columnist Vic Pollard wrote in 2005.[81]

Following defeat by his Republican challenger, on his last day as a California assemblyman, Gonzales wrote a letter to César Chávez. His letter assessed the future of farm labor policy in the California legislature, as well as the future of the UFW in Kern County:

> The majority of Chicano farm laborers are not impressed with your operation.... They are either tired of the struggle or disillusioned with the entire movement.... They are enraged by the violent and insulting tactics employed by some of your supporters.... There is a growing resentment toward the union and I feel it stems from the poor public relations policy carried out by your union officials.... In your effort to carry on your boycott at the national and international levels you have lost contact with your true constituency.... Only Jack Henning's pressure and money, and the fact that it was an election year got you the 41 labor votes from the Democrats [for AB 3370].... Unless you begin to mend your fences with a majority of Mexican American farmworkers you will not be winning elections when and if a farm labor bill is passed.... I hope I have not offended you again with these candid remarks. I only make them because, contrary to the belief of some of your volunteers, I am concerned about the destiny of farm workers in this country. I worked in the Delano grape fields before most of them had ever heard of the place.... The growers ... blinded by their own greed, bigotry, and disgust for your movement ... will never trust a Chicano.[82]

Gonzales's words foreshadowed some of the challenges the UFW would encounter with winning elections in the fields following passage of the Agricultural Labor Relations Act in 1975. Additionally, as recent UFW historians have documented, internal conflicts within the UFW's rank-and-file leadership in the late 1970s and early 1980s, as well as limited strategic capacity, ultimately hamstrung the union's success in organizing farmworkers.[83]

CONCLUSION

The election loss of Ray Gonzales to Bill Thomas for the California Assembly in 1974 marked a turning point in the shifting fortunes of grassroots political action among multiracial liberal coalitions in greater Bakersfield.

Multiracial alliances from below had propelled Gonzales from academia into the political arena in 1972. He drew on the multiracial heritage of the civic unity movement and, at the same time, on the growing political importance of young Chicana/os during the heyday of the Chicana/o Power movement.[84] Holding together racial alliances, however, proved untenable for the Chicano Democrat in conservative Kern County. Moreover, the controversy surrounding UFW-sponsored farm labor legislation guaranteeing the preservation of the secondary boycott was equally divisive among Gonzales's core constituents. In the end, conservative political mobilization for Bill Thomas unseated the Chicano Democrat, eclipsing the political progress grassroots multiracial coalitions had made in Kern County up until this point. For Thomas, 1974 marked the beginning of a remarkable career as a Bakersfield Republican legislator, leading to his chairmanship of the US House Committee on Ways and Means until his retirement from Congress in 2007. Along the way, Thomas would mentor a young staffer, Kevin McCarthy, who would eventually replace Thomas as the Republican representing Bakersfield in Congress.

Following the election defeat, Ray Gonzales worked in Governor Jerry Brown's administration; was appointed to the Public Employment Relations Board, adjudicating labor disputes among teachers, state employees, and management; and undertook federal service in the diplomatic corps in Latin America.[85] He later taught political science at CSU Monterey Bay until retirement. He would run unsuccessfully for Kern County supervisor against the former *Bakersfield Californian* reporter (who covered much of Gonzales's tenure in the state assembly) and Republican Mary K. Shell. Despite his political misfortunes, Gonzales maintained a steadfast commitment to civil rights and political empowerment, particularly among Latina/os. His work in the 1990 redistricting efforts in southeast Bakersfield proved crucial to establishing a Latina/o seat for Kern County's growing Latina/o population—at the supervisorial level, as well as in both houses of the California State Legislature and in the US House of Representatives. In 2018, after having served for a time as a Bakersfield City School Board trustee in retirement, he passed away in Bakersfield at the age of eighty.[86]

Yet, the multiracial grassroots coalition building that characterized his 1972 campaign has not been replicated in Kern County Latina/o politics. Corporations have since played a more significant role in financing candidates. In more recent times, while the diversification of the Delano, Arvin, and Bakersfield City Councils has brought hope to grassroots organizers and multiracial civil rights and social justice groups, much work remains to be done to challenge entrenched Republican politics in greater Bakersfield.[87]

The political dynamics of historical grassroots civil rights organizing beyond the fields are an important part of Bakersfield's lost civil rights history. Recounting these stories more fully demonstrates the broad scope of civil rights reform and political empowerment in Bakersfield and Kern County among the region's historical racial minority populations.

6 | POLICE VIOLENCE, FAIR MEDIA, RURAL HEALTH CARE, AND CIVIL RIGHTS ACTIVISM IN GREATER BAKERSFIELD

Bakersfield is a sociologically backward community, a racist community.
Robert Powers, former chief of the Bakersfield Police Department, 1969

I am so mad, I can't even tell you. [The] Kern County Liberation Movement has received a $2 . . . million dollar grant for a migrant health center for southeast Bakersfield from H.E.W. I say get rid of H.E.W. & O.E.O. and it would be a step in the right direction toward restoring sanity in Washington D.C. . . . Cesar Chavez is allowed to run roughshod . . . over all of us in the valley, here with his own brand of Revolution.
Bakersfield resident Helen Graf to California senator George Murphy, 1971

On July 23, 1969, fifteen Bakersfield Police Department (BPD) officers confronted two hundred (mostly Black) teenagers outside Fraternal Hall on East California Avenue in Bakersfield, where a city-sponsored dance was being held. The cause of the confrontation was, and continues to be, a matter of racial animosity, controversy, and sensitivity in the community's collective memory.[1] Bakersfield National Association for the Advancement of Colored People (NAACP) chapter president Ralph Anthony described the events of that night in a September 1969 letter to the NAACP West Coast (WC) regional office: "the police of the city of Bakersfield, in force, viciously and without provocation, attacked a large group of teenagers and their chaperones who were attending a regularly scheduled teen dance at the Teen Center, under the aegis of the Bakersfield City Department of Recreation. . . . About 160 teen-agers, 8 chaperones and 5 members of the band were in attendance. . . . All of those present were black with the exception of two white men, the Director of the Center, David Hashim and the director of another Center, Jack Brigham."[2] Police reports indicated that two nineteen-year-olds—Julius Brooks Jr. and Wayne Johnson—along with chaperone Terry Larkin, were charged, tried, and eventually convicted by an all-white jury for "resisting arrest and failure to disperse" outside Fraternal Hall.[3]

This chapter addresses the scope of civil rights activism beyond the fields in the late 1960s and early 1970s in greater Bakersfield. The diversity of civil rights activism manifested beyond farm labor, including struggles against police violence toward racial minority groups, the fair media movement, and struggles over expanding access to rural health care. The "Fraternal Hall incident" in July 1969 was a catalyst for civil rights mobilization in southeast Bakersfield. Black and Brown activists mobilized in an effort to fight legacies of racial segregation and inequality. White racial liberals also played a key role in helping speak truth to power concerning racism toward Bakersfield's Black and Brown communities. Taken together, the three efforts to expand civil rights beyond the fields illustrate the depth and diversity of civil rights reform in greater Bakersfield during the heyday of the farmworker movement.

RACIAL POLITICS AND POLICE BRUTALITY

Within the racially charged atmosphere of Bakersfield, city politics split along the lines of grape boycott supporters and opponents. Other civil rights struggles also manifested in greater Bakersfield. Police brutality strained relations between southeast city residents and Kern County law enforcement. This conflict became an especially mobilizing force for civil rights leaders in 1969. Abusive law enforcement practices were nothing new in Kern County. Events in 1969, however, seemed to mark a turning point. Law enforcement agencies, local government, and civil rights leaders stressed the need to improve relations between Bakersfield's segregated racial minority communities and law enforcement. The means by which to achieve this lofty end were not clear. War on Poverty proponents lobbied the city council to support development programs to temper youth, economic, and social marginalization—often with mixed results.

In April 1969, Eddie Hare, a member of the NAACP Youth Council, requested information from the Bakersfield City Council regarding available grants for a summer recreation program for southeast Bakersfield. He asked for an appointment with the appropriate city council committee to discuss the NAACP proposal. Bakersfield mayor Don Hart responded that the

Auditorium and Recreation Committee was the appropriate group to discuss the matter and referred the request to that committee.[4] The local NAACP's interest in working with the city to provide recreational opportunities for Black youth was an important step in quelling racial tensions in late 1960s Bakersfield. Nevertheless, events between spring and summer 1969 proved confrontational for racial minority groups in southeast Bakersfield and law enforcement, particularly when it came to the use of public funds to create tax-sponsored teen activities for Black youth. Controversy surrounding the use of public funds in southeast Bakersfield was nothing new, but rather a continuation of local backlash toward antipoverty programs first noticeably demonstrated in 1966.

From the local African American community's perspective, police officers physically beat several Black teenagers in attendance at Fraternal Hall in a vulgar display of police brutality. What gave this interpretation of events community credibility was the testimony of former police officer Steve Powers during the Brooks, Johnson, and Larkin trial in the fall of 1969. Powers's testimony "prompted many persons to question the story handed out by police officials about exactly what went on outside . . . Fraternal hall."[5] Powers—who had been on the scene as one of the responding officers—testified that five officers beat one Black youth seriously and that many other indiscriminate beatings by BPD occurred. When Powers dictated his official police report to the stenographer back at the station, she mentioned that the other officers involved had indicated that the criminal provocation had emanated from the Black teenage crowd outside Fraternal Hall, not the police. Powers recalled the *official* story of what happened at Fraternal Hall, according to the BPD, as follows: "I walked across the street. I walked up and the [Black] youth hit me. So I hit him and he fell down and hit his face on the cement." For Powers, the uniformity of the officers' reports was "code that the police were making up a story and would [have all officers present outside Fraternal Hall] stick by it."[6] Not willing to compromise his integrity, Powers resigned from the BPD on August 4, 1969, one week after the incident, despite his long admiration for law enforcement.

What happened after this courtroom testimony prompted Powers's father, Robert Powers—who had served in the 1930s and 1940s as BPD chief and then state director of law enforcement services under California attorney general Robert Kenny—to publicly condemn the BPD and local government for perpetuating and tolerating abuses against the constitutionally protected rights of citizens. In October 1969, Robert Powers told the *Fresno Bee* that the city of Bakersfield was "a sociologically backward community, a racist community . . . where police can be used to harass private citizens."[7] The former

BPD chief issued his statement after law enforcement officers harassed both him and his son Steve, because of the latter's testimony at the Brooks, Larkin, and Johnson trial. Newspapers reported that "following his testimony, [Steve] Powers left the courtroom with Bakersfield NAACP President Ralph Anthony and . . . [they] were followed by a motorcycle police unit and a patrol car. They drove to Robert Powers' home, outside the city limits, and . . . two police units 'surrounded' the house."[8] Deciding to test the BPD's motives, Robert Powers took his son out for an afternoon drive.[9] The two police cars followed and pulled over the father and son. The former chief asked the officers why they were being stopped, and the police informed Powers that he and his son were being detained until special prosecutor Gary T. Friedman arrived to serve a subpoena on the latter. When asked whether either man was under arrest, the police answered no. Immediately Robert Powers and his son drove away. The police followed and pulled the two men over again, this time blocking Powers's car from both front and back until Friedman arrived. Escorted by a Bakersfield police captain and two sergeants—one of whom was the officer in charge of the anti-riot force that Steve Powers had reported on—Friedman had secured the subpoena from the district attorney's office, with the intent of recalling to the stand that BPD "coward turncoat," Steve Powers. Friedman's efforts were in vain. "The next morning . . . a superior court . . . judge quashed the subpoena without any opposition from Friedman."[10]

Although protesting racial discrimination and police harassment such as what occurred at Fraternal Hall in July 1969 was not new in southeast Bakersfield, Robert Powers's public criticism of the city and law enforcement, coupled with his son Steve's testimony against the BPD, was both new and peculiar, given their white racial identity and mutual careers in law enforcement. Publicly calling out racial discrimination and abusive officers within the BPD, the two Powers men brought a heightened level of credibility to ongoing (and future) citizen complaints about racial discrimination in Kern County law enforcement. By speaking their truth about police practices, father and son encouraged racial minority activists and racial coalitions to champion civil rights reform, including efforts against police brutality.[11]

Unfortunately, despite Steve Powers's testimony, the Fraternal Hall trio was convicted of the charges against them, and the police were not held accountable. Civil rights groups and supportive citizens voiced their opposition to the local court's decision to exonerate the BPD. In December 1969, Bakersfield NAACP president Ralph Anthony charged that "the Bakersfield Police Department . . . fail[ed] in its responsibility to a large segment of the community."[12] Three incidents in the previous six months—the Fraternal Hall incident, the arrests of Black students during the Bakersfield Christmas

Parade, and the allegedly unprovoked police beating of a Black youth, Jimmy Stewart—inflamed the city's Black community. Anthony believed that the city council was derelict in its duty as an elected body because it had ignored complaints from the Black community. Parents, ministers, attorneys, businessmen, and students had all filed petitions before the city council to report police brutality. The city council consistently denied the existence of police violence, particularly since the Kern County grand jury failed to indict any police officers following the Fraternal Hall incident in July 1969. "We have come to the conclusion that the Bakersfield Police Department is rapidly becoming a racist institution," Anthony admonished the city council.[13]

Cyrille Duzen, a member of the local NAACP Legal Redress Committee, spoke before the city council in January 1970, voicing a typical reaction to the police brutality. "Not all . . . cases [of abuse] are limited to black people, but the vehemence and the seemingly [sic] relish for hurting, the dirty racist name calling that goes on in the name of law enforcement, seems most often directed to them [and] . . . is done in our name and with our money," she opined.[14] Duzen recounted a community meeting in 1968 where "over 300 shocked citizens from all segments of Bakersfield, met in a hot, airless church, on a boiling August night, because a sixteen-year old black youngster had been beaten unconscious by at least two law enforcement officials and dragged around a vacant lot . . . while other policemen [either] assisted or stood by." She continued, noting that "because the police officers changed their testimony between appearances before the juvenile [court] referee and the superior court judge, the boy was convicted." After recounting these instances of abuse, Duzen reiterated what had happened at Fraternal Hall six months prior. "This innocent recreation was turned into a nightmare which became community-wide," she said.[15] She read aloud an excerpt from an official summary of the Fraternal Hall incident that had been sent to the US Commission on Civil Rights:

> About half of the youngsters were out of the hall, when Sgt. Benfield yelled "Charge." The police came running across the street whaling their riot clubs, hitting indiscriminately at the fleeing youngsters and chaperones who attempted to show their official buttons. Women and girls, as well as adult men and boys, were repeatedly struck. Some were singled out for severe beatings, as the youngsters ran back into the building to escape the onslaught of the police who followed them into the hall and continued to club and curse them. Mace was used on people who were obviously trying to leave the premises. Shots were fired, seven arrests were made. Four juveniles

and three adults, all of whom were severely beaten. . . . Squad cars and the paddy wagon roamed the neighborhood, chasing youngsters on foot and in cars as far as Lakeview Avenue, about a mile away.[16]

Bakersfield City Council members decried Duzen's allegations of police abuse. Councilman Kenneth Vetter remarked that "this California Avenue incident has been hashed and re-hashed over and over. . . . It was referred to the Grand Jury, and the Grand Jury investigated it, and as I understand took testimony from a number of people, and the[n] declined to bring back any indictment of anyone. How long do we have to keep going over the same thing?"[17] Since the grand jury had failed to indict the BPD and the only persons convicted were Black youths and a chaperone, there was no reason for Duzen and others to complain, Vetter reasoned. Patterns of police abuse did not legally exist in his view. "These people you mentioned, the defendants that were arrested, they were also convicted, as well," Vetter reminded Duzen. At that point in the meeting, Councilman Keith Bleecker interjected, "I don't want to hear any more of this." Vetter completed his thought: "you [Duzen] keep going over and over the same thing. . . . Perhaps in your own mind you feel that they are the truth. In my own mind, they're not."[18]

After members of the city council questioned why Duzen had made allegedly erroneous statements regarding police misconduct, Del Rucker, the single African American city councilman, intervened to clarify why Duzen had brought her concerns to the city council. After a back-and-forth between Rucker, community members, and the other city council members, Alvin Lacey Henry, chair of the NAACP Labor and Industry Committee, cut to the chase: "understand this, if we didn't have problems, we wouldn't be here."[19] Dan Wade, editor of the local Black newspaper, the *Observer*, added his support. Speaking directly to Republican councilman Richard Stiern, Wade said, "You asked Mrs. Duzen why she didn't go to the grand jury. The grand jury did not invite her there. They didn't invite me there. They [only] invited people they wanted there, the people who would tell them what they wanted to hear. We are asking you to give us a chance to work with you, . . . [to] stop things like the Watts Riots, we [certainly] don't want that here in Bakersfield."[20] David Hashim, a city employee and one of the two white men who had helped organize and chaperone the dance, corroborated statements made against the official BPD line and grand jury finding. According to Hashim, who had been making security walks around the building every quarter hour, there had been no African American teenagers outside Fraternal Hall when the police arrived. Moreover, speaking forty years later, Hashim still did not know who had initially contacted the police or why they had done so.[21]

Remembering the controversy years later, Steve Powers suspected that the entire incident at Fraternal Hall had been orchestrated by the police department, particularly since there was notable controversy surrounding the use of public funds to provide recreation programs for Black youth in southeast Bakersfield.[22] Such programs were part of Kern County's War on Poverty and thus were politically controversial and locally contested. If Black youth could be seen as troublesome and unruly, willing to start confrontations with police, then Bakersfield taxpayers would be justified in a critique of subsidizing social programs in southeast Bakersfield. Following the Fraternal Hall incident, Hashim submitted an official report to Bakersfield police chief Jack Towle, noting the indiscriminate beatings of Black youth by police officers. According to Hashim, the chief buried the report. "I lost a tremendous amount of faith in law enforcement after that incident," Hashim later recalled.[23]

Black youth were enraged by the apparent collusion between city government and law enforcement to cover up the truth of what had happened at Fraternal Hall. Don Clarke, campus community coordinator for the Bakersfield College Black Student Union, later told the city council that a lot of the "youngsters" at the Fraternal Hall dance "have gone to Oakland with hopes of joining the Black Panther Party."[24] In a rebuttal to Bakersfield mayor Don Hart, Clarke offered a poignant observation: "don't tell me about sharing responsibility because . . . for 400 years we didn't share any responsibility, so don't try to give it to me now." In response, Mayor Hart told Clarke, "Let's try to make things equate and come to a mutual understanding. That's all I asked you to do, the same thing that *you people* have asked of us."[25]

NAACP chapter president Ralph Anthony tried to reason with the city council in light of such inflammatory remarks and misunderstanding. He made concrete recommendations to quell racial tension between the police department and the southeast community, including the creation of a citizens patrol to monitor teen dances and social functions, a police-community athletic league, and citizen committees charged with improving relations between the police and community.[26] Councilman Stiern encouraged Anthony to help steer Black youth toward careers in law enforcement. Stiern stressed the need for Anthony, as well as other Black leaders like Charles Siplin, to encourage Black youth to join the BPD. "Now what I want to know is, are you, Ralph Anthony, head of the NAACP . . . [and] Charles Sipplin [sic], who also exerts considerable influence as you do among the young kids in our community, . . . [and] people like Art Shaw . . . doing everything they can to funnel these kids down to the Police Department to make applications for the job," Stiern asked. He then questioned Anthony about the NAACP position. "It's possible that by inflammatory statements like we have heard tonight, we could be driving suitable kids away from the Police Department. Has that occurred to you?" Stiern cautioned.[27] Anthony remarked in turn, "we got educational problems, we got economic problems, we got a community that is sitting out there that is becoming stagnated only because there is no money being [re]turned back into the community, and the multiplex of problems there [is so large] that we do not have the resources to bring this community up."[28] Stiern's suggestion to increase minority applications to the police department appeared reductionist in light of Anthony's remarks on the structural barriers faced by southeast Bakersfield's Black community.

Black church leaders also spoke out against police abuse. Reverend Dewitt Graham had taken over the leadership of the Cain Memorial African Methodist Episcopal (AME) Church from Julius Brooks by 1970. Like Brooks, Reverend Graham took a strong position on civil rights, but he didn't use the gentle and diplomatic approach of his predecessor and former Intergroup Relations Board (IRB) chair. Graham lambasted the city council: "Seems we want to make the police a sacred cow, so to speak, the untouchables.... There is police brutality [in the community] and we must come to this realization." The reverend's rhetoric was effective. He stated that for those in the community who did not acknowledge that there was police brutality, such thinking echoed the perpetrators' belief that "this is a necessary act to keep n———rs in their place. And this is the way it is, you know, so we will get tough on these n———rs, so they won't get tough like they were in Watts, [or] as they are in Chicago, in Detroit, and other places."[29] Graham was exceptionally blunt. "You can't understand it, Mr. Stiern, because you're white. Mr. Bleecker, you can't understand it, because you're white. But we are saying that as people who have been born black, we are subject to police brutality."[30]

Such thinking as expressed by Graham lingered long in Bakersfield. In 1984, following a mistaken arrest where police officers drew loaded guns at William McCullough, school principal and the city's first Black chairman of the Police Commission, local Black leaders remembered the origins of local hostility toward the police as rooted in the aftermath of Fraternal Hall, fourteen years prior. Indeed, it was following Fraternal Hall that local Black leaders began to pressure authorities to have "a black named to the Police Commission," noted NAACP activist Ralph Anthony to the *Los Angeles Times*. It wasn't until 1979, however, that the first African American was appointed to the commission, that being McCullough. The *Times* further reported in 1984 that "critics of the Police Department point out that of

Bakersfield's 209 police officers, only 14 are Latino and 10 are black. They also charge that the department avoids public scrutiny by keeping its internal investigation records confidential and by limiting the role of the Police Commission."[31]

MULTIRACIAL ACTIVISM AND THE NATIONAL FAIR MEDIA MOVEMENT

At the same time that police violence was helping mobilize multiracial civil rights activism in Bakersfield, the national fair media reform movement was affecting institutional culture vis-à-vis the position of African Americans and Mexican Americans in greater Bakersfield. The fair media reform movement sought to reshape programming and media practices to better reflect minority interests. Chicana/o civil rights leaders in Bakersfield became aligned with this national movement through the formation of a five-city, multistate coalition that helped introduce Chicana/o nationalism into local civil rights discourse. Their efforts yielded one of the most fruitful campaigns of the Chicana/o movement period: the 1972 McGraw-Hill concessions. In the spring of that year, McGraw-Hill bought four regional television networks from the Time Life company, with Federal Communication Commission (FCC) approval. In order to have a legitimate operating license, McGraw-Hill committed significant resources to minority programming and hiring, as well as changes in labor practices. Since 1969, Chicana/os and the multiracial civil rights group the Kern Council for Civic Unity (KCCU) had pressured local and national media outlets to be more inclusive of minority interests in news coverage, fair labor standards, and the creative development of programming. Bakersfield civil rights leaders pressured local media outlets by aligning themselves with the national media reform movement.

With its roots in the former Jim Crow South, where the (predominantly white) United Church of Christ (UCC) and African American civil rights groups fought against racist practices in Mississippi, the fair media movement in the late 1960s was a decentralized movement that operated in local communities throughout the United States. Civil rights attorneys interested themselves in test cases where local civil rights groups forced media outlets to change labor and programming standards to reflect minority interests. What makes Bakersfield significant in this discussion is that its reform efforts were *not* relegated to the local. Rather, by partaking of a five-city coalition—alongside San Diego, California; Denver, Colorado; Indianapolis, Indiana; and Grand Rapids, Michigan—it was able to have a meaningful effect against a media conglomerate at the national level. Given Kern County's multiracial population, the KCCU sought alliances with national Mexican American organizations to pursue reform in the public media industry. The National Mexican-American Anti-Defamation Committee (NMAADC) and the Mexican American Legal Defense and Educational Fund (MALDEF) were two national Mexican American civil rights organizations interested in fair media issues for Mexican Americans. In the late 1960s, their respective leadership, Domingo "Nick" Reyes and Mario Obledo, pressed their organizations to coordinate a national strategy for Chicana/os specific to media reform. Reyes and Obledo were important contacts for the KCCU after it initiated a challenge against KERO-Bakersfield, which in turn spawned the five-city coalition against McGraw-Hill.

The KCCU challenge against KERO-23 occurred in the context of the national media reform movement. The NMAADC gained national recognition as a fair media leadership organization in the late 1960s by pressuring Frito-Lay to drop its controversial but wildly popular "Frito Bandito" commercials. These commercials caricatured the Frito Bandito as the typical Mexican outlaw, evoking memories of the Mexican bandits who had stormed the deserts of the American Southwest in the late nineteenth and early twentieth centuries.[32] "Begun in 1967, Frito-Lay Corporation launched a national advertising campaign featuring an 'unshaven, unfriendly, and leering' Frito Bandito who stole Anglos' corn chips at gunpoint," notes media scholar Chon A. Noriega.[33] Chicana/o civil rights organizations challenged these negative caricatures of Mexican Americans, so typical of standard practices in the American broadcasting industry. Frito-Lay officially stopped running the commercials in the summer of 1971. Protest against such racialized imagery helped refashion the image of Mexican Americans in the United States.

The actor Bill Dana's portrayal of the fictional character José Jiménez is another case in point. National Chicana/o media organizations mobilized against negative media stereotypes early in the fair media movement. Dana's character spoke broken English and seemed good natured but dim witted, eager to please a white audience. Due to the NMAADC's pressure on Frito-Lay and the ensuing rise of the Chicana/o civil rights movement, Dana (who was not Mexican but Turkish) eventually stopped performing the character. "On April 4, 1970, after nearly two years of battle with Chicano media groups, Bill Dana announced . . . that José Jiménez was dead," wrote scholar Francisco J. Lewels Jr.[34] Along with the NMAADC, several other organizations—the Involvement of Mexican-Americans in Gainful Endeavors (IMAGE) in San Antonio, Texas, the Council to Advance and Restore the Image of Spanish-Speaking and Mexican Americans (CARISSMA) in Los

Angeles, and the Midwest Chicano Mass Media Committee in Chicago—pressured Dana to drop the character. Stressing the significance of these efforts, NMAADC president Nick Reyes recalled, "their efforts . . . resulted in thwarting . . . the Frito Bandito and José Jiménez. . . . [Such efforts helped] . . . breach . . . the gap between the Chicano community and the higher levels of mass media."[35]

Prior to the KCCU-initiated blockade of McGraw-Hill's buyout of Time Life stations, Mexican Americans across the Southwest had already involved themselves in the national fair media movement. The success of African Americans in the American South encouraged Mexican Americans to launch reform challenges of their own. The Community Relations Service (CRS) of the US Department of Justice (DOJ) in the late 1960s "generated minority-media conferences in a score of cities, . . . the first meeting [occurring among] a local Hispanic community . . . in San Antonio in 1969."[36] In June 1970, the newly formed National Chicano Media Council solicited Ruben Salazar of the *Los Angeles Times* as its chair. Two months later Salazar was shot and killed by a Los Angeles sheriff during the Chicano Moratorium against the Vietnam War in East Los Angeles, weakening the overall impact of the newly formed national Hispanic media organization.[37] One important fair media group formed from the CRS meeting was the Colorado Committee on Mass Media and the Spanish Surnamed. Organized in June 1970, the group challenged license renewals for four major television stations in Denver, gaining concessions in the hiring of Hispanics and the formation of Hispanic advisory committees.[38] These early successful efforts set the stage for the major concessions granted to Chicana/os during the 1972 McGraw-Hill negotiations.

Strategies employed by African Americans in the Jim Crow South helped activists out west foment legal strategies and approaches in the fight for fair media representation. Chicana/o civil rights activists in Bakersfield built alliances with the national fair media movement with full awareness of these strategies. Former CRS associate director Bertram Levine, whose office helped facilitate and mediate the national media reform movement, recalled that "in the early 1960s, radio and television were practically lily-white, and print media were strictly Jim Crow."[39] The UCC led the endeavor to change media practices on a local network basis through FCC policy. The church's efforts reaped national results. Dr. Everett Parker, who served as director of the UCC Office of Communication from 1954 to 1983, had "long been involved in citizen challenges to radio and television licenses" by the time the McGraw-Hill company made the first major media concessions to Chicana/os in 1972.[40] Parker "doggedly challenged the broadcast industry and the FCC when they ignored minority concerns or showed contempt for the public's right to have a say in what goes on the air," wrote *New York Times* columnist Charles Austin in 1983. When Parker retired, he was quoted as saying that "the public still has to bang on the doors of the FCC in order to assure [sic] that justice is done."[41] According to media scholar Julian Williams, Parker "was convinced that the right of access to communications channels was not only basic to democratic functioning, but that the church has a moral responsibility to fight for it."[42]

The fair media movement gained its first legal victory when a group of African American students at Tougaloo College in Jackson, Mississippi, challenged the local television stations WLBT and WJTV for "ignoring their interests [and] presenting a one-sided, anti-Negro version of the civil rights [movement]."[43] Such was the first time a church or any public interest group had taken on the FCC on behalf of a segment of the public.[44] Journalist Kay Mills wrote that "blatant misrepresentation had political ramifications within both white and black communities. Whites could not fully understand what they could not see. Blacks could not feel the courage of their numbers [nor] their leaders argue the merits of their cause on television."[45] According to legal documents, "the first complaints [in Jackson] went back to 1955 when it was claimed that WLBT had deliberately cut off a network program about race relations problems on which the General Counsel of the NAACP was appearing and had flashed on the viewers' screens a 'Sorry, Cable Trouble' sign."[46]

The UCC assisted in monitoring the stations for several years and pushed the FCC to deny the stations' license renewal applications.[47] Finally, a June 1969 legal decision written by Justice Warren E. Burger of the Court of Appeals in Washington (later chief justice of the US Supreme Court) "declared that members of the public had the right to intervene in license proceedings." Burger's decision and the *Tougaloo* case "stripped WLBT of its license and established a new pattern in the relationship between broadcast licensees and the members of their public, . . . [as well as] provided practical lessons in how pressure could be brought [and] the broadcast establishment . . . challenged."[48] Earl K. Moore, who represented the constituency groups against the television station in Jackson, would later represent the KCCU in Bakersfield in challenging McGraw-Hill. By September 1971, with the help of the UCC Office of Communication, there were nearly fifty license renewals being challenged across the country.[49] Civil rights groups challenged the license renewals of media stations failing to serve the public interest in their respective service areas. The problem with petitions to deny license renewals, however, was that even after they were filed with the FCC, the incumbent network could continue to operate and earn revenue. But major transactions were leverage points, particularly when networks were interested in finalizing a deal in order to expand revenues from acquisitions and transfers.[50]

Within this context of national media reform, Bakersfield civil rights leaders launched their own strategic attacks against local media outlets and helped win landmark concessions for Chicana/os in the national fair media movement. Given the strong Black Protestant community in southeast Bakersfield interested in social and economic justice, the message of the UCC resonated with the larger community. Charles Siplin, the Black director of the Friendship House Community Center in the late 1960s, partnered with Ray Gonzales in the KCCU to spearhead media reform in Bakersfield in the struggle against McGraw-Hill. Their collegial and working relationship was powerful and symbolic, given the men's respected positions within the African American and Mexican American communities. The Friendship House was a nondenominational religious outreach center affiliated with the National Council of Churches, and it had been at the forefront of the civil rights struggle in East Bakersfield since the late 1950s. Gonzales had taught since 1965 as a professor of modern languages, first at Bakersfield College and then later at California State University (CSU), Long Beach, and CSU Bakersfield.

The civic unity interest in fair media was rooted in opposition to right-wing talk radio in Bakersfield. Talk show conservatives, such as Bakersfield Republican activist Georgia Johnson, railed against African Americans, Mexican Americans, and white liberals with vitriolic criticism. Richard Cotten, a nationally known right-wing writer, radio broadcaster, and erstwhile resident of Bakersfield, had relocated to the South but still maintained an office in Bakersfield and another in Washington, DC, for lobbying politicians.[51] A segregationist and defender of the White Citizens' Council, Cotten was, according to the FBI, associated with the Christian Laymen of Kern, a "closeted Ku Klux Klan group, functioning under the auspices of the American Council Christian Laymen."[52] Within this local media context, civic unity activists pressured local media outlets to give more balanced coverage and eliminate hate speech in public programming. KGEE radio, according to the KCCU, had a number of right-wing conservative talk shows that failed to offer a countervailing viewpoint in equivalent airtime. The KCCU invoked the Fairness Doctrine to expand the ideological landscape of Kern County's media marketplace. From 1949 until 1987, "the Fairness Doctrine required broadcasters to present controversial issues facing their community in a balanced manner as a condition for obtaining a broadcast license."[53] After the KCCU notified the FCC, the commission issued a letter to KGEE regarding its failure to control the content. The FCC also warned KGEE that it needed to comply with federal regulations regarding personal attacks made against individuals and groups. The KCCU concluded that "the FCC Fairness Doctrine is a major tool which can be used to protect the public's right to hear all sides of [an] issue."[54]

The KCCU allied with the fair media movement and Chicana/o civil rights groups across multiple cities. The NMAADC and MALDEF acted as liaison organizations in forming the five-city coalition against McGraw-Hill. The Chicano Federation of San Diego, formed in 1968 by a group of local Chicana/o leaders, fought for access and greater public services and advocated for the rights and dignity of the Chicana/o and Mexicana/o community.[55] In Denver, Rodolfo "Corky" Gonzales's organization, Crusade for Justice, mobilized aggressively against local police brutality.[56] Young Chicana/os credited Gonzales with articulating the tenets of Chicana/o nationalism.[57] Chicana/o nationalism, according to movement activists, united a theretofore philosophically diverse and regional Mexican American population. According to historian Lorena Oropeza, Chicana/o nationalism redefined patriotism away from military service and more toward community service for Chicanas and Chicanos in local barrios.[58] This rethinking affected older barrio communities as well. By allying with leaders in other cities in the media reform movement, Bakersfield civil rights leaders established a critical support network that aided their efforts to enact local civil rights reform. Regional alliances provided Chicana/os in Bakersfield with a sense of racial and ethnic unity, distinct from earlier racial coalitions built through the KCCU, which were more county oriented and for a time statewide. Thus, as the Chicana/o fair media movement grew from its roots in the multiracial politics of the KCCU, its development represented something new within the national fair media movement. Changing how Mexican Americans were perceived in mainstream media was central to furthering Chicana/o nationalism, and the battle against McGraw-Hill became a front line in this struggle for civil rights reform.

The national media reform movement, particularly among Chicana/os, helped facilitate Chicanismo and cultural nationalism among activists and thereby shape how media and television depicted Mexican Americans. Prior to the fair media movement, Mexican Americans were stereotyped negatively, epitomized by Bill Dana's caricature José Jiménez and the Frito Bandito character. Media thus became a battleground in the war over ethnicity. At the same time, the state tried to "contain social movements in the name of corporate capitalism" through federal communications policy.[59] In brief, social movements from below helped create their own ethnic identities by establishing a place within the corporate media world, working through

FCC policy. In Bakersfield, civil rights organizations such as the KCCU and the Community Service Organization (CSO) faced down media stations to enact reforms for minorities and women. They challenged local stations under threat of filing petitions to deny FCC license renewals, unless civil rights concessions were made. The FCC license renewal process, mandated by the Communications Act of 1934, offered an effective method for local organizations to challenge an industry that had vast resources and that otherwise might operate with impunity toward the general public and minority interests. "The movement was about getting diversity integrated into the corporate world, not about changing the corporate world," recalled attorney Al Kramer. "The notion was that if you got diversity into the corporate world, you would get a different output."[60]

McGraw-Hill made landmark concessions to largely Chicana/o civil rights organizations in spring 1972. After three long years of paperwork and negotiations between civil rights groups, McGraw-Hill, and the FCC, the company's concessions represented a new direction in the corporate media reform movement. "[McGraw-Hill] was really the first major deal Chicanos had gotten involved in, getting the same kind of leverage that other ethnic civil rights groups were getting, mainly African Americans," said Kramer.[61] One editorial in *Broadcast* magazine described the results of the McGraw-Hill concessions as "regulatory anarchy," relegating the US government to a subsidiary role in broadcast regulation, courtesy of a professional solicitor of minority protest—Al Kramer.[62] The McGraw-Hill concessions represented a shift in the media reform movement because Chicana/os led the drive. Chicana/os, however, were not the only racial group in Kern County and Bakersfield pushing for fair media practices.

Diverse racial activists within the KCCU helped propel the fair media movement in Kern County. African Americans and white liberals invested heavily with Mexican Americans in the eventual success or failure of the fair media movement. As activists mobilized, the majority of organizations involved in the five-city coalition against McGraw-Hill, especially in Denver and San Diego, were predominately Chicana/o civil rights groups. The groups involved from Denver included the Colorado Committee on Mass Media and the Spanish Surnamed, La Raza Unida Party, the Latin American Council, Sociedad Mutualista Círculo Mexicano, Latino Jalisco, the Associated Migrant Opportunity Services, and the Community Services Organization. In San Diego, in addition to the Chicano Federation of San Diego, individual petitioners Louis Trujillo, Antonio Mojica, Daniel Vargas, Abraham Ortega, José Álvarez, Jesse Arizola, Marcelina Espinosa, Andrew Cervantes, Mike Uriegas, Ernestine Sovala, Margarita Dunquez, Martin

Morales, Simón Aguilar Jr., José Trevino, Tony Rios, and Agustín Chávez led the effort. The catalyst for their actions was a proposal by McGraw-Hill to buy stations in five regional media markets: WFBM-TV in Indianapolis, WOOD-TV in Grand Rapids, KLZ-TV in Denver, KOGO-TV in San Diego, and KERO-TV in Bakersfield. Through the activists' efforts, the entire deal was stalled and multiyear negotiations were undertaken between Time Life, McGraw-Hill, and civil rights organizations in the five cities between 1969 and 1972. Educator and civil rights activist Ray Gonzales recalled, "we found out Channel 23, owned by Time Life, was being sold to McGraw-Hill in a five-channel deal that included Bakersfield, Denver, San Diego, Indianapolis, and Chicago. There were five media market places. The other four were in the top 50 market. Bakersfield was the throwaway in the group. It was not in the top 200 market."[63] Bakersfield civil rights leaders thus played a foundational role (much bigger than their market share) in initiating and facilitating fair media negotiations with McGraw-Hill.

McGraw-Hill's planned acquisition of KERO and the other four networks was blocked by the KCCU's petition to deny a license renewal for KERO in 1969. The KCCU worked in concert with the UCC and Department of Communication at Stanford University to document bias and unfair practices at the local television station. Through the UCC, KCCU members established contact with the Washington attorneys who had successfully gained concessions in the 1969 landmark Court of Appeals case *Office of Communication of the United Church of Christ v. F.C.C.* Ray Gonzales remembered that the "United Church of Christ [sent] a hotshot group of lawyers that had won some successful cases in the South. . . . They . . . gave us some free advice and we started putting this plan together, and started checking out the [FCC's] fourteen points. The UCC sent a lawyer [Leonard Moore], and they said we can file against McGraw-Hill when they get ready for the transfer of the license."[64] Having threatened a petition to deny KERO's operating license, the KCCU learned that KERO was being bought by McGraw-Hill. It also learned that other cities were involved in the proposed transaction. Earl K. Moore, the attorney who had represented and won the suit in Jackson, Mississippi, against WLBT, became representing attorney for the KCCU against KERO. After the five-city coalition formed through organizational efforts by the NMAADC and MALDEF to challenge McGraw-Hill's proposed buyout, joint petitions were submitted in all five cities to deny the right of the licensed stations to operate. At that point, the target cities voted to give representation responsibility to attorney Al Kramer.

In the five cities, Chicana/o activists were interested in diversifying ownership and providing institutional opportunities to gain a foothold in local and national media broadcasting. Strategically, Chicana/os pushed beyond what African Americans had accomplished in the South, arguing for "increased minority programming [and] . . . basic regulatory issues resolved: namely, concentration of control, anti-competitive effects, and potential conflicts of interest."[65] The coalition pointed out that if the FCC approved McGraw-Hill's acquisition of the five regional markets, an "ownership pattern" in "clear violation of FCC multi ownership rules" would ensue. According to Kramer, the McGraw-Hill license renewal blockade was "the first test of whether or not the Commission [would] enforce these [specific] policies" of the 1934 Communications Act.[66] The UCC Office of Communication recognized the significance of the coalition's blockade, noting that it had "the potential of setting a precedent for change in the entire broadcasting industry."[67]

Bakersfield civil rights leaders charged local media with excessive commercialization practices. KCCU members complained that KERO played commercials up to twenty minutes per hour, even during prime-time programming. According to KERO, extensive commercialization was required for financial profit and economic viability. The KCCU challenged the argument, demanding that KERO's financial records be released so that this claim could be verified. KERO denied the request, and the UCC Office of Communication prepared in the fall of 1971 to go to court and demand the station turn over financial records to the KCCU.[68] The demand for disclosure was important. The FCC had just months before denied the Alianza Federal de Pueblos Libres (Alliance of Free City-States) its financial disclosure request against major networks in New Mexico.[69] Representing the KCCU in 1971, attorney Earl K. Moore declared KERO's excessive commercialization and inferior service in the Bakersfield market unjustified, with full financial disclosure the only recourse to prove legitimacy.[70]

The KCCU worked with other local civil rights groups such as the United Farm Workers (UFW) and the CSO in broadening media reform and leveraging power against local media in greater Bakersfield. César Chávez of the UFW and Anthony P. Rios, president of the California CSO, "filed a petition on behalf of their organizations against radio station KWAC in Bakersfield, which specialized in Spanish-language programs," in the fall of 1971.[71] "KWAC was openly anti-union," recalled CSO activist Jesse Alcala.[72] With KWAC the only Spanish-language station in the southern San Joaquin Valley at the time, its anti-unionism, particularly the public sentiments expressed by its co-owner and popular radio personality Maria Elena, became a target for local activists. There were "books-[worth of] FCC irregularities . . . income tax evasion . . . payola . . . affidavits from former employees saying that they got fired because they were supporting the farmworkers . . . [saying that] they couldn't talk about the farmworkers," Alcala recalled of KWAC.[73] The KCCU also broadened its public confrontation to include KJTV (channel 17), accusing it of "failing to provide adequate locally-produced public affairs programming, news, and [also] discriminating against minorities in hiring practices."[74] As broadcasters had feared, the FCC license renewal process offered citizens and labor leaders a window of opportunity to challenge standard media practices that had long been used to forestall progressive reforms such as diverse programming and minority hiring, and to avoid issues of concern to minority communities.

As the media movement in Bakersfield built alliances with Chicana/o organizations across the five cities, the political expediency of civil rights racial coalitions was tested. After Kramer assumed representation of the five-city coalition, Nick Reyes and the NMAADC were cut out of the coalition's legal representation. Given the NMAADC's active role in the Chicana/o fair media movement, Reyes accused the UCC and Kramer of "seducing away" Chicana/o groups that the NMAADC was trying to aid. According to Reyes, "white groups ought to work among whites, or enable minority groups to do the work themselves.... Their whole philosophy is not to let us do it for ourselves. It's super white to the rescue."[75] Racial coalitions, in Reyes's view, were secondary to the need to build an independent Chicana/o presence in the American media industry, one not dependent on relationships with African Americans and white liberals. Reyes did not come to his position lightly. In addition to his work with the NMAADC, he "had a varied background in the Federal Government, as Special Assistant to the Commissioners of the Equal Employment Opportunity Commission (EEOC) and Public Affairs and Education Programs at the EEOC."[76] Testifying before the FCC in 1971, Reyes argued that "there seems to be an attitude on the part of advertisers that America is basically a racist society: that it is good business to capitalize on this proclivity by making the Chicano (Mexican American) appear as a figure to be laughed at, scorned and otherwise demeaned ... as a stupid, dirty, shiftless, immoral, servile bandito."[77] Ending these racial stereotypes would have to be accomplished by Chicana/os, not others, Reyes reasoned. Kramer, for his part, recalled, "there were tensions with having white lawyers.... I had my own share of flare-ups with people who thought I was being an arrogant white guy. I don't know if I was or wasn't.... I deal[t] with ... more important issue[s]."[78] Both Reyes and Kramer knew the possible financial and leadership benefits gained by representing the five cities against McGraw-Hill, particularly in an age of the expansion of the public interest legal movement.[79]

Beyond ideological tensions over the merits of racial coalitions, the slowness of the litigation process thwarted immediate results and was a delicate issue for KCCU members. By 1971, the KCCU had been fully involved with the coalition for nearly two years. Its members' impatience was rooted in the organization's experience years earlier, with the lack of action by organizations such as the Bakersfield IRB and the city council to enact civil rights changes at home. The KCCU had since 1969 exerted leverage against local media outlets by threatening to petition the FCC to deny license renewals. Bargaining with local media outlets rather than waiting for a litigation deal brokered with the five cities, however, had its drawbacks. Even if such bargaining led to positive gain in the national media reform movement, the small size of the Bakersfield market—as compared to, say, Denver and San Diego—meant smaller potential concessions. As McGraw-Hill negotiated with Kramer in late 1971, part of McGraw-Hill's proposals included terms not equal to what KERO was ready to concede to the KCCU independently.[80] And yet, the KCCU did not cease negotiating with local media stations amid the drawn-out litigation process with McGraw-Hill. KCCU activist Ray Gonzales recalled the local negotiations: "we had rented rooms out at the Hacienda hotel. We had our negotiating team, and we had [attorneys] Gabe Solomon and Tim Lemucchi willing to do some initial legal filings, and we had [the media] lined up and . . . signing agreements, agreeing to do what we asked them to do. We always said it wasn't only going to be a minority thing, but also public service announcements, and all kinds of stuff. We were focused in Kern County on three TV stations and about ten radio stations."[81] The KCCU was interested in changing media practices and culture throughout Kern County, not only at KERO.

The KCCU pressed locally for immediate and direct action that bore concrete results. Charles Siplin and Ray Gonzales, representing the racial minority leadership within the KCCU, challenged local media television and radio stations to meet demands from local civil rights groups. In an August 1971 open letter to the "Managers of the Electronic Media in Kern County," Gonzales pressured local media outlets to negotiate the demands of several coalitions by September of that same year. He wrote, "if negotiations are not fruitful we will file a petition to deny [the FCC license] in each situation that warrants it."[82] The threat alone was intimidating for small networks, whose budgets would have trouble sustaining any residual litigation costs. Gonzales reminded broadcasters of recent legal decisions upholding the efforts of the UCC in the Jackson case, as well as the broad-based national civil rights organizations the KCCU had helped organize in support of its efforts in Bakersfield.[83]

The civil rights groups that signed the KCCU's open letter genuinely represented minority interests in Bakersfield. In addition to the umbrella civil rights organization KCCU, the following organizations joined the fight for fair media: the American Civil Liberties Union (ACLU); the Black and Brown Coalition; Black Citizens for Better Education; the Black Students Union of Bakersfield College; Chicanos Interested in Democracy of California State College, Bakersfield; Kern County Welfare Rights Association; the NAACP; the Mexican American Political Association (MAPA); and the Mexican Heritage Association.[84] In their multiracial nature, the groups presented a comprehensive picture of the minority communities in Bakersfield. The KCCU organized this broad coalition in order to represent what the Kern County radio and TV networks deemed the *public interest*. One requirement for stations in the process of FCC license renewal was that they conduct ascertainment studies of the community to make sure that the programming reflected the interests of the public. Network television and radio stations were supposed to conduct community service assessments with representative leaders of local communities. Writing in August 1971, Michael Dutton, chair of the KCCU Public Relations Committee, declared, "we are concerned that in our brief investigation of the 'community needs' analysis at several stations, very few, and sometimes no members of the minority community were interviewed, nor were interviews conducted with individuals under the age of twenty-five."[85] Ray Gonzales confirmed: "we were never contacted for an interview, nor was Charles [Siplin]. And we were the ones who initiated the proceedings. Only later, after we brought in MALDEF and NMAADC, did the stations consult with us for their ascertainment studies."[86]

Negotiations between the KCCU and local media outlets were eventually challenged by the relationship of the KCCU to the five-city coalition. Gonzales expressed concerns over this challenge to attorney Kramer in late 1971: "Because of the KCCU's efforts to cooperate in the 5-city matter, we have for all practical purposes lost a very meaningful agreement with the major T.V. station in this area. . . . We insist that Bakersfield receive equal treatment regardless of the size of the market. . . . We feel that in your desire to deal only with the regulatory issues, the local coalitions may not even have a pie to deal with. At this point we have to consider what is best for the minorities of this area."[87] Following his letter to Kramer, as KCCU liaison to the five-city coalition, Gonzales withdrew the KCCU as official petitioner of the "request to deny" for KERO—but the Bakersfield CSO maintained its corresponding position as petitioner. The strategy indicates discontent within the ranks of the KCCU over the slow pace of the proceedings, as well as a desire to strike a deal with local media outlets. The fact that the CSO petitioned with the KCCU's consent also indicates that the fair media movement in Bakersfield was coming to be seen as a Chicana/o issue, since the CSO was more exclusively a Mexican American organization, while the KCCU was more multiracial. In a legal rebuttal to the CSO petition to deny, McGraw-Hill used this fact in its defense, noting that the CSO was "a Spanish surnamed organization" and not truly representative of minorities or community interests in Kern County and the Bakersfield market.[88]

By withdrawing its petition against McGraw-Hill, the KCCU was able to broker immediate reforms for women and minorities with local broadcasters in Bakersfield. At the time of the McGraw-Hill negotiations, the KCCU had gained the support of the local chapter of the National Organization for Women, which was also supportive of the racial minority goals of the KCCU. The KCCU withdrawal from the McGraw-Hill negotiations did not halt its support for the CSO and MALDEF to carry on the fight at the national level. Gonzales believed it most important to win immediate concessions from local broadcasters, rather than risk losing potential gains by waiting until the conclusion of the long McGraw-Hill negotiations.[89]

The actual concessions made by McGraw-Hill to the five-city coalition, nevertheless, were pivotal. In early spring 1972, the FCC approved McGraw-Hill's proposed purchase of the Time Life networks. In turn, the consolidated coalition threatened to file a lawsuit against the new deal, effectively stalling the transfer again. In order to avoid more potential litigation costs and lost revenue due to delayed acquisition, McGraw-Hill settled, meeting the demands of the coalition. Media diversity ownership was one significant outcome of the concessions. McGraw-Hill was forced to drop purchase of one of the five proposed networks, in this case WOOD-TV in Grand Rapids. The concession forced McGraw-Hill to acknowledge the FCC's Top 50 Market policy, which was designed to promote "diversity of ownership of television stations and prohibit a broadcaster from acquiring more than two VHF stations in the top-50 markets without making a 'compelling public interest showing.'"[90] Even so, the concession to drop the fifth network upset the FCC, since it had previously ruled that McGraw-Hill had demonstrated a compelling case for public interest in the sale. The five cities now circumvented the FCC's ruling and pressed for diversity of media ownership by threatening to file additional paperwork in order to prevent transfer from Time Life. Rather than fight an endless regulatory battle and lose the financial benefits of the transfer, McGraw-Hill settled with the coalition.

The formation of minority advisory councils (MACs) was a significant concession of the McGraw-Hill agreement. In each of its purchased network regions, MACs were to act as official liaisons between the media industry and minority communities. Local MACs consisted of up to five members representing minority groups that had challenged the original license renewals with the FCC. A regional MAC coordinator was also created; Mario Obledo of MALDEF nominated a young Moctesuma Esparza (future Hollywood film director) for the position.[91] According to the agreement, local MACs would "be involved from the beginning in the development of local programming related to minorities," as well as a host of other responsibilities related to labor recruitment.[92]

Perhaps the most significant McGraw-Hill concession was the agreement to produce an eighteen-part *La Raza* program to be presented in the four regional markets, to cover the history and identity of the Mexican people, from their Mesoamerican origins through the twentieth century. The stations, "in consultation with a coordinating committee made of members suggested by local MACs, [were to] produce . . . the programs dealing with Mexican American culture and history."[93] In 1974, the first parts received an honorable mention from the Robert F. Kennedy Journalism Award, as they were deemed "the first television documentary series to take a comprehensive look at the role of Mexican Americans in the U.S."[94] The first seven volumes won a Peabody Award for documentary journalism and were titled: "An Introduction," "The History and the Heritage," "Learning in Two Worlds: Education," "Survival: The Chicanos' Struggle for Human Dignity," "Celebración: The Chicanos' Pursuit of Happiness," "A Political Renaissance: Examining the Chicanos' Re-Emerging Role in Government," and "A Working People: Chicanos in the Workforce."[95] From 1975 to 1979, as the documentary series continued production, Moctesuma Esparza directed six episodes of the series, which eventually ran in national syndication.[96]

THE POLITICS OF RURAL HEALTH CARE

Another important manifestation of multiracial civil rights activism beyond the fields was the fight to expand access to rural health care in greater Bakersfield. Transnational migration of Mexican immigrants helped perpetuate anti-statist opposition to civil rights reform in rural Kern County. The expansion of federally subsidized health care among migrant populations became a battlefront in the ongoing struggle to expand civil rights in the San Joaquin Valley. In the late 1960s, Kern County was selected to become a recipient site for federally subsidized rural health-care funding, much to the dismay of the county's anti-statist medical establishment. For the county and city's racially marginalized populations, access to basic health care became a civil rights issue. Federally funded rural health care meant servicing a predominantly ethnic Mexican population. The success of the UFW in calling attention to the plight of migrant farmworkers played a significant role in the selection of Kern County as a target site for federal grants designed to expand the healthcare infrastructure in poor rural communities. While the UFW developed modest access to health-care services for migrant workers, its clinics only covered workers under union contract, thus limiting the number of patients served.[97]

As federal resources expanded into rural Kern County, tensions arose between Mexican American and African American community activists over access to and control of subsidized low-income health care. Federal monies were awarded initially to a predominantly African American group called the Kern County Liberation Movement (KCLM). The fact that federal money was given to a Black organization instead of a Mexican American organization angered some Mexican American leaders. The KCLM believed, conversely, that Bakersfield's segregated Black community deserved the money and would use it wisely to serve the rural farmworker community. African Americans in Kern County had a deep history of migrant agricultural labor, dating back to the late nineteenth century. The KCLM argued that grant monies would develop rural health-care facilities in the southeast section of Bakersfield, an area that was largely unincorporated yet home to a historically stable African American community and in proximity to Bakersfield's semi-urban and rural ethnic Mexican community in the county periphery.[98] The KCLM argued that both racial communities, Mexican Americans and African Americans, would be served. Over the course of the 1970s, competition and discord between the UFW and the grant recipients behind what became known as Clinica Sierra Vista (formerly Clinica de los Campesinos or Farmworkers Clinic) deepened. The conflict illustrates the limitations of the UFW in its efforts to champion all aspects of labor and civil rights reform in Kern County and across rural California. Furthermore, the conflict over rural health care highlights the connections between the farmworker movement and the variant strains of African American and Mexican American civil rights reform, as well as the anti-statist opposition these activists encountered.

Controversy surrounding rural health-care funds centered on the question of who would be in charge of administering programs. Representative William Ketchum of California's Thirty-Sixth Congressional District was a moderate Republican who supported subsidized rural health-care programs but moved away from supporting the project as tensions mounted on the political right. On April 6, 1973, Ketchum released a statement attempting to "set the record straight" concerning his alleged support for the migrant health clinic La Clinica de los Campesinos in Lamont, California. While noting that he supported well-administered clinics for farmworkers, Ketchum reiterated that "at no time . . . have I specifically indicated my support of the administrative practices of La Clinica de los Campesinos as the clinic indicates that I have."[99] Through this political posturing, Ketchum signaled support for "well-administered" migrant health clinics such as those operated by the Kern County Medical Society (KCMS) but distanced himself from farmworker clinics run by the KCLM, even after the latter changed its name to the less politically divisive Kern County Health Committee.

The expansion of federally subsidized rural health care was politically divisive over the question of local control and administration of grant programs. The rural health-care debate in 1973 echoed debates over control of federally subsidized War on Poverty programs as early as 1965. What was new in the debate over rural health care in the early 1970s was the racial tension between African Americans and Mexican Americans. In the mid-1960s, interracial tensions within the antipoverty movement were nominal compared to the conflict that arose among multiracial grassroots organizations concerning debates over the rural welfare state in the early 1970s.[100]

To counter skepticism over subsidized health-care programs, the city of Arvin (just southeast of Bakersfield) declared April 14, 1973, as Clinica de Los Campesinos Day (Farmworkers Clinic Day). The Arvin resolution noted that the health clinic served a community need both inside and outside of Arvin, worked in collaboration with existing agencies, and did so in such a manner to maintain the integrity of "local control and local involvement without the requirements of handouts and allowing people to help themselves without being social parasites on other segments of our society."[101] The wording of the resolution appealed to Kern County's anti-statist political traditions and the larger political culture, which was hostile toward the welfare state and subsidized programs for the poor.[102] Federally subsidized farm health-care programs provided basic access to health care for migrant workers who lacked health-care services provided by employers (i.e., agribusiness). As the UFW argued, farmworkers had been excluded from New Deal–era labor protections; modestly funded federal health-care programs improved the lives of migrant workers just as New Deal–era legislation had done for industrial workers. At the same time, federal assistance acted as a form of corporate welfare to agricultural interests by providing subsidized medical benefits to the migrant labor population, relieving growers of the responsibility of providing medical benefits to their workers through contracts, as did other corporate industries. Liberal policymakers, while perhaps genuine in intent (or pragmatically seeking to win over potential voters) and sympathetic to the farm labor struggle, affirmed through legislation the myth of agrarian exceptionalism by relieving growers of the need to provide their workers with adequate health care.

Labor conditions for farmworkers in California's Central Valley commanded significant national attention in the late 1960s. National policymakers reacted with political aplomb to this perceived rural labor crisis. Minnesota senator Walter Mondale, a Democrat who served on the Subcommittee on Migratory Labor, led the charge, drafting legislation authorizing $11 million for migrant health programs for the 1970 fiscal year. The US Department of Health, Education, and Welfare (HEW) directed its region 9 (West Coast) branch to implement grants in areas with large migrant populations. Bakersfield was selected as a grant recipient site.[103] Given that federal dollars were intended to offer an expanded health-care infrastructure for migrant workers, the focus was naturally to service a predominantly ethnic Mexican farm labor population. In Bakersfield, the search for an appropriate organization to implement health-care services was racially divisive and mobilized opposition to federally subsidized health care. As HEW sought out Chicana/o organizations to fund the project, no suitable organization emerged. The predominantly African American KCLM was thereby awarded $2.6 million to immediately establish a health center for migrant workers. As a result of the award, Kern County's health establishment opposed what it viewed as wasteful federal spending, as the KCMS already administered a small, regional, migrant health-care program.

According to the official KCMS agency history, "until the mid-fifties, the practice of medicine was relatively free from government regulation and influence, although numerous political and legislative attempts were mounted to do so, and vigorously opposed by organized medicine. Cracks in the dam appeared . . . in . . . 1958 . . . [when] Carroll Goss, MD, presented a list of proposed principles for the administration of medical cards for welfare recipients."[104] Goss thereafter (and prior to the post-1970 influx of federal funds) pioneered migrant health clinics in rural Kern County. In 1966, the California State Department of Health contracted with the KCMS to provide a medical facility for migrant workers in the Lamont area, and in 1968, Goss established two mobile migrant health-care trailers in the Lamont area, each providing basic medical services for farmworkers south of Bakersfield. The program was called the Migrant Workers Health Clinic.[105] Goss headed the implementation of migrant clinics for the KCMS; by the end of the 1970 harvest season,

Goss reported servicing 3,200 visits with a volunteer staff for his two trailers, one at the historical Sunset labor camp in Weedpatch, California, and the other northwest of Bakersfield in the small community of Wasco.[106]

Goss's migrant clinics were an important expansion of health-care access for the migrant population in greater Bakersfield. Although inadequately funded, they had the official sanction and sponsorship of the county's medical establishment. KCMS minutes note that the "Kern County Liberation Movement (KCLM) had applied for a federal grant to establish a 'migrant' health clinic in SE Bakersfield, by-passing the State Department of Health. This . . . duplicate[d] the program sponsored by KCMS, which opposed the movement."[107] Despite the fact that the KCMS had already established a functioning migrant health clinic, the KCLM felt that working with the KCMS was not worthwhile. KCLM members charged the KCMS with having no genuine interest in improving medical services in the migrant community, and with being part of the valley's larger anti-statist political culture. The KCLM was interested in taking administrative control of federally funded rural health-care programs. As a result of KCMS dissatisfaction with the KCLM, Goss suggested that the KCMS consider moving its migrant health operations to northern Kern County, since the KCLM was already in operation in the southern part of the county.[108]

KCMS officials described the KCLM as "reminiscent of Berkeley in the 1960s," an organization run by a "group of quasi-altruistic populists." The KCMS was furious that the federal government had funded the KCLM with taxpayer dollars, at the very same time that a KCMS migrant health clinic had been expanding service (with a $325,645 grant received in 1970). Criticism of Kern County's medical establishment, however, eclipsed the work done by Goss's migrant health clinics. In 1973, the KCMS migrant health-care program would come to an end. That was also the same year that the KCLM changed its name to the Kern County Health Committee, dropping the more politically charged "liberation movement." In the end, the KCLM disbanded with the establishment of the Clinica de Los Campesinos, which would become the Clinica Sierra Vista, providing federally subsidized health care in rural California into the twenty-first century.[109]

In May 1973, as tensions mounted over which agency controlled rural health care in Kern County, the *Bakersfield Californian* ran an exposé series by staff writer Gordon Anderson on the nature of Kern County's medical practices. Anderson's series opened by noting that Eldon E. Geisert controlled the three branches of Kern County medicine: the KCMS, the Foundation for Medical Care, and the Houchin Community Blood Bank. Inquiries into the nature and workings of these three branches were, according to Anderson, met with "silence, subsequent denial of prior statements, fear and verbal abuse."[110] Anderson's series pointed to the county's overall anti-statist political culture and the medical establishment's emphasis on local control.

Kern County's medical establishment was also called into question by a HEW audit in 1971. Dr. Vernon Wilson, HEW health services director, "ordered a site team to visit five California counties in November–December 1971," in order to evaluate organized medicine. Kern County was among the counties visited. The site team's investigation was highly critical of and damaging to the KCMS. The HEW team found "the Kern Society's summer migrant care program to be at best, superficial. It is episodic, non-continuous medical care with no follow-up or integrated medical social services. The Medical Society controls the program and doles out the $25 hour opportunities to its physicians, both the needy and the greedy."[111] The HEW site team recommended that the KCMS migrant program be terminated and its funds transferred elsewhere. HEW further recommended that the KCLM migrant health care project receive funding, particularly in light of the fact that the KCMS had "no pretense at tolerance, compassion or interest in the problems of the migrant [workers]," and that "efforts to establish a viable and ultimately . . . durable program must be prepared for great hostility."[112]

Subsidized health care for migrant farmworkers prompted significant backlash from Kern County's conservative base. Bakersfield resident Helen Graf wrote to her Republican senator George Murphy in July 1970, protesting the expansion of rural health-care clinics for migrant workers in Kern County. "I am so mad, I can't even tell you. [The] Kern County Liberation Movement has received a $2 . . . million dollar grant for a migrant health center for southeast Bakersfield from H.E.W. I say get rid of H.E.W. & O.E.O. [the Office of Economic Opportunity] and it would be a step in the right direction toward restoring sanity in Washington D.C. I am opposed to supporting revolution. . . . Cesar Chavez is allowed to run roughshod . . . over all of us in the valley, here with his own brand of Revolution."[113] Graf's commentary characterizes the broader Kern County conservative electorate, which viewed the expansion of rural health care through an anticommunist lens, ultimately conflating various strains of labor and civil rights initiatives as part of the same revolutionary agenda. Tehachapi homemaker Gertude Pool echoed Graf. Writing to Representative Ketchum, Pool opined: "It is so disgusting for these foreigners to come in our country to work and make a good living send much of the money out of our country, and then rise up as Cesar Chavez has done. . . . Almost all the people believe he is backed by Communists a lot of money coming from somewhere nobody seems to know where from."[114]

Tensions over language and perceived exclusion also divided African Americans and Mexican Americans in the implementation of federal programs in Kern County. Local African American leaders expressed dissatisfaction that Mexican Americans and African Americans were being pitted against each other over federal programs. Writing to OEO's Washington office in early 1972, Bakersfield NAACP president Robert Mosley voiced concern about the OEO migrant division's director, Pete Morales, who was scheduled to evaluate the Bakersfield Target Area Poverty (TAP) programs. "It seems a paranoia permeates that division that inhibits the true meaning of O.E.O. and definitely stagnates the effectiveness of the War on Poverty.... It is with concern for the Black and Anglo Farmworkers in Kern and King Counties and as President of the Bakersfield Chapter of the N.A.A.C.P. that I request that Mr. Ralph Anthony . . . accompany your evaluating team."[115] Mosley was inflamed that OEO's migrant division seemed to give preference to the migrant Mexican population at the cost of equal services to Anglo and African American farmworkers. "That Division has implemented policy that extends to the point of calling for more Campesino representatives within the structure of those programs operating.... It is my belief that the term Campesino means farmworker of Mexican or Latin extraction; and this leaves the Black and Anglo farmworker to believe that O.E.O. is purposely excluding them."[116] The local NAACP also complained that some federally funded programs had meetings conducted entirely in Spanish, without bilingual translators available for non-Spanish-speaking attendees.

Bakersfield's multiracial civil rights leaders were highly conscious of the growing tensions between African Americans and ethnic Mexicans in the early 1970s. The appointment of a local African American to head an antipoverty agency caused alarm among many Mexican Americans, since the agency was designed to "provide day care to the children of migrant workers." Commenting on growing tensions between the two racial groups, local college professor (and soon-to-be political candidate) Ray Gonzales lamented in the local NAACP press, "How can this matter be resolved? How can the minority people avoid the fights that occur over the trickling of funds that fall from government tables? . . . If the minority people in this community cannot get themselves together, it almost seems pointless to try to influence the rest of this society."[117] Gonzales's criticism of infighting between Black people and Chicana/os was reflected by Duane Goff, who worked on Gonzales's 1972 election campaign. "My experience with the Chicanos and the blacks vis-à-vis KCEOC [the Kern County Economic Opportunity Commission] was that a lot of both the blacks and the Chicanos who were struggling for superiority power in the KCEOC were not even the political leaders in the community. A lot of them were not even respected by us. We called them triple P people—*poverty program prostitutes* or *poverty program parasites*—because they were fighting more for their own power and their own titles more than they were fighting for us."[118]

CONCLUSION

The struggle against police brutality, the fair media movement, and efforts to expand federally subsidized rural health care illustrate how civil rights reform manifested beyond the fields of the San Joaquin Valley. These various reform efforts show the diversity of activists fighting to expand social justice among the region's racialized populations, particularly its Black and Brown populations in southeast Bakersfield. Following the Fraternal Hall incident, a local chapter of the ACLU was formed and the civic unity movement, which had waned since 1967, was reinvigorated. Police reform was championed by African American, Mexican American, and white liberal civil rights activists through the 1970s. Fraternal Hall would also live on in the collective memory of the multiracial activists and Black community in southeast Bakersfield as evidence of racial bias within law enforcement in Bakersfield.[119]

Like the struggle against police brutality, the fair media movement was another important strand of multiracial civil rights activism in Bakersfield. An interesting outgrowth of the McGraw-Hill concessions was an effort to form a national civil rights pressure group in Washington, DC, to take on the telecommunications industry. In a letter to Gilbert Pompa, assistant director of conciliation at the DOJ CRS, Pete Vigil of the Chicano Federation of San Diego suggested that "a National Organization representative of Chicanos is very urgently needed now, if we are to counter the efforts of the National Association of Broadcasters to pass legislation which would limit progress."[120] According to Vigil, the time was right, especially after the landmark concession gained by the five cities over McGraw-Hill. Vigil was worried that under the Richard Nixon administration, FCC policies, especially the Fairness Doctrine, the petition to deny, and the Communications Act, would be threatened, potentially eliminating the leverage power of minority groups so aptly demonstrated by the McGraw-Hill proceedings. Thirteen civil rights and fair media activists, including Al Kramer and Earl K. Moore, sent a letter to President Nixon in July 1972 about the "extreme resistance [and] . . . recalcitrance from . . . broadcast licensees," following a meeting between President Nixon and "30 executives of major broadcast companies across the country."[121] Civil rights groups were concerned especially with Nixon's advisors who suggested major changes for broadcasting, including updating the Communications Act, eliminating the Fairness Doctrine, and instituting changes to the license renewal process in order to curb activists from using the process to "threat[en] the broadcasting industry's stability and profitability."[122] To the national fair media movement, such proposals seemed to be a direct response to local civil rights groups that had successfully blocked or stalled the license renewal process and won concessions for minority groups along the way. The power fair media groups had claimed at the local level, illustrated by the McGraw-Hill proceedings and the UCC's actions in the American South, encouraged the Nixon administration to deregulate the media industry in the early 1970s. In a memorandum to President Nixon, Clay Whitehead, director of the White House Office of Telecommunications Policy from 1970 to 1974, said: "we stand to gain substantially from an increase in the relative power of the local stations. They are generally less liberal and more concerned with education than with controversial national affairs. Further, a decentralized system would have far less influence and be far less attractive to social activists."[123] No national media lobbying group for Chicana/os emerged to challenge this deregulatory movement among conservatives.[124]

Finally, the fight to expand access to rural health care in the southern San Joaquin Valley, although contentious, underscores the difficulties in advancing health care for all in one of California's most underserved regions. The UFW had marginal success with its own medical plan for unionized farmworkers—the Robert F. Kennedy Farm Workers Medical Plan—but greater efforts to expand access to rural populations were clearly on the agenda of Black and Brown activists in the early 1970s. The UFW medical plan obligated employers of unionized workers to "contribute 10 cents for every hour worked by every worker."[125] "True, our medical plan is small when compared to other long established unions," read the plan's brochure, "but as we grow in numbers and as our members continue to sacrifice and work for social justice, we will be able to win more benefits for our children."[126] Thirty-four Delano area growers, who signed the first UFW Organizing Committee contract, financed the plan. On October 21, 1971, the Rodrigo Terronez Memorial Clinic opened in Delano on the Forty Acres property.[127]

The UFW wanted to make sure that its Delano medical clinic serviced only unionized workers, not scab labor. In November 1973, a sign was placed in front of the clinic noting that anyone who used the services at the clinic would have to show a check stub or proof that they were on the boycott picket line. UFW employee Esther Uranday reported to César Chávez thereafter, "I have seen people come to the door and stand and read the sign and turn around."[128] While the UFW's inroads into rural medical care were important, its limited capacity to provide health care access, coupled with the administrative challenges it faced and the competition among activist organizations for federal contracts, underscores the scale of the problem of rural health care access. This problem ultimately surpassed the capacity of activists and unions alike in rural California.

7 | A NEW BATTLEGROUND FOR CIVIL RIGHTS

The Desegregation of the Bakersfield City School District, 1969–1984

I think it's the best thing that could have happened to the Bakersfield school system. Bakersfield always had this thing where you dare not question—you just take it. That time is gone now.

"A young Negro," interviewed by Los Angeles Times reporter Noel Greenwood, 1969

The Bakersfield school district is a bastion of conservatism in California. Its location in the center of Kern County has long made it the center of civil rights activity, but for the most part non-judicial. This suit could provide unique relief in a previously untouched legal area for Chicanos. I need not emphasize the dramatic impact of this . . . case.

Mexican American Legal Defense and Educational Fund (MALDEF) official, 1974

The post-*Brown* mandate to desegregate public schools in the United States with all deliberate speed ushered in a period of legal and social conflict. Proponents of racial integration battled against those committed to localism, anti-statism, and, at worst, racial segregation, over the question of civil rights reform in American education. Historians have noted that the false binary of de facto and de jure racial segregation created and sustained a myth of southern exceptionalism, situating the historical narrative of school desegregation as primarily a southern problem.[1] Other regions of the country have resultingly been marginalized from school desegregation narratives.[2] As historians have noted, however, the problem of the proverbial color line in America was enforced not only by explicit southern Jim Crow laws, but also through variant social policies and practices from housing to employment across the northern and western states.³

Regional and multiracial considerations in the American West help reorient the historiography of school desegregation in the United States. This final chapter helps fill a gap in the historiography by addressing a multiracial narrative of school desegregation beyond the American South. Specifically, this chapter examines the roles Mexican Americans and African Americans played in the desegregation of the Bakersfield City School District (BCSD) between 1969 and 1984. At the time, the BCSD was one of the largest public elementary school districts in California. The 1970s were an especially active era of civil rights struggle in California's interior region, given the farm labor struggle and conservative counterresistance toward labor and civil rights. Urban Mexican Americans and African Americans mobilized racial alliances and used the legal apparatus of the state and federal government to challenge a long tradition of racial segregation in Bakersfield city schools.

A landmark event in the history of school desegregation during the post-*Brown* era, the 1984 Bakersfield Consent Decree ended a fifteen-year struggle among civil rights leaders, the BCSD, and federal officials over de facto and de jure racial segregation in Bakersfield. The US Department of Health, Education, and Welfare (HEW), after the lengthiest administrative hearings in the agency's history, concluded in 1978 that the BCSD was guilty of deliberate segregation practices in 1978. Rather than admit guilt, BCSD officials adopted magnet school programs seen by Reagan-era officials as a national blueprint for voluntary school desegregation and a viable alternative to the racial conflict wrought by forced busing, mandatory racial integration, and public admonishment by civil rights activists. The story of desegregating the BCSD reveals further how grassroots civil rights leaders built coalitions across racial lines—challenging institutional racism in an area referred to pejoratively as "Mississippi West," based on the region's history of race relations, segregation, and racial conflict. While racial coalitions among civil rights leaders helped sustain the long struggle for school desegregation in Bakersfield, such alliances were by no means natural or logical. Racial segregation, continuous Mexican immigration, white flight, and the farm labor movement affected racial coalition building in complex ways. Moreover, like many of the civil rights campaigns of this era, school desegregation sparked mobilization at the local and national levels to halt the advancement of civil rights reform.

INDICTMENT AND ALLEGATIONS OF RACIAL SEGREGATION

In 1965 the Bakersfield chapter of the National Association for the Advancement of Colored People (NAACP) submitted its annual report to its West Coast (WC) regional directors. The report chronicled the chapter's various civil rights activities of the previous year. Among the activities noted were the efforts of the Target Area Poverty (TAP) council to fight poverty. The report also noted significant challenges concerning the education of racial minority children. While the local NAACP had succeeded in pressuring local officials to remove Jim Crow segregation signs in public spaces within municipal boundaries by 1950 and had been involved in a number of civil rights struggles between 1950 and 1965, tackling school segregation was another feat all together. Legal filings note that in 1950–1951 the BCSD racial minority population was roughly 25 percent of the district-wide population and that the majority of African American and Mexican American children attended six of the nineteen BCSD elementary schools—Fremont (95 percent minority), Potomac (99 percent minority), Jefferson (70 percent minority), Mount Vernon (95 percent minority), Casa Loma (50 percent minority), and McKinley (40 percent minority)—as well as Lincoln Junior High, which was 100 percent minority.[4] The construction of school boundaries clearly reflected the pattern of racial segregation in Bakersfield, reenforced through the racially segregated housing market and use of restrictive covenants to keep Black and Brown populations in southeast Bakersfield and the city's rural periphery.

Between 1950 and 1965, racial minority enrollments increased and segregated schools grew more entrenched within the BCSD. Reflecting on his childhood experience in southeast Bakersfield's schools, Chuck Ford, who became Fremont School's principal and the first Black educational administrator in Kern County, commented in a civic unity newsletter interview that, "Lincoln, as I recall, had few white students—mostly blacks and browns. I wondered where the white children went to school, because they used to live all around Lincoln, but didn't attend Lincoln."[5] Principal Ford further recalled a growing disconnect between African American and Mexican American children as he grew older. "Mexican children, who were pals and friends at Lincoln, suddenly became very distant at the Jr. high scene. They were trying to make the white scene. I lost what I thought were some of my real good friends in elementary school behind that scene."[6]

To challenge racial segregation and isolation in the schools, the Bakersfield NAACP branch secured an African American candidate for the elementary school board in 1964. While the candidate failed to win, the school board election effort yielded positive results. School officials thereafter advanced African American teachers to permanent teaching positions within the district. Even so, such efforts dramatized the BCSD's tendency to isolate Black educators in racially imbalanced schools. "De facto segregation is commonplace in our community with 50% of the High Schools (3 of 6) having no Negro students in attendance nor do the Elementary or Jr. High School from which they draw. . . . Negro teachers . . . are systematically assigned to predominantly Negro Schools," the Bakersfield NAACP reported to its regional office.[7] To fight job discrimination, NAACP officers filed a complaint with the California Fair Employment Practices Commission (FEPC), "alleging discrimination in teacher placement and student assignment." In summation to the regional office, the local branch declared that high schools and elementary schools were "under pressure from the Mexican and Negro communities to develop programs designed to expand services."[8]

The Bakersfield NAACP's early efforts to fight school segregation were a significant part of the chapter's long history of civil rights activism. The passage of civil rights legislation in 1964–1965 shifted the NAACP-WC's organizational focus toward fair housing. After the California Supreme Court overturned Proposition 14 in 1967, essentially upholding the 1963 Rumford Fair Housing Act, Congress passed the Fair Housing Act in 1968. The NAACP-WC again shifted its limited resources, this time toward tackling the thorny issue of so-called de facto racial segregation in public schools. This shift had unintended consequences for racial coalition building. In California, "the educational civil rights goals pursued through litigation for race-based discrimination . . . and language-based discrimination . . . translate[d] into *conflicting* avenues of redress," notes Mark Brilliant.[9] In Bakersfield, however, tensions between African Americans and Mexican Americans over school integration and bilingual education did not significantly divide racial minorities; rather, they indicated an institutionalized racism that marginalized the needs of both Black and Brown students.

By 1969, civil rights groups in Bakersfield were spearheading an effort to desegregate the BCSD. In April of that year, NAACP activists pressured the local school board to hire a Black principal at the majority Black Lincoln Junior High School. At the time, only one Black principal worked in the entire district, which comprised thirty-six schools and sixteen thousand students.[10] Geraldine Owens, president of Lincoln's parent-teacher association and equal education activist, told school board members, "if we're to continue to be subjected to de facto segregation then we demand a suitable administrator and experienced teachers who understand [the] problems existing at Lincoln School."[11] NAACP officials opined that Lincoln was a perfect example of how mandated school boundaries reinforced racially imbalanced schools. The school's northern boundary was three blocks from the school site, whereas the southern boundary was nine blocks south. Meanwhile, many white families lived just north of the northern attendance boundary and, if brought to Lincoln, would have helped achieve racial balance.[12] According to a National Institute of Education report published in 1974, "as a consequence of the growing Chicano population [in southeast Bakersfield] . . . boundary line gerrymandering has been practiced in the area for years." The report further noted that illustrating such claims, including identifying what were commonly known to parents as Chicana/o or Black schools within the district, was difficult because "the local school district office would not supply the school boundary lines of the last few years" at the time the report was published.[13]

In 1969 the Kern Council for Civic Unity (KCCU) supported closing Lincoln Junior High School due to the severity of its racial isolation and academic achievement gaps. Lincoln's principal, Al Thoman, recommended to the BCSD board that the best way to help Lincoln children, nearly all African American, was to integrate them into other schools. "Given the location of this school and the housing segregation of this community, Lincoln Junior High can never be integrated," read one civic unity newsletter.[14] In March 1970, Duane Belcher, civic unity activist and chair of the ad hoc committee Citizens for Better Schools, presented an integration plan to the BCSD board. His plan articulated a means to achieve forced compliance with the State Board of Education's 15 percent rule for racially balanced schools, all with minimal transportation needs and cost to the district. Several local civil rights groups supported Belcher's proposal, including the local chapters of the NAACP, Community Service Organization (CSO), Mexican American Political Association (MAPA), American Civil Liberties Union (ACLU), and KCCU. The school board, however, ignored the plan.[15] Jack Brigham, a white teacher at Lincoln Junior High School and civic unity activist, admonished school board president Bennet Seaman for the board's neglect of conditions at Lincoln. "Would the . . . Board members . . . allow their own child to attend this school? Would you want your child to be educated in a junior high where approximately 80% of the students enter the high schools at the lowest 2 levels in a system that has 5 levels? IF LINCOLN IS NOT GOOD ENOUGH FOR YOUR CHILD OR THE CHILDREN OF YOUR FRIENDS, IT IS NOT GOOD ENOUGH FOR ANY CHILD."[16]

The KCCU worked in conjunction with southeast Bakersfield residents to encourage state action against segregated schools. In early March 1969, nearly six hundred residents met at East Bakersfield High School and held "a workshop conducted by poor people."[17] Among the issues discussed was the poor-quality education. Summarizing the day's events, the KCCU newsletter reported that area residents had lamented the racial status quo. "We were told to . . . preach to our children the benefits of acquiring an education . . . [yet] they look around and see no examples of educated minority group members getting anywhere . . . one black principal, no browns, low percentages of black and brown teachers, and in many schools no minority teachers of any kind," the newsletter reported.[18] Such public statements were significant, given the media bias of the city's main newspaper, the *Bakersfield Californian*, particularly in its coverage of labor and civil rights issues. Southeast Bakersfield residents further complained, "we were told to fight for more taxes, but we know that . . . some administrators don't even bother to ask for money that is available to them to help our kids, for example, the National School Lunch Program, A.B. 1331, [and] Elementary and Secondary Education Act funds."[19] Efforts to desegregate schools were bolstered by newly adopted State Board of Education requirements that schools be racially balanced against the larger community. "Any school within any district must have its majority/minority student distribution conform with a plus or minus 15% deviation from the district majority/minority student distribution," the KCCU reported.[20] Civic unity activists noted that the "majority/minority distribution for the Bakersfield City School District is 63% majority (white) and 37% minority students (black and brown). Therefore at any school within the district the percentage of majority students should not exceed 78% (63+15=78) and the minority student population should never exceed 52% (37+15=52). Any school in the district that exhibits a majority student population of 79% or greater, or a minority student population of 53% or greater would be in technical violation of the State Board's approved formula."[21]

In light of the newly adopted California standard, the KCCU's reporting was dramatic. "Only one major elementary school representing 923 students conformed to the State Board of Education's formula. . . . [Twenty-five] schools representing more than 18,000 of the 19,210 students in the district did not. The one complying school had 3 of the 2,852 Blacks in the district."[22] KCCU chairman Belcher summarized the problem of racial concentration in the BCSD by using a simple hypothetical to showcase the reality of racial isolation in Bakersfield schools: "If a circle 1.75 miles in radius is imposed upon the city of Bakersfield with Potomac School at its center, all eight of the schools violating the State Board formula for over concentration of *minority* students falls [*sic*] inside, while none of the *majority* violating schools fall inside. Even more significantly, if a circle 1.2 miles in radius is imposed upon the city of Bakersfield using Fremont School as its center, 2,654 of the 2,852 Black students in the district fall within its confines. Or, there are 198 Black students out of 2,852 who are attending a Bakersfield city school outside a 1.2 mile radius from Fremont school."[23] As Belcher indicated, the racial concentration of African American children in southeast Bakersfield schools was extreme. While the racial segregation of Spanish-surnamed students was simultaneously significant and dramatic in terms of discrimination, the racial isolation of Black children was egregious and demanded immediate response, local civil rights activists argued.

As part of an effort to seek outside assistance, local NAACP officers, led by chapter president Ralph Anthony, considered filing a lawsuit against the BCSD board. The NAACP-WC advised Anthony, however, not to file suit. Regional director Leonard Carter reminded Anthony that not only was HEW investigating the BCSD, but the California state attorney general had filed a lawsuit in May 1969 against the BCSD. According to Carter, the attorney general sought the elimination of racial imbalance in accordance with the state administrative code. Rather than waste valuable legal resources on a double or possibly triple indictment, Carter advised caution. He affirmed that the NAACP would likely file an amicus curiae brief (friend of the court document) spelling out NAACP support for the state's lawsuit against the BCSD. The simultaneous charges Carter described against the BCSD from the state attorney general and HEW were "unprecedented in California school history."[24]

The state attorney general (SAG) office filed its petition in Kern County Superior Court in May 1969. The petition asked the court "to order the district to select a plan 'insofar as reasonably feasible' to alter attendance zones in a manner that will prevent, alleviate or eliminate racial imbalance, and to implement the plan by September that year."[25] The basis for the petition revolved around the fact that most students in the BCSD attended racially imbalanced schools. Enforcing the State Board of Education's racial balance policy was an important legal approach. In making this argument, the SAG office used the logic of racial discrimination that had led to the *Brown* decision years before; namely, that racial segregation had a negative impact on children psychologically and that racially imbalanced schools denied children equal educational opportunity, in violation of the Fourteenth Amendment's equal protection clause. The SAG petition charged the district, as composed of "27 elementary schools and 7 junior high schools," with significant "student racial imbalance."[26] The petition for writ also noted that for a number of years, "demands and requests . . . by parents and organizations" were made on the district "to prevent, alleviate, and eliminate the racial imbalance existing in the schools."[27] Parents pleaded that racial isolation caused by district policy had negative psychological effects on their children. "Racially imbalanced schools den[y] students an equal educational opportunity, cause social and psychological injury . . . and thwart the ability of students to learn and exchange views with other students," the petition read.[28]

The BCSD board sidestepped the charges levied by the SAG. The district canceled its compensatory education program, which was designed to increase achievement levels of students from poverty-level homes. Shortly after the school board canceled the program, a group of concerned citizens and civil rights leaders protested the board's decision. At a June 1969 school board meeting, the Kern County Democratic Central Committee declared that the actions of the BCSD board were "a deliberate attempt" to "punish innocent children" in light of the fact that the district was being sued by the SAG.[29] Drawing connections between federal intervention into civil rights reform and local resistance was key for civil rights activists in Bakersfield. Local Mexican American civil rights leaders declared the school board action to be blatantly racist. Ray Gonzales, at the time vice president of the Association of Mexican American Educators and a civic unity activist, accused the school board of "not [being] responsive to the true educational needs of this community. . . . Only a shortsighted, unimaginative, and yes, racist group . . . could deny the educational benefits of ESEA [Elementary and Secondary Education Act] funds to the needy children of this community."[30]

Local parents protested the elimination of the BCSD's compensatory program. In early June 1969, more than two hundred protesters "picketed four junior high graduations where board members were speaking, held rallies, marched on the Board of Education building and held a 'sleep in' on the building's steps."[31] Such protest inspired and reflected a civil rights awakening among Bakersfield's Black and Brown community. The school board's elimination of the compensatory program was protested by a multiracial alliance of civil rights and community groups. The local NAACP chapter, MAPA, the Association of Mexican American Educators, the Bakersfield parent-teacher association, the American Association of University Women, the League of Women Voters, the Kern County Democratic Central Committee, church groups, and the multiracial KCCU all participated. The school board also drew visible support during its meetings, "all of it from white residents," the *Los Angeles Times* reported.[32] At a school board meeting where the elimination of the compensatory program was discussed, one white teacher summarized comments he regularly heard from white parents on the subject of southeast Bakersfield's Black and Brown residents: "A lot of these people don't pay much taxes. They don't raise their kids as responsible citizens. You talk to a postman and find out how many welfare checks he carried each month and what addresses he takes them to."[33] Such sentiments echoed the way white residents racialized their views of welfare and the use of taxpayer resources in southeast Bakersfield and the city's rural periphery.

By July 1969, reforming racially imbalanced schools was at the forefront of the civil rights struggle in Bakersfield. The legality of so-called de facto segregation in Bakersfield schools was in flux, as civil rights activists working in tandem with state and federal officials exerted political pressure. Hearings on the SAG lawsuit were set to begin the week of July 7, 1969, in Kern County Superior Court. Journalists described the event as a "classic example . . . test case" against de facto segregation, led by California attorney general Thomas Lynch.[34] The hearings were the first of their kind in California. When hearings began, members of the right-wing Kern County White Citizens' Council protested outside the courthouse in downtown Bakersfield, carrying antibusing signs and handing out literature against forced integration. C. J. Thompson, head of the local White Citizens' Council, was recorded as saying, "It's about time our people woke up."[35] After two days of hearings, imported Fresno judge Kenneth Andreen was set to rule on what county counsel Ralph Jordan (representing the BCSD in the case) deemed as having "far-reaching effect[s] on the city school system and perhaps . . . other school districts in California."[36] The Bakersfield case—alongside simultaneous charges filed by the SAG against the San Diego Unified School District—would serve as a test case of the state's definition of de facto segregation and the state's options to legally force integration.[37]

Following the two-day July hearings, Andreen's ruling was expected by the start of the 1969 fall school term. Delays, however, prevented Andreen from reaching a decision by the projected date. The BCSD, meanwhile, deliberated how to handle concurrent charges levied by HEW against the district. The federal government's first issuance of a desegregation warning in California was against the BCSD, that same summer. HEW determined the BCSD to be in violation of the 1964 Civil Rights Act and gave the district forty-five days to reply as to how the district would remedy racially imbalanced schools. Civil rights law granted HEW the legal authority to enforce racial integration in public schools.[38] To add teeth to HEW's warning, $1 million in federal funds were threatened to be withheld from the district. HEW accused the district of "deliberately segregating Negro pupils by gerrymandering attendance areas, strategically locating new schools to prevent integration, restricting Negro children to overcrowded schools while other schools were below capacity, using bussing to reinforce segregation, and following inconsistent pupil assignment policies."[39] HEW further claimed that racial minority teachers were not actively recruited and, when hired, were segregated to majority Black schools. Lastly, services for Spanish-surnamed children proportional to their numbers and needs were often insufficient and inadequate. HEW official Gordon Rubin told reporters that Bakersfield had been investigated by HEW and that no specific timetable was given to the district to implement a desegregation plan. Rather, good-faith progress was expected, and, as a last resort, HEW would eliminate federal funding if non-compliance continued.[40]

In October 1969, Judge Andreen issued a five-page memorandum of intended decision on the SAG case. Andreen concluded, "the state may have a case under California law, [but] if so it has not proved it yet."[41] By February 1970, his decision was final. Despite Andreen's dismissal of the complaints, BCSD board president Bill Curran was not satisfied. Curran issued a cautionary warning to what he saw as judicial encroachment on local schools. As Judge Andreen had indicated possible future legal action against de facto racial segregation in public schools, Curran declared, "I should hope not. The course [of legal rulings] should refrain from blazing pathways when such matters lie in the legislative province of government. I firmly believe that the responsibilities and the authority of Congress and the Legislature should be carefully guarded from encroachment by the judiciary."[42]

Curran's fellow school board member Marguerite Shaw, wife of NAACP and KCCU activist Art Shaw, took aim at Curran's remarks. She rebutted that the school board needed to move in a positive direction and begin forcing integration in southeast Bakersfield schools.[43] Her nephew Joe Hopkins, who attended McKinley Elementary, would years later reflect on his own experience in Bakersfield city schools. "My childhood was filled with violence and being called 'n——r' by white classmates in public school (McKinley). . . . Though they bullied me, I overcame."[44] Shaw's election to the local school board during the spring of 1969 resulted from an intensive grassroots campaign to elect new thinking to the school board. Reflecting on the significance of her seat, Shaw remarked, "the most important thing about the election was the participation of the people who made it possible. There were many people active who were not ordinarily involved. The number was surprisingly large (more than 200 financial contributions alone and about 150 active campaign workers). It was less a personal victory for me than a victory for them. . . . My supporters came in all sizes, shapes and colors. Negro, white, Mexican American, Republican and Democrat, liberal, moderate and conservative."[45] Shaw's election to the school board symbolized the hopes of racial liberals and local activist groups to enact positive change in Bakersfield's burgeoning civil rights movement.

Shortly after Shaw's public admonishing of Curran, the remaining three school board members issued a joint statement supporting Curran's position. Shaw refused to sign the statement, demonstrating the division in the school board over extending desegregation plans to racially imbalanced schools.[46] Despite Curran and the school board's general recalcitrance toward racial integration, the local NAACP pressed on. Harold Tomlin, education committee chair of the Bakersfield NAACP, expressed optimism. Andreen's "decision has not changed one iota of our determination to bring about a better racial balance in the schools, to upgrade the quality of education our children receive. We will push forward and institute another suit . . . and try to change the attitude of the board that the neighborhood school system is the best for all children," he remarked.[47] Tomlin had previously testified against and protested the BCSD, and his actions were used by the SAG to show that the BCSD had been pressured by community leaders and parents to take steps to alleviate racially imbalanced schools. Tomlin testified that school officials responded to his requests by affirming that "there was nothing in the rules that would command [the district] to [racially integrate] . . . [and that the district] believed in the neighborhood [school] concept and . . . no law or anything . . . would compel them to . . . end . . . that."[48] The SAG office appealed its case against the BCSD but, in April 1972, withdrew its case. This was because a law went into effect the previous month requiring districts with racial and ethnic imbalances to submit desegregation plans to the California Department of Education for compliance review.[49]

Despite Andreen's ruling in the SAG suit, local civil rights leaders had faith in HEW investigations, believing that the federal agency would ultimately force the district to desegregate. In January 1969, the Office for Civil Rights (OCR) for region 9 initiated an on-site compliance review of the BCSD. The goal of the review was to determine the district's compliance with Title VI of the 1964 Civil Rights Act. The OCR investigation was part of HEW's official inquiry into "specific findings of non-compliance with regard to the operation of racially imbalanced schools, the assignment of faculties to schools within the district, the denial of services to Spanish-speaking pupils, and the availability of special services to minority pupils."[50] After an initial investigation, OCR officials alerted the BCSD of their findings of noncompliance, yet the district ignored these findings. Data gathered by the OCR included racial statistics within BCSD schools. The OCR reported that the BCSD had a total enrollment of 22,072 students across its twenty-eight elementary schools and eight junior high schools (as of the time the report was completed). Of the enrolled students, 58 percent were Anglo, 15 percent Black, and 24 percent Spanish-surnamed.[51] The OCR delved into some schools, including the predominantly Mexican American Mount Vernon Elementary, in more depth. The OCR found of Mount Vernon's third grade population, for example, that "60% of all Spanish surnamed students were noted by classroom teachers as having Spanish as the primary home language."[52] Further data indicated that Mount Vernon enrolled 907 Spanish-surnamed students of a total population of 1,128; thus, Spanish-surnamed students accounted for 80 percent of the total school population. The OCR also found that Mexican American enrollment across the district increased by 41 percent between 1963 and 1969, or from 3,943 to 5,606 students.

Summarizing their conclusions, OCR officials reasoned that an educational performance gap existed between Anglo, Black, and Spanish-surnamed students and increased "significantly as . . . students progressed through the educational system." The assignment of curriculum within BCSD schools was "highly correlatable with race and ethnicity."[53] With regard to Chicana/o students, the OCR highlighted that "the district although receiving federal monies for Title VII and Title I programs for Spanish speaking children ha[d] not expanded those programs to serve the numbers of children identified . . . as Spanish speaking and in need of such services."[54] Regarding bilingual education, the OCR determined that "the district employ[ed only] one Spanish surnamed teacher in the Title VII program and no Spanish surnamed teachers in the district bilingual education and Title I language development programs. [Furthermore,] only 18 Spanish surnamed teachers . . . [were] employed by the district which enroll[ed] over 4300 Spanish surnamed children at the elementary level." "Black and Spanish surnamed students . . . [were] discriminatorily over-included in classes for the . . . mentally retarded [so-called educable mentally retarded, EMR] . . . [and were] located in predominantly minority schools," the OCR concluded.[55]

As HEW's investigation into the BCSD dragged into the 1970s, the NAACP-WC looked for additional ways to challenge institutional discrimination in public education. The reality of unequal schools and outcomes mobilized civil rights activists, despite the slowness of government bureaucracy. In August 1971, a KCCU newsletter reported that "Kern County is the last of the counties left which had not yet voted on unification." Proposed plans for district unification to enact desegregation included dividing greater Bakersfield into three districts: north, central, and south. Civil rights groups opposed such a plan, given that among the three districts, the assessed valuation of money spent per pupil would vary from $16,000 in the northern (white) district to $5,600 and $8,600 in the central and southern districts, respectively (these having a majority of the city's Black and Brown population). Civil rights groups proposed instead creating a "single district plan for the county" that would promote strict equalization in terms of monies spent and ethnic distribution.[56]

In January 1973, the Bakersfield NAACP chapter contacted NAACP regional offices regarding school unification in greater Bakersfield's outlying districts. Regional NAACP-WC officer Virna Canson wrote to her Bakersfield colleagues, highlighting an important legal issue regarding this question. The battle over unification represented a new front in the fight with school officials in Kern County, since many smaller outlying districts were also segregated. Civil rights activists argued that unification would help create a more equitable tax base to fund local schools and uniform desegregation plans. Referencing the actions of the Kern County Committee on School District Organization, Canson observed, "Kern repeatedly defies the law. I see where this stalling is more and more eroding any strong basis on which we can fight back. . . . This is a hot, hot issue. . . . How has Kern County gotten by without holding a unification election? What kind of conspiracy exists between the State of California and Kern County?"[57] Canson's perceived conspiracy among Kern County educators and government officials highlights the scale of resistance mounted by local school officials toward civil rights reform. Canson's comments also show a continued hope of the NAACP-WC in ongoing investigations into the BCSD as a new front in civil rights struggles to desegregate California public schools.[58]

DESEGREGATION IN BLACK AND BROWN

As the HEW 1972 compliance review documented, racial discrimination in the BCSD concerned not only African Americans, but Mexican Americans as well. At about this same time, therefore, MALDEF activists were corresponding with Bakersfield Mexican American civil rights leaders to discuss the merits of a lawsuit against the BCSD. MALDEF was specifically interested in potential violations of the ESEA Title I criteria, used to allocate federal funding to programs targeting children from low-income families. This legal approach was innovative. The SAG suit and HEW's concurrent investigation both argued that the BCSD was in violation of Title VI requirements of the 1964 Civil Rights Act. Gaining legal ground against the BCSD proved tenuous, however, in light of Judge Andreen's dismissal of the SAG suit in October 1969. MALDEF's Title I criteria emphasis, therefore, offered a potentially new avenue for civil rights reform against racial discrimination in Bakersfield's public schools.

MALDEF attorneys focused on the lack of resources for Spanish-speaking students. Its officials argued that Mexican Americans were the largest disadvantaged minority group in the American Southwest and suffered the greatest in educational achievement, due primarily to inadequate resources.[59] Such neglect, MALDEF reasoned, was caused in part by "the criteria for selecting target schools for participation under ESEA [Title] I that used factors which tend[ed] to exclude Mexican-American children from participation. . . . In Bakersfield, the school district used AFDC [Aid to Families with Dependent Children] criteria exclusively rather than AFDC plus other factors which would take into account the language problems of a substantial number of poor children."[60] Nearly 20 percent of all students (not just Mexican American) in the BCSD during the 1968–1969 school year came from homes receiving AFDC.[61] Racial demographics would change dramatically within the district in the early 1970s. White flight affected the BCSD as white people began settling in the suburban developments of southwest Bakersfield, leaving a trail of depleted neighborhood tax bases and segregated schools behind. The BCSD, in turn, incorporated more Spanish-surnamed students as Mexican immigration and settlement increased in central and southeast Bakersfield. MALDEF, in coordination with local Chicana/o activists, took an interest in making civil rights a focus within this changing urban racial landscape.

To give direction to a potential Bakersfield case, MALDEF officer Lupe Martinez informed Bakersfield civil rights leaders of successful Title I models used in Los Angeles to increase federal resources for Spanish-speaking students. Martinez advised Bakersfield activists to consider certain questions: "What school districts in California use[d] language as a factor in determining Title I eligibility? How predominately are Mexican American schools ranked using this criteria? . . . The LA city schools include[d] language as a criteria and . . . balanced monies for black and Mexican American children so far as Title I [was concerned]," Martinez reported.[62] Bakersfield civil rights leaders thereafter began advocating new criteria for the distribution of federal resources for Spanish-speaking children. Jess Alcala and Josie Jamie of the Concerned Parents Committee (CPC) criticized the BCSD's policy of allocating Title I monies based on the percentage of students from families receiving AFDC. Alcala pleaded that although many Mexican American families qualified for welfare, a low percentage of qualified applicant parents living in the district received benefits. The BCSD's allocation of Title I federal resources thus discriminated against Spanish-speaking students not on welfare, even though they qualified for benefit services, Alcala concluded.[63]

Beyond Title I, Alcala and other CPC members protested the inferior conditions at the predominantly Mexican American Mount Vernon Elementary School. The CPC lambasted the school board because regular heating and lighting services were not connected in the portable classrooms at the start of the fall 1969 term until school had been in session for four weeks. Such negligence from the school board, Alcala noted scornfully, continued to "the highest degree . . . discrimination against Mexican American children. . . . When will you stop discriminating against Mexican American children; when will you stop discriminating against all minority groups—both Mexican and Negro?"[64] The CPC orchestrated a letter-writing campaign by parents to protest inferior conditions in minority schools. CPC members wrote to MALDEF regional director Lupe Anguiano in the fall of 1969 to obtain her assistance in expanding Title I services at Mount Vernon. Anguiano, a former nun, was a longtime civil rights activist and grassroots organizer who honed her community organizing through volunteer work with the United Farm Workers (UFW) and the grape boycott campaign.[65] Parent Jose Garcia wrote to Anguiano, "porque está el distrito de la escuela discriminando contra México Americano?" (why does this school district discriminate against Mexican Americans?).[66] Parents argued that a preponderance of limited resources and poor conditions in southeast Bakersfield schools warranted greater utilization of Title I monies. Frank Espinoza, a local activist and Employment Development Department employee, noted that Jefferson Elementary School was composed of nearly 75 percent Mexican American children and that working parents had a limited education and suffered underemployment. "Not having the proper percent of families on welfare," Espinoza proclaimed, had unjustly kept Title I funds out of the poverty-stricken Jefferson Elementary School.[67]

While MALDEF maintained close interest in the BCSD through the early 1970s, the organization also supported HEW efforts to charge the district with discrimination. According to MALDEF's 1974 annual report, the organization had been involved in twenty-one cases concerning education litigation from Texas to California in 1973. Cases focused on violations of Title VII of the Civil Rights Act, use of dual-tracking systems, violations of the Fourteenth Amendment, failure to provide bilingual or bicultural instruction, and other forms of legal discrimination. Only one of the twenty-one cases, however, concerned Kern County: *Irene Peña v. Board of Trustees of the Delano Union School District*.[68] The *Peña* lawsuit challenged placement and hiring practices in the Delano school district, as well as school racial segregation.

Both MALDEF and California Rural Legal Assistance argued that Delano's "six elementary schools, divided by Highway 99, included three schools on the west side in which Mexican Americans and nonwhites comprised 99 percent, 98 percent, and 97 percent of the student populations respectively, while those on the east side were overwhelmingly white," further noting that the school board "refused to redraw attendance zones on an east/west axis that would integrate the town's schools."[69] While *Peña* was briefed and argued, the case was ultimately delayed until the California Supreme Court ruled on the constitutionality of Proposition 21 in January 1975 (Assignment of Students to Schools Initiative).[70] The language of Proposition 21 limited pupil placement remedies based on race, so that "no public school student shall, because of his race, creed, or color, be assigned to or be required to attend a particular school." The proposition also repealed the section of the California Education Code "establishing policy that racial and ethnic balance in pupil enrollment in public schools shall be prevented or eliminated."[71] The latter provision of California's Education Code had motivated Bakersfield's civil rights leaders to challenge school discrimination in the first place. Indeed, as Daniel Martinez HoSang notes, "Proposition 21 did have a chilling effect on many local school desegregation efforts."[72] The legal precariousness of school desegregation efforts encouraged MALDEF to limit its approach in spearheading civil rights reform in greater Bakersfield. MALDEF's limited funding operation and commitment to numerous legal cases counterbalanced the organization's support of HEW efforts to promote school desegregation and bicultural awareness in Bakersfield. Relying on HEW did not mean, however, that MALDEF neglected civil rights in Bakersfield. MALDEF was intimately involved with other civil rights reforms in Bakersfield throughout the 1970s, including the fair media movement.

In 1974, MALDEF involved itself in another issue concerning racial discrimination toward Mexican American children in the BCSD. The suicide of thirteen-year-old Barbara Renee Arvizu in May 1973 prompted MALDEF attorneys to reevaluate their organization's legal interest in institutional racism and discrimination against Mexican Americans in the district. MALDEF officials and Chicana/o parents in Bakersfield were convinced that racial discrimination played a role in the death of the young girl. MALDEF records show that Barbara Arvizu was suspended from school on four separate occasions between February and May 1973, her last suspension coming only days before her suicide. While her death proved tragic for the Arvizu family, MALDEF's investigation revealed how patterns of racial discrimination in the school contributed to Barbara's death.

MALDEF attorneys gathered a variety of startling statistics regarding racial inequities at Compton Junior High School. MALDEF attorneys reported that the ethnic composition of the school during the 1972–1973 year was 26 percent Chicana/o and 62 percent Anglo. Conversely, in summer 1969, when the SAG filed its petition for writ against the BCSD, legal documents record that Compton was 97 percent white. Within those few short years, a limited district busing plan had transferred greater numbers of Mexican American and African American students—including Barbara Arvizu—to Compton.[73] MALDEF reports further revealed that during the 1972–1973 school year, "the people suspended were overwhelmingly minority with the vast majority being Chicano: 19 blacks, 49 Chicanos, and 20 Anglos. Chicanos were 56% of the students suspended and blacks 22%[,] for a total of 78% minority suspensions as against a minority enrollment of 36%. Suspensions of both Chicanos and blacks were [also] longer [in time] than those of Anglos."[74] And while Compton "enrolled only 2% of the Chicanos in the district the year of Barbara's death, [it] . . . accounted for 26% of all suspensions of Chicanos . . . that year." Lastly, MALDEF learned of the tense relationship between Compton principal Donald Pruett and the minority students at his school. "Mr. Pruett [200-plus pounds] put an 80-pound black student through a glass door for a minor infraction, the year of Barbara's death[,] and had similar incidents with Chicanos," MALDEF investigators reported.[75]

After gathering evidence from the Bakersfield Chicana/o community, MALDEF attorneys discussed the potential of their involvement with the Arvizu case. They were interested particularly in the roles Principal Pruett and the school counselor had played in the wrongful death of thirteen-year-old Barbara Arvizu. In the aftermath of Barbara's death, Principal Pruett was transferred to Longfellow Elementary School. MALDEF investigators could not determine, however, whether Pruett's transfer was a consequence of the Chicana/o community's demand for an official investigation into his conduct at Compton Junior High School. In July 1973, just two months after Barbara's death, the *Bakersfield Californian* reported that the BCSD board had voted three to two to transfer thirteen principals, "during a stormy board meeting . . . attended by more than 450 residents. . . . Most controversial were [the] transfers of Pruett, Compton Junior High principal," and two others.[76] Pruett's transfer to Longfellow was both criticized and supported by many in attendance, but no testimony against Pruett was more significant than that of Steve Arvizu, uncle of the deceased and at the time a doctoral student in anthropology at Stanford University.[77] "I don't see the relationship between stern discipline and a successful education program. . . . Many here share concerns about [the] loss of a principal but some of us here tonight have concerns which run much deeper than education," Arvizu told the school board.[78] Newspapers reported that rumor had it that Assemblyman Ray Gonzales had asked the school district administration to recommend Pruett's transfer, although Gonzales's office officially denied any participation in BCSD personnel decisions.[79] Barbara's parents eventually filed a cause of action against the district in May 1974. Discussing the significance of the Arvizu case, a MALDEF official remarked internally that "the Bakersfield school district is a bastion of conservatism in California. Its location in the center of Kern County has long made it the center of civil rights activity, but for the most part non-judicial. This suit could provide unique relief in a previously untouched legal area for Chicanos. I need not emphasize the dramatic impact of this suicide case."[80]

In their official complaint against the BCSD, filed in Kern County Superior Court, Rene and Esther Arvizu accused district officials of having "for several months intentionally and outrageously harassed, menaced, intimidated, maligned and embarrassed Barbara Arvizu . . . made false accusations about her and imposed unreasonable and unjust punishments upon her. . . . Barbara Arvizu was caused to suffer great humiliation, embarrassment and severe mental pain and suffering."[81] According to Barbara's parents, the young girl was physically pushed by the school counselor, in an incident that was witnessed by nine students and that left Barbara "on all fours to keep from sprawling."[82] In issuing a formal complaint to the school board, prior to submitting their case to the superior court, Barbara's parents questioned "the legal and ethical practices of the Principal and Counselor as evidenced by the behavior and statements [made] toward [their] daughter—threatening her with non-graduation, insinuating she was like a 'bar-lady' [and] being very quick to administer suspensions and document disciplinary actions but being reluctant . . . to facilitate . . . [Barbara's] well-being and success in school."[83]

Barbara's suicide note stated her reason for taking her own life. "I have decided for myself that my time has come. For instance, if I don't pass this year I never will and I know I won't. . . . I am doing this for my weeks suspension and I would rather be dead before my dad gets a hold of me and my mom will just make things worse."[84] Prior to her suicide, in school conferences with Barbara and her parents, school officials had noted that "Barbara was very mature appearing for a junior high school girl. She was physically well-developed. She wore a great deal of make-up rather well applied. . . . Barbara's problems seem[ed] to stem from the fact that she dawdled with her friends during the recess period. She is consistently late to classes, has been involved in fighting, defies adult authority, and generally has a poor attitude."[85] In making recommendations to Barbara's parents, school officials stressed that Barbara needed to arrive at school and individual classes on time, and that "in all other manners she is to conduct herself as a lady."[86]

In April 1974, MALDEF officials interviewed Barbara Arvizu's parents and family. Among the facts gathered included that prior to eighth grade, Barbara had never been suspended or failed academically. Her parents reported that Principal Pruett had told Barbara before her death that "she was to fail . . . and that the school counselor told Barbara that she looked like a 'bar lady' and had thrown Barbara to the ground in front of 8 witnesses," although the counselor denied the claim.[87] MALDEF officials noted that Compton Junior High had been predominantly Anglo throughout most of Pruett's tenure as principal, beginning in the early 1960s, and that rumor had it that "Pruett picked on bussed kids because he resented minority kids in [the] Anglo school." MALDEF also noted that "[Pruett was a] right-wing darling [and] does not hide [the] fact that he is prejudiced."[88]

THE BCSD VERSUS HEW

In June 1975, amid the tumult of federal and civil rights investigations into the BCSD, HEW denied federal aid funds not yet approved to the BCSD in the amount of $200,000.[89] The funds were part of a grant for a bilingual teacher training program between the BCSD and California State College, Bakersfield. Under federal law, HEW could not provide funding for any new program when administrative proceedings were scheduled (HEW hearings began in Bakersfield the following week).[90] Bakersfield civil rights leaders thereafter issued a joint statement condemning rumors that the federal government had eliminated school funding. In an open letter to Bakersfield school board president Mel Magnus, local civil rights leaders declared, "you have the ethical responsibility to correct erroneous allegations that HEW has 'cut-off' or 'terminated' federal funds. The vast majority of federal financial assistance to BCSD continues unabated. . . . Under law, HEW was . . . prohibited from increasing the level of federal funding."[91] The BCSD in response refuted HEW's rationale for withholding funding. The school district saw the action as unfair, arguing that the language used by HEW in official inquiries was too vague. The BCSD contended that the district could not adequately provide information to counter allegations made by HEW, nor implement any procedural reforms consistent with federal requests. According to this argument, HEW's nonspecific requests for racial and ethnic statistics actually prevented the district's compliance.

The controversy over whether HEW had technically denied federal funds to the district marked a turning point in the relationship between the BCSD and HEW. HEW first contacted the district in 1969 and maintained correspondence with district officials through 1975, the year HEW administrative hearings began. District officials characterized HEW correspondence as "replete with errors and false charges."[92] In the view of BCSD officials, "no person in the District, ha[d], on the grounds of race, color, or national origin, been excluded from participation in, been denied the benefits of, or been otherwise subject to discrimination under any program in the District."[93] School officials accused HEW of desperately trying to "fasten upon the District charges of noncompliance with law," rather than practice legal fairness, given the organization's federal authority to investigate and amend racially imbalanced schools.[94]

District officials also accused HEW of using racist terminology. The word *Chicano* was a highly politicized term in California's Central Valley in the early 1970s. Federal officials used the term when referencing Spanish-surnamed students within the BCSD. The district "demand[ed] that term [Chicano] be stricken from every place it appears in the [HEW] Notice," on the grounds that "among persons within and without the employ[ment] of the District and conversant with the Spanish language . . . the term 'Chicano' . . . means and connotes 'pig' or 'swine' . . . and [such a term] never is applied to a human being except in a derogatory sense."[95] The district's antipathy to the term echoed the rhetorical tactics generally utilized by the grassroots right and backlash against the Chicana/o movement. School officials reversed charges of discrimination against the BCSD, arguing instead that HEW officials were using discriminatory language and thereby insulting Mexican Americans and others who found the term *Chicano* offensive. HEW's intrusive legal proceedings abused federal investigatory powers, or so BCSD officials reasoned.

By 1974, five years had elapsed since the first legal charges of racial discrimination had been brought against the BCSD, and the remedy period had long since passed for the BCSD to comply with Title VI. Even so, HEW claimed that the BCSD was noncompliant in several areas, including faculty recruitment and assignment, student assignment, comparability of services, and denial of services. HEW argued that African American and Mexican American students were discriminated against and that racial minority teachers did not experience equal levels of recruitment, placement, and promotion as white teachers. After five long years of legal correspondence between HEW and the BCSD, government officials thus maintained that there was "no basis . . . found by OCR for withdrawing the charges."[96]

In preparation for administrative hearings, HEW officials stated what sections of the Civil Rights Act the BCSD had violated. Lloyd Henderson, director of the OCR Elementary and Secondary Education Division, noted that section B of Title VI required that school systems "take affirmative action to eliminate officially caused or sanctioned segregation and . . . ensure that nondiscriminatory equal educational opportunity [existed] for all pupils."[97] Notably, the district had never admitted to sanctioning segregation of its students. The BCSD, while acknowledging its racially imbalanced schools, argued that the racial imbalance was caused by city housing patterns, not district policy. Henderson found that the district provided "inferior educational services" to minority children, especially Spanish-speaking children, who were subsequently at a major disadvantage due to inferior and inadequate curriculum. BCSD officials maintained racially identifiable special education classes, HEW noted, in addition to schools that were racially identifiable by means of zone changes and grade manipulation. Of the two thousand students in the 1974–1975 academic year whose dominant language was not English, only 25 percent received bilingual education or intensive English training. Such negligence, federal officials reasoned, constituted discrimination in light of the then-recent Supreme Court decision in *Lau v. Nichols*. In this January 1974 ruling, the court held that HEW could require school districts, under the threat of withholding federal funding, to take affirmative steps to "insure [*sic*] that non-English speaking national origin minority students . . . [were] provided truly equal access to the full benefits of the educational process."[98] HEW also alleged that the BCSD repeatedly altered school boundary zones and manipulated school capacities to keep schools racially identifiable. "Data shows that white children living in the area of Fremont [Elementary School] were bussed through the Mayflower [district] to Mount Vernon, while blacks living in the Mayflower area went to Lincoln and Owens," Henderson reiterated to Bakersfield superintendent Walter Hauss. "The district consistently adopted a course of action which increased or failed to alleviate the racially identifiable Lincoln and Owens [schools]. Such a pattern constituted de jure segregation," Henderson concluded.[99] OCR director Peter Holmes wrote to Hauss, "all efforts to persuade officials of your district to submit an acceptable compliance plan have failed. . . . I must conclude that compliance by your district cannot be secured by voluntary means."[100]

In response to HEW's threats, Hauss highlighted the district's extraordinary efforts to abide by the law. The superintendent reaffirmed that the BCSD was "the first district in Kern County to institute a bilingual program." While Hauss admitted that there were "racially identifiable special education classes, the district ha[d] taken steps to eliminate" such classes and made "positive steps to reduce the percentage of blacks [in such classes] as rapidly as possible."[101] The serious allegation of de jure segregation within the BCSD commanded strong attention from Hauss: "[we are] aware that a number of schools are racially imbalanced. . . . [Yet] the Bakersfield City School District can find no formal record in Board Minutes nor in administrative regulations which evidences a pattern of boundary zone changes, site selections, and capacity manipulation for the purpose of maintaining racially identifiable schools."[102] Hauss reminded HEW that Fresno County judge Kenneth Andreen had found that "the racial imbalance in the schools of the Bakersfield City School District . . . [was] caused by residential patterns and not by any gerrymandering of school attendance boundaries." Andreen's ruling affirmed what the superintendent argued, namely, that "de facto racial balance in . . . the district innocently caused by residential patterns does not constitute [nor] . . . compromise deprivation of the equal protection of the laws guaranteed by the Fourteenth Amendment."[103] No court, Hauss emphasized, had issued a writ of mandamus, or direct command, to desegregate.

Despite competing statements issued by Judge Andreen, HEW, and school officials, the suggestion of innocence on the part of BCSD officials obscured the role that racial segregation had long played in creating racially restrictive residential areas in Bakersfield. Settlement patterns in Bakersfield were far from the result of freedom of choice. Racial housing covenants, a segregated labor force, and gerrymandered school attendance zones had maintained racial segregation in southeast Bakersfield schools since the early twentieth century. As Thomas J. Sugrue and others have shown, the false binary of de jure and de facto segregation obscures more than clarifies how historical state-sanctioned racial segregation in American cities outside of the Jim Crow South limited educational opportunities and shaped economic outcomes for racial minority children.[104]

In late July 1975, HEW launched formal administrative hearings against the BCSD, first in Bakersfield and later in San Francisco. But the process had dragged on for too long. Within the context of government action against segregation in Bakersfield, the NAACP launched a class-action lawsuit against HEW. Bakersfield civil rights leaders participated in the process, helping gather signatures for the suit locally. Bakersfield NAACP president Ralph Anthony contacted NAACP-WC regional officer Virna Canson, forwarding her a taped copy of a BCSD board meeting from July of that year. He noted that among the subjects discussed at the meeting were developments at Emerson Junior High, one of the schools that had experienced "tremendous integrational changes within the past five (5) years from [a] predominantly white [school] to predominantly black and brown [school]."[105] Anthony informed Canson that African American educator Fred Haynes had become principal of Emerson and had received NAACP support when he first became principal of Lincoln Junior High School in 1969. The local NAACP believed that HEW needed to be pressured to force integration, hence its participation in the class-action suit. "HEW has been dragging its feet," NAACP activist Harold Tomlin told reporters covering the class-action suit. "I feel HEW, due to various political reasons, simply has been reluctant to force desegregation."[106] As the HEW administrative hearings began in late July, the hearings became local political theater, pitting integrationists against anti–civil rights conservatives. The latter were more dominant locally and caricatured HEW as an invasive and abusive taxpayer-funded organization in need of prompt dismantling.

FROM BAKERSFIELD TO SAN FRANCISCO

While the HEW administrative hearings did not reveal a substantial amount of new information in the case against the BCSD (beyond what had already been alleged and documented by civil rights groups), the politicization of the HEW hearings had repercussions locally. Republican congressman William Ketchum utilized the hearings to energize his base. Ketchum especially opposed the moving of the hearings to San Francisco in early 1976. According to a congressional press release in March 1976, Ketchum declared, "in no way may the interests of justice, economy, good education, and protection of all citizens' civil rights be served by moving these [HEW] proceedings. . . . Such an irresponsible action can only serve the selfish motives of bureaucratic minions within HEW, while at the same time effectively foreclosing any possibility for Bakersfield city school officials to complete their defense against the vast array of allegations heaped upon them by HEW's lawyers."[107] Ketchum's statement echoed his Republican constituents' criticism of allegations made against the school district. Right-wing supporters inundated Ketchum's office, urging him to support keeping the HEW hearings in Bakersfield. "Bakersfield is where the alleged problem is, Bakersfield is where the people most directly concerned are, and Bakersfield is where these proceedings should be conducted until their conclusion," Ketchum declared.[108] Ketchum was especially critical of HEW attorneys, whom he characterized as using "sledgehammer" tactics against district school officials.

Congressman Ketchum's constituents were up in arms over the presence of HEW in Bakersfield. His form letters to constituents expressed disappointment: "Never in my life have I had a conversation quite like the hour-and-a-half long one which took place in my office with HEW's General

Counsel! Over and over, I made one simple point very clear: the rights of the people of Bakersfield would be denied if such a move took place."[109] Other community members joined the fight. The 930-member Kern Division of the Retired Teachers Association (RTA), specifically its board of directors, wrote to the HEW secretary in protest. The RTA opposed the move on the grounds that relocation posed economic hardship for defense witnesses who had yet to testify, and that genuine community interest and pride would be lost if the proceedings moved to San Francisco.[110]

The decision to move the hearings was debated among BCSD legal representatives, HEW officials, and the presiding administrative law judge, John Ohanian. According to BCSD officials, HEW staff perpetuated the idea of moving the hearings out of Bakersfield. Ohanian stated publicly that the benefits of moving the hearings to San Francisco included "limiting the hearing to more relevant and more material testimony by the district."[111] Dennis Reid, a BCSD legal representative who handled the district's objection to the move, delayed and frustrated the hearings by "putting on witnesses having little or no relevance to the matter," Ohanian commented publicly.[112] While the BCSD lamented government largesse and wasted taxpayer dollars accrued by the lengthy hearings, its legal representatives prolonged the proceedings and, in turn, created an opportunity for grassroots mobilization on the political right to protest civil rights reform.

Correspondence between county counsel Ralph Jordan (who led the BCSD defense effort) and Congressman Ketchum charts the legal efforts of Bakersfield conservatives to stymie civil rights reform. In early April 1976, Jordan wrote to Ketchum, encouraging the congressman to enact legislation to weaken HEW's investigative powers. Jordan suggested that "hearing officers (administrative law judges) must be truly independent.... Our experience indicated that it is extremely unfortunate and ill-advised to have presiding officers in such cases whose background is one affiliated with the Federal Government."[113] Judge Ohanian had enacted "bureaucratic tyranny" over Bakersfield citizens, Jordan intimated. The county counsel suggested further that civil rights charges against school districts should require that hearings be conducted in the community where the charges were made. Lastly, the attorney suggested that the cost of defending school districts outside of the school's jurisdiction ought be subsidized by HEW, not local taxpayers.[114] Congressman Ketchum responded to Jordan by affirming that he was already in the "process of drafting legislation to insure [*sic*] the independence of administrative law judges and to require that a locality be reimbursed for expenses incurred when the hearings . . . moved out of the locality."[115] In 1976, Ketchum contacted the Speaker of the House of Representatives, Carl

Albert, to press the Democrat into launching a congressional investigation into the Bakersfield hearings. "The [HEW] hearings have been distorted by continual actions on the part of the hearing judge.... HEW lawyers ... have made a mockery of the words 'fair and impartial.' ... The most outrageous action ... to move the hearings from ... Bakersfield to San Francisco ... can only be construed as a violation of the most severe magnitude of the civil rights of the people of Bakersfield," Ketchum informed the Speaker.[116]

The fight with HEW occurred more broadly within a right-wing agenda for educational reform. Correspondence between Ketchum and his constituents reveals a preference for vocational training and cuts to higher education. "I do agree that way too much emphasis has been put upon 'higher education' so much so that a myth of 'unlimited opportunities' has led to over-enrollment in our institutions of higher learning.... Many people are not suited to college study," Ketchum responded to one constituent.[117] Referring to his fruitless efforts to convince HEW officials to keep the hearings in Bakersfield, Ketchum remarked, "the sum and substance of *those* conversations was about the same as talking to the wind! This experience has jolted me even further into the realization that government is becoming an unresponsive and uncaring monster."[118] One constituent letter to Ketchum encapsulated the sentiment of the average conservative Bakersfieldian—namely, the notion that the entire HEW proceedings were a "cruel hoax ... perpetuated upon the tax-paying citizens of Bakersfield."[119] Some Ketchum constituents suggested radical solutions. Writing under the pseudonym "Disgusted citizen," Arthur Doland opined, "what would happen if everybody in Bakersfield refused to pay any more income tax and would pay it directly to our local agencies rather than the people in Washington whom [*sic*] do not know how to spend it."[120] Claire Hanson, an eighteen-year veteran teacher with the BCSD, expressed exasperation for the federal bureaucracy. "To me, this [HEW hearing] is an example of the need to put control back into the hands of local citizens and eliminate federal controls of matters which can and should be handled locally!"[121]

Grant Jensen, assistant superintendent for the Kern High School District, was especially disturbed by what he saw as intrusive requests by HEW regarding language practices. The founding principal of Bakersfield's South High School (the "Rebels") in 1957, Jensen professed administrative prerogatives that reflected larger views of Bakersfield's white population toward civil rights reform.[122] HEW requested that the district submit a quantitative report noting the number of students whose first acquired language was other than English, the language most spoken by any student other than English, and the language most spoken in the home other than English.[123]

To illustrate the absurdity of such a request, Jensen responded on behalf of BCSD officials that "our school personnel have no way of knowing whether the student's primary language under this definition is Italian, Greek, Danish, German, Spanish, or what have you; nor do we feel it is any of our business. . . . This might well be called an invasion of the privacy of youngsters and families."[124] Jensen's rhetorical response was a straw man, since local school districts, in their own acknowledgment, were experiencing not a massive influx of Scandinavian or European immigrants but rather immigration from Mexico and Spanish-surnamed students. HEW's request for such information was part of a larger trend across San Joaquin Valley school districts. Eighteen school districts throughout the valley were targeted for investigation by HEW regarding student language statistics, including: Clovis Unified, Corcoran Joint Unified, Delano Joint Union Elementary, Delano Joint Union High, Dinuba Elementary, Fowler Unified, Kern High School, Kings Canyon Unified of Reedley, Madera Unified, Mendota Unified, Mendota Union Elementary, Merced City Elementary, Merced Union High, Parlier Unified, Porterville Elementary, Sanger Unified, Tulare City Elementary, and Visalia Unified.[125] These districts collectively constituted the agrarian heartland of California's interior region, where the labor force consisted heavily of Mexican immigrant workers and their families.

At the conclusion of the HEW hearings in 1978, Judge Ohanian issued a 220-page decision chronicling the results of HEW's 111-day investigation into the BCSD, the longest in the agency's history. Ohanian determined that the district was guilty of creating a "de jure dual school system by intentionally segregating black and Hispanic students from white students."[126] Ohanian noted several key areas of racial discrimination, including:

a) gerrymandering school attendance zones to comport with racially restrictive land covenants in subdivision areas
b) using temporary facilities at majority white schools rather than transferring white students to minority schools
c) assigning students to schools outside their geographic attendance zones solely on the basis of race
d) establishing a vocational school solely for minority students in grades K–12
e) selecting school location sites with the intent to segregate students
f) busing students past their nearest school to more distant segregated schools
g) failing to implement a 1972 desegregation plan sponsored by the California Department of Education[127]

Ohanian surmised that the district had also "violated Title VI by failing to assess properly the . . . English language ability of its students . . . discriminat[ing] against black and Hispanic children by using racially and culturally biased placement criteria . . . [and] failing to evaluate properly such students prior to placement in EMR classes."[128]

Following Ohanian's ruling, the desegregation of the BCSD seemed imminent. Enforcing desegregation in Bakersfield schools, however, proved difficult for federal officials. Local resistance to busing and forced integration mirrored the nationwide backlash against forced busing in the late 1970s. Such backlash reaped political action at the national level. The passage of the Eagleton-Biden Amendment in 1978 prohibited the OCR "from requiring desegregation plans which utilize[d] additional transportation of students."[129] To avoid busing, on March 27, 1979, the BCSD board voted to close Lincoln Junior High School, after over a decade of civil rights leaders calling for the dispersal of the heavily concentrated African American student body into other area schools to promote racial integration. As a result, the attendance areas for Curran, Compton, and Chipman Junior High Schools were modified to include the Lincoln attendance area.[130]

Local officials and parents, however, proved resilient in resisting integration efforts. In 1979 desegregation efforts expanded to include the Kern High School District. At the time, the district was in the process of formulating a master plan for desegregation, based on guidelines from the California State Board of Education. Carey Scott, a local attorney and NAACP officer, was appointed to the master plan committee and contacted NAACP-WC regional officer Virna Canson for advice about how to proceed with a problem that had arisen within the committee. Scott was alarmed that the district's desegregation plan permitted North High School in Oildale to keep its 98 percent white student body. Oildale was historically exclusively white, Scott informed Canson, and had been known locally as a racist enclave. Scott wanted to go on record as opposing any master plan that permitted the existence of a white racially isolated school.[131] For Scott, a desegregation plan for North High School would mean more than integrating just one school. North High and Oildale's school district had been a bastion of white racial conservatism and regressive racial thinking for most of the twentieth century. Integrating North High through a desegregation plan would be a symbolic victory. Furthermore, not integrating North High would mark a victory for racial conservatives and minimal change in the status quo of race relations in Bakersfield.

The BCSD petitioned for a review of Ohanian's ruling while implementing piecemeal changes to alleviate gross manifestations of racially imbalanced schools. "The decision of the ALJ [administrative law judge] was subsequently affirmed by the Civil Rights Reviewing Authority and discretionary Secretarial review was denied, making final the ALJ's decision," notes a legal complaint filed against the BCSD by assistant attorney general William Bradford Reynolds.¹³² The BCSD's petition for review of Ohanian's decision was ruled moot by an agreement between the Department of Education and the BCSD in January 1981. The 1981 compliance agreement was designed to leverage "significant changes . . . within the District . . . includ[ing] an entirely new Governing board being elected, a new superintendent being hired, changes in other administrators, a change in legal counsel, . . . and the manner of delivery of the District's programs in each of the . . . areas cited by the Administrative law Judge as being in noncompliance." Furthermore, the district made a commitment to "reduce racial isolation in its schools by adjusting school attendance boundary lines so as to allow children to attend the school that is located the closest walking distance from the children's place of residence, if such adjustment will have the effect of reducing racial isolation."¹³³ The compliance agreement, however, did not state specifically whether the district's plan was in compliance with the law; rather, it helped grease the wheels for a forthcoming settlement, which followed shortly after Reynolds filed complaint against the district in 1983.

By 1982, federal proceedings against the BCSD had been ongoing for thirteen years. And while the district had taken steps to remedy racial imbalance in its schools, racially isolated schools remained. In July of that year, the Department of Education, having exhausted its agency's legal redress following Ohanian's ruling, referred the case to the DOJ for enforcement. Upon review of the Bakersfield case, DOJ officials determined that "judicial action [should] be initiated but . . . not limited to consideration of mandatory transportation remedies."¹³⁴ White flight from city schools to southwest Bakersfield, coupled with Mexican immigration and settlement in the southeast parts of the city, had altered the racial composition of the district. Between 1967 and 1979, the BCSD lost nearly six thousand of its white students, who dropped from 63 to 50 percent of the district's total population. At the same time, enrollments grew "in several of the predominately white elementary districts just beyond Bakersfield City School District boundaries, including Panama, Fruitvale, Rosedale, and Norris districts."¹³⁵ DOJ officials remarked that "the past fourteen years has [*sic*] seen a decline in the total [BCSD] student population and an increase in the percentage of minorities, especially Hispanics, within the [school] system. . . . It is estimated that 8% to 11% of the total student population transfers in or out of the District schools each month."¹³⁶ DOJ attorneys noted that Judge Ohanian had found that "most of the District's segregative conduct had occurred prior to *Brown* but concluded that the segregative effects of that conduct, along with more recent acts and omissions, resulted in the segregative conditions extant at the time of the [HEW] hearing."[137]

Compliance agreements between the BCSD and federal agencies responded to plans drawn up locally in Bakersfield. Following Ohanian's initial decision, the BCSD formed an integration steering council (ISC) to formulate plans for racial integration. The district's motivation was in part to comply with the California Supreme Court's 1976 ruling in *Crawford v. Board of Education of the City of Los Angeles*. This decision "imposed a duty on school districts to eliminate school segregation regardless of cause." While the ISC formulated desegregation plans to recommend to the district, BCSD officials did not wait to implement changes. In March 1979, the district "started to close schools and modify attendance areas, including taking action which effectively desegregated the District's junior high schools."[138] The district implemented "mini-magnet" programs during the 1981–1982 school year that "offered to all 4–6 grade students . . . an elective enrichment program not lasting more than 15 school days of approximately two hours per day." The intent of the mini-magnet programs, district officials noted, was to "break down the resistance of parents and children to attending schools in unfamiliar neighborhoods."[139] With these mini-magnet programs, in conjunction with efforts to enhance compensatory programs and reading improvement in minority schools, district attorneys declared that "no further action" by the DOJ was warranted, despite the Department of Education's referral to the DOJ for enforcement. BCSD attorneys maintained that the "District had never engaged in deliberately segregative practices."[140] In their review of the case, DOJ officials observed that "since the initiation of the administrative proceedings against the Bakersfield City School District in 1968, the once prevalent segregated conditions have diminished and the segregative practices have apparently ceased. . . . Demographically, the District and its schools are quite different from what they were in 1975 when the administrative hearing commenced[,] or 1978 [when Ohanian issued his ruling]." Nevertheless, DOJ officials concluded that "the District student assignment violations remained inadequately remedied."[141]

The DOJ noted further that the BCSD "mini-magnet" programs utilized transportation on a short-term basis to transfer students to and from the magnet schools throughout portions of the school week.[142] By 1984, the Hispanic population of the district had grown to 7,167 (38 percent of the district total), while the white population had fallen to 8,357 (44 percent). The Black student population held at 2,936 (16 percent).[143] Thus, such action was not precluded by the Eagleton-Biden Amendment's "prohibition against the use of transportation to effect compliance with Title VI."¹⁴⁴ DOJ officials lauded the ISC's vision of a magnet school program that "would involve students attending schools other than neighborhood schools for an entire year to receive instruction in both magnet and basic courses . . . [all the while] continu[ing] to serve as a neighborhood school [rather than] . . . draw[ing] its entire enrollment from throughout the District."¹⁴⁵ In light of the seemingly good-faith steps taken by the BCSD toward racial integration, along with the pressure from parents and civil rights activists to integrate southeast Bakersfield's schools, DOJ officials recommended "fil[ing] suit against the Bakersfield School District but attempt[ing] to resolve [the] matter by consent prior to the filing of suit." Specifically, they called for a consent agreement that "embodie[d] the additional desegregation concepts proposed by the District's Integration Steering Council."¹⁴⁶

In 1984, the historic Bakersfield Consent Decree brought a formal ending to the protracted struggle by civil rights groups to desegregate the BCSD. Of the district's twenty-five elementary schools at this time, four became magnet schools designed to "attract white students to predominately black and Hispanic schools by establishing special programs in science, computer-assisted instruction and the creative and performing arts, as well as special classes for gifted and talented youngsters," the *New York Times* reported.¹⁴⁷ What made Reagan-era officials declare the Bakersfield plan a national "blueprint for desegregation" was that while "previous Administrations . . . supported the use of magnet schools [they] often insisted that such voluntary means of desegregation be accompanied by court-ordered busing."¹⁴⁸

Legal scholars critical of the DOJ's role in prosecuting desegregation cases noted problems with the Bakersfield Consent Decree, particularly with regard to the idea of it being a national blueprint. Randolph D. Moss, commenting on the negative impact of community involvement when the DOJ filed suit as opposed to when community groups and parents did so, noted that "where the Department of Justice is the plaintiff . . . the process of institutional reform is potentially closed to other interested persons; the multipolar nature of public law litigation is transformed into a bipolar process. . . . [Ultimately, this] undermines the effectiveness and integrity of the process of institutional reform through consent decree."¹⁴⁹ Referencing the Bakersfield case specifically, Moss noted that the Bakersfield decree was "exceptionally weak" and had "done little to desegregate the schools of Bakersfield."¹⁵⁰ Another scholar noted that the Bakersfield decree presented "no 'fall-back,' mandatory assignment provisions to take effect in the event [that] no appreciable desegregation occur[ed]."¹⁵¹

While the institutionalization of the magnet program was welcomed by many Bakersfield residents as a positive step toward dealing with racially imbalanced schools, the magnet programs' real significance rested in the triumph of the conservative right against forced busing programs and what was perceived as too much federal intervention into local affairs. Judge Ohanian, who had found the district guilty of de jure segregation in 1978, was interviewed by reporters following the 1984 consent decree. Ohanian remarked, "here's a school system that had deliberately segregated for many years, including busing to maintain segregation. Now, when they're finally brought to justice, it would seem appropriate to me that since they had compelled busing to create segregation, they ought to be required to use busing to correct the segregation that was brought about."[152] African American BCSD assistant superintendent Paul Cato remarked of the magnet programs: "the Bakersfield community wanted to use voluntary techniques and tried every avenue to prevent the Federal Government from coming in here with a mandatory busing program."[153] Media coverage reported that the Bakersfield Consent Decree reflected "President Reagan's opposition to affirmative action programs and to mandatory busing for school desegregation."[154]

Reagan-era officials praised Bakersfield's voluntary desegregation program. In a letter to Clarence Pendleton of the US Commission on Civil Rights, assistant attorney general William Bradford Reynolds wrote, "the decree provides for the establishment of magnet schools in each of the racially imbalanced schools of the district. Magnet schools are those schools which are structured to attract students notwithstanding existing attendance or zone requirements."[155] In March 1985, members of the BCSD board contacted the White House, informing the administration of the success of magnet programs in the district. Local resident Marjorie Holt expressed her gratitude to President Reagan, writing, "thank you for trusting . . . this community enough to allow us to integrate voluntarily. It is working! You and your administration need not feel embarrassed by your decision, which in my mind has always been sensitive to both minority and non-minority civil rights."[156] William Taylor, who at the time was director of the Center for National Policy Review at the Catholic University of America, criticized the Bakersfield deal. "The reason it was sent to the Justice Department was that it was determined that there were deliberate segregative practices in Bakersfield, mandatory practices that assign[ed] children to segregated schools. . . . The Supreme Court has made it clear that under those circumstances freedom of choice is not enough, whether you call them 'magnets' or whatever. . . . The Justice Department . . . did not protect the rights of the children of Bakersfield."[157]

National media and civil rights organizations were also skeptical of magnet programs. Many saw voluntary desegregation as a questionable and ultimately weak means of breaking racial isolation in America's public schools. Mary Frances Berry, then a member of the US Commission on Civil Rights, noted in *Time* magazine, "magnet schools by themselves do not achieve desegregation."[158] Others doubted that in the absence of provisions for mandatory busing, magnet schools' reliance on community voluntarism could create significant racial integration. Ralph G. Neas, executive director of the Leadership Conference on Civil Rights (and the person Senator Edward Kennedy described on the floor of the Senate as the 101st senator for civil rights), described the result of the Bakersfield Consent Decree: "it would seem once again the Justice Department is refusing to enforce our civil rights law."[159] An op-ed in the *New York Times* remarked of the Bakersfield case that "it's certainly a blueprint: for evasion and for continuing the Administration's lax approach to school desegregation."[160] In the end, the Bakersfield Consent Decree marked a triumph of conservatism and anti-statism against federal intervention into civil rights reform in Bakersfield.

CONCLUSION

The state of magnet programs in the early twenty-first century begs the need to properly contextualize the emergence of such school programs within the larger history of civil rights reform. Within the BCSD, as of 2011, there were seven magnet schools. Such schools are highly desirable to local residents. Magnet schools offer a number of services that other district schools do not necessarily match. Many parents want their children to attend magnet schools, which have become synonymous with academic excellence. One article reflecting on the success of the BCSD magnet school program noted in a local Bakersfield magazine that one parent signed her child up for a magnet program the day after the child was born. The article portrayed magnet programs as successful offerings that had moved beyond their original purpose of providing a multicultural educational experience in racially isolated schools.[161] Steve Gabbitas, a former spokesperson for the BCSD, noted in 2009 that "all schools within the BCSD meet federal guidelines based on demographics."[162] Gabbitas's statement may be true of the magnet schools within the BCSD, but schools throughout the rest of the BCSD, southeast Bakersfield, and the outlying districts of Kern County are more racially segregated than ever. Segregation in the twenty-first century, in comparison to the civil rights era, is much more of a "Hispanic problem," to borrow the language of social conservatives.[163]

It is ironic that the BCSD was proclaimed a national model for school desegregation in 1984, given the resegregation of American schools.[164] Remarks made by a young Republican legislator from Bakersfield in the late 1970s speak to the irony of the Bakersfield model: "Kern County has a vested interest in keeping people where they are, especially racially and instituting minimal change." Similarly, the editor of the *Bakersfield Californian* described his hometown as "the most harmoniously segregated community in America. . . . There is absolutely no crossing of racial and cultural lines," he claimed, adding that "many prominent businessmen here literally deny the existence of Blacks and Mexican-Americans. . . . Their problems don't exist because *they* don't exist."[165] Magnet schools in Bakersfield, while lauded for achieving academic excellence and making gains toward racial balance, beg a revisiting of their origins in Bakersfield's long struggle for civil rights reform in the post–World War II era. Racial tensions gave birth to the school integration movement and fomented conservative countereffects in support of voluntary desegregation. The twenty-first-century magnet school narrative in Bakersfield blurs the historical reality of the origins of desegregation in Bakersfield and its connection with the school integration movement and various strands of civil rights activism in greater Bakersfield.

CONCLUSION

In the aftermath of Hurricane Katrina in 2005, two Bakersfield teenagers garnered national attention in their efforts to help New Orleans residents. ABC News reported that thirteen-year-old twins Lamb and Lynx Gaede, like many other children across the country, decided to help victims of Hurricane Katrina; in their case, however, the sisters' efforts were aimed at helping *only* white people after the disaster. "The girls' donations were handed out by a White Nationalist [group] that also left a pamphlet promoting its [organization] and beliefs."[1] As the media followed the girls' story, the nation learned of the girls' cultural roots in Bakersfield. The city provided a nurturing environment for the girls' musical career—music grounded in a message of white supremacy. Dubbed Prussian Blue, the Gaede twins' musical act achieved national popularity among white supremacists. A British media outlet reported that the twins were so popular that the former presidential candidate and outspoken white supremacist David Duke used the girls to attract support.[2] Bakersfield residents, however, tolerated the negative attention the music duo brought to their city for only so long. A few months after Katrina, Prussian Blue was scratched from the musical program for the annual Kern County Fair. For April Gaede, the mother of the twins, such treatment reinforced her suspicion that Bakersfield was "not white enough" for her family. The family soon resettled to an undisclosed location somewhere in the Pacific Northwest.[3]

The suggestion that Bakersfield was "not white enough" for the Gaedes is revealing of changing racial demographics in greater Bakersfield. Latina/o immigration dramatically changed the racial composition of the city and county in the post–civil rights era.[4] While the course of civil rights history in Bakersfield did not proceed in the mirror image of the Deep South, the long civil rights movement in Bakersfield was propelled by multiracial activism rooted in the farm labor struggle, from which sprung various manifestations of urban civil rights reform. In this rural California hinterland, Kern County and Bakersfield institutions have struggled with the realities of a burgeoning racial minority population. The southern diaspora in Bakersfield is unmistakable. The southern background of many of the region's white residents formed the historical milieu in which the course of civil rights reform unfolded. While civil rights struggles in the region were not as dramatically resisted as those propagated in the American South by Alabama governor George Wallace and Birmingham commissioner of public safety Eugene "Bull" Connor, the historical impact of racial segregation and discrimination on racial minority populations in the city and county was equally egregious.

As the racial composition in Bakersfield has shifted from a white majority to a Hispanic majority, part of that evolution has included a parallel growth in the institutionalization of how the farmworker movement is remembered. In March 2014, Mexican actor and director Diego Luna's biopic *Cesar Chavez* was released. According to Luna, the film brought much-needed attention to the life and legacy of the farm labor activist. Most Americans, Luna noted, were ignorant of who Chávez was and what he did to improve the lives of farmworkers. The film was screened across the United States, including in the aging but still glamorous Bakersfield Fox Theater, the historical United Farm Workers (UFW) headquarters at Forty Acres in Delano, and Maya Cinemas in southeast Bakersfield. Local residents remembered the tumultuous years and heyday of the UFW, both celebrating and lamenting the film's premiere in the proverbial ground zero of the farm labor struggle.[5]

At the same time, the rise of Congressman Kevin McCarthy of Bakersfield has marked the steadfast importance of the Republican Party and its grip on political power within the region.[6] These two seemingly unrelated events correlate to recent scholarship documenting the long history of farm labor struggle in rural California. *Cesar Chavez*, the movie, highlights the growing recognition among historians of the ways the UFW shaped American labor history and social justice movements in the post–World War II era. McCarthy's political ascendancy marks a triumph of the political right for Bakersfield Republicans. Central Valley conservatives organized themselves for decades at the grassroots level in opposition to many of the labor and civil rights reforms engendered by the farm labor movement. Bakersfield conservatives, moreover, have been quick to point out the mixed legacy of César Chávez. His celebrated status as an American icon obscures, they reason, the reality of his grassroots legacy in Kern County. Writing in 1993, shortly after Chávez's death, Ray Gonzales, the former California assemblyman and (in 1972) first Chicano elected to the state legislature from the Central Valley, reflected on this gap between Kern County and the outside world: "the Kern County Board of Supervisors, the five Republicans who would have traditionally been put in office by the money of growers . . . had not bothered to recognize the death of their county's most famous national [labor] leader," despite the fact that the "Pope, the President, and numerous foreign leaders had sent envoys or ... condolences."[7]

SOCIAL JUSTICE ACTIVISM IN A POST–UFW MOVEMENT ERA

On June 25, 2014, the Bakersfield City Council held its regular monthly meeting. In attendance that night were over one hundred students, activists, and citizens in support of a resolution proposed by First Ward city councilman Willie Rivera, representing southeast Bakersfield. The resolution called for the city council to voice support for comprehensive immigration reform. For over an hour, activists spoke passionately about the need for the city council to support immigration reform and to advise House majority leader McCarthy that his constituents would not stand for continued congressional inaction.[8] Turning the city council into a forum of protest was an old political strategy, as multiracial activists had done so successfully in the decades following World War II. Ultimately, however, the city council's Republican majority voted to table Rivera's resolution indefinitely.[9]

The meeting echoed strikingly of the past. In the 1960s, the Bakersfield City Council became a nexus of civil rights protest, often to the chagrin of the Republican majority vote. Ward 1, both in the mid-1960s and half a century later, has historically been a "racial borderhood" represented by African Americans, until it became a predominantly Latina/o seat with the election of Rudy Salas in 2010 and Eric Arias in 2020. The gulf between southeast Bakersfield and other areas of greater Bakersfield remains striking. Wealth and resources are largely concentrated in the northwest and suburban developments in the southwest part of the city, while the southeastern city remains racially segregated, impoverished, and disproportionately policed.[10]

In 2015, the UFW celebrated the fifty-year anniversary of the Delano grape strike. Yet, Chávez's popular memory in the region where he based his life's work remains ambiguous. The Delano School Board's 2003 decision to name Cesar Chavez High School in recognition of the labor leader proved controversial.[11] Most of my students at the Bakersfield College Delano Campus, while intimately familiar with the struggles of migrant farmworkers, are woefully ignorant of the history of the Delano grape strike. Emeritus professor of history at Yale University Jon Butler, who served on the founding faculty at California State College (now University), Bakersfield, remarked that the college "opened in 1970 and I came in 1971. We were quickly instructed NEVER to mention the grape workers or Cesar Chavez.... The then vice president . . . glowered at any mention of Chavez."[12] Butler's recollections are striking, given public outcry against a proposed noncredit course series at Bakersfield College focused on teaching farm labor history through landmark site visits in Delano and to the National Chavez Center.[13] Kern County's ambivalence about acknowledging the legacy of the farmworker movement is still a flash point in local politics, although federal intervention has helped cement his local legacy. In 2010, the UFW headquarters at Forty Acres in Delano was designated a national historic landmark.[14] A number of other locations throughout California honoring César Chávez have been petitioned to be designated historic landmarks, many of them centered in Kern County.[15] In 2012, President Barack Obama visited La Paz in Keene, California, designating the UFW headquarters a national monument. In 2022, California Democratic senator Alex Padilla introduced legislation to designate various sites associated with César Chávez and the farmworker movement as a national park, in order to increase the capacity of the National Park Service to preserve the story of the farmworker movement for generations to come.[16]

Issues of historical memory beyond the farmworker movement have also been battled over in Kern County. In the 2010s the Kern County Board of Supervisors was successfully sued by the Mexican American Legal Defense and Educational Fund (MALDEF). MALDEF attorneys argued that the county's governing board had racially gerrymandered its voting districts, denying Latina/os the opportunity of fair representation on the county's governing board despite the significance of the region's Latina/o population. A key part of the plaintiff's argument against the board was the county's long history of racially discriminatory practices, as presented by consulting Stanford historian Albert Camarillo. "County lawyers tried to dismiss Camarillo's well-documented research as 'hearsay.'" After a federal judge agreed with the plaintiff that the board had in fact been guilty of racial gerrymandering, MALDEF opined: "that the county would allow attorneys representing them in court to . . . attempt to whitewash documented accounts of Kern's racist history speaks volumes about the living legacy of discrimination."[17]

The legal victory for MALDEF has proven both evasive and fruitful for social justice groups in Bakersfield. David Couch, the white Republican supervisorial incumbent, was reelected to the board in a majority Latina/o district following the creation of a more equitable map, against challenger Emilio Huerta, son of longtime local activist Dolores Huerta.[18] Yet, in 2022, a coalition of social justice organizations led by the Dolores Huerta Foundation's organizers pressured the Bakersfield City Council to adopt fair maps based on the 2020 census data. Their public arguments invoked the 1965

Voting Rights Act and the potential threat of a lawsuit, using the same legal arguments against racial gerrymandering put forth by MALDEF. Through weeks of public debates, local Republican strategists spoke publicly against the fair maps, lambasting the Dolores Huerta Foundation and its organizers on local talk radio, referring to the foundation as "evil," and attributing vast left-wing conspiracies in Bakersfield to the foundation and the UFW.[19] Ninety-two-year-old activist Dolores Huerta, who has been on the ground organizing in greater Bakersfield for more than half a century, reflected on the city council's action: "I think it is going to bring our community closer together and, of course, give representation to many people that have been left out of representation here in the city."[20] The fair maps coalition in Kern experienced another victory in 2022 when Governor Gavin Newsom signed Assembly Bill 2494, authored by Bakersfield assemblyman Rudy Salas, which effectively moves the power of approving redistricting maps from the Kern County Board of Supervisors to a Citizens Redistricting Commission.[21]

The UFW today, as well as the Dolores Huerta Foundation, champions immigration reform. The immigrant rights movement is now front and center in the civil rights movement in rural California. This was not the case in 1965. The UFW was historically opposed to undocumented workers, a reaction to their use as strikebreakers. The UFW moreover did not have a monopoly over the discourse surrounding Mexican immigration to Kern County during the civil rights era. Servicing the undocumented in rural Kern County was part of the panoramic focus of labor and civil rights activism in Kern County. Chicana/o activists in Bakersfield helped bridge relations with Mexico and promoted *Chicanismo sin fronteras* (without borders). The expansion of the rural welfare state, while on one level a relief to agribusiness because it provided worker benefits, also provided valuable and much-needed services to mostly undocumented farmworkers. Those two developments—*Chicanismo sin fronteras* and rural health care—provided significant social and economic resources for migrants and their children to carve out spaces of political, economic, and social stability in the heart of California's rural interior.

CIVIL RIGHTS BEYOND THE FIELDS

Understanding the historiography of this region in terms of political development and social justice history is important. The horticulturalist ideological school clearly shows the complex evolution of political conservatism and its opposition to farm labor activism and the welfare state. Effective challenges to the political right will likely emerge through demographic change and a growing awareness of the region's multiracial civil rights history. Conversely, if the political right seeks to maintain its stronghold in greater Bakersfield, continued organizational focus on courting Hispanic conservative voters will be of utmost importance. Recent scholarship on the UFW advances some of these important themes. Examinations of the internal dynamics of the union, the use of the boycott, and external UFW relations (including ties built by the boycott) chronicle the ways power shifted in the region, in addition to showing leadership dynamics. This book combines these historiographical currents by connecting the UFW to its surroundings at the local level. The southern San Joaquin Valley produced two important political forces in the American West—multiracial civil rights activism and rural white conservatism—whose historical developments are complexly intertwined. The leadership of César Chávez, including his flaws and unique ability to cultivate leadership in others, was critical in the rise, fall, and longevity of these two competing ideologies. Ultimately, however, the social justice and civil rights activism engendered in part by the UFW went well beyond the fields of Kern County, spatially and temporally. The multiracial activism in greater Bakersfield's racial borderhoods is a critical legacy of the story of civil rights in the American West and a space where people of color still struggle in the twenty-first century to build on the activism of previous generations.

New scholarship sustains this position, but paints a grim picture of the course of labor and civil rights reform in a post–UFW movement era. This development within California's rural historiography is connected to social and political issues outside the scope of the farm labor movement. Major public policy issues such as immigration reform, prison realignment, the establishment of a high-speed rail, efforts to curb the use of methamphetamine, and the rise of Bakersfield's conservative brand illustrate the centrality of the southern San Joaquin Valley to historical and contemporary issues of economic and social justice in the American West.[22] Rural California, while peripheral to Southern California, US West, and borderlands historiography, is a critical space where issues of race, civil rights, and political mobilization have affected social and political life well beyond its regional confines.

The fundamental conflict in Bakersfield's civil rights struggle was in many ways covert. The institutions of government, education, housing, labor, and politics were for the most part rhetorically open to racial minority residents. Yet, in reality, these venues were segregated on a racial basis until civil rights reformers challenged racial discrimination in the postwar years. The struggle for civil rights in Bakersfield was, moreover, not without its heroes and villains. The opponents of civil rights, even if convinced that their actions were nothing less than good conservative institutional management, proved detrimental to the struggle for racial equality and civil rights reform. The parochial nature of civil rights in this area of California seldom attracted the sexy media coverage of larger metropolises like Los Angeles or San Francisco—outside of the farmworker movement. Nevertheless, the struggles and institutional complications of urban civil rights reform were no less real to the Mexican Americans, African Americans, and white racial liberals who confronted the ugly head of racism, segregation, and discrimination in California's rural hinterlands.

Along with white liberals, African American and Mexican American civil rights leaders brought a new element to community politics, one that did not exist prior to the mid-twentieth century. Bakersfield's white liberals came mostly from an educated elite that was both professional and community oriented in terms of progressive politics and efforts to form racial majority-minority relationships between white people and people of color. The city of Bakersfield was primarily white for much of the twentieth century, with a growing Latina/o population and a small but well-established African American population. The minority neighborhoods and ethnic enclaves were distinguishable and usually sat outside of the city's legal municipal boundaries, which protected the city coffers from sharing tax revenue with these poorer and darker areas of greater Bakersfield. City-sponsored sidewalks, sewers, parks, and public lighting were conspicuously absent from these Black and Brown spaces. Relations between law enforcement and minority residents were tense. While individuals of Chinese, Basque, and Italian backgrounds also came to Bakersfield, these racial and ethnic groups were mostly integrated in a generation or two into mainstream city life. Many white ethnic groups began life in the minority corridor of East Bakersfield or what was known historically as Kern Island and Sumner but were—like the Earl Warren family—soon able to transition out of this corridor. Residents of Black or Brown skin hue, however, ultimately found it more difficult to overcome the institutional roadblocks of Kern County and Bakersfield society. As late as 1984, long after fair housing laws went into effect, the *Los Angeles Times* reported that "the State Department of Fair Employment surveyed 50 apartment houses and found that in all but one landlords were illegally discriminating against minority renters."[23]

Bakersfield and Kern County in many ways showcased a dramatic confrontation between the growing political factions involved in the struggle for labor and civil rights in the American Far West. The interface of workers and growers in California agriculture went beyond, however, matters of wages and labor. The topic of the constitutional rights of the poor expanded the dialogue and conversation of labor rights for workers and citizens beyond the fields. Racial liberals inundated politicians with pleas for assistance to investigate poverty, racism, and discrimination in California's Central Valley. Conservative resistance to federal and state intervention into local matters complicated such efforts. The hardships endured by Okie migrants, having assumed a status of popular cultural folklore, set the grounds for the ensuing political battle over civil rights, which would define the postwar years in California's Central Valley. The fallacy of this protracted struggle is that it was exclusively about labor rights in California's agricultural fields; in actuality, it was also a struggle for urban civil rights reform. While farm labor issues inspired political reformers in urban venues, urban civil rights struggles mainly occurred separate from the farm labor movement.

Agriculture has always been a darling of American folklore and, not by coincidence, politics as well, but farm labor confrontations in California's Central Valley sowed the seeds for the urban struggle for civil rights reform. In Bakersfield and Kern County, the fight in the fields came to fruition under the aegis of César Chávez and the UFW in the 1960s, with their national and international boycott of California grapes. The War on Poverty simultaneously bolstered racial conservatives and civil rights reformers through federal assistance programs for the poor. While poverty programs advanced civil rights reform for African Americans and Mexican Americans, conservative resistance to the War on Poverty and the expansion of the rural welfare state, coupled with racial minority competition for federal resources, ultimately undermined the grassroots aspect of antipoverty programs and encouraged civil rights reform in other public venues.

The political awakening of ethnic Mexicans developed simultaneously in the late 1960s and early 1970s in Bakersfield. Many Mexican Americans became Chicana/o by choice, a nomenclature designated to show a political maturation. The formation of a Chicana/o studies program in the Kern Community College District mobilized young Chicana/os for civil rights reform in higher education. The multiracial fair media movement, led by the African American and Mexican American civic unity activists, also resulted in employment and opportunity advances for women and minority groups in Bakersfield media outlets, as well as for Chicana/os more generally at the national level, through the McGraw-Hill media concessions.

The rise of Latina/o political activism complicated the idea of race and politics in the region, since the nexus of Latina/o politics is transnational and not necessarily local in character. This reality produced a broader political conflict between Latina/os and the local political establishment in Bakersfield and Kern County. As witnessed in the 1972 election of Raymond

Gonzales, the conservative establishment opened its arms to him as a person of quality even as a Latino, but he was later vilified by both the conservative right and the liberal left when he attempted to serve his broad constituency with fairness and deft politics. Evidently, in order to work in Kern County politics, Gonzales had to be a conservative or liberal with no goal of political consensus. Yet, his journey opened the door for other Latina/os from the region to follow into local, state, and national politics.[24]

Contemporary politics in Bakersfield and Kern County remain in the post–civil rights era generally one and the same: conservative. Even today, white people dominate Bakersfield's governing institutions, much as they did in the mid-1950s. This point is offered not as criticism per se, but as an observation of how this area is still politically and institutionally segregated. The legacy of the liberal advances of the 1960s and 1970s in Bakersfield is mixed and far from accepted in political power circles. As this book shows, conservatives mobilized powerfully to stymie civil rights reform in the postwar era. The final chapter of this book documents the long struggle to desegregate the Bakersfield City School District (BCSD), a struggle in which African Americans, Mexican Americans, and white liberals fought side by side to change institutional segregation in education. At the same time, the struggle culminated with the creation of the BCSD magnet program—a voluntary desegregation program brokered by the BCSD and the Reagan administration. While the Department of Justice officially closed its case against the BCSD in 2011, schools in Kern County and greater Bakersfield remain highly segregated by race.[25]

The mobilization of racial minority groups to fight for civil rights reform has nevertheless had a lasting legacy. In Kern County, long-permeating racism remains spatially oriented. The southeast part of Bakersfield remains the ethnic enclave of yesteryear, and the residents are the poorest of the city's poor. Most west Bakersfield citizens still do not drive to these spaces as they represent poverty, crime, dark-skinned residents, and a potential for violence. Yet, my hope is that this book shows that Bakersfield's multiracial civil rights history, much of which occurred in the poor and marginalized corridors of southeast Bakersfield and in the county's rural periphery, is rich in historical memory and can provide its residents a "usable past"—one that situates the struggle in the city and county in the twenty-first century within a genealogy of modern California civil rights history.

ACKNOWLEDGMENTS

This book project has been a long time coming. The seeds were planted in 2003 in the downtown Bakersfield office of Heritage of America, over long conversations with Jess Nieto about the Chicana/o movement in Bakersfield for my first graduate seminar paper. So many good people in Bakersfield and beyond have contributed along the way toward its completion. To everyone I acknowledged in my University of California, Santa Barbara, dissertation in 2012, I say "ditto" here! Since then, lots of Santa Barbara folks have continued to nourish my work and inspire me, especially Mario T. García, who recently retired after forty-seven years of teaching and service. The biannual Sal Castro Memorial Conference and all its participants over the past decade have helped me better understand the local, national, and international dimensions of the long struggle for Chicana/o and Mexican American civil rights and social justice. Participating in the Routledge anthology based on the initial conference was a thoroughly enjoyable experience. I thank Routledge for allowing me to republish portions of that chapter here. Special thanks to Brian Behnken, another Sal Castro conference alumnus, for helping shape my thinking on the diversity of Latina/o activism in the twentieth century. Thank you to the University of Georgia Press for allowing me to republish portions of my chapter on that important work. Thank you, Kerry Webb, my favorite acquisitions editor with roots in Bakersfield, and the entire team at the University of Texas Press, who have supported and offered critical feedback on this project for several years as it's moved slowly toward completion. Thank you to Max Krochmal, Carlos Blanton, Luis Alvarez, Kathryn Olmsted, Lauren Araiza, and the anonymous reviewers who provided critical feedback to the manuscript at various stages.

The Kern Community College District has been a wonderful place to work while writing the history of civil rights in greater Bakersfield. Former college president and now California state chancellor Sonya Christian has always inspired me with her clear vision, administrative leadership, and focus on student equity. I'll forever appreciate our mutual love and respect for Delano, rural communities, and the rich history of the farmworker movement at the home of the Renegades. I am grateful to the Norman Levan Center for the Humanities at Bakersfield College for supporting my work, including important research travel and board membership to California Humanities. Numerous colleagues have supported or inspired my work, especially my humanities comrades Andrew Bond, Javier Llamas, Rosa Garza, Robert Torres, Randal Beeman, Bruce Meier, Olivia Garcia, Ishmael Kimbrough, Jenny Grohol, Shawn Newsom, Jeff Newby, Tina Mendoza, Omar Gonzales, Abraham Castillo, Elias Medina, Kim Chin, Nicole Carrasco, Octavio Barajas, and Fernando Serrano. Thank you as well to my past and current administrative deans, Emmanuel Mourtzanos, Cornelio Rodriguez, and Richard McCrow, for always supporting me. I am also grateful for fruitful collaboration with brilliant scholars across town at California State University, Bakersfield, including Gonzalo Santos, Adam Sawyer, Brittney Beck, Mustafa Dhada, Chris Livingston, Donato Cruz, Miriam Vivian, and all the folks at the Public History Institute, Historical Research Center, and Department of History. Special thanks as well to all the visiting scholars and public intellectuals hosted by the Bakersfield College Social Justice Institute since 2015, especially Shawn Schwaller, LeRoy Chatfield, José Luis Benavides, Lori Flores, Sarah Wald, Gabriel Thompson, Steve Pitti, Ray Rast, Mark Arax, Eladio Bobadilla, James Gregory, Ashley Adams, Linda Esquivel, Dolores Huerta, Marissa Aroy, Marco E. López-Quezada, and the late Dawn Mabalon. Your collective work on civil rights, social justice, and the Central Valley energized my thinking beyond measure. And to my students, especially those at the Bakersfield College Delano Campus, I've learned so much from your family histories of migration, farm labor, and lives across borders. I hope you have enjoyed learning from me as much as I have from you.

Short of a global pandemic, this project may have been completed sooner, but it has been all the more enjoyable for the great folks in the world of public humanities who have supported my work over the years. I am especially thankful to the National Endowment for the Humanities for funding several grant projects that have helped me preserve and better teach the history of the farmworker movement and social justice activism in the San Joaquin Valley. I thank former CEO and president Julie Fry at California Humanities for inviting me to serve on our state humanities council years ago. I've met so many wonderful people by serving on the board, including my fellow historians and board alumni Bill Deverell and Natalia Molina, whose passion for California never ceases to inspire me to be a better historian. I have learned so much about public humanities from my board colleagues Rachel Hatch, Nina Malton, Neha Balram, Daniel Summerhill, John Szabo, and Nora Chapman, as well as the entire California Humanities staff, especially Felicia Kelly and John Lightfoot.

A number of civil rights and social justice groups in greater Bakersfield have inspired this book. The historical legacy of the United Farm Workers (UFW), while now being excavated to a major extent by historians, has left a lasting yet largely unexplored impact in the San Joaquin Valley. Activists and community organizers with the Cesar Chavez Foundation, UFW Foundation, Dolores Huerta Foundation, Kern Sol News, California Rural Legal Assistance, Center on Race, Poverty and the Environment, and other organizations have inspired my thinking about the legacy of labor, civil rights, and social justice struggle in greater Bakersfield. I also want to thank the many activists themselves, many of whom have passed since the publication of my dissertation, who shared their intimate histories and personal archives so I could better understand the diverse and complex legacy of civil rights history in greater Bakersfield, especially Jack Brigham, Ray Gonzales, Jess and Peggy Nieto, Milt Younger, Carlos and Rosalio Bañales, Hortencia Solis, Josie Triplett, Janet Florez, Duane Goff, Emily Gonzalez, Steve Barber, Ralph Anthony, Laurie Coyle, Sasha Biscoe, Alex Edillor, Roger Gadiano, Andres Chavez, and Marc Grossman.

Most importantly, I want to thank my family. My parents, David and Irene Rosales, have supported me in countless measures, from proofreading, to funding research and writing space, to sharing our family history since I was a little guy. I love you both dearly. To my siblings, David and Miranda, thank you for providing a good example regarding the importance of education, family, and joy in life. To my aunts, uncles, cousins, and extended family, I hope you appreciate this history of the place we've called home for more than a century. I dedicate this book to the memory of my grandmother Nancy Rosales, and my dear mother, Irene Ramos Rosales—two women who loved family without limits. To my *suegros*, Elias and Carolina Valadez, you have inspired the *regeneración* of my identity, if only through lots of *chiles, nopales y español. Gracias por su apoyo y ayuda*. Most of all, I thank Brenda Valadez for making my life as a historian, husband, and father immeasurably better than it would be otherwise. And to my children, Oliver Jr., Olivia, and baby Oceann-Alexander, your father loves you infinitely and hopes that each of you will one day appreciate this history of civil rights struggle in Bakersfield—forever part of your family's legacy and California roots. Finally, I dedicate this book to the good people of Bakersfield. I hope reading gives you greater appreciation for our city's people and history, all the while stirring your imagination toward a better future.

NOTES

INTRODUCTION

1. "Bakersfield Landmarks Eyed to Honor Celebs," *Bakersfield Californian*, March 28, 2009. Some scholars chronicling the life of Chávez have chosen not to accent his name because he did not do so generally in correspondence. The mispronunciation of his name, however, particularly outside the American Southwest, is reason enough to do so.

2. The UFW has undergone name changes in the institutional history of the union. It began in 1962 as the National Farm Workers Association (NFWA), which merged with the Agricultural Workers Organizing Committee (AWOC), led by labor leader Larry Itliong, in 1966. Those two organizations would become the United Farm Workers Organizing Committee (UFWOC) and later change its name again to the United Farm Workers (UFW), as it is known today. See Lauren Araiza, *To March for Others: The Black Freedom Struggle and the United Farm Workers* (Philadelphia: University of Pennsylvania Press, 2014), 173n3.

3. On the Okie migration to California, see James N. Gregory, *American Exodus: The Dust Bowl Migration and Okie Culture in California* (New York: Oxford University Press, 1989).

4. Adam J. Ramey, "The Grapes of Path Dependency: The Long-Run Political Impact of the Dust Bowl Migration," *Journal of Historical Political Economy* 1, no. 4 (2021): 531, 532.

5. Thomas R. Wellock, "Stick It in L.A.! Community Control and Nuclear Power in California's Central Valley," *Journal of American History* 84, no. 3 (December 1997): 942–978.

6. I use the term *ethnic Mexican* to refer to Mexican immigrants and their descendants across generations in Kern County and greater Bakersfield. When appropriate, I utilize the terms *Mexican American*, *Chicano*, and *Chicana* to refer to specific generational experiences of ethnic Mexicans in the United States during what historian Mario T. García refers to as the Mexican American and Chicana/o generations and the distinct historical events that helped shape their identity in the United States between 1940 and 1980. See Mario T. García, "Chicana/o History: A Generational Approach," in *Routledge Handbook of Chicana/o Studies*, ed. Francisco A. Lomelí, Denise A. Segura, and Elyette Benjamin-Labarthe (New York: Routledge, 2019), 27–42.

7. While some scholars have not capitalized Central Valley in their work, I follow Linda Nash's example in *Inescapable Ecologies: A History of Environment, Disease, and Knowledge* (Berkeley: University of California Press, 2006). She argues that the Central Valley is a unique ecological region with environmental problems that separate the region from other areas of California and the American Far West, most

notably Southern California. On the Central Valley's historical distinctiveness through historical travel accounts, see Janet Firemen, "Between Horizons: Traveling the Great Central Valley," *Pacific Historical Review* 81, no. 1 (February 2012): 1–20.

8. For scholarship on the UFW, see Miriam Pawel, *The Union of Their Dreams: Power, Hope, and Struggle in Cesar Chavez's Farm Worker Movement* (New York: Bloomsbury, 2009); Miriam Pawel, *The Crusades of Cesar Chavez* (New York: Bloomsbury Press, 2014); Randy Shaw, *Beyond the Fields: Cesar Chavez, the UFW, and the Struggle for Social Justice in the 21st Century* (Berkeley: University of California Press, 2008); Frank Bardacke, *Trampling Out the Vintage: Cesar Chavez and the Two Souls of the United Farm Workers* (London: Verso, 2011); Todd Holmes, "The Economic Roots of Reaganism: Corporate Conservatives, Political Economy, and the United Farm Workers Movement, 1965–1970," *Western Historical Quarterly* 41, no. 1 (Spring 2010): 55–80; Matt Garcia, *From the Jaws of Victory: The Triumph and the Tragedy of Cesar Chavez and the Farm Worker Movement* (Berkeley: University of California Press, 2012); Araiza, *To March for Others*; Christian Paiz, *The Strikers of Coachella: A Rank-and-File History of the UFW Movement* (Chapel Hill: University of North Carolina Press, 2023).

9. Garcia, *From the Jaws of Victory*, 11.

10. Albert Camarillo, "Navigating Segregated Life in America's Racial Borderhoods, 1910s–1950s," *Journal of American History* 100, no. 3 (December 2013): 645–662. Camarillo's characterization of borderhoods is appropriate for describing the position of East Bakersfield, formerly known as Sumner, to Bakersfield proper, given the role of racial segregation in shaping urban development in southeast Bakersfield.

11. See David Vaught, "State of the Art—Rural History, or Why Is There No Rural History of California?," *Agricultural History* 76 (Spring 2002): 326–337. For an earlier assessment, see Richard Steven Street, "Rural California: A Bibliographic Essay," *Southern California Quarterly* 70, no. 3 (1988): 299–328.

12. On the origins of California conservatism amid the 1930s struggle between agricultural labor and big business, see Kathryn S. Olmsted, *Right Out of California: The 1930s and the Big Business Roots of Modern Conservatism* (New York: New Press, 2017).

13. Wellock, "Stick It in L.A.!," 944. Comedian Conan O'Brien joined the tradition among late-night comedians, including most famously Johnny Carson, of jokingly criticizing Bakersfield conservatism vis-à-vis the rest of the state. On Twitter, O'Brien (@ConanOBrien) remarked, "Massachusetts was just named the most liberal state. Researchers almost picked California, but then they stopped for gas in Bakersfield." Twitter, October 29, 2014, 10:22 a.m.

14. This cultural recognition was confirmed by the awarding of Bakersfield's other favorite son beside Buck Owens, Merle Haggard, with a prestigious Kennedy Center Honor in December 2010, as well as the hosting of the *Bakersfield Sound* exhibit at the Country Music Hall of Fame and Museum in Nashville, Tennessee, in 2012–2014. See "Kennedy Center Honors 2010: Merle Haggard, Chita Rivera, Paul McCartney Honored," *Washington Post*, December 29, 2010. The emergence of "the Bakersfield Sound" has been an important development in American music culture and modern political conservatism. See Shane Hamilton, *Trucking Country: The Road to America's Walmart Economy* (Princeton, NJ: Princeton University Press, 2008), 192–193; Robert Price, *The Bakersfield Sound: How a Generation of Displaced Okies Revolutionized American Music* (Berkeley, CA: Heyday, 2015).

15. Gregory, *American Exodus*, xvi–xvii; see also James N. Gregory, *The Southern Diaspora: How the Great Migrations of Black and White Southerners Transformed America* (Chapel Hill: University of North Carolina Press, 2005).

16. David Igler, *Industrial Cowboys: Miller and Lux and the Transformation of the Far West, 1850–1920* (Berkeley: University of California Press, 2001), 183.

17. David Vaught, *Cultivating California: Growers, Specialty Crops, and Labor* (Baltimore, MD: Johns Hopkins University Press, 1999), 2. Vaught disagrees with Carey McWilliams's interpretation of California agribusiness in the latter's landmark text, *Factories in the Field: The Story of Migratory Farm Labor in California* (Boston: Little, Brown, 1939). While Vaught's work does not document the political imaginaries of farmworkers themselves, his description of grower ideology is salient.

18. On grower ideology in response to farm labor organizing, see Lizzie Lamoree, "The Managed Crisis: Labor Relations and Management in California Agriculture, 1930–1980" (PhD diss., University of California, Santa Barbara, 2012).

19. Vaught, *Cultivating California*, 191. Vaught notes Victor Davis Hanson, a fifth-generation raisin and plum grower in Fresno County, as proof that the horticultural ideal remains prevalent in the valley today. Interestingly, Hanson is well known for his condemnation of Chicana/o studies. See Victor Davis Hanson, *Mexifornia: A State of Becoming* (San Francisco: Encounter Books, 2003).

20. On California farm labor history and activism, see Devra Weber, *Dark Sweat, White Gold: California Farm Workers, Cotton, and the New Deal* (Berkeley: University of California Press, 1994); Richard Steven Street, *Beasts of the Field: A Narrative History of California Farmworkers, 1769–1913* (Stanford, CA: Stanford University Press, 2004); Donald H. Grubbs, "Prelude to Chavez: The National Farm Labor Union in California," *Labor History* 16, no. 4 (Winter 1975): 453–469; Ernesto Galarza, *Spiders in the House and Workers in the Field* (Notre Dame, IN: University of Notre Dame Press, 1970); Dionicio Nodín Valdés, *Organized Agriculture and the Labor Movement before the UFW: Puerto Rico, Hawai'i, and California* (Austin: University of Texas Press, 2011).

21. Galarza, *Spiders in the House and Workers in the Field*, 23.

22. Grubbs, "Prelude to Chavez." On the NFLU, see also Richard Steven Street, "Poverty in the Valley of Plenty: The National Farm Labor Union, DiGiorgio Farms, and Suppression of Documentary Photography in California, 1947–66," *Labor History* 48, no. 1 (February 2007): 25–48; Garcia, *From the Jaws of Victory*, 12–23.

23. Franklin Williams to Walter White, November 17, 1950, carton 77, folder 2, NAACP, Region 1, Records, BANC MSS 78/180 c, Bancroft Library, University of California, Berkeley.

24. See, e.g., John Gregory Dunne, *Delano: The Story of the California Grape Strike* (New York: Farrar, Straus and Giroux, 1967); Peter Matthiessen, *Sal Si Puedes: Cesar Chavez and the New American Revolution* (Berkeley: University of California Press, 2000); Jacques E. Levy, *Cesar Chavez: Autobiography of La Causa* (Minneapolis: University of Minnesota Press, 2007).

25. See, e.g., Steven W. Bender, *One Night in America: Robert Kennedy, César Chávez, and the Dream of Dignity* (Boulder, CO: Paradigm, 2008); Richard Griswold del Castillo, *César Chávez: A Triumph of Spirit* (Norman: University of Oklahoma Press, 1995); Susan Ferriss and Ricardo Sandoval, *The Fight in the Fields: Cesar Chavez and the Farmworkers Movement* (New York: Harcourt Brace, 1997); Richard W. Etulain, ed., *Cesar Chavez: A Brief Biography with Documents* (New York: Palgrave, 2002).

26. See Margaret Rose, "Women in the United Farm Workers: A Study of Chicana and Mexicana Participation in a Labor Union, 1950–1980" (PhD diss., University of California, Los Angeles, 1988); Rose, "'Woman Power Will Stop Those Grapes': Chicana Organizers and Middle-Class Female Supporters in the Farm Workers' Grape Boycott in Philadelphia, 1969–1970," *Journal of Women's History* 7, no. 4 (Winter 1995): 6–36; Rose, "'From the Fields to the Picket Line: Huelga Women and the Boycott,' 1965–1975," *Labor History* 31, no. 3 (Summer 1990): 271–293; Rose, "Traditional and Non-traditional Patterns of Female Activism in the United Farmworkers of America, 1962–1980," *Frontiers* 11, no. 1 (1990): 26–32.

27. Rose, "Woman Power Will Stop Those Grapes," 7.

28. See Rose, "Traditional and Non-traditional Patterns of Female Activism."

29. On recent historians dethroning Chicana/o movement icons, see Rodolfo F. Acuña, "It's a Wonderful Life? Too Many Chicana/o Academics Sacrifice Needs of Community or Students for Career Advancement," *Mexmigration: History and Politics of Mexican Immigration* (blog), February 13, 2013.

30. On the intersection of the UFW and religious activism, see Mario T. García, ed., *The Gospel of César Chávez: My Faith in Action* (Lanham, MD: Rowman and Littlefield, 2007); Keith Douglass Warner, "The Farm Workers and the Franciscans: Reverse Evangelization as Social Prompt for Conversion," *Spiritus: A Journal of Christian Spirituality* 9, no. 1 (Spring 2009): 69–88; Kevin J. O'Brien, "La Causa and Environmental Justice: César Chávez as a Resource for Christian Ecological Ethics," *Journal of the Society of Christian Ethics* 32, no. 1 (Spring/Summer 2012): 151–168; Luis D. León, "Cesar Chavez in American Religious Politics: Mapping the New Global Spiritual Line," *American Quarterly* 59, no. 3 (September 2007): 857–881; Andrew Jacobs, "Friends and Foes: Religious Publications and the Delano Grape Strike and Boycott (1965–1970)," *American Catholic Studies* 124, no. 1 (Spring 2013): 23–42; Alan J. Watt, *Farm Workers and the Churches: The Movement in California and Texas* (College Station: Texas A&M University Press, 2010); Marco G. Prouty, *César Chávez, the Catholic Bishops, and the Farmworkers' Struggle for Social Justice* (Tucson: University of Arizona Press, 2006).

31. Miriam Pawel, "Farmworkers Reap Little as Union Strays from Its Roots," *Los Angeles Times*, January 8 , 2006. The UFW publicly admonished Pawel's series, charging that she never allowed the union to respond in kind to the accusations made against it. See "The Los Angeles Times Series on the United Farm Workers: A Disservice to Readers and the Farm Worker Movement: Executive Summary," United Farm Workers (website), accessed July 3, 2023.

32. Pawel, *The Crusades of Cesar Chavez*; Pawel, *The Union of Their Dreams*. As Fernando Gapasin notes in a review of Pawel's work, the union's success and failure still hinged upon decisions made by Chávez and that ultimately Pawel's interviewees, in relaying their own stories about the rise and fall of the UFW, have their own legacies to protect. See Fernando Gapasin, "Perspectives on César Chávez and the Farm Workers Movement," *New Labor Forum* 21, no. 3 (Fall 2012): 116.

33. Ana Raquel Minian, "'Indiscriminate and Shameless Sex': The Strategic Use of Sexuality by the United Farm Workers," *American Quarterly* 65, no. 1 (March 2013): 78.

34. Garcia, *From the Jaws of Victory*, 4.

35. On liberalism in American political history, see Allen J. Matusow, *The Unraveling of America: A History of Liberalism in the 1960s* (Athens: University of Georgia Press, 2009).

36. Garcia, *From the Jaws of Victory*, 15.

37. See Lauren Araiza, "For Freedom of Other Men: Civil Rights, Black Power, and the United Farm Workers, 1965–1973" (PhD diss., University Of California, Berkeley, 2006); Araiza, "'In Common Struggle against a Common Oppression': The United Farm Workers and the Black Panther Party, 1968–1973," *Journal of African American History* 94, no. 2 (Spring 2009): 200–223; Araiza, *To March for Others*.

38. Brilliant writes: "the presence of multiple 'race problems,' each of which tended to attach itself to the state's different racial groups in different ways or degrees, mitigated against the making of a single civil rights movement. . . . The bulk of California's civil rights litigation and legislation action took place in the wide space between the poles of cooperative interracial coalitions and contentious conflicts between coalition members." Mark Brilliant, *The Color of America Has Changed: How Racial Diversity Shaped Civil Rights Reform in California, 1941–1978* (Oxford: Oxford University Press, 2010), 6–7.

39. Araiza, *To March for Others*. On the scope of Black-Brown relations during the civil rights era, see Brian D. Behnken, *Fighting Their Own Battles: Mexican Americans, African Americans, and the Struggle for Civil Rights in Texas* (Chapel Hill: University of North Carolina Press, 2011); Behnken, ed., *The Struggle in Black and Brown: African American and Mexican American Relations during the Civil Rights Era* (Lincoln: University of Nebraska Press, 2011); Neil Foley, *Quest for Equality: The Failed Promise of Black-Brown Solidarity* (Cambridge, MA: Harvard University Press, 2010); Gordon K. Mantler, *Power to the Poor: Black-Brown Coalition and the Fight for Economic Justice, 1960–1974* (Chapel Hill: University of North Carolina Press, 2013); Josh Kun and Laura Pulido, eds., *Black and Brown in Los Angeles: Beyond Conflict and Coalition* (Berkeley: University of California Press, 2014).

40. See Araiza, *To March for Others*, 90, 108–109. Both Roy Wilkins and Martin Luther King Jr. offered only tepid support for the UFW because of financial donations to the NAACP and the SCLC by industry groups (including agribusiness or those industries affected by UFW boycotts) and the Teamsters Union, the UFW's archrival in the fields.

41. While this introduction offers a brief overview of the new farm labor history's connections to the main themes in this book, much more could be said about the growth of this historiography. A longer historiographical examination of this topic is certainly warranted.

42. Camarillo, "Navigating Segregated Life," 651.

43. Historian Annelise Orleck notes that Las Vegas, Nevada, was also referred to as the "Mississippi of the West," given the impact of African American migration from Mississippi to that Sunbelt city. See Annelise Orleck, *Storming Caesars Palace: How Black Mothers Fought Their Own War on Poverty* (Boston: Beacon Press, 2005).

44. Mario T. García explores the connections between educational reform and civil rights in *Blowout! Sal Castro and the Chicano Struggle for Educational Justice* (Chapel Hill: University of North Carolina Press, 2011).

45. See Oliver A. Rosales, "'Hoo-ray Gonzales!': Civil Rights Protest and Chicano Politics in Bakersfield, 1968–1974," in *The Chicano Movement: Perspectives from the Twenty-First Century*, ed. Mario T. García (New York: Routledge, 2014), 73–94.

46. See Nancy MacLean, *Freedom Is Not Enough: The Opening of the American Workplace* (Cambridge, MA: Harvard University Press, 2008), 155–184.

CHAPTER 1: "A LABORATORY OF RACES"

The chapter epigraphs are from, respectively, Office File, 1914–1927, Survey of Race Relations records, box 20, Hoover Institution Library and Archives, Stanford University, Stanford, CA; Johnie Mae (Lothridge) Parker, interview by Irma Weill and Orville P. Armstrong, March 28, 1971, p. 4, San Joaquin Valley Oral History Project, Bakersfield Sound, California State College, Bakersfield.

1. "Chapters in City's Black History Recalled," *Bakersfield Californian*, February 24, 2007.

2. "Residents of Sunset-Mayflower Area Push Annexation Vote," *Bakersfield Californian*, March 8, 1949.

3. I use the term *greater Bakersfield* to refer to land within the municipal city limits, unincorporated communities on the outskirts of the city, and several surrounding smaller rural communities, such as Delano, Shafter, McFarland, Lamont, and Arvin, that have strong historical ties to Bakersfield. While the municipal boundaries of Bakersfield grew over the twentieth century, growth often excluded communities of color. The growth of Bakersfield vis-à-vis that of the aforementioned smaller rural towns solidified Bakersfield as the urban capital of the southern San Joaquin Valley, in relation to smaller rural communities that predominantly comprised ethnic Mexicans, with notable Black communities in Wasco, Shafter, and, especially, Allensworth (in southern Tulare County, just northwest of Delano).

4. Albert Camarillo, "Report of Dr. Albert M. Camarillo" (November 8, 2016), *Luna v. County of Kern*, 291 F. Supp. 3d 1088 (E.D. Cal. 2018), statement in author's possession, 4. I thank Al Camarillo for sharing a copy of his testimony.

5. See, e.g., George Harwood Phillips, *"Bringing Them under Subjection": California's Tejón Indian Reservation and Beyond, 1852–1864* (Lincoln: University of Nebraska Press, 2004). While native displacement is an important facet of the region's history, indigenous peoples in the San Joaquin Valley have struggled, with varying degrees of success, to preserve their cultural identity and history, including through federal recognition. See, e.g., "Tejon Tribe Fought for Recognition throughout History," *Bakersfield Californian*, September 7, 2016.

6. US Department of the Interior, Census Office, *Report on Population of the United States at the Eleventh Census: 1890*, part 1 (Washington, DC: Government Printing Office, 1895), 378; US Department of the Interior, Census Office, *Twelfth Census of the United States, Taken in the Year 1900: Population*, part 1 (Washington, DC: US Census Office, 1901), 11.

7. Quoted in "Mexicans File," William Harland Boyd Papers, Vertical Files, William Harland Boyd Collection, Beale Memorial Library, Bakersfield, CA (hereafter WHBC).

8. Linda Nash, *Inescapable Ecologies: A History of Environment, Disease, and Knowledge* (Berkeley: University of California Press, 2006), 68–69.

9. On racial scripts, see Natalia Molina, *How Race Is Made in America: Immigration, Citizenship, and the Historical Power of Racial Scripts* (Berkeley: University of California Press, 2014).

10. William Harland Boyd, *The Chinese of Kern County, 1857–1960* (Bakersfield, CA: Kern County Historical Society, 2002), 49.

11. Boyd, *The Chinese of Kern County*, 121. Interestingly, two distinct Chinatowns formed in Bakersfield: the "older" location, from Twentieth to Twenty-Second Street between K and N Streets; and the "newer" Chinatown, just a few blocks southeast of there, on Q Street between Seventeenth and Eighteenth Streets. See Boyd, 50–51.

12. Quoted in Gilbert Gia, "Bakersfield and the Anti-Chinese Pogroms of 1893," 2, Historic Bakersfield and Kern County (website), accessed May 31, 2022.

13. Gia, "Bakersfield and the Anti-Chinese Pogroms of 1893," 2. Gregory Kimm notes that the "Chinese Section" of Union Cemetery in Bakersfield is located on the east side of the cemetery and has compiled a useful list of 168 individual plots located at Bakersfield's oldest cemetery. For Kimm's list, see Boyd, *The Chinese of Kern County*, 240–245.

14. Boyd, *The Chinese of Kern County*, 35.

15. Anti-Chinese sentiments in Fresno, for example, manifested as greater hostility and violence comparative to Bakersfield, rooted in the long history of racial segregation in west Fresno. See Ramon D. Chacon, "The Beginning of Racial Segregation: The Chinese in West Fresno and Chinatown's Role as Red Light District, 1870s–1920s," *Southern California Quarterly* 70, no. 4 (1988): 371–398.

16. Gia, "Bakersfield and the Anti-Chinese Pogroms of 1893," 16.

17. Quoted in "Mexicans File," WHBC.

18. Quoted in "Mexicans File," WHBC.

19. Quoted in "Mexicans File," WHBC.

20. "Morning Echo," September 16, 1874, quoted in F. Javier Llamas, "Mexican Pioneers and the Origins of the Mexican Colonia in Bakersfield" (presentation, Western History Association annual meeting, Las Vegas, NV, October 17, 2019).

21. David Igler, *Industrial Cowboys: Miller and Lux and the Transformation of the Far West, 1850–1920* (Berkeley: University of California Press, 2001), 45, 97.

22. Ruben Mendoza, *Herencia Mexicana: The Mexican Americans of Kern County, 1870–1955* (Bakersfield, CA: Mexican Heritage Project Fund, 1986), 6.

23. William Harland Boyd, *A California Middle Border: The Kern River Country, 1772–1880* (Richardson, TX: Havilah Press, 1972), 8–9.

24. Igler, *Industrial Cowboys*, 126.

25. Thelma B. Miller, *History of Kern County, California*, vol. 1 (Chicago: S. J. Clarke, 1929), 563.

26. Wallace Smith, *Garden of the Sun: A History of the San Joaquin Valley, 1772–1939*, 2nd ed. (Fresno, CA: Linden, 2004), 612–613.

27. On the influence of the railroad in transforming California, see William F. Deverell, *Railroad Crossing: Californians and the Railroad, 1850–1910* (Berkeley: University of California Press, 1996).

28. Jeffrey Marcos Garcílazo, *Traqueros: Mexican Railroad Workers in the United States, 1870–1930* (Denton: University of North Texas Press, 2016), 9.

29. See Boyd, *A California Middle Border*, 124.

30. William Harland Boyd, *Lower Kern River Country, 1850–1950: Wilderness to Empire* (Bakersfield, CA: Kern County Historical Society, 1997), 29.

31. Richard J. Orsi, *Sunset Limited: The Southern Pacific Railroad and the Development of the American West, 1850–1930* (Berkeley: University of California Press, 2007), 19.

32. Boyd, *A California Middle Border*, 196.

33. Boyd, *Lower Kern River Country*, 35.

34. John Leonard Compton, "A Study of Non-attendance in the Elementary Schools of Bakersfield, California" (master's thesis, University of Southern California, 1929), 69.

35. Compton, "A Study of Non-attendance," 69–70.

36. David Rosales, "A History of the Rosales and Ramos Families," unpublished essay, in author's possession.

37. Llamas, "Mexican Pioneers and the Origins of the Mexican Colonia in Bakersfield."

38. Quoted in "Mexicans File," WHBC.

39. "Traditional Mexican Dancers Help Revitalization Efforts in East Bakersfield," *Bakersfield Californian*, January 12, 2020.

40. See the presentation by F. Javier Llamas in "Sociedad Juarez Mutualista Mexicana 110th Anniversary, Bakersfield Calif.," YouTube video, uploaded January 1, 2021, by Salon Juarez, 1:31:41 at 46:15.

41. Llamas, "Mexican Pioneers and the Origins of the Mexican Colonia in Bakersfield."

42. *Morning Echo*, August 25, 1912, WHBC.

43. *Morning Echo*, August 25, 1912, WHBC.

44. Zaragosa Vargas, *Crucible of Struggle: A History of Mexican Americans from Colonial Times to the Present Era* (New York: Oxford University Press, 2011), 188.

45. US Department of Commerce, Bureau of the Census, *Fifteenth Census of the United States: 1930; Population*, vol. 3, part 1 (Washington, DC: Government Printing Office, 1932), 243, 247, 266.

46. John King, "An Inquiry into the Status of Mexican Segregation in Metropolitan Bakersfield" (master's thesis, Claremont College, 1946), 15.

47. Mendoza, *Herencia Mexicana*, 30, 40 (qtd.).

48. One of Ignacia's early grammar school teachers at Hawthorne Elementary School in Bakersfield renamed Ignacia "Nancy," as it was easier for her to pronounce. The name remained Nancy's preference for the rest of her life.

49. Rosales, "A History of the Rosales and Ramos Families."

50. Michael Eissinger, "Kern County: California's Deep South" (conference presentation, Critical Ethnic Studies and the Future of Genocide: Settler Colonialism/White Supremacy/Heteropatriarchy, University of California, Riverside, March 2011), 2.

51. Other historians have noted similar trends north of Kern, in Fresno County. Historian Patrick Fontes notes in his study of the Mexican population of Fresno County that "when Mexican immigrants entered the Fresno region in large numbers in the early twentieth century . . . they encountered a society founded on White American ideals of class and race. . . . Mexican 'peon' immigrants . . . were bogeymen in the minds of many Southern migrants in Fresno County." See Patrick Fontes, "Peons, Prisons, and Probation: The Criminalization of the Mexican Immigrant in Fresno County, 1880–1930," (PhD diss., Stanford University, 2016), 19.

52. Camarillo, "Report of Dr. Albert M. Camarillo," 9.

53. "*Luna v. County of Kern*: MALDEF and Latino Voters Achieve Landmark Victory," *MALDEF in History* (blog), MALDEF, March 26, 2019.

54. Eissinger, "Kern County: California's Deep South," 7–8.

55. Camarillo, "Report of Dr. Albert M. Camarillo," 10.

56. Tarea Hall Pittman, "NAACP Official and Civil Rights Worker," interview by Joyce Henderson, May 20, 1971, p. 4, Earl Warren Oral History Project, Bancroft Library, University of California, Berkeley.

57. Alicia E. Rodriquez, "'No Ku Klux Klan for Kern': The Rise and Fall of the 1920s KKK in Kern County, California," *Southern California Quarterly* 99, no. 1 (2017): 10.

58. Rodriquez, "No Ku Klux Klan for Kern," 9n7.

59. *Southern Californian and Kern County Weekly Courier*, December 27, 1877; William D. Carrigan and Clive Webb, *Forgotten Dead: Mob Violence against Mexicans in the United States, 1848–1928* (Oxford: Oxford University Press, 2017), 203.

60. Rodriquez, "No Ku Klux Klan for Kern," 37.

61. Rodriquez, "No Ku Klux Klan for Kern," 45.

62. Camarillo, "Report of Dr. Albert M. Camarillo," 11.

63. Camarillo, "Report of Dr. Albert M. Camarillo," 5.

64. Devra Weber, *Dark Sweat, White Gold: California Farm Workers, Cotton, and the New Deal* (Berkeley: University of California Press, 1994), 66–67.

65. Walter Goldschmidt, *As You Sow: Three Studies in the Social Consequences of Agribusiness* (New York: Harcourt Brace, 1947), vii–viii.

66. Goldschmidt, *As You Sow*, vii, vii, 6.

67. Quoted in Daniel J. O'Connell and Scott J. Peters, *In the Struggle: Scholars and the Fight against Industrial Agribusiness in California* (New York: New Village Press, 2021), 18.

68. Goldschmidt, *As You Sow*, 59.

69. O'Connell and Peters, *In the Struggle*, 15.

70. Nelson A. Pichardo Almanzar and Brian W. Kulik, *American Fascism and the New Deal: The Associated Farmers of California and the Pro-industrial Movement* (Lanham, MD: Lexington Books, 2013), 70.

71. Weber, *Dark Sweat, White Gold*, 9.

72. "Mexican Group Will Oppose Strike Move," *Bakersfield Californian*, April 5, 1934. Devra Weber notes that in Bakersfield, Mexican fraternal organizations reflected class differences, for example: "Bakersfield's Mexican Rotary and athletic clubs reflect[ed] the older and more prosperous middle class" that had developed in East Bakersfield since the early twentieth century. Weber, *Dark Sweat, White Gold*, 252n86.

73. "Force, Violence during Harvests in Valley Urged," *Bakersfield Californian*, April 5, 1934.

74. Lillie Ruth Ann Counts Dunn, "California Odyssey: The 1930s Migration to the Southern San Joaquin Valley," interview by Judith Gannon, February 14 and 16, 1981, p. 17, Oral History Program, California State College, Bakersfield.

75. Pichardo Almanzar and Kulik, *American Fascism and the New Deal*, 67.

76. Pichardo Almanzar and Kulik, *American Fascism and the New Deal*, 68.

77. Gabriel Thompson, *America's Social Arsonist: Fred Ross and Grassroots Organizing in the Twentieth Century* (Berkeley: University of California Press, 2019), 33.

78. Thompson, *America's Social Arsonist*, 34, 36–37, 40.

79. Thompson, *America's Social Arsonist*, 40.

80. Eissinger, "Kern County: California's Deep South," 4.

81. Eissinger, "Kern County," 4, 5.

82. Photographer Ernest Lowe captured Black rural to rural migration in the 1950s and 1960s. His collection can be found online at "Ernest Lowe Photography Collection," Calisphere, University of California Libraries (website), accessed August 26, 2022.

83. Parker, interview by Weill and Armstrong, March 28, 1971, 4.

84. Parker, interview by Weill and Armstrong, 5–6.

85. On Black rural migration to California, see *We Are Not Strangers Here*, podcast series, 2021, Cal Ag Roots (website), accessed August 26, 2022.

86. Lynn M. Hudson, *West of Jim Crow: The Fight against California's Color Line* (Champaign: University of Illinois Press, 2020), 93–94.

87. Hudson, *West of Jim Crow*, 96.

88. Delores Nason McBroome, "Harvests of Gold: African American Boosterism, Agriculture, and Investment in Allensworth and Little Liberia," in *Seeking El Dorado: African Americans in California*, ed. Lawrence B. de Graaf, Kevin Mulroy, and Quintard Taylor (Los Angeles: Autry Museum of Western Heritage, 2001), 154.

89. Hudson, *West of Jim Crow*, 92.

90. Hudson, *West of Jim Crow*, 102.

91. Hudson, *West of Jim Crow*, 109.

92. McBroome, "Harvests of Gold," 157. UNIA, actually the Universal Negro Improvement Association, was founded by Marcus Garvey in 1914.

93. Hudson, *West of Jim Crow*, 111.

94. Bakersfield educator Fred Luther Haynes compiled useful portraits of Black women in Kern County history; see *African American Women Trailblazers: A Celebration of Africa's Gift to Kern County* (n.p.: Xlibris, 2009).

95. Josephine Triplett, "History, Family, and Making a Difference" (presentation, Bakersfield College, November 6, 2014), YouTube video, uploaded September 11, 2021, by Michelle Hart, 52:29.

96. Triplett, "History, Family, and Making a Difference."

97. Hudson, *West of Jim Crow*, 106.

98. Hudson, *West of Jim Crow*, 95.

99. McBroome, "Harvests of Gold," 151.

100. McBroome, "Harvests of Gold," 156.

101. Peter LaChapelle, "'Shadows of the Dust': The Expectation and Ordeal of California's African-American Dust Bowl Migrants; Southern San Joaquin Valley, 1929–1941" (master's thesis, California State University, Bakersfield, 1997), 11.

102. Haynes, *African American Women Trailblazers*, 35–37.

103. Quoted in Haynes, *African American Women Trailblazers*, 32–34.

104. Igler, *Industrial Cowboys*, 123.

105. Quoted in LaChapelle, "Shadows of the Dust," 74.

106. Christina Veola Williams McClanahan, "California Odyssey: The 1930s Migration to the Southern San Joaquin Valley," interview by Judith Gannon, June 20, 1981, p. 14, Oral History Program, California State College, Bakersfield.

107. McClanahan, "California Odyssey," 15, 18.

108. Brent McClanahan Sr., interview by John Purcell, May 31, 2016, p. 3, San Joaquin Valley Oral History Project, Bakersfield Sound, California State College, Bakersfield.

109. Quoted in Haynes, *African American Women Trailblazers*, 48.

110. Irene Rosales, interview by author, May 30, 2022.

111. Rosales, interview by author.

112. On the role of realtors in creating racially restrictive housing, see Gene Slater, *Freedom to Discriminate: How Realtors Conspired to Segregate Housing and Divide America* (Berkeley, CA: Heyday, 2021).

113. Camarillo, "Report of Dr. Albert M. Camarillo," 6.

114. Camarillo, "Report of Dr. Albert M. Camarillo," 7.

115. Office File, 1914–1927, Survey of Race Relations records, box 20, Hoover Institution Library and Archives, Stanford University, Stanford, CA; Slater, *Freedom to Discriminate*, 90.

116. Office File, 1914–1927, Survey of Race Relations records.
117. "Restriction Requirements—Hillcrest Tract No. 1095," June 10, 1939, Hall of Records, Bakersfield, CA.
118. Office File, 1914–1927, Survey of Race Relations records.
119. Untitled article, *Bakersfield Californian*, March 5, 1941.
120. "Kern County Town Struggling to Overcome Its Racist Image," *Los Angeles Times*, August 9, 1992; "Conservative Oildale Could Be a Bellwether of How Trump's Message Translates in California," *Los Angeles Times*, April 4, 2016.
121. Edgar Combs, "California Odyssey: The 1930s Migration to the Southern San Joaquin Valley," interview by Judith Gannon, April 2, 1981, p. 6, Oral History Program, California State College, Bakersfield.
122. Quoted in "Chapters in City's Black History Recalled," *Bakersfield Californian*, February 24, 2007.
123. Donato Cruz, "'America's Newest City': 1950s Bakersfield and the Making of the Modern Suburban Segregated Landscape" (master's thesis, California State University, Bakersfield, 2020), 49.
124. John Dunne, *Delano: The Story of the California Grape Strike* (Berkeley: University of California Press, 2008), 10–11.
125. Mark Day, *Forty Acres: Cesar Chavez and the Farm Workers* (New York: Praeger, 1971), 125.
126. Olen Cole, *The African-American Experience in the Civilian Conservation Corps* (Gainesville: University Press of Florida, 1999), 25.
127. Quoted in James N. Gregory, *American Exodus: The Dust Bowl Migration and Okie Culture in California* (New York: Oxford University Press, 1989), 167.
128. King, "An Inquiry into the Status of Mexican Segregation," 52.
129. Gilbert Gia, "Chinese Parents and the School Boycott of 1910," 4, quoting *Bakersfield Californian*, January 15, 1896, Historic Bakersfield and Kern County (website), accessed May 31, 2022.
130. Gia, "Chinese Parents and the School Boycott of 1910," 1.
131. *Morning Echo*, September 23, 1921, quoted in "Mexicans File," WHBC.
132. King, "An Inquiry into the Status of Mexican Segregation," 58.
133. McClanahan, "California Odyssey," 14.
134. Vivian Leah Barnes Kirschenmann, "California Odyssey: The 1930s Migration to the Southern San Joaquin Valley," interview by Michael Neely, April 22 and May 5, 1981, p. 26, Oral History Program, California State College, Bakersfield.
135. King, "An Inquiry into the Status of Mexican Segregation," 19.
136. King, "An Inquiry into the Status of Mexican Segregation," 20–21.
137. James Franklin Johnston, "A Study of Retardation in an Elementary School of California" (master's thesis, University of Southern California, 1927), 33.
138. George G. Perkins, "Survey of Racial Attitudes in Three Communities, Kern County, California" (master's thesis, Montana State University, 1952), 13 (qtd.), 11–12.
139. King, "An Inquiry into the Status of Mexican Segregation," 60.
140. "Elbo-In Incident," *Blue and White Newspaper*, January 30, 1950, Bakersfield High School Archives, Bakersfield, CA; "Unique Plans Laid for Café," *Bakersfield Californian*, January 19, 1950. I thank Bakersfield High School archivist Ken Hooper for pointing me to this story.
141. Rodriquez, "No Ku Klux Klan for Kern," 12.
142. "Elbo-In Incident," *Blue and White Newspaper*, January 30, 1950.
143. Letter to the editor, *Blue and White Newspaper*, January 31, 1950.

144. "Racial Sign Removal from Cafes Urged," *Bakersfield Californian*, February 22, 1950.

CHAPTER 2: CIVIC UNITY
The epigraphs are from, respectively, Franklin Williams to Walter White, November 17, 1950, carton 77, folder 2, NAACP, Region 1, Records, BANC MSS 78/180 c, Bancroft Library, University of California, Berkeley (hereafter NAACP Records); Christina Pazzanese, "What Is Compelling to Do Right Now?," *Harvard Gazette*, September 26, 2023.

1. Mark Brilliant, *The Color of America Has Changed: How Racial Diversity Shaped Civil Rights Reform in California, 1941–1978* (Oxford: Oxford University Press, 2010), 9.

2. For an overview of the activities of the NFLU, see Donald H. Grubbs, "Prelude to Chavez: The National Farm Labor Union in California," *Labor History* 16, no. 4 (Winter 1975): 453–469.

3. Ernesto Galarza, *Spiders in the House and Workers in the Field* (Notre Dame, IN: University of Notre Dame Press), 20–21.

4. On the decline of the NFLU, see Zaragosa Vargas, *Crucible of Struggle: A History of Mexican Americans from Colonial Times to the Present Era* (New York: Oxford University Press, 2011), 278; Richard Steven Street, "Poverty in the Valley of Plenty: The National Farm Labor Union, DiGiorgio Farms, and Suppression of Documentary Photography in California, 1947–66," *Labor History* 48, no. 1 (February 2007): 25–48.

5. Franklin Williams to Walter White, November 17, 1950, carton 77, folder 2, NAACP Records.

6. Williams to White, November 17, 1950.

7. "A Report on Housing in the San Joaquin Valley to the San Joaquin Valley Agricultural Labor Resources Committee," August–September 1950, Governor's Committee to Survey the Agricultural Resources of the San Joaquin Valley Records, F3845, California State Archives, Sacramento.

8. On rural Black migration to Central California, see Michael Eissinger, "Re-Collecting the Past: Rural Historically African American Settlements in the San Joaquin Valley" (PhD diss., University of California, Merced, 2017).

9. Obituary of Rabbi Sanford E. Rosen, *San Francisco Chronicle*, September 1, 2006.

10. Sanford E. Rosen, "Dec 1949 Sermon," box 1, folder 1, "Sermons. 24 Aug 1945–9 Dec 1949," Sanford E. Rosen Papers, Manuscript Collection no. 682, American Jewish Archives, Cincinnati, OH.

11. Rosen, "Dec 1949 Sermon."

12. "Board of Directors meeting, January 28, 1950," box 7, folder 13, CFCU Records, Bancroft Library, University of California, Berkeley.

13. Obituary of Rabbi Sanford E. Rosen, *San Francisco Chronicle*, September 1, 2006.

14. "Discriminatory Signs Hit by Minister Group," *Bakersfield Californian*, March 7, 1950.

15. Ordinance 860 (1950), Ordinances of the Bakersfield City Council.

16. "Annexed District Wants Sewers, Better Streets," *Bakersfield Californian*, March 29, 1953.

17. Measure 4 advertisement, *Bakersfield Californian*, March 23, 1953.

18. Margaret Govea, interview, October 30, 2005, box 10, folder 10, Community Service Organization History Project records, M1669, Special Collections and University Archives, Stanford University Libraries, Stanford, CA.

19. Fred Ross to Cesar Chavez, April 6, 1955, CSO Collection, University of California, San Diego, now held at Special Collections and University Archives, Stanford University Libraries, Stanford, CA.

20. "Statement of Congressman Harlan Hagen before House Judiciary Committee—a Bill to Outlaw the Communist Party," March 1954, box 43, Misc. Correspondence 1954–1964, 11.8.26, Harlan Hagen Papers, Walter Stiern Library Special Collections, California State University, Bakersfield (hereafter HHP).

21. Brilliant, *The Color of America Has Changed*, 151.

22. Justina and Daniel Arias to Harlan Hagen, n.d., box 106, Immigration 1953–1957, 11.25.14, HHP.

23. José R. Burciaga to Harlan Hagen, June 22, 1955, box 106, Immigration 1953–1957, 11.25.14, HHP.

24. Jack White to General Joseph Swing, June 28, 1955, box 106, Immigration 1953–1957, 11.25.14, HHP.

25. Henry Martinez to Harlan Hagen, June 9, 1955, box 106, Immigration 1953–1957, 11.25.14, HHP.

26. "12 Kern CSO Delegates See Bill Signed," *Bakersfield Californian*, July 25, 1961.

27. Brilliant, *The Color of America Has Changed*, 122.

28. "Collins, Sullivan Visit Oakland to Study Job Laws," *Bakersfield Californian*, April 23, 1957.

29. On the civic unity of Los Angeles, see Zaragosa Vargas, *Labor Rights Are Civil Rights: Mexican Workers in Twentieth-Century America* (Princeton, NJ: Princeton University Press, 2005), 258–260.

30. Brilliant, *The Color of America Has Changed*, 90.

31. Ordinance 1146 (1957), Ordinances of the Bakersfield City Council.

32. "Secrecy Is Dangerous," *Bakersfield Californian*, August 26, 1957.

33. Vargas, *Labor Rights Are Civil Rights*, 258.

34. "A Negro Moves into a White Neighborhood," *California Crossroads* 2, no. 10 (October 1960), Jack Maguire Local History Room, Beale Memorial Library, Bakersfield, CA (hereafter JMLHR).

35. "Black Man, White Man," *California Crossroads* 2, no. 11 (November 1960), JMLHR.

36. Edna Buster to Harlan Hagen, September 26, 1962, box 43, Misc. Correspondence 1954–1964, 11.8.28, HHP.

37. "Patriotic Meet Held by DAR," *Bakersfield Californian*, February 12, 1954.

38. Arthur J. Kolatch, "Human Relations Commission," *California Crossroads* 3, no. 7 (July 1961), JMLHR.

39. Resolution 47-63 (1963), Resolutions of the Bakersfield City Council.

40. Resolution 47-63 (1963).

41. West Coast regional NAACP field report, October 17–21, 1963, carton 77, folder 3, NAACP Records.

42. G. E. Stevens to Tarea Hall Pittman, December 20, 1962, carton 77, folder 3, NAACP Records.

43. Minutes of the Bakersfield City Council, August 3, 1964.

44. KCCU newsletter, 1965, Jack Brigham Collection, in author's possession (hereafter JBC).

45. KCCU membership pamphlet, n.d., JBC.

46. KCCU pamphlet, n.d., JBC.

47. Ray Gonzales, interview by author, May 11, 2009.

48. "1000 Join Bakersfield Procession," *Bakersfield Californian*, March 15, 1965. For an overview of the march, see Johnie Mae Parker, *How Long? Not Long! The Battle to End Poverty in Bakersfield* (Bakersfield, CA: self-pub., 1987), 20.

49. Quoted in "1000 Join Bakersfield Procession," *Bakersfield Californian*.

50. Quoted in "1000 Join Bakersfield Procession," *Bakersfield Californian*.

51. Marshall Ganz, email to author, February 28, 2009. For an overview of Marshall Ganz's work in Mississippi and its impact in shaping his worldview, see Pazzanese, "What Is Compelling to Do Right Now?"; Marshall Ganz, *Why David Sometimes Wins: Leadership, Organization, and Strategy in the California Farm Worker Movement* (New York: Oxford University Press), 2009.

52. "Grand Jury Files Report on KKK," *Bakersfield Californian*, May 19, 1922. On the activities of the Ku Klux Klan in Bakersfield, Kern County, and surrounding areas, see Alicia E. Rodriquez, "'No Ku Klux Klan for Kern': The Rise and Fall of the 1920s KKK in Kern County, California," *Southern California Quarterly* 99, no. 1 (Spring 2017): 5–45; Kenneth E. Farmer, "The Invisible Empire in Kern County, 1922" (essay, California Polytechnic State University, 1972); Edward Humes, *Mean Justice* (New York: Simon and Schuster, 1999); David Mark Chalmers, *Hooded Americanism: The History of the Ku Klux Klan* (Durham, NC: Duke University Press, 1987), 125. On the connection between the Klan and the Kern County Board of Supervisors, see Rick Wartzman, *Obscene in the Extreme: The Burning and Banning of John Steinbeck's "The Grapes of Wrath"* (New York: PublicAffairs, 2008).

53. Neil R. McMillen, *The Citizens' Council: Organized Resistance to the Second Reconstruction, 1954–64* (Urbana: University of Illinois Press, 1971), xii.

54. "Huelga, Citizens Council, the NAACP," *California Crossroads* 8, no. 2 (February 1966), JMLHR.

55. "Segregationists Stalled by Sit-In," *Bakersfield Californian*, January 19, 1966.

56. "Segregationists Stalled by Sit-In," *Bakersfield Californian*.

57. "Segregationist More Viewed by IGR [Inter-Group Relations] Board," *Bakersfield Californian*, January 21, 1966.

58. "Segregationist More Viewed by IGR Board," *Bakersfield Californian*.

59. "City Urged to Denounce Segregationist," *Bakersfield Californian*, January 26, 1966; "Segregationist Controversy Sparks City Council Meeting," *Bakersfield Press*, January 26, 1966.

60. Minutes of the Bakersfield City Council, January 31, 1966.

61. Minutes of the Bakersfield City Council, January 31, 1966.

62. "Cannot Outlaw Group—Says Council," *Bakersfield Californian*, February 2, 1966.

63. Minutes of the Bakersfield City Council, January 31, 1966.

64. Minutes of the Bakersfield City Council, March 7, 1966.

65. Brilliant, *The Color of America Has Changed*, 7.

66. On Black-Brown coalitions, see Lauren Araiza, *To March for Others: The Black Freedom Struggle and the United Farm Workers* (Philadelphia: University of Pennsylvania Press, 2013).

CHAPTER 3: "MAXIMUM FEASIBLE PARTICIPATION" AND OPPOSITION

The epigraph is from Henry Fuller to Harlan Hagen, October 1965, box 2, Office of Economic Opportunity War on Poverty, San Joaquin Valley Farm Labor Collection, Sanoian Special Collections Library, California State University, Fresno (hereafter OEO, SJVFLC).

1. On the impact of southern migration on US history in the twentieth century, see James N. Gregory, *The Southern Diaspora: How the Great Migrations of Black and White Southerners Transformed America* (Chapel Hill: University of North Carolina Press, 2005); Gregory, *American Exodus: The Dust Bowl Migration and Okie Culture in California* (New York: Oxford University Press, 1989)

2. See, e.g., Todd Holmes, "The Economic Roots of Reaganism: Corporate Conservatives, Political Economy, and the United Farm Workers Movement, 1965–1970," *Western Historical Quarterly* 41, no. 1 (Spring 2010): 55–80. On the conservative ascendency in California, see Kurt Schuparra, *Triumph of the Right: The Rise of the California Conservative Movement, 1945–1966* (Armonk, NY: M. E. Sharpe, 1998); Matthew Dallek, *The Right Moment: Ronald Reagan's First Victory and the Decisive Turning Point in American Politics* (New York: Free Press, 2000).

3. See Peter LaChapelle, "'Shadows of the Dust': The Expectation and Ordeal of California's African-American Dust Bowl Migrants; Southern San Joaquin Valley, 1929–1941" (master's thesis, California State University, Bakersfield, 1997).

4. See, e.g., Annelise Orleck, *Storming Caesars Palace: How Black Mothers Fought Their Own War on Poverty* (Boston: Beacon Press, 2005); Gordon K. Mantler, *Power to the Poor: Black-Brown Coalition and the Fight for Economic Justice, 1960–1974* (Chapel Hill: University of North Carolina Press, 2013); William S. Clayson, *Freedom Is Not Enough: The War on Poverty and the Civil Rights Movement in Texas* (Austin: University of Texas Press, 2010); Marc S. Rodriguez, "Migrants and Citizens: Mexican American Migrant Workers and the War on Poverty in an American City," in *Repositioning North American Migration History: New Directions in Modern Continental Migration, Citizenship, and Community*, ed. Marc S. Rodriguez (Rochester, NY: University of Rochester Press, 2004), 328–352; Robert Bauman, *Race and the War on Poverty: From Watts to East L.A.* (Norman: University of Oklahoma Press, 2008).

5. Scholars have assessed the limits of the War on Poverty in its operational framework of maintaining racial capitalism vis-à-vis the mantra of "maximum feasible participation" and community action, while at the same time mitigating radical movements among racialized populations. In addition, case studies have evaluated locally where the War on Poverty proved lasting and impactful. See, e.g., Alyosha Goldstein, *Poverty in Common: The Politics of Community Action during the American Century* (Durham, NC: Duke University Press, 2012); Noel A. Cazenave, *Impossible Democracy: The Unlikely Success of the War on Poverty Community Action Programs* (Albany: State University of New York Press, 2007); Robin Marie Averbeck, *Liberalism Is Not Enough: Race and Poverty in Postwar Political Thought* (Chapel Hill: University of North Carolina Press, 2018).

6. Thomas R. Wellock, "Stick It in L.A.! Community Control and Nuclear Power in California's Central Valley," *Journal of American History* 84, no. 3 (December 1997): 942–978.

7. "Tri-County Agency Gets Federal Grant," *Visalia Times-Delta*, October 6, 1965, box 2, OEO, SJVFLC.

8. For a general overview of how antipoverty programs functioned in major US cities, see Allen J. Matusow, *The Unraveling of America: A History of Liberalism in the 1960s* (Athens: University of Georgia Press, 2009).

9. See, e.g., Charles Murray, *Losing Ground: American Social Policy, 1950–1980* (New York: Basics Books, 1994); Daniel P. Moynihan, *Maximum Feasible Misunderstanding: Community Action in the War on Poverty* (New York: Free Press, 1969).

10. On the impact of deindustrialization in the United States vis-à-vis the urban crisis, see Thomas J. Sugrue, *The Origins of the Urban Crisis: Race and Inequality in Postwar Detroit* (Princeton, NJ: Princeton University Press, 2005). See also Carey McWilliams, *Factories in the Field: The Story of Migratory Farm Labor in California* (Boston: Little, Brown, 1939).

11. See Michael Harrington, *The Other America: Poverty in the United States* (New York: Macmillan, 1962); Maurice Isserman, *The Other American: The Life of Michael Harrington* (New York: PublicAffairs, 2000).

12. Matusow, *The Unraveling of America*, 245–246.

13. Johnie Mae Parker, *How Long? Not Long! The Battle to End Poverty in Bakersfield* (Bakersfield, CA: self-pub., 1987), 33.

14. Matusow, *The Unraveling of America*, 246.

15. Parker, *How Long? Not Long!*, 35.

16. "Governing Body," California/Bakersfield Anti-Poverty Council, Grant Files, 1966–1971, Migrant Division, Office of Operations, OEO, Community Services Administration, record group 381, National Archives at College Park, MD (hereafter Migrant Division, RG 381, NACP-MD).

17. The TAP area included Bakersfield census tracts 15, 20, 21, 22, 23, 25, and 31. Tract 22 was the most important, given the density of the area's population and its location in southeast Bakersfield, bordering municipal boundaries, as opposed to the more distant rural parts of Kern County. The square mileage of Kern County is larger than that of the state of Massachusetts.

18. Dolores Huerta to Ruth Graves, July 26, 1965, California/National Farm Workers Association, Grant Files, 1966–1971, Migrant Division, RG 381, NACP-MD.

19. Parker, *How Long? Not Long!*, 41.

20. Obituary of Melvin Brown, *Bakersfield Californian*, April 2, 2005.

21. Parker, *How Long? Not Long!*, 43.

22. Parker, *How Long? Not Long!*, 45.

23. For an early history of the CSO, see Katherine Underwood, "Pioneering Minority Representation: Edward Roybal and the Los Angeles City Council, 1949–1962," *Pacific Historical Review* 66, no. 3 (August 1997): 399–425; Kenneth C. Burt, "The Power of a Mobilized Citizenry and Coalition Politics: The 1949 Election of Edward R. Roybal to the Los Angeles City Council," *Southern California Quarterly* 85, no. 4 (Winter 2003): 413–438. On the importance of the Govea family to the Bakersfield CSO chapter and the farmworker movement, see Miriam Pawel, *The Union of Their Dreams: Power, Hope, and Struggle in Cesar Chavez's Farm Worker Movement* (New York: Bloomsbury, 2009), prologue.

24. For a brief history of East Bakersfield through the lens of one of its notable residents, see Ed Cray, *Chief Justice: A Biography of Earl Warren* (New York: Simon and Schuster, 1997), 15–34; Jim Newton, *Justice for All: Earl Warren and the Nation He Made* (New York: Penguin, 2006), 19–34.

25. Carlos and Rosalio Bañales, interview by author, 2009.

26. "TAP Operated Many Faceted Program to Help Its People," *Bakersfield Californian*, November 23, 1966.

27. Parker, *How Long? Not Long!*, 47–53.

28. See Patty Newman, *Pass the Poverty, Please!* (Whittier, CA: Constructive Action, 1966). On women in the modern conservative movement, see Michelle Nickerson,

Mothers of Conservatism: Women and the Postwar Right (Princeton, NJ: Princeton University Press, 2012).

29. For a history of conservative mobilization around this rhetoric and its effects on the history of politics and society in the United States, see Michael W. Flamm, *Law and Order: Street Crime, Civil Unrest, and the Crisis of Liberalism in the 1960s* (New York: Columbia University Press, 2005).

30. Minutes of the Bakersfield City Council, May 16 and May 23, 1966.

31. "Unrest Erupts Briefly; Boy Hit by Bullet; 33 Persons Arrested," *Bakersfield Californian*, May 23, 1966; "Young Folk Need Jobs, Aide Says," *Bakersfield Californian*, May 24, 1966. The farmworker movement also resulted in acts of violence, by both union supporters and law enforcement. The principled nonviolence of César Chávez, however, may have been integral in preventing large-scale racial riots and, although acknowledged by scholars, is still understudied as it relates to a local history of the region. On the nonviolent strategies of Chávez, see José-Antonio Orosco, *Cesar Chavez and the Common Sense of Nonviolence* (Albuquerque: University of New Mexico Press, 2008).

32. Pawel, *The Union of Their Dreams*, 7–8.

33. "Hagen, Harlan Francis, (1914–1990)," *Biographical Directory of the United States Congress* (online), accessed August 28, 2023.

34. "The National Farm Workers Poverty Program," California/National Farm Workers Association, Grant Files, 1966–1971, Migrant Division, RG 381, NACP-MD.

35. OEO press release, October 5, 1965, box 2, OEO, SJVFLC.

36. OEO press release, October 5, 1965.

37. On the Americanization of Mexican immigrants in early twentieth-century Los Angeles, see George J. Sánchez, *Becoming Mexican American: Ethnicity, Culture, and Identity in Chicano Los Angeles, 1900–1945* (New York: Oxford University Press, 1993), 87–107.

38. "Summary of Proposed Program of the National Farm Workers Association to Aid Agricultural Workers under the Poverty Program," box 2, OEO, SJVFLC.

39. "Summary of Proposed Program of the National Farm Workers Association."

40. "Summary of Proposed Program of the National Farm Workers Association."

41. Harlan Hagen to Dolores Huerta, July 14, 1965, box 2, OEO, SJVFLC.

42. Harlan Hagen to Gillis W. Long, May 24, 1965, box 2, OEO, SJVFLC.

43. Harlan Hagen to Dolores Huerta, May 25, 1965, box 2, OEO, SJVFLC.

44. Fay C. Short to Harlan Hagen, October 8, 1965, box 2, OEO, SJVFLC.

45. Resolution 81-65 (October 7, 1965), Delano City Council, box 2, OEO, SJVFLC.

46. Thomas H. Kuchel to Clifford F. Loader, October 11, 1965, box 2, OEO, SJVFLC. On Loader, see Jacques E. Levy, *Cesar Chavez: Autobiography of La Causa* (Minneapolis: University of Minnesota Press, 2007), 186.

47. Thomas H. Kuchel to Robert Sargent Shriver, October 21, 1965, box 2, OEO, SJVFLC.

48. César Chávez to Thomas H. Kuchel, October 9, 1965, box 2, OEO, SJVFLC. On the career of Kuchel, see Todd Holmes, "Demise and Ascent: The Career of Thomas Kuchel and the Advent of the Reagan Right," *BOOM California* 1, no. 4 (Winter 2011): 20–25.

49. "OEO Fund Grant Only Delayed: Agency Turns Down Review," *Bakersfield Californian*, December 23, 1965.

50. Ivan G. McDaniel to Bernard Boutin, January 1, 1966, State OEO Records, F3751:151, California State Archives, Sacramento.

51. Austin P. Morris, "Agricultural Labor and National Labor Legislation," *California Law Review* 54, no. 5 (December 1966): 1959n85.

52. Ivan G. McDaniel and Leon L. Gordon, "Comment: Agricultural Labor Relations. The Other Problem: A Rebuttal," *Stanford Law Review* 15, no. 4 (July 1963): 616–637. On the Bracero Program, see Robert S. Robinson, "Taking the Fair Deal to the Fields: Truman's Commission on Migratory Labor, Public Law 78, and the Bracero Program, 1950–1952," *Agricultural History* 84, no. 3 (Summer 2010): 381–402; Deborah Cohen, *Braceros: Migrant Citizens and Transnational Subjects in the Postwar United States and Mexico* (Chapel Hill: University of North Carolina Press, 2011).

53. Dolores Huerta to Ruth Graves, July 26, 1965, California/National Farm Workers Association, Grant Files, 1966–1971, Migrant Division, RG 381, NACP-MD.

54. Memo to Mr. Shriver, October 12, 1965, California/National Farm Workers Association, Grant Files, 1966–1971, Migrant Division, RG 381, NACP-MD.

55. Memo to Mr. Shriver, October 12, 1965.

56. John Daum to Ed May and Bob Clampitt, September 10, 1965, California/National Farm Workers Association, Grant Files, 1966–1971, Migrant Division, RG 381, NACP-MD.

57. Noel Klores to Fred Hayes, October 12, 1965, California/National Farm Workers Association, Grant Files, 1966–1971, Migrant Division, RG 381, NACP-MD.

58. Klores to Hayes, October 12, 1965.

59. Kirke Wilson to Ruth Graves, October 21, 1965, California/National Farm Workers Association, Grant Files, 1966–1971, Migrant Division, RG 381, NACP-MD.

60. "General Letter from Cesar Chavez," California/National Farm Workers Association, Grant Files, 1966–1971, Migrant Division, RG 381, NACP-MD.

61. Frank E. Dyer to Harlan Hagen, October 7, 1965, box 2, OEO, SJVFLC.

62. Clifford F. Loader to Harlan Hagen, October 5, 1965, box 2, OEO, SJVFLC.

63. Mr. and Mrs. Alejandro Fetalvero to Harlan Hagen, October 8, 1965, box 2, OEO, SJVFLC.

64. *Citizens for Facts from Delano*, no. 1 (1966), box 2, OEO, SJVFLC.

65. Letter to Mrs. Joe Luque, November 3, 1965, California/National Farm Workers Association, Grant Files, 1966–1971, Migrant Division, RG 381, NACP-MD.

66. Eduardo Quevedo to Larry Itliong, November 19, 1965, National Farm Workers Association Collection, box 11, folder 6, Archives of Urban and Labor Affairs, Wayne State University, Detroit, MI.

67. Letter to Mrs. Joe Luque, November 3, 1965, California/National Farm Workers Association, Grant Files, 1966–1971, Migrant Division, RG 381, NACP-MD.

68. Robert Aguilar et al. to California CSO chapters, n.d., box 2, OEO, SJVFLC.

69. Vance A. Webb to Robert Sargent Shriver, October 10, 1965, box 2, OEO, SJVFLC.

70. "C of C Takes Stand Opposing 'Rights' Issue," *Delano Record*, November 11, 1965.

71. "C of C Takes Stand Opposing 'Rights' Issue"; Abe Goertzen to Harlan Hagen, November 11, 1965, box 2, OEO, SJVFLC.
72. David S. Fairbairn to John J. McFall, September 23, 1966, box 2, OEO, SJVFLC.
73. Council of California Growers newsletter, no. 169 (October 11, 1965), box 2, OEO, SJVFLC.
74. Stephen Pavich to Harlan Hagen, October 18, 1965, box 2, OEO, SJVFLC.
75. Stanley E. Willis to Robert Sargent Shriver, October 25, 1965, box 2, OEO, SJVFLC.
76. Herbert A. Watkins to Harlan Hagen, October 26, 1965, box 2, OEO, SJVFLC.
77. Paul Perlin to Thomas H. Kuchel, November 23, 1965, box 2, OEO, SJVFLC.
78. Everett B. Krackov to Harlan Hagen, October 18, 1965, box 2, OEO, SJVFLC.
79. Doug Adair to Adam C. Powell, October 12, 1965, box 2, OEO, SJVFLC.
80. SNCC, "Hagen Hits Federal Funds for Strikers; Ignored Federal Subsidies for Growers," n.d., box 2, OEO, SJVFLC. On alliances between the SNCC and the United Farm Workers (UFW), see Lauren Araiza, "For Freedom of Other Men: Civil Rights, Black Power, and the United Farm Workers, 1965–1973" (PhD diss., University of California, Berkeley, 2006).
81. SNCC, "Hagen Hits Federal Funds for Strikers."
82. Henry Fuller to Harlan Hagen, October 12, 1965, box 2, OEO, SJVFLC.
83. Mel Brown to Harlan Hagen, n.d., box 2, OEO, SJVFLC.
84. Brown to Hagen, n.d.
85. Harlan Hagen to William G. Phillips, January 19, 1966, box 2, OEO, SJVFLC.
86. Hagen to Phillips, January 19, 1966.
87. Stanley E. Willis to Harlan Hagen, January 31, 1966, box 2, OEO, SJVFLC.
88. See John Dunne, *Delano: The Story of the California Grape Strike* (Berkeley: University of California Press, 2008); Mark Day, *Forty Acres: Cesar Chavez and the Farm Workers* (New York: Praeger, 1971), 125–139.
89. 112 Cong. Rec. H24,446 (1966), box 2, OEO, SJVFLC.
90. Harlan Hagen to Robert Sargent Shriver, February 22, 1966, box 2, OEO, SJVFLC.
91. Hagen to Shriver, February 22, 1966.
92. Harlan Hagen to Donald T. Appell, March 6, 1966, box 2, OEO, SJVFLC.
93. Harlan Hagen to David Bowers, March 6, 1966, box 2, OEO, SJVFLC.
94. Telegram to Harlan Hagen from constituents, n.d., box 2, OEO, SJVFLC.
95. Harlan Hagen to Robert Sargent Shriver, June 24, 1966, box 2, OEO, SJVFLC.
96. Hagen to Shriver, June 24, 1966.
97. James Wrightson, "Mathias Nearly Announces as He Blasts Hagen," *Fresno Bee*, November 19, 1965.
98. See Dunne, *Delano*; Peter Matthiessen, *Sal Si Puedes: Cesar Chavez and the New American Revolution* (Berkeley: University of California Press, 2000).
99. See Susan Ferris and Ricardo Sandoval, *The Fight in the Fields: Cesar Chavez and the Farmworkers Movement* (New York: Harcourt Brace, 1997); "Robert Kennedy Took On the Kern County Sheriff," March 1966, YouTube video, uploaded August 18, 2015, by UFW, 1:34.
100. Minutes of the Bakersfield City Council, September 6, 1966.

101. "Board Can't Put Poverty Up to People," *Bakersfield Californian*, May 25, 1966.
102. "Board Can't Put Poverty Up to People," *Bakersfield Californian*.
103. "Roland Fires Back at CAP Clinic," *Bakersfield Californian*, March 7, 1966.
104. "Roland Resigns as Director of CAP Program," *Bakersfield Californian*, March 6, 1966.
105. "Roland Resigns as Director of CAP Program," *Bakersfield Californian*.
106. Obituary for William H. Park, *Los Angeles Times*, May 24, 1988.
107. "Poverty War Foes Told: Quit," *Bakersfield Californian*, March 17, 1966.
108. "Poverty War Foes Told: Quit," *Bakersfield Californian*.
109. "$492,577 Cost Set for Anti-Poverty Projects in Area," *Bakersfield News Bulletin*, May 1, 1966.
110. "Director Is Due June 27 for CAP Job," *Bakersfield Californian*, June 19, 1966.
111. "Probe Asked on 'Sabotage' Allegations," *Bakersfield Californian*, March 22, 1966.
112. "Arthur Shaw, Prasad Take New Posts," *Bakersfield Californian*, August 9, 1966.
113. "Two Men Clash on Poverty," *Bakersfield Californian*, May 3, 1966.
114. Ralph Jordan to Board of Supervisors, May 24, 1966, carton 77, folder 3, NAACP, Region 1, Records, BANC MSS 78/180 c, Bancroft Library, University of California, Berkeley (hereafter NAACP Records).
115. "Sore 'Attitude' of Three," *Bakersfield Californian*, May 17, 1966.
116. "Poverty War to Cut Welfare," *Bakersfield Californian*, June 2, 1966.
117. Mary Rourke, "Virna Canson, 81; Activist, Director of NAACP's 9-State Western Region," *Los Angeles Times*, May 21, 2003.
118. Virna Canson to Leonard Carter, June 17, 1966, carton 77, folder 3, NAACP Records.
119. Leonard Carter to Art Shaw, June 23, 1966; Virna Canson to Leonard Carter, June 17, 1966; both letters in carton 77, folder 3, NAACP Records.
120. "Resolution," 1966, carton 77, folder 3, NAACP Records.
121. Terry L. Baum to John C. Williamson, May 22, 1966, carton 77, folder 3, NAACP Records.
122. Art Shaw to Leonard Carter, June 26, 1966, carton 77, folder 3, NAACP Records.
123. Kenneth Hoagland to Mayor and City Council, June 1, 1966, carton 77, folder 3, NAACP Records.
124. "Report of the Kern County Economic Opportunity Corporation Programs," October 16, 1967, State OEO Records, R3751:151, California State Archives, Sacramento.
125. "Report of the Kern County Economic Opportunity Corporation Programs."
126. For an overview of CAP programs and the ideological battles between liberals, conservatives, and political radicals in the northern United States, see Thomas J. Sugrue, *Sweet Land of Liberty: The Forgotten Struggle for Civil Rights in the North* (New York: Random House, 2008), 356–399.
127. "Report of the Kern County Economic Opportunity Corporation Programs," October 16, 1967, State OEO Records, F3751:151, California State Archives, Sacramento.
128. Art Shaw to Gene De la Torre, September 14, 1967, California/Bakersfield

Anti-Poverty Council, Grant Files, 1966–1971, Migrant Division, RG 381, NACP-MD.

CHAPTER 4: AGRARIAN CHICANISMO

The epigraph is from Jesus Gilberto Nieto, "A Proposal for the Establishment of a Chicano Cultural Center and a Proposal for the Establishment of a Chicano Studies Department, Bakersfield College," Spring 1974, Jess Nieto Collection, in author's possession (hereafter JNC).

1. George Mariscal, *Brown-Eyed Children of the Sun: Lessons from the Chicano Movement, 1965–1975* (Albuquerque: University of New Mexico Press, 2005), 3.

2. Lorena Oropeza, *¡Raza Sí! ¡Guerra No! Chicano Protest and Patriotism during the Vietnam War Era* (Berkeley: University of California Press, 2005), 71–72.

3. Michael Soldatenko, *Chicano Studies: The Genesis of a Discipline* (Tucson: University of Arizona Press, 2009), 11.

4. Ignacio M. García, *The Forging of a Militant Ethos among Mexicans Americans* (Tucson: University of Arizona Press, 1997), 4.

5. Marisol Moreno, "'Of the Community, for the Community': The Chicana/o Student Movement in California's Public Higher Education, 1967–1973" (PhD diss., University of California, Santa Barbara, 2009), 3.

6. Moreno, "Of the Community, for the Community," viii.

7. See, e.g., Frank P. Barajas, *Mexican Americans with Moxie: A Transgenerational History of El Movimiento Chicano in Ventura County, California, 1945–1975* (Lincoln: University of Nebraska Press, 2021).

8. See Carlos Muñoz Jr., *Youth, Identity, Power: The Chicano Movement* (London: Verso, 1989).

9. Muñoz, *Youth, Identity, Power*, 192.

10. Michael Soldatenko, "The Genesis of Academic Chicano Studies, 1967–1970: The Emergence of Empirical and Perspectivist Chicano Studies," *Latino Studies Journal* 9, no. 2 (Spring 1998): 3–25.

11. Moreno, "Of the Community, for the Community," 212.

12. Jess Nieto, interview by author, November 2003.

13. Nieto, interview by author.

14. Ray Gonzales, interview by author, May 11, 2009.

15. Nieto, interview by author.

16. Nieto, interview by author.

17. See Seferino Ayala, "Mexican Americans Achieving New Goals," *Renegade Rip*, May 1, 1970, Bakersfield College Archives, Bakersfield, CA (hereafter BCA).

18. Nieto, interview by author.

19. Nieto, interview by author.

20. According to a now-defunct version of the Deganawidah-Quetzalcoatl University homepage, "D-Q University is a private, independent, non-profit, accredited, open access, multi-campus, two-year college, dedicated to the progress of indigenous peoples through education."

21. Nieto, interview by author.

22. "Finlinson Views BC," *Renegade Rip*, January 14, 1972, BCA.

23. "Finlinson Views BC," *Renegade Rip*.

24. Fred Lewis, "Reps Approve Chicano Center," *Renegade Rip*, October 15, 1971, BCA.
25. Ruben Felix, "United Mexican Students," *Renegade Rip*, October 15, 1971, BCA; "La Raza," *Renegade Rip*, December 3, 1971, BCA.
26. Ben Jones, "'Cultural Awareness' Made as New Grad Requirement," *Renegade Rip*, March 9, 1973, BCA.
27. Nieto, interview by author.
28. Nieto, interview by author.
29. Randy Shaw, *Beyond the Fields: Cesar Chavez, the UFW, and the Struggle for Social Justice in the 21st Century* (Berkeley: University of California Press, 2008), 47.
30. Ron Johnson, "MECHA Demanding 100% UFW Lettuce," *Renegade Rip*, March 1, 1974, BCA.
31. Duane Goff, interview by author, March 7, 2010.
32. Johnson, "MECHA Demanding 100% UFW Lettuce."
33. Frank P. Barajas, "Chicana-Chicano Agonists," *BOOM California*, November 2, 2021.
34. Goff, interview by author.
35. Goff, interview by author.
36. Gus García to Graduation Requirements Committee, Bakersfield College, February 21, 1973, JNC.
37. García to Graduation Requirements Committee.
38. D. J. Whipple, "Collins Overrules Senate," *Renegade Rip*, March 22, 1974, BCA.
39. Barajas, "Chicana-Chicano Agonists."
40. Gaylen Lewis, evaluation of Jess Nieto, 1973, JNC. Lewis's attempt to draw a distinction between the assimilationist orientation of the League of United Latin American Citizens (LULAC) and a more radical Chicana/o identity highlights the importance of reevaluations of LULAC in the development of Chicana/o movement historiography. See, e.g., Mario T. García, *Mexican Americans: Leadership, Ideology, and Identity, 1930–1960* (New Haven, CT: Yale University Press, 1991), 25–61; Benjamin Márquez, *LULAC: The Evolution of a Mexican American Political Organization* (Austin: University of Texas Press, 1993); Carlos Kevin Blanton, *George I. Sánchez: The Long Fight for Mexican American Integration* (New Haven, CT: Yale University Press, 2015).
41. Nieto, interview by author.
42. "Gonzales Climaxes Semana de la Raza," *Renegade Rip*, May 11, 1973, BCA.
43. Francine Filoteo, "Professor Feels Unity of BC Chicanos," *Renegade Rip*, May 3, 1974, BCA.
44. Quoted in Filoteo, "Professor Feels Unity of BC Chicanos."
45. Chicano Cultural Center pamphlet, 1975–1977, BCA.
46. Chicano Cultural Center and Chicano Studies, Bakersfield College, pamphlet, 1976, JNC.
47. The Title IX Ethnic Heritage Studies Program of the Elementary and Secondary Education Act was approved in 1972 under President Richard Nixon. See "Ethnic Heritage Studies Program," in *Harvard Encyclopedia of American Ethnic Groups*, ed. Stephan Thernstrom (Cambridge, MA: Presidents and Fellows of Harvard College, 1980), 343–344.
48. Jesus Gilbert Nieto, "A Descriptive Analysis of an International and Intercultural Approach in a Community College Setting" (EdD diss., University of Southern California, 1975), 1–6.

49. Nieto, "A Descriptive Analysis of an International and Intercultural Approach," 48–49.
50. Jess Nieto, "Project MECHICA Students Continue Studies in Mexico," *Renegade Rip*, September 27, 1974, BCA.
51. Nieto, "A Descriptive Analysis of an International and Intercultural Approach," 58.
52. "Estudiantes de Bakersfield Saludaron Ayer al Gobernador," *Carteles del Sur*, April 15, 1976, JNC.
53. Jess Nieto, "Socializing Americans: School and Community, a Chicano Perspective," *Renegade Rip*, April 19, 1976, BCA.
54. "Dr. Nieto Named Dean at Delano College Center," *Delano Record*, September 6, 1977.
55. Nieto, interview by author.
56. Nieto, interview by author.
57. Nieto, interview by author.
58. Jess Nieto, "Statement by the Minority Coalition of Kern County Delano Chapter Presented to the Delano City Council," February 6, 1978, JNC.
59. Susan Cox, "Police Charged with Harassment," *Delano Record*, April 23, 1980.
60. "Mexican-American Communication Gaps in Delano Area Discussed," *Delano Record*, September 1, 1977.
61. Jorge Pérez Ponce (Internacional División, El Congreso Nacional de Asuntos de Colegiales) to Jesus Nieto, March 21, 1978, JNC.
62. "Ethnic Music Delivered by Folkloristas Group," *Bakersfield Californian*, April 28, 1982.
63. Alex Edillor, "Los Folkloristas Bring Spectacular Musical Texture," *Delano Record*, November 29, 1977.
64. Jess Nieto, "El Nuevo Canto: Los Folkloristas," *Somos Magazine*, May 1979, JNC.
65. The two documentary films were titled *Where Are the Roots of Men?* and *Pre-Columbian World View of the Universe*. See Greg Lipford, "BC Pair Receive $30,000 for TV Script," *Renegade Rip*, October 3, 1977, BCA.
66. Key letters of support came from, for example, UCLA scholar Juan Gómez-Quiñones; Ignacio Bernal, director of Mexico's National Museum of Anthropology; Jerry Apodaca, then governor of New Mexico; and Ray Gonzales, member of the California Fair Employment Committee.
67. César E. Chávez to Jesus Nieto, October 11, 1978, JNC.
68. Jesus Gilberto Nieto, "A Proposal for a New Partnership between Private Enterprise in the United States of America and the Republic of Mexico: Gemini Foundation and Fossil Energy Corporation," Fall 1980, JNC.
69. Julian Nava, *Julian Nava: My Mexican American Journey* (Houston: Arte Publico Press, 2002), 144.
70. "Pact for Project with Mexico Signed," *Jottings: The League for Innovation in the Community College* 8, no. 1 (September 1980): 1, JNC.
71. Nava, *Julian Nava*, 169.
72. Alfonso J. García, "Otorgaran Becas a Jóvenes Estudiantes Mexicanos, Anuncia el Embajador J. Nava," *Novedades: El Mejor Diario De México*, January 23, 1981, JNC. See also "Colaboración entre iguales, las relaciones de México y EU," *El Universal: El Gran Diario de México*, January 23, 1981, JNC.

73. Jess Nieto, interview by author, May 12, 2006.

74. On the continuation of Nieto's international and transnational initiatives, see "Highlights from Dr. Gonzalo Santos' Talk at the 1st Annual Jess Nieto Memorial Conference," April 2018, YouTube video, uploaded March 18, 2021, by Bakersfield College Social Justice Institute, 14:08.

75. "Educator, Philanthropist, and Activist Jess Nieto Touched Many Lives," *Bakersfield Californian*, October 9, 2017.

76. On tensions between the UFW and undocumented workers, see Frank Bardacke, *Trampling Out the Vintage: Cesar Chavez and the Two Souls of the United Farm Workers* (London: Verso, 2011), 488–506.

CHAPTER 5: "HOO-RAY GONZALES!"

The chapter title, "Hoo-ray Gonzales!," was the phrase on the promotional button for Ray Gonzales's 1972 campaign for the California State Assembly. The chapter epigraphs are from, respectively, Raymond Gonzales, "Will Parra-Florez Assembly Race Turn into the Family Feud Part II," *La Voz de Kern*, 2010, in author's possession; Maureen McCloud, "The Kern Brand of Politics—Conservative, Populist, Humorless," *California Journal*, July 1978.

1. Resolution 87-68 (September 16, 1968), Resolutions of the Bakersfield City Council.

2. César Chávez, "A Dialogue with Congress," transcript, October 1, 1969, Farmworker Movement Documentation Project (website), last updated 2014.

3. For an overview of the historical development of Central Valley towns with regard to tensions between growers and labor, see Devra Weber, *Dark Sweat, White Gold: California Farm Workers, Cotton, and the New Deal* (Berkeley: University of California Press, 1994), 17–47.

4. Marshall Ganz, interview by LeRoy Chatfield, 2009, oral history audio files, 1:03:00 and 41:29, Farmworker Movement Documentation Project (website), last updated 2014.

5. On Jessica Govea, see Gloria Alday, "Organizing a Movement: Jessica Govea—Chicana, Feminist & Labor Organizer" (undergraduate honor's thesis, Yale College, 2007); Mireya Loza, "How One Girl Helped Build a Latinx Civil Rights Movement," *O Say Can You See?* (blog), National Museum of American History, December 16, 2020.

6. On the role of Filipinos in the farm labor movement, see Craig Scharlin and Lilia V. Villanueva, *Philip Vera Cruz: A Personal History of Filipino Immigrants and the Farmworkers Movement* (Los Angeles: University of California, Los Angeles, Labor Center, 1992); Christian O. Paiz, *The Strikers of Coachella: A Rank-and-File History of the UFW Movement* (Chapel Hill: University of North Carolina Press, 2023).

7. Minutes of the Bakersfield City Council, April 28, 1969.

8. Minutes of the Bakersfield City Council, April 28, 1969.

9. Lauren Araiza, "For Freedom of Other Men: Civil Rights, Black Power, and the United Farm Workers, 1965–1973" (PhD diss., University of California, Berkeley, 2006), 59.

10. On contemporary politics in Kern County, see Steve Singiser, "Forget Mark Sanford: Here Is a Special Election with Real Lessons for 2014," *Daily Kos Elections*, June 2, 2013.

11. Statement by Raymond Gonzales, Californian Radio, September 13, 2011.

12. Campaign flyer, 1972, P1010543, book 1, Ray Gonzales Collection, in author's possession (hereafter RGC).

13. "Brochure on bio of Ray Gonzales," 1972, P1010546-47, book 1, RGC.

14. See, e.g., Armando Navarro, *La Raza Unida Party: A Chicano Challenge to the US Two-Party Dictatorship* (Philadelphia: Temple University Press, 2000).

15. Raymond Gonzales, email to author, October 5, 2011.

16. See James N. Gregory, *The Southern Diaspora: How the Great Migrations of Black and White Southerners Transformed America* (Chapel Hill: University of North Carolina Press, 2005), 286–290.

17. Ray Gonzales, interview by author, May 11, 2009.

18. "The 14th Annual Convention of the California Democratic Council," 1966, box 31, folder 10, California Democratic Council Records, Southern California Library, Los Angeles.

19. Duane Goff, interview by author, March 2010.

20. On white supremacy and the Ku Klux Klan in Taft, see Edward Humes, *Mean Justice* (New York: Simon and Schuster, 1999); Rick Wartzman, *Obscene in the Extreme: The Burning and Banning of John Steinbeck's "The Grapes of Wrath"* (New York: PublicAffairs, 2008); Alicia E. Rodriquez, "'No Ku Klux Klan for Kern': The Rise and Fall of the 1920s KKK in Kern County, California," *Southern California Quarterly* 99, no. 1 (Spring 2017): 5–45.

21. Gonzales, interview by author.

22. Steve Barber, interview by author, October 26, 2023.

23. Ray Gonzales, political campaign flier, 1972, P1010546, book 1, RGC.

24. "Ray Gonzales Opens Campaign," *La Voz*, August 10, 1972, P1010549, book 1, RGC.

25. "Ray Gonzales Reviews Busy First Year in State Assembly," March 1, 1974, P1010785, book 2, RGC.

26. "Ray Gonzales Spends Busy Day Stumping," *Bakersfield Californian*, November 1, 1972. Many Kern County Democrats still echo Gonzales's moderate liberalism. See, e.g., Ben Christopher and Ariel Gans, "'Overlooked': How the Central Valley Became California's Most Fiercely Contested Political Turf," KQED, October 21, 2022.

27. Although there needs to be more work done on the historical religiosity of California's Central Valley residents, for a useful introduction on the impact of southern migration to the American West in terms of religiosity, see Gregory, *The Southern Diaspora*, 197–235.

28. "East Students to Join in Celebrating Cinco de Mayo," May 3, 1972, P1010516, book 1, RGC.

29. "He Feels Council Acted Out of Turn," May 16, 1972, P1010575, book 1, RGC. On Chicana/o opposition to the war in Vietnam, see Lorena Oropeza, *¡Raza Sí! ¡Guerra No! Chicano Protest and Patriotism during the Vietnam War Era* (Berkeley: University of California Press, 2005).

30. "Gonzales Campaign," October 12, 1972, P1010574, book 1, RGC.

31. "Blowing the Whistle: Assemblyman Fights System," n.d., P1010573, book 1, RGC.

32. See Todd Holmes, "The Economic Roots of Reaganism: Corporate Conservatives, Political Economy, and the United Farm Workers Movement, 1965–1970," *Western Historical Quarterly* 41, no. 1 (Spring 2010): 55–80.

33. "More Tolerant of Its Shortcomings: Gonzales Mellows after Year in Legislature," January 15, 1974, *Los Angeles Times*, P1010774, book 2, RGC.
34. "Foe of Cussing and Gratuities: A Maverick Legislator," *San Francisco Chronicle*, March 12, 1973, P1010607, book 1, RGC.
35. "Gonzales Assails Williamson Act," n.d., P1010554, book 1, RGC.
36. "Ag Preserves: Need or Sham?," January 20, 1974, P1010720, book 2, RGC.
37. "Ag Preserves," January 20, 1974.
38. "Gonzales Asked to Clarify 'Tax Fraud,'" April 5, 1973, P1010517, book 1, RGC.
39. "Dr. Gonzales Scores Open Space Act," March 22, 1972, P1010544, book 1, RGC.
40. Mary K. Shell, "Nothing but a 'Sham and Fraud,'" *Bakersfield Californian*, April 1, 1973.
41. "Tempers Flare over Name for Library," *Bakersfield Californian*, February 20, 1974, P1010533, book 1, RGC.
42. Raymond Gonzales, email to author, October 5, 2011.
43. Letter to the editor, *Bakersfield Californian*, March 1, 1974, P1010733, book 2, RGC.
44. "Let Citizens Decide," editorial, February 24, 1974, P1010735, book 2, RGC.
45. James Richardson, *Willie Brown: A Biography* (Berkeley: University of California Press, 1996), 129.
46. Richardson, *Willie Brown*, 226.
47. Barber, interview by author.
48. Miriam Pawel, *The Crusades of Cesar Chavez* (New York: Bloomsbury Press, 2014), 246.
49. Herman Sillas, "Mexican-Americans and the Political Mainstream," *Los Angeles Times*, November 22, 1972.
50. Randy Shaw, *Beyond the Fields: Cesar Chavez, the UFW, and the Struggle for Social Justice in the 21st Century* (Berkeley: University of California Press, 2008), 151.
51. "Candidates Booed, Grilled," n.d., P1010569, book 1, RGC.
52. For examples of this tendency of Alatorre during speaking engagements, see, e.g., "Statements and Speeches," 1973–1974, box 6, folder 4, Richard Alatorre Collection, John F. Kennedy Memorial Library, California State University, Los Angeles.
53. Barber, interview by author.
54. Raymond Gonzales, "The California Farmworker: Forgotten Man in History of Agribusiness," *Sacramento Bee*, April 22, 1973, P1010616, book 1, RGC.
55. Raymond Gonzales, email to author, October 5, 2011.
56. Art Torres to Raymond Gonzales, August 16, 1973, box 13, folder 28, UFW Administration Files, UFW Organizing Committee, Archives of Urban and Labor Affairs, Wayne State University, Detroit, MI (hereafter UFW Files, ULA-WSU).
57. Raymond Gonzales to Art Torres, August 9, 1972, box 13, folder 28, UFW Files, ULA-WSU.
58. Ray Gonzales to Cesar Chavez, November 25, 1972, box 13, folder 28, UFW Files, ULA-WSU.
59. Cesar Chavez to Ray Gonzales, November 30, 1972, box 13, folder 28, UFW Files, ULA-WSU.
60. "The Gonzales Report," August 30, 1973, P1010666, book 1, RGC.

61. Mary K. Shell, "How Our Very Own Legislators Voted," October 14, 1973, P1010719, book 2, RGC.

62. Ray Gonzales to Cesar Chavez, July 27, 1973, box 3, folder 34, UFW Work Department, UFW Organizing Committee, ULA-WSU.

63. Gonzales, interview by author.

64. Ernest Gallo to William Ketchum, June 27, 1974; Fred L. Starrh to John Tunney, May 8, 1974; both letters in Unions folder, William Ketchum Papers, Walter Stiern Library, California State University, Bakersfield.

65. Ray Gonzales, email to author, October 20, 2011.

66. Jerry Gillam, "Assembly OKs Secret Farm Ballot Measure," *Los Angeles Times*, August 20, 1974.

67. See Miriam Pawel, *The Union of Their Dreams: Power, Hope, and Struggle in Cesar Chavez's Farm Worker Movement* (New York: Bloomsbury, 2009), 147–149.

68. Quoted in Frank Bardacke, *Trampling Out the Vintage: Cesar Chavez and the Two Souls of the United Farm Workers* (London: Verso, 2011), 488.

69. Pawel, *The Union of Their Dreams*, 149.

70. Pawel, 148.

71. Susan Ferris and Ricardo Sandoval, *The Fight in the Fields: Cesar Chavez and the Farmworkers Movement* (New York: Harcourt Brace, 1997), 197.

72. Gonzales, interview by author.

73. Gonzales, interview by author.

74. "The Workers Are Ignored," editorial, *Bakersfield Californian*, Aguust 26, 1974, P1010725, book 2, RGC.

75. "Compare the Issues [with Thomas]," advertisement, *Bakersfield Californian*, October 31, 1974, P1010618, book 1, RGC.

76. "Thomas Raps Gonzales for Farm Labor Bill Role," *Bakersfield Californian*, August 22, 1974, P1010724, book 2, RGC.

77. Gonzales, interview by author.

78. "Candidate Thomas Asks Gonzales to Debate Now," *Bakersfield Californian*, June 6, 1974, P1010814, book 2, RGC.

79. Walter W. Stiern, oral history interview by Enid Hart Douglass, May 27 and June 4, 1987, 141, State Government Oral History Program, California State Archives, Sacramento.

80. Gonzales, interview by author.

81. Vic Pollard, "Kern's Mercurial Mastermind: Bill Thomas (R-CA) Will Leave Indelible Mark," *Bakersfield Californian*, October 30, 2005.

82. Ray Gonzales to Cesar Chavez, December 1, 1974, box 45, folder 28, UFW Office of President, ULA-WSU.

83. On the alleged decline of the UFW, see Bardacke, *Trampling Out the Vintage*; Pawel, *The Union of Their Dreams*; Shaw, *Beyond the Fields*; Matt Garcia, *From the Jaws of Victory: The Triumph and the Tragedy of Cesar Chavez and the Farm Worker Movement* (Berkeley: University of California Press, 2012).

84. On the civic unity movement in California, see Mark Brilliant, *The Color of America Has Changed: How Racial Diversity Shaped Civil Rights Reform in California, 1941–1978* (Oxford: Oxford University Press, 2010); Shana Bernstein, *Bridges of Reform: Interracial Civil Rights Activism in Twentieth-Century Los Angeles* (New York: Oxford University Press, 2011).

85. Raymond Gonzales, email to author, October 5, 2011.

86. "Raymond Gonzales, 'Catalyst' for Change in Kern County, Area's First Latino Assemblyman, Dead at 80," *Bakersfield Californian*, September 5, 2018.

87. On growing racial diversity among local politics in greater Bakersfield, see, e.g., Gabriel Thompson, "Meet the Millennial Mayor Who Took on Big Oil—and Won," *Nation*, July 12, 2019; Alejandra Reyes-Velarde, "Race for Central Valley's Soul," *Los Angeles Times*, November 7, 2022.

CHAPTER 6: POLICE VIOLENCE, FAIR MEDIA, RURAL HEALTH CARE, AND CIVIL RIGHTS ACTIVISM IN GREATER BAKERSFIELD

The first epigraph is from Ron Taylor, "Ex-Police Chief Calls Bakersfield Backward, Racist," *Fresno Bee*, October 12, 1969. Powers had served as chief of police between 1933 and 1945. The second epigraph is from Helen Graf to George Murphy, July 13, 1970, folder 1, box 34, California/Bakersfield Anti-Poverty Council, Grant Files, 1966–1971, Migrant Division, Office of Operations, Office of Economic Opportunity, Community Services Administration, record group 381, National Archives at College Park, MD (hereafter Migrant Division, RG 381, NACP-MD).

1. "Dance Hall Incident Still Has Repercussions," *Bakersfield Californian*, October 21, 1969; Ralph Anthony, interview by author, May 8, 2007.

2. Ralph Anthony to Nathaniel Colley, September 9, 1969, carton 77, folder 4, NAACP, Region 1, Records, BANC MSS 78/180 c, Bancroft Library, University of California, Berkeley (hereafter NAACP Records).

3. "An Open Letter to the People of Bakersfield," *Bakersfield Californian*, October 19, 1969.

4. Minutes of the Bakersfield City Council, April 21, 1969.

5. "Dance Hall Incident Still Has Repercussions," *Bakersfield Californian*, October 21, 1969.

6. Steve Powers, email to author, May 11, 2007.

7. Ron Taylor, "Ex-Police Chief Calls Bakersfield Backward, Racist," *Fresno Bee*, October 12, 1969.

8. Taylor, "Ex-Police Chief Calls Bakersfield Backward."

9. Anthony, interview by author.

10. Taylor, "Ex-Police Chief Calls Bakersfield Backward."

11. Oliver Rosales, "Racial Liberalism on California's Racial Frontier: The Career of Robert B. Powers" (paper presented at the annual meeting of the California Council for the Promotion of History, San Luis Obispo, October 2008). On Powers, see Robert B. Powers, "Law Enforcement, Race Relations: 1930–1960," interview by Amelia R. Fry, 1969, Earl Warren Oral History Project, Bancroft Library, University of California, Berkeley. On police violence in Kern County, see Shawn Schwaller, "Greetings from Bakersfield! Law Enforcement Corruption, White Supremacy, and Latinx Lives in California's Deep Red South," *Boom California*, October 16, 2018.

12. Minutes of the Bakersfield City Council, December 22, 1969.

13. Minutes of the Bakersfield City Council, December 22, 1969.

14. Minutes of the Bakersfield City Council, January 5, 1970.

15. Minutes of the Bakersfield City Council, January 5, 1970.

16. Minutes of the Bakersfield City Council, January 5, 1970.

17. Minutes of the Bakersfield City Council, January 5, 1970.

18. Minutes of the Bakersfield City Council, January 5, 1970.

19. Minutes of the Bakersfield City Council, January 5, 1970.
20. Minutes of the Bakersfield City Council, January 5, 1970.
21. David Hashim, interview by author, September 22, 2009.
22. Steve Powers, pers. comm., 2007.
23. Hashim, interview by author.
24. Minutes of the Bakersfield City Council, January 5, 1970.
25. Minutes of the Bakersfield City Council, January 5, 1970 (emphasis added).
26. Minutes of the Bakersfield City Council, January 5, 1970.
27. Minutes of the Bakersfield City Council, January 5, 1970.
28. Minutes of the Bakersfield City Council, January 5, 1970.
29. Minutes of the Bakersfield City Council, January 5, 1970.
30. Minutes of the Bakersfield City Council, January 5, 1970.
31. Ronald Taylor, "Turmoil in 'Mississippi West': Bakersfield Police Practices Rekindle Debate on Treatment of Blacks, Latinos," *Los Angeles Times*, March 14, 1984.
32. Chon A. Noriega, *Shot in America: Television, the State, and the Rise of Chicano Media* (Minneapolis: University of Minnesota Press, 2000), 48–50.
33. Noriega, *Shot in America*, 35.
34. Francisco J. Lewels Jr., *The Uses of the Media by the Chicano Movement: A Study in Minority Access* (New York: Praeger, 1974), 57.
35. Armando Rendon and Domingo Nick Reyes, *Chicanos and the Mass Media* (Washington, DC: National Mexican-American Anti-Defamation Committee, 1971).
36. Bertram Levine, *Resolving Racial Conflict: The Community Relations Service and Civil Rights, 1964–1989* (Columbia: University of Missouri Press, 2005), 222.
37. Levine, *Resolving Racial Conflict*, 223. On the death of Ruben Salazar, see Lorena Oropeza, *¡Raza Sí! ¡Guerra No! Chicano Protest and Patriotism during the Vietnam War Era* (Berkeley: University of California Press, 2005), 172–182.
38. Levine, *Resolving Racial Conflict*, 222.
39. Levine, *Resolving Racial Conflict*, 218.
40. "UCC Agency Backs Challenge to Transfer of TV Stations," *Religious News Service*, October 20, 1971, box 677, folder 5, MALDEF Records, Department of Special Collections and University Archives, Stanford University Libraries, Stanford, CA (hereafter MALDEF Records).
41. Charles Austin, "After 30 Years, This Media Watchdog Still Vigilant," *New York Times*, August 28, 1983.
42. Julian Williams, "Broadcast Segregation: WJTV's Early Years," *American Journalism* 19, no. 3 (2002): 87–103.
43. "The Pool of Experts on Access," *Broadcasting*, September 20, 1971, box 677, folder 5, MALDEF Records.
44. Austin, "After 30 Years, This Media Watchdog Still Vigilant."
45. Kay Mills, *Changing Channels: The Civil Rights Case That Transformed Television* (Jackson: University of Mississippi Press, 2004), 4.
46. *Office of Communication of the United Church of Christ v. Federal Communications Commission*, 359 F.2d 994 (D.C. Cir. 1966).
47. "The Pool of Experts on Access," *Broadcasting*.
48. Austin, "After 30 Years, This Media Watchdog Still Vigilant."
49. "The Struggle over Broadcast Access," *Broadcasting*, September 20, 1971, box 677, folder 5, MALDEF Records.
50. Al Kramer, interview by author, March 10, 2010.

51. Donato Cruz, "'America's Newest City': 1950s Bakersfield and the Making of the Modern Suburban Segregated Landscape" (master's thesis, California State University, Bakersfield, 2020), 176.

52. Cruz, "America's Newest City," 185.

53. Mara Einstein, *Media Diversity: Economics, Ownership, and the FCC* (Mahwah, NJ: Lawrence Erlbaum, 2004), 22.

54. KCCU newsletter, November 1967, Jack Brigham Collection, in author's possession (hereafter JBC). The Fairness Doctrine was repealed during the first Reagan presidential administration. Many media activist groups argue that reinstating the Fairness Doctrine would help mitigate the partisan nature of media journalism and curb the role of corporations in defining media news programming. See Robert W. McChesney and John Nichols, *The Death and Life of American Journalism: The Media Revolution That Will Begin the World Again* (Philadelphia: Nation Books, 2010).

55. Roberto L. Martínez, "The Border and Human Rights: A Testimony," in *Chicano San Diego: Cultural Space and the Struggle for Justice*, ed. Richard Griswold del Castillo (Tucson: University of Arizona Press, 2007), 224–225. On the Chicana/o movement in San Diego, see Jimmy Patiño, *Raza Sí, Migra No: Chicano Movement Struggles for Immigrant Rights in San Diego* (Chapel Hill: University of North Carolina Press, 2017).

56. On the Chicana/o movement in Denver, see Ernesto B. Vigil, *The Crusade for Justice: Chicano Militancy and the Government's War on Dissent* (Madison: University of Wisconsin Press, 1999).

57. George Mariscal, *Brown-Eyed Children of the Sun: Lessons from the Chicano Movement, 1965–1975* (Albuquerque: University of New Mexico Press, 2005), 63.

58. Oropeza, *¡Raza Sí! ¡Guerra No!*, 63.

59. Noriega, *Shot in America*, xii.

60. Kramer, interview by author.

61. Kramer, interview by author.

62. Editorial, *Broadcast*, May 15, 1972, box 677, folder 5, MALDEF Records.

63. Ray Gonzales, interview by author, May 11, 2009.

64. Ray Gonzales, interview by author, April 15, 2009.

65. "McGraw Hill Negotiates with Groups," *Black Communicator*, October 1971, box 677, folder 5, MALDEF Records.

66. Quoted in "McGraw Hill Negotiates with Groups."

67. Memorandum, December 3, 1971, UCC Office of Communication, box 677, folder 5, MALDEF Records.

68. "Parker in Corner of T-L Challengers," *Broadcasting*, October 25, 1971, box 677, folder 5, MALDEF Records.

69. Lewels, *The Uses of the Media by the Chicano Movement*, 110–111.

70. "UCC Agency Backs Challenge to Transfer of TV Stations," *Religious News Service*, October 20, 1971, box 677, folder 5, MALDEF Records.

71. "Church Agency Aids Minorities Opposing Radio-TV Licensing," *Religious News Service*, November 9, 1971, box 677, folder 5, MALDEF Records.

72. Jesse Alcala, interview by author, October 11, 2019.

73. Alcala; see also Abraham Castillo, "*La* KWAC: Understanding the Origins of Spanish-Language Radio in Kern County," unpublished paper in author's possession, 19.

74. "Church Agency Aids Minorities Opposing Radio-TV Licensing," *Religious News Service*.

75. "A Rift in the Challengers' Ranks," *Broadcasting*, October 4, 1971, box 677, folder 5, MALDEF Records.

76. Domingo Nick Reyes, "Testimony on Modern Advertising Practices" (paper, National Mexican American Anti-Defamation Committee, November 18, 1971), 1.

77. Reyes, "Testimony on Modern Advertising Practices," 1. See also Rendon and Reyes, *Chicanos and the Mass Media*.

78. Kramer, interview by author.

79. Noriega, *Shot in America*, 85.

80. Raymond Gonzales to Albert Kramer, n.d., box 677, folder 5, MALDEF Records.

81. Gonzales, interview by author, February 2010.

82. KCCU newsletter, August 1971, JBC.

83. KCCU newsletter, August 1971, JBC.

84. KCCU newsletter, August 1971, JBC.

85. KCCU newsletter, August 1971, JBC.

86. Gonzales, interview by author, February 2010.

87. Raymond Gonzales to Albert Kramer, late 1971, box 677, folder 5, MALDEF Records.

88. Memorandum Opinion and Order (file no. BRCT-286, FCC 72-220), "In Re Application of Time-Life Broadcast, Inc.," March 1972, box 677, folder 2, MALDEF Records.

89. Raymond Gonzales, email to author, April 27, 2012.

90. "McGraw-Hill Sets Record for Concessions to Minorities," *Broadcasting*, May 15, 1972, box 677, folder 5, MALDEF Records.

91. Mario Obledo to McGraw-Hill, n.d., MALDEF Records.

92. Draft agreement, April 26, 1972, box 678, folder 1, MALDEF Records.

93. Draft agreement, April 26, 1972.

94. "Programs, Initiatives, and Awards," McGraw-Hill Companies (archived website), accessed April 30, 2012.

95. See the *La Raza* listing in the Peabody Awards Collection, Walter J. Brown Media Archives, University of Georgia, Athens, accessed August 30, 2023.

96. "Moctesuma Esparza," UCLA School of Theater, Film, and Television Alumni Network (archived website), accessed April 30, 2012. Esparza is also the founding CEO of Maya Cinemas and has produced feature films such as *Selena* (1997).

97. On the connections between welfare and civil rights, see Felicia Kornbluh, *The Battle for Welfare Rights: Politics and Poverty in Modern America* (Philadelphia: University of Pennsylvania Press, 2007); Annelise Orleck, *Storming Caesars Palace: How Black Mothers Fought Their Own War on Poverty* (Boston: Beacon Press, 2005)

98. For a brief treatment of Bakersfield's Black community and its proximity to Mexican Americans, see Peter LaChapelle, "'Shadows of the Dust': The Expectation and Ordeal of California's African-American Dust Bowl Migrants; Southern San Joaquin Valley, 1929–1941" (master's thesis, California State University, Bakersfield, 1997).

99. Arvin-Lamont Migrant Health Clinic, press release, April 6, 1973, William Ketchum Papers, Walter Stiern Library, California State University, Bakersfield (hereafter WKP).

100. Conservatives across the United States used the bureaucratic apparatus of War on Poverty programs to undermine grassroots civil rights organizing. See, e.g., Joseph

Crespino, *In Search of Another Country: Mississippi and the Conservative Counterrevolution* (Princeton, NJ: Princeton University Press, 2007); Thomas J. Sugrue, *Sweet Land of Liberty: The Forgotten Struggle for Civil Rights in the North* (New York: Random House, 2008).

101. "Resolution of the City of Arvin," 1973, WKP.

102. See Thomas R. Wellock, "Stick It in L.A.! Community Control and Nuclear Power in California's Central Valley," *Journal of American History* 84, no. 3 (December 1997): 942–978.

103. Michael Aron, "Dumping $2.6 Million on Bakersfield (or How *Not* to Build a Migratory Farm Workers' Clinic)," *Washington Monthly*, October 1972, 23–32. The first Migrant Health Act was signed by President John F. Kennedy in 1962, and has been continually reauthorized by Congress. In 1970, the wording of the law changed to include "other seasonal farmworkers," which expanded the number of eligible recipients under the program—an important expansion as UFW union worker healthcare coverage was limited vis-à-vis that of the entire farmworker population of the southern San Joaquin Valley. See "History of America's Agricultural Workers and the Migrant Health Movement," National Center for Farmworker Health (website), accessed August 30, 2023.

104. Phillips Dunford, ed., *Kern County Medical Society: The First 100 Years, 1897–1997* (Bakersfield, CA: Kern County Medical Society, 1997), 226.

105. Dunford, *Kern County Medical Society*, 235.

106. Dunford, *Kern County Medical Society*, 299.

107. Dunford, *Kern County Medical Society*, 299.

108. Dunford, *Kern County Medical Society*, 257.

109. Dunford, *Kern County Medical Society*, 300.

110. Gordon Anderson, "Kern Medicine: 3-Pronged Establishment Set Up," *Bakersfield Californian*, May 23, 1973.

111. Gordon Anderson, "Kern Medicine: Reform Committee 'Moribund,'" *Bakersfield Californian*, May 26, 1973.

112. Gordon Anderson, "Kern Medicine: HEW Rips Society," *Bakersfield Californian*, May 27, 1973.

113. Helen Graf to George Murphy, July 13, 1970, folder 1, box 34, California/Bakersfield Anti-Poverty Council, Grant Files, 1966–1971, Migrant Division, RG 381, NACP-MD.

114. Gertrude Pool to William Ketchum, n.d., Unions, WKP.

115. Robert Mosely to Dan Cox, February 20, 1972, carton 77, folder 6, NAACP Records.

116. Robert Mosely to Bob Mathias, February 23, 1972, carton 77, folder 6, NAACP Records.

117. Ray Gonzales, "Black and Brown Together," *Observer*, November 6, 1970, Beale Memorial Library, Bakersfield, CA.

118. Duane Goff, interview by author, March 2010.

119. Robert Price, "For the Anthonys It's about Jesus but Also about Justice," *Bakersfield Californian*, February 8, 2021.

120. Pete Vigil to Gilbert Pompa, n.d., box 677, folder 1, MALDEF Records.

121. William D. Wright et al. to the president, July 17, 1972, box 677, folder 5, MALDEF Records.

122. Wright et al. to the president, July 17, 1972.
123. Dennis Hevesi, "Clay T. Whitehead, Guide of Policy That Helped Cable TV, Is Dead at 69," *New York Times*, July 31, 2008.
124. Lewels, *The Uses of the Media by the Chicano Movement*, 109.
125. Memorandum, August 1, 1969, box 7, folder 9, UFW Administration Files, UFW Organizing Committee, Archives of Urban and Labor Affairs, Wayne State University, Detroit, MI (hereafter UFW Files, ULA-WSU).
126. Robert F. Kennedy Farm Workers Medical Plan brochure, August 21, 1969, box 7, folder 9, UFW Files, ULA-WSU.
127. Rodrigo Terronez Memorial Clinic, brochure, n.d., box 3, folder 6, UFW Work Department, UFW Files, ULA-WSU.
128. Esther Uranday to Cesar Chavez, October 26, 1973, box 3, folder 6, UFW Work Department, UFW Files, ULA-WSU.

CHAPTER 7: A NEW BATTLEGROUND FOR CIVIL RIGHTS

The epigraphs are from, respectively, Noel Greenwood, "School System of Bakersfield in Center of New Battleground," *Los Angeles Times*, July 20, 1969; memorandum about Barbara Arvizu suicide, September 4, 1974, box 1137, folder 3, MALDEF Records, Department of Special Collections and University Archives, Stanford University Libraries, Stanford, CA (hereafter MALDEF Records).

1. See Matthew D. Lassiter and Joseph Crespino, eds., *The Myth of Southern Exceptionalism* (Oxford: Oxford University Press, 2010). On southern resistance to desegregation in Mississippi, see Joseph Crespino, *In Search of Another Country: Mississippi and the Conservative Counterrevolution* (Princeton, NJ: Princeton University Press, 2007).
2. On the history of school desegregation in the American Southwest and Far West, see Guadalupe San Miguel Jr., *Brown, Not White: School Integration and the Chicano Movement* (College Station: Texas A&M University Press, 2001); Brian D. Behnken, *Fighting Their Own Battles: Mexican Americans, African Americans, and the Struggle for Civil Rights in Texas* (Chapel Hill: University of North Carolina Press, 2011); José F. Moreno, ed., *The Elusive Quest for Equality: 150 Years of Chicano/Chicana Education* (Cambridge, MA: Harvard Educational Review, 2003); Carlos Kevin Blanton, *The Strange Career of Bilingual Education in Texas, 1836–1981* (College Station: Texas A&M University Press, 2007); Mark Brilliant, *The Color of America Has Changed: How Racial Diversity Shaped Civil Rights Reform in California, 1941–1978* (Oxford: Oxford University Press, 2010); Emily E. Straus, *Death of a Suburban Dream: Race and Schools in Compton, California* (Philadelphia: University of Pennsylvania Press, 2014); Danielle R. Olden, *Racial Uncertainties: Mexican Americans, School Desegregation, and the Making of Race in Post–Civil Rights America* (Oakland: University of California Press, 2022).
3. See Thomas J. Sugrue, *Sweet Land of Liberty: The Forgotten Struggle for Civil Rights in the North* (New York: Random House, 2008).
4. Supplemental trial brief, *People of the State of California v. Bakersfield City School District*, no. 106 225 (September 15, 1969), box 1137, folder 4, MALDEF Records.
5. Kern Council for Civic Unity (KCCU) newsletter, August 1971, Jack Brigham Collection, in author's possession (hereafter JBC). See also obituary for Charles D. Ford, *Bakersfield Californian*, November 6, 2008.
6. KCCU newsletter, August 1971, JBC.

7. NAACP Bakersfield Branch annual report, 1965, carton 77, folder 3, NAACP, Region 1, Records, BANC MSS 78/180 c, Bancroft Library, University of California, Berkeley (hereafter NAACP Records).

8. NAACP Bakersfield Branch annual report.

9. Brilliant, *The Color of America Has Changed*, 229.

10. "Lincoln School Trouble Brews," *Bakersfield Californian*, April 17, 1969.

11. "Lincoln School Trouble Brews." See also obituary for Geraldine Vera Owens, *Bakersfield Californian*, August 23, 2007.

12. "City School Integration by Fall Goal," *Bakersfield Californian*, May 29, 1969.

13. Rodolfo G. Serrano, "Desegregation in the South San Joaquin Valley," National Institute of Education, August 1976, 19.

14. KCCU newsletter, May–June 1969, JBC.

15. Jack Brigham to Bennett Seaman, September 27, 1971, JBC.

16. Brigham to Seaman.

17. KCCU newsletter, March–April 1969, JBC.

18. KCCU newsletter, March–April 1969, JBC.

19. KCCU newsletter, March–April 1969, JBC.

20. KCCU newsletter, March–April 1969, JBC.

21. KCCU newsletter, March–April 1969, JBC.

22. KCCU newsletter, March–April 1969, JBC.

23. KCCU newsletter, March–April 1969, JBC.

24. "School System of Bakersfield in Center of New Battleground," *Los Angeles Times*, July 20, 1969.

25. "State Charges Racial Imbalance," *Bakersfield Californian*, May 28, 1969.

26. Petition for writ of mandate, *People of the State of California v. Bakersfield City School District*, no. 106 225 (June 3, 1969), box 1071, folder 19, MALDEF Records.

27. Petition for writ of mandate, *People of the State of California v. Bakersfield City School District*.

28. Petition for writ of mandate, *People of the State of California v. Bakersfield City School District*.

29. "Board Draws Fire for Canceling Program," *Bakersfield Californian*, June 17, 1969.

30. "Board Draws Fire for Canceling Program," *Bakersfield Californian*.

31. "School System of Bakersfield in Center of New Battleground," *Los Angeles Times*, July 20, 1969.

32. "School System of Bakersfield," *Los Angeles Times*.

33. "School System of Bakersfield," *Los Angeles Times*.

34. "City School Hearing Set for Monday," *Bakersfield Californian*, July 8, 1969.

35. "State Opens Hearing in School Case," *Bakersfield Californian*, July 8, 1969.

36. "State Opens Hearing in School Case," *Bakersfield Californian*.

37. "State Opens Hearing in School Case," *Bakersfield Californian*.

38. "Bakersfield School Gets Warning on Integration," *Los Angeles Times*, July 13, 1969.

39. "Bakersfield School Gets Warning on Integration," *Los Angeles Times*.

40. "Bakersfield School Gets Warning on Integration," *Los Angeles Times*.

41. "Integration Suit Rejected," *Bakersfield Californian*, October 24, 1969.

42. "Curran Individual Views on Suit Told," *Bakersfield Californian*, October 29, 1969.

43. "Racial Imbalance Brings Increasing Pressure on Board," *Bakersfield Californian*, November 5, 1969.

44. Joe C. Hopkins, "American Insurrection Mars Dr. King's Dream and Celebration of Kamala as Our First Black Woman Vice President," editorial, *Pasadena/San Gabriel Valley Journal*, January 14, 2020.

45. KCCU newsletter, May–June 1969, JBC.

46. "Three Board Members Back Curran," *Bakersfield Californian*, November 6, 1969.

47. "No Integration Move Needed Now—Curran," *Bakersfield Californian*, October 28, 1969.

48. Supplemental trial brief, *People of the State of California v. Bakersfield City School District*, no. 106 225 (July 23, 1969), box 1137, folder 4, MALDEF Records.

49. "Bakersfield Wins School Appeal," *Bakersfield Californian*, April 7, 1972.

50. Bakersfield City School District Title VI compliance review, 1969, box 1137, folder 5, MALDEF Records.

51. Bakersfield City School District Title VI compliance review.

52. Bakersfield City School District Title VI compliance review.

53. Bakersfield City School District Title VI compliance review.

54. Bakersfield City School District Title VI compliance review.

55. Bakersfield City School District Title VI compliance review.

56. KCCU newsletter, August 1971, JBC.

57. Virna Canson to Ann Everly, January 17, 1973, carton 77, folder 6, NAACP Records.

58. For more information on civil rights activist Virna Canson, see Kendra Gage, "Creating the Black California Dream: Virna Canson and the Black Freedom Struggle in the Golden State Capitol, 1940–1988" (PhD diss., University of Nevada, Las Vegas, 2015).

59. Lupe A. Martinez to Jerry Lopez, memo, January 20, 1970, box 1071, folder 19, MALDEF Records.

60. Martinez to Lopez, January 20, 1970.

61. "School System of Bakersfield in Center of New Battleground," *Los Angeles Times*, July 20, 1969.

62. Lupe A. Martinez to Jerry Lopez, Joe Ortega, Jean Fairfax, and Phyllis McClure, memo about addition to the Bakersfield criteria research, February 4, 1970, box 1071, folder 19, MALDEF Records.

63. Jess Alcala to Walter Stiern et al., October 30, 1969, box 1071, folder 19, MALDEF Records.

64. "Discrimination Must End," *Bakersfield Californian*, October 28, 1969.

65. On Anguiano, see Lupe Anguiano, interview by Virgina Espino, April–September 2011, Center for Oral History Research, University of California, Los Angeles.

66. Jose Garcia to Lupe Anguiano, n.d., box 1071, folder 19, MALDEF Records.

67. Frank Espinoza to Lupe Anguiano, October 1, 1969, box 1071, folder 19, MALDEF Records.

68. *Irene Peña v. Board of Trustees of the Delano Union School District*, no. 120061

(Sup. Ct. Cal. Kern 1973); annual report to the Board of Directors, 1973, box 7, folder 3, MALDEF Records.

69. Albert Camarillo, "Report of Dr. Albert M. Camarillo" (November 8, 2016), *Luna v. County of Kern*, 291 F. Supp. 3d 1088 (E.D. Cal. 2018), statement in author's possession, 20.

70. On the rise and fall of Proposition 21 and California racial politics, see Daniel Martinez HoSang, *Racial Propositions: Ballot Initiatives and the Making of Postwar California* (Berkeley: University of California Press, 2010), 93–104.

71. Voter Information Guide for 1972, General Election, p. 55, University of California College of the Law, San Francisco, Repository.

72. HoSang, *Racial Propositions*, 104.

73. Supplemental trial brief, *People of the State of California v. Bakersfield City School District*, no. 106 225 (July 23, 1969), box 1137, folder 4, MALDEF Records.

74. Memorandum about Barbara Arvizu suicide, September 4, 1974, box 1137, folder 3, MALDEF Records.

75. Memorandum about Arvizu suicide.

76. "Trustees Approve Transfers of 13 Principals," *Bakersfield Californian*, July 11, 1973.

77. Steve Arvizu later became the founding provost of California State University, Monterey Bay, and president of Oxnard College. See Steve Arvizu, interview by Kristin Sevilla, April–May 1996, California Revealed, California State University, Monterey Bay, Library Archives.

78. "Trustees Approve Transfers of 13 Principals," *Bakersfield Californian*, July 11, 1973.

79. "Trustees Approve Transfers of 13 Principals," *Bakersfield Californian*.

80. Memorandum about Barbara Arvizu suicide, September 4, 1974, box 1137, folder 3, MALDEF Records.

81. Complaint, May 23, 1974, *Rene Arvizu and Esther Arvizu v. Bakersfield City School District*, no. 128573 (Sup. Ct. Cal. Kern 1974), box 1137, folder 3, MALDEF Records.

82. Mr. and Mrs. Reynaldo Arvizu to Bakersfield City School District, June 5, 1973, box 1137, folder 3, MALDEF Records.

83. Mr. and Mrs. Arvizu to Bakersfield City School District.

84. Barbara Arvizu, suicide letter, box 1137, folder 3, MALDEF Records.

85. Report of conference, April 23, 1973, box 1137, folder 3, MALDEF Records.

86. Report of conference, April 23, 1973.

87. Arvizu family, interview, April 20, 1974, box 1137, folder 3, MALDEF Records.

88. Arvizu family, interview, April 20, 1974.

89. *Bakersfield City School District of Kern County v. Ernest Boyer et al.*, 610 F.2d 621 (9th Cir. 1980).

90. W. J. McCance, "Kern Loses Another $242,000 Funds," *Bakersfield Californian*, July 22, 1975.

91. Harold Tomlin et al., open letter to Mel Magnus, n.d., JBC.

92. Administrative proceedings in the Department of Health, Education, and Welfare, June 25, 1975, carton 77, folder 6, NAACP Records.

93. Administrative proceedings in the Department of Health, Education, and Welfare.

94. Administrative proceedings in the Department of Health, Education, and Welfare.

95. Administrative proceedings in the Department of Health, Education, and Welfare. According to the historian David G. Gutiérrez, the term *Chicano* was "long used as a slang or pejorative in-group reference to lower-class persons of Mexican descent.... The term *Chicano* was adopted by young Mexican Americans as an act of defiance and self-assertion and as an attempt to redefine themselves by criteria of their own choosing." See David G. Gutiérrez, *Walls and Mirrors: Mexican Americans, Mexican Immigrants, and the Politics of Ethnicity* (Berkeley: University of California Press, 1995), 184.

96. Lloyd Henderson to Walter Hauss, July 1, 1974, carton 77, folder 6, NAACP Records.

97. Henderson to Hauss, July 1, 1974.

98. Henderson to Hauss, July 1, 1974. See also *Lau v. Nichols*, 414 U.S. 563 (1974).

99. Henderson to Hauss, July 1, 1974.

100. Peter Holmes to Walter Hauss, April 21, 1975, carton 77, folder 6, NAACP Records. On Holmes's involvement with the Office of Civil Rights and school desegregation efforts, see Peter Holmes, interview by William Link, April 18, 1991, Southern Oral History Program Collection, L-0168, Documenting the American South.

101. Walter Hauss to Peter Holmes, May 12, 1975, carton 77, folder 6, NAACP Records.

102. Hauss to Holmes, May 12, 1975.

103. Hauss to Holmes, May 12, 1975.

104. See Thomas J. Sugrue, *The Origins of the Urban Crisis: Race and Inequality in Postwar Detroit* (Princeton, NJ: Princeton University Press, 2005); Gene Slater, *Freedom to Discriminate: How Realtors Conspired to Segregate Housing and Divide America* (Berkeley, CA: Heyday, 2021).

105. Ralph Anthony to Virna Canson, July 23, 1975, carton 77, folder 6, NAACP Records.

106. "Class Action Suit against HEW Names City School District," *Bakersfield Californian*, July 4, 1975.

107. US Congress, news release, March 6, 1976, HEW Hearings, William Ketchum Papers, Walter Stiern Library, California State University, Bakersfield (hereafter WKP).

108. US Congress, news release, March 6, 1976.

109. William Ketchum to Glen Wahlquist, March 18, 1976, HEW Hearings, WKP.

110. Florence Moody to David Mathews, March 9, 1976, HEW Hearings, WKP.

111. W. J. McCance, "Taxpayers Lose, Jordan Says of Move," *Bakersfield Californian*, March 6, 1976.

112. McCance, "Taxpayers Lose, Jordan Says of Move."

113. Ralph Jordan to William Ketchum, April 2, 1976, HEW Hearings, WKP.

114. Jordan to Ketchum, April 2, 1976.

115. William Ketchum to Ralph Jordan, April 12, 1976, HEW Hearings, WKP.

116. William Ketchum to Carl Albert, March 18, 1976, HEW Hearings, WKP.

117. William Ketchum to Mrs. C. Swanson, February 27, 1976, Office of Education, WKP.

118. William Ketchum to Arthur D. Doland, March 25, 1976, HEW Hearings, WKP.

119. Merle Cassidy to William Ketchum, March 6, 1976, HEW Hearings, WKP.

120. Arthur Doland to William Ketchum, March 21, 1976, HEW Hearings, WKP.

121. Claire Hanson to William Ketchum, February 22, 1976, HEW Hearings, WKP.

122. On recent controversy over the changing of the South High School mascot from the Rebels to the Spartans, see Nicholas Belardes, "South Bakersfield's Confederate Remains," *Boom California*, June 2, 2020.

123. Grant Jensen to William Ketchum, February 4, 1975, Office of Education, WKP.

124. Jensen to Ketchum, February 4, 1975.

125. Jim Boren, "Schools Face Charges of Language Discrimination," *Fresno Bee*, January 24, 1975.

126. Thomas Keeling to Myron Lehtman, April 27, 1983, P/Entry 214—Subject Files of Roger Clegg, Bakersfield Independent School District (ff), box 463, record group 60, National Archives at College Park, MD (hereafter RG 60, NACP-MD).

127. Keeling to Lehtman, April 27, 1983.

128. Keeling to Lehtman, April 27, 1983.

129. Keeling to Lehtman, April 27, 1983.

130. "Chronology of Major Integration Related Activities—1954 through 1983," BCSD, in author's possession. I thank former BCSD communications director Steve Gabbitas for providing access to this timeline.

131. Carey Scott to Virna Canson, March 26, 1979, carton 77, folder 7, NAACP Records.

132. Complaint, *United States v. Bakersfield City School District and School Board*, no. CV-F-84-39 (E.D. Cal. January 25, 1984), P/Entry 214—Subject Files of Roger Clegg, Bakersfield Independent School District (ff), box 463, RG 60, NACP-MD.

133. US Department of Education, "Assurance of Compliance and Compliance Agreement," January 15, 1981, P/Entry 214—Subject Files of Roger Clegg, Bakersfield Independent School District (ff), box 463, RG 60, NACP-MD.

134. Carey Scott to Virna Canson, March 26, 1979, carton 77, folder 7, NAACP Records.

135. "White Flight or No, They're Leaving," *Bakersfield Californian*, March 16, 1979.

136. Thomas Keeling to Myron Lehtman, April 27, 1983, p. 3, P/Entry 214—Subject Files of Roger Clegg, Bakersfield Independent School District (ff), box 463, RG 60, NACP-MD.

137. Keeling to Lehtman, April 27, 1983, 4.

138. Keeling to Lehtman, April 27, 1983, 7.

139. Keeling to Lehtman, April 27, 1983, 8, 15.

140. Keeling to Lehtman, April 27, 1983, 16.

141. Keeling to Lehtman, April 27, 1983, 17, 18.

142. Keeling to Lehtman, April 27, 1983, 22.

143. First annual report of the Bakersfield City School District, *United States v. Bakersfield City School District and School Board*, no. CV-F-84-39 (E.D. Cal. January 25, 1984), in author's possession.

144. Thomas Keeling to Myron Lehtman, April 27, 1983, p. 21, P/Entry 214—Subject Files of Roger Clegg, Bakersfield Independent School District (ff), box 463, RG 60, NACP-MD.
145. Keeling to Lehtman, April 27, 1983, 22.
146. Keeling to Lehtman, April 27, 1983, 23–25.
147. Robert Pear, "U.S. Shifts Tactics on Desegregation of Lower Schools," *New York Times*, January 26, 1984.
148. Pear, "U.S. Shifts Tactics on Desegregation."
149. Randolph D. Moss, "Participation and Department of Justice School Desegregation Consent Decrees," *Yale Law Journal* 95, no. 8 (July 1986): 1815.
150. Moss, "Participation and Department of Justice School Desegregation Consent Decrees," 1812–1813.
151. Drew S. Days III, "Turning Back the Clock: The Reagan Administration and Civil Rights," *Harvard Civil Rights–Civil Liberties Law Review* 19 (1984): 327.
152. Quoted in Judith Cummings, "Voluntary Desegregation of Schools Divided Bakersfield, Calif.," *New York Times*, February 12, 1984.
153. "Desegregation, Reagan Style," n.d., box 151, folder 19, MALDEF Records.
154. Cummings, "Voluntary Desegregation of Schools."
155. William Bradford Reynolds to Clarence Pendleton, May 15, 1984, P 184, Subject Files of William Bradford Reynolds, Civil Rights Division, Bakersfield School District, box 217, RG 60, NACP-MD.
156. Marjorie Holt to Ronald Reagan, March 25, 1985, P 184, Subject Files of William Bradford Reynolds, Civil Rights Division, Bakersfield School District, box 217, RG 60, NACP-MD.
157. Quoted in Cummings, "Voluntary Desegregation of Schools."
158. Quoted in Ellie McGrath, "Another Retreat From Busing," *Time*, February 6, 1984.
159. "Desegregation, Reagan Style," n.d., box 151, folder 19, MALDEF Records.
160. "A Blueprint All Right—for Segregation," *New York Times*, February 1, 1984, box 151, folder 19, MALDEF Records.
161. Natalie Erlendson, "The Draw of Magnet Schools," *MAS Magazine*, January 25, 2009.
162. Quoted in Erlendson, "The Draw of Magnet Schools."
163. On the so-called Hispanic problem, see Samuel P. Huntington, *Who Are We? The Challenges to America's National Identity* (New York: Simon and Schuster, 2004); Victor Davis Hanson, *Mexifornia: A State of Becoming* (San Francisco: Encounter Books, 2003).
164. See, e.g., Gary Orfield et al., *Harming Our Common Future: America's Segregated Schools 65 Years after Brown*, Civil Rights Project/Proyecto Derechoes Civiles, Center for Education and Civil Rights, University of California, Los Angeles, May 10, 2019.
165. Quoted in Camarillo, "Report of Dr. Albert M. Camarillo," 28. See also Maureen McCloud, "The Kern Brand of Politics—Conservative, Populist, Humorless," *California Journal*, July 1978.

CONCLUSION

1. "Young Singers Spread Racist Hate," ABC News, October 20, 2005.
2. Catherine Elsworth, "Twin Pop Stars with Angelic Looks Are New Faces of Racism," *Telegraph*, October 25, 2005.
3. "Young Singers Spread Racist Hate," ABC News.

4. On Mexican settlement in the Central Valley, see Juan-Vicente Palerm, "The New Rural California: Farmworkers Putting Down Roots in Central Valley Communities," *California Agriculture* 54, no. 1 (January–February 2000): 33–34.

5. Joe Moore, "Director Diego Luna Brings the Story of Cesar Chavez to the Silver Screen," Valley Public Radio, KVPR, March 18, 2014; Jennifer Self, "Introducing Cesar Chavez: Film Intended to Preserve legacy," *Bakersfield Californian*, March 22, 2014.

6. Abby Sewell and Richard Simon, "Kevin McCarthy, Would-Be Majority Leader, at Home in D.C., Bakersfield," *Los Angeles Times*, June 12, 2014.

7. See Raymond Gonzales, "Some Came to Praise César, While Others Stood Far Away," *Hispanic Link*, May 10, 1993, reprinted in *A Lifetime of Dissent: Passionate and Powerful Articles on the Critical Issues of Our Times*, by Raymond Gonzales (n.p.: Xlibris, 2006), 154.

8. For a transcript of the city council's response to Rivera's resolution, see Minutes of the Bakersfield City Council, June 25, 2014.

9. Jose Gaspar, "Bakersfield City Council Tables Immigration Reform Resolution," *Bakersfield Now*, June 25, 2014; Jennifer Medina, "McCarthy's Role Is Debated in His Land of Immigrants," *New York Times*, June 22, 2014.

10. My thinking on the movement of the white population in Kern County to northwest Bakersfield has been informed by Navjyot Gill, "The Construction of Racial Boundaries and Redistricting in Kern" (paper presented at the annual meeting of the Western Historical Association, Las Vegas, NV, October 2019).

11. For an overview of the controversy, see "What's in a School Name? Plenty," *Bakersfield Californian*, September 7, 2003.

12. Jon Butler, email to author, March 6, 2016.

13. See, e.g., Perry Smith, "BC's New Course on History of Agricultural Labor Draws Ire, Discussion," *Bakersfield Californian*, November 11, 2022; Jose Gaspar, "Despite Rhetoric, BC Committee Approves Farm Labor History Courses," *Bakersfield Californian*, October 24, 2022.

14. "Forty Acres Designated a National Historic Landmark," *Bakersfield Californian*, February 19, 2011.

15. For a list of historic sites proposed for preservation, see Final Cesar Chavez Special Resource Study, National Park Service (website), October 24, 2013.

16. César E. Chávez and the Farmworker Movement National Historic Park Act, S. 4371, 117th Cong. (2022).

17. "*Luna v. County of Kern*: MALDEF and Latino Voters Achieve Landmark Victory," *MALDEF in History* (blog), MALDEF, March 26, 2019.

18. "Supervisor David Couch Earns Victory in Unofficial Final Election Results," *Bakersfield Californian*, March 19, 2020.

19. See, e.g., the public comment section of the October 20, 2022, curriculum meeting at Bakersfield College. The public debated the merits of a proposed noncredit course sequence for students to visit local landmark sites associated with the farmworker movement, illustrating the longevity of anti-UFW sentiment within the region and its use as a mobilization tool on the political right. See "Public Communication," 4 parts, Curriculum Committee Meeting, October 20, 2022, Bakersfield College, Bakersfield, CA. See also Jose Gaspar, "Proposed Courses at BC Draw Scrutiny," *Bakersfield Californian*, October 16, 2022.

20. "Bakersfield City Council Formally Approves Unity Map," *Bakersfield Californian*, April 7, 2022.

21. "Newsom Signs Bill to Create Kern Redistricting Commission, Stripping Power from County Supervisors," *Bakersfield Californian*, September 19, 2022; County of Kern Citizens Redistricting Committee, CA assembly bill no. 2494 (2022).

22. One of the most significant social issues facing Central Valley residents, particularly in the southern San Joaquin Valley, is the production, distribution, and consumption of methamphetamine. "Eighty percent of the nation's meth labs and 97 percent of its 'superlabs' are located there," notes Ray Winter. See Ray Winter, "New Factories in the Fields," *Boom* 1, no. 4 (Winter 2011). On the politics behind efforts to begin California's high-speed rail project in Central California, see James Fallows, "California's High-Speed Rail no. 3: Let's Hear from the Chairman," *Atlantic*, July 14, 2014.

23. Ronald Taylor, "Turmoil in 'Mississippi West': Bakersfield Police Practices Rekindle Debate on Treatment of Blacks, Latinos," *Los Angeles Times*, March 14, 1984.

24. Harold Pierce, "Raymond Gonzales, 'Catalyst' for Change in Kern County, Area's First Latino Assemblyman, Dead at 80," *Bakersfield Californian*, September 5, 2018.

25. See Jorge Barrientos, "Historic Desegregation Order on BCSD Lifted," *Bakersfield Californian*, January 26, 2011.

INDEX

Page numbers in italics indicate images.

ACLU, 129, 166, 175, 183
Acuña, Rudy, 113–114
Adair, Doug, 85–86
African Americans: and antipoverty movement, 62, 68, 71–72; and Black-Brown unity, 8, 47, 48, 50, 57–58, 126, 133, 134; and Elbo-In boycott, 44–45; and election of Ray Gonzales, 127, 135; and fair media movement, 155, 157–158, 159, 161, 163, 164, 166; and farmworker movement, 6, 8, 30, 49–50, 64, 126, 231n40; and health care, 169, 170, 171, 174; and housing segregation, 15–16, 39, 40–41, 56–57; and policing, 42, 147–148, 149–155; as racialized labor force, 29, 37; and recreation programs, 147, 148–149, 153; and school segregation, 43–44, 181, 184–185, 187–188, 190, 195, 204; and settlement in greater Bakersfield, 15, 24–25, 33–38, *34*, 49–50, 68, 232n3; and tensions with Mexican American activists, 99, 142, 169, 170, 174, 182; and white supremacy, 37–38, 41–42, 43, 56, 188
agribusiness: and antipoverty opposition, 82, 87, 89; and anti-unionism, 30, 31–32, 125–126; and conservative politics, 4–5, 132, 133; and displacement of Mexican landowners, 19–20; and health care, 170–171, 217; and racialized labor force, 2, 19–20, 26, 28–29, 37. *See also* growers
Aid to Families with Dependent Children (AFDC), 192
Alatorre, Richard, 135, 139, 140

Albert, Carl, 202–203
Alcala, Jesse, 163–164, 192–193
Allensworth (Tulare County, CA), 33–36, 232n3
Allensworth, Allen, 33, 35
American Federation of Labor and Congress of Industrial Organizations (AFL-CIO), 32, 128, 136–137
Anderson, Gordon, 172–173
Andreen, Kenneth, 187, 188, 189, 191, 200
Anguiano, Lupe, 193
Anthony, Ralph, *129*, 147–148, 150, 153–154, 174, 185, 200
antipoverty movement, 11, 56, 59–60, 62, 63–64, 67–99, 148–149, 153. *See also* War on Poverty
Araiza, Lauren, 8
Arias, Eric, 215
Armstrong, James, 62
Arvin (Kern County, CA), 29, 32, 40, 49, 130, 144, 170, 232n3
Arvizu, Barbara Renee, 194–197
Arvizu, Steve, 195–196, 262n77
Assembly Bill (AB) 3370, 139–140, 143
Associated Farmers (AF), 31–32
Associated Students of Bakersfield College (ASBC), 108
Atha, Fleming, 128, 131, 136

Bakersfield (Kern County, CA): African American settlement in, 15, 24–25, 34, 35, 36, 68, 232n3; borderhoods in, 4, 9, 215, 218, 228n10; Chinese settlement in, 17–18; and conservative politics, 218–219, 221, 228n13; ethnic Mexican

269

settlement in, 18, 20, 24–25, 28, 42; and housing segregation, 15–16, 38–41, 43, 56–57, 215; and racial discrimination, 41–42, 44–45, 51; and school segregation, 42–44, 210–211, 221; and settlement in unincorporated areas, 24–25, 39, 50, 232n3; sociopolitical history of, 1–2, 4, 16–18; and War on Poverty, 91–97

Bakersfield Californian, 56, 131, 140, 172–173, 184, 211

Bakersfield City Council: and anti-poverty movement, 68, 70, 73, 74, 90–92, 94, 95, 96–97; and conservative politics, 123, 144, 215; and discriminatory signs, 45, 51; and farmworker movement, 124–126; and immigration reform, 215; and multiracial coalitions, 48–49, 57–59; and police brutality, 151–154; and racial gerrymandering, 216–217; and Vietnam War, 131; and White Citizens' Council, 62–64, 73; and youth recreation programs, 148–149

Bakersfield City School District (BCSD), 43, 73, 111, 180, 181–211

Bakersfield College: Chicana/o student movement at, 106–107, 108–110, *111*, 112, 113, *121*; and Chicana/o studies, 103, 104, 106, 107–108, 112, 113–114, 115, 121; and ethnic studies requirement, 110–113; and faculty activism, 59, 68; and legacy of farmworker movement, 215, 216; and Semana de la Raza, 113–114, 130, 131

Bakersfield Consent Decree, 180, 208, 209, 210

Bakersfield Council of Churches, 57

Bakersfield High School, 21, 22, 44–45, 105

Bakersfield Police Commission, 154, 155

Bakersfield Police Department (BPD), 147–148, 149–155

Barber, Steve, *128*, 129, *129*, 134, 142

Basques, 1, 17, 219

Belcher, Duane, 59, 60, 183, 184–185

bilingual education, 8, 182, 190, 193, 197, 199

Black Muslims, 62
Black Panthers, 8, 126, 153
Black Power movement, 49, 64, 65
Bleecker, Keith, 152, 154
Boatwright, Dan, 140
borderhoods, 4, 9, 228n10
boycotts: and Chicana/o student movement, 107, 109–110, *111*, 113; and discriminatory signs, 44–45; and legacy of UFW, 6, 7, 218; and legislation, 135, 137–140, 141, 143, 144; of non-UFW lettuce, 109–110, *111*. *See also* Delano grape strike/boycott

Bracero Program, 52, 79, 90, 105
Bradley, Tom, 126
Brigham, Jack, 148, 183
Brilliant, Mark, 8, 48, 182, 231n38
Brooks, Julius, 58, 62, 63, 154
Brooks, Julius, Jr., 148, 149, 150
Brown, Melvin (Mel), 59, 62, 72, 87, 92, 93–94, 96
Brown, Pat, 55, 89, 128
Brown v. Board of Education, 61, 179, 180, 185, 206
Burger, Warren E., 158
busing, school: conservative opposition to, 4, 187, 205, 208, 209; and Ray Gonzales, 141; and school segregation, 180, 195, 197, 204, 210
Butler, Jon, 215–216
Buttonwillow (Kern County, CA), 37–38, 43

Cain Memorial African Methodist Episcopal Church, 38, 58, 60, 154
California Crossroads, 56
California Federation for Civic Unity (CFCU), 48, 50, 51
California State University (CSU), 104, 105, 106, 127
Camarillo, Albert, 4, 9, 16, 26–27, 28, 39, 216, 228n10
camps, labor, 28, 30, *31*, 32, 38, 40, 50
Cannery and Agricultural Workers Industrial Union, 31, 32
Canson, Virna, 96, 191, 200, 205
Carter, Leonard, 8, 96, 97, 126, 185
Cato, Paul, 209

INDEX | 271

Central Valley (CA), 1, 3–5, 13, 214, 220, 227n7, 251n27, 267n22. *See also* San Joaquin Valley
Chávez, César: and CSO, 8, 53; and Delano grape strike, 51, 101, 109, 125; and fair media movement, 163; and health care, 173, 176; legacy of, 1, 5, 6, 7, 214–216, 218, 227n1, 230n32; and Jess Nieto, 116, 119; and NFWA poverty grant, 69, 75, 78–80, 81, 82, 84, 87, 89–90; and nonviolent struggle, 125, 243n31; and racialized political campaigns, 142; and secondary boycott legislation, 136, 137, 138, 140, 143
Chicana/o movement: at Bakersfield College, 106–107, 108–110, *111*, 112, 113–114, *121*; conservative opposition to, 67, 83, 198; and election of Ray Gonzales, 124, 130–131, 144; and fair media movement, 155, 160; and farmworker movement, 101–102, 107, 109–110, 113, 122; and higher education, 102, 107, 121; and LULAC, 248n40; and multiracial coalitions, 49, 65, 144
Chicana/os: and election of Ray Gonzales, 124, 128, 135, 144; and fair media movement, 155, 160, 161–163, 164, 166, 167, 175, 176; and farmworker movement, 101–102; and higher education, 103–104, 108–109, 115; and policing, 117–118; and term *Chicano*, 198, 220, 227n6, 263n95. *See also* Mexican Americans; Mexicans, ethnic
Chicana/o studies, 103, 104, 105–106, 110, 112, 113–116, 121, 229n19
Chicanismo, 104, 160, 217
Chicano Cultural Center (CCC), 103, 108–109, 113, 114, 118
Chicanos Unidos for Progress, 111
Chinese Americans, 17–18, 33, 39, 42, 219, 232n11, 233n13, 233n15
Christianity, 6–7, 27
churches, 24, 25, 71, 154, 158, 186
citizenship classes, 53, 54, 76–77, 80, 81
city services, 2, 15, 36, 37, 49, 52, 92, 219

Civil Rights Act of 1964, 187, 189, 191, 193, 199. *See also* Title VI; Title VII
civil rights movements. *See* urban civil rights movements
Clinica de los Campesinos (Clinica Sierra Vista), 169, 170, 172
Collins, John, 110, 112, 113
Comisión Honorifica Mexicana, 30–31, 72, 83
Communications Act of 1934, 161, 163, 175, 176
communism: and antipoverty movement, 75, 86, 87–88, 89–90; and Chicana/o student movement, 109; and labor movements, 31, 48, 52, 173; and Mexican American constituents, 52, 53
Community Action Program (CAP) Committees, 62, 70–71, 85. *See also* Kern County CAP Committee
community colleges, 103–104, 118, 119–121. *See also* Bakersfield College
Community Relations Service (CRS), 157, 175
Community Service Organization (CSO): and antipoverty movement, 68, 72–73, 83, 98; and civil rights efforts, 8, 47, 52–55, 59, 80; and fair media movement, 161, 163, 166–167; and school desegregation movement, 183
Compton, John, 21
Compton School, 195, 197, 205
Concerned Parents Committee (CPC), 192–193
conservatism: Bakersfield brand of, 1–2, 4–5, 214–215, 217–221, 228nn13–14; and Chicana/o movement, 67, 83, 198; and ethnic studies, 110–111, 112–113; and housing opposition, 51–52, 59; and local government collaboration, 48, 59, 63–64; and poverty programs, 68–69, 74–76, 80, 88, 89, 91–92, 99, 257n100; and Ray Gonzales campaigns, 127–128, 130, 137, 144; and right-wing media, 159, 176; and rural health care, 168, 173; and school segregation, 196, 201–204, 205, 209, 210–211
Cotten, Richard, 159

cotton, 15, 30, 31, 33, 68
Crawford v. Board of Education, 207
Crocker, J. C., 18–19
Cruz, Donato, 40–41
CSO. *See* Community Service Organization
Curran, Bill, 188, 189
Curran, Thomas, 93

Dana, Bill, 156–157, 160
Davis, Tom, 110–113
death penalty, 141, 142
Deganawidah-Quetzalcoatl (D-Q) University, 108, 247n20
Delano (Kern County, CA): African American settlement in, 33, 41, 232n3; ethnic Mexican settlement in, 25, 28, 41; and opposition to NFWA grant, 76, 77, 78, 79, 81–83, 84, 88; police harassment in, 116–118; segregation in, 39, 41, 88, 193–194. *See also* Delano grape strike/boycott
Delano Center, 116–117
Delano City Council, 68, 78, 79, 80–81, 84, 117–118, 144
Delano grape strike/boycott: and Chicana/o movement, 10, 101, 107, 110, 113; conservative reaction to, 2, 62, 67, 69, 75, 76, 97, 124–126; and law enforcement, 91; legacy of, 215–216; and multiracial coalitions, 7, 51, 64; and NFWA poverty grant, 75–82, 84, 86, 87–90; and undocumented workers, 54, 139, 217
Delano High School Adult Education Program, 78, 81, 84
Delano Police Department, 116–118
Democratic Party: and agribusiness, 133, 135; and boycott legislation, 137, 138, 139–140, 143; and New Deal, 4, 133; and NFWA poverty grant, 75–76, 78, 80, 82, 87, 88, 89, 90; and Ray Gonzales campaigns, 127–128, 129–130, 131, 132, 135, 144, 251n26; and War on Poverty, 74, 93, 186
Denver (CO), 155, 157, 160, 161, 162, 165

Department of Education, California, 189, 204
Department of Education, US, 206, 207
Department of Health, Education, and Welfare, US (HEW): and rural health care, 171, 173; and school segregation, 180, 185, 187–188, 189, 190, 191, 193, 197–207
Department of Justice, US (DOJ), 157, 206–208, 209, 210, 221
DiGiorgio, Joseph, 40
DiGiorgio strike, 5, 6, 49
discrimination, racial: in Bakersfield, 18, 51, 214; and democratic participation, 26, 28, 53, 216–217; and education, 21–22, 43, 182, 185, 190, 191–194, 198–199, 204–205; and employment, 55–56, 164, 182, 194, 198; and farmworkers, 7, 28, 67, 103; and housing, 39–40, 60, 219; in Kern County, 26–28, 36–37, 39, 216; and multiracial coalitions, 2, 6, 58; in policing, 149–150; and public accommodations, 41–42, 44–45, 51
Dolores Huerta Foundation, 216–217
Dust Bowl, 2, 15, 37, 40, 43, 73
Duzen, Cyrille, 151–152
Dyer, Frank E., 81, 82

Eagleton-Biden Amendment, 205, 207–208
East Bakersfield, 20–25, *22, 34*, 43, 72, 219, 228n10, 235n72
Economic Opportunity Act of 1964, 70, 73, 74, 79, 81, 88, 90–91, 95
education: bilingual, 8, 182, 190, 193, 197, 199; citizenship, 53, 54, 76–77, 80, 81; higher, 102, 103–104, 106–107, 115, 119–121, 121, 203; and magnet programs, 180, 207–211, 221; and public school segregation, 21, 42–44, 179–211, 221; special, 190, 199, 205; vocational, 38, 203, 204
Eissinger, Michael, 26, 33
Elbo-In, 44–45
El Centenario, 24
Elementary and Secondary Education

Act (ESEA) of 1965, 186, 191, 192.
    See also Title I
El Paso (TX), 24, 42, 105
El Plan de Santa Bárbara, 104
Emerson School, 200–201
environmental regulation, 4–5, 127
España, Sal, 97, 98
Esparza, Moctesuma, 168, 257n96
Espinoza, Frank, 193
ethnic power movements, 64–65. *See also*
    Chicana/o movement
ethnic studies, 102–103, 107, 108,
    110–113, 115, 121, 248n47. *See also*
    Chicana/o studies

Fairbairn, David S., 84, 93
Fair Employment Practices Committee
    (FEPC), 47, 48, 55–56, 58, 64
fair housing movement, 38–41, 47, 48,
    49–52, 56–57, 59–60, 182, 219
fair maps movement, 216–217
fair media movement, 155–168, 175–176,
    194, 220, 256n54
Fairness Doctrine, 159, 160, 175, 176,
    256n54
farmworker movement: and Chicana/o
    movement, 101–102, 107, 109–110,
    113, 122; and early strike efforts, 5–6,
    28–32, *30*; legacy of, 1, 3, 166n19, 214,
    215–216; and multiracial coalitions,
    2–3, 6–8, 45, 124, 126, 169, 213; and
    national attention, 29, 50, 62, 91, 116,
    143, 171; and undocumented workers,
    54, 139, 217; and violence, 28, 31, 110,
    125, 243n31. *See also* Delano grape
    strike/boycott; United Farm Workers
farmworkers: African American, 33, 50,
    68, 174; and education, 75, 76–77,
    81–82; and health care, 169–172,
    176–177, 217, 258n103; and poor
    living conditions, 29, 33, 37, 38, 49–50;
    as racialized labor force, 19, 24, 28, 29,
    37. *See also* farmworker movement;
    United Farm Workers
Federal Communications Commission
    (FCC), 155, 158–161, 163–164, 165,
    166, 167, 175

Filipinos, 2, 41, 75, 80, 82, 118
Finlinson, Burns, 107, 108
Fontes, Patrick, 234n51
Ford, Chuck, 181
Fourteenth Amendment, 185, 193, 200
Fraternal Hall incident, 147–148,
    149–153, 154, 175
fraternal organizations, 30–31, 235n72
Fremont School, 43, 181, 185, 199
Fresno (Fresno County, CA), 18, 27, 28,
    229n19, 233n15, 234n51
Friendship House Community Center,
    71, 72, 95, 159
Frito Bandito, 156, 157, 160

Galarza, Ernesto, 5, 49, 53–54
Ganz, Marshall, 60, 61, 125
Ganz, Sylvia, 60
García, Gus, 111–112
García, Mario T., 227n6
Garcia, Matt, 3, 7
Gemini Proposal, 119–121
General Agreement on Tariffs and Trade
    (GATT), 120
gerrymandering, racial, 26, 28, 183, 187,
    200, 204, 216–217
Gia, Gilbert, 18, 42
GI Bill, 129, 204
Goff, Duane, 109, 110, *121*, 129,
    174–175
Goldschmidt, Walter, 29
Gonzales, Ray, *128*, *141*; and César
    Chávez, 142–143, 214–215; and
    Chicana/o studies, 105; and fair media
    movement, 159, 162, 165, 166, 167;
    and grassroots election, 124, 126–144,
    220–221; and school desegregation,
    186, 196
Gonzales, Rodolfo "Corky," 113, 160
Goss, Carroll, 171–172
Govea, Jessica, 53, 125, 130
Govea, Juan, 53, 72
Govea, Margaret, 53, 130
Graham, Dewitt, 154
Grand Rapids (MI), 155, 162, 167
Grapes of Wrath, The (Steinbeck), 29, 32
Gregory, James N., 4, 41, 128

274 | INDEX

growers: and antipoverty opposition, 75, 79, 80, 81, 83, 84–85, 86, 88; and antiunion efforts, 4, 5–6, 31–32; and Chicana/o movement, 116, 117, 118, 143, 229n19; and grape boycott, 124, 125, 126, 135, 137, 139, 140; and health care, 170–171, 176; and recruitment of labor, 33, 40; and tax breaks, 132–133, 170–171; and Teamsters Union, 109, 136. *See also* agribusiness

Hagen, Harlan: and INS office, 53, 54; and NFWA poverty grant, 76, 77–78, 79, 80, 81, 82, 85, 86–90
Haggard, Merle, 228n14
Hall, William Henry Bud, 35–36
Hanson, Victor Davis, 229n19
Hare, Eddie, 148
Harrington, Michael, 70
Hart, Don, 148–149, 153
Hashim, David, 148, 152, 153
Hauss, Walter, 199, 199–200
Havilah (Kern County, CA), 16, 19
Hawthorne School, 42, 234n48
Haynes, Fred Luther, 236n94
health care, 35, 38, 72, 142, 168–175, 176–177, 217, 258n103
Henning, Jack, 128, 140, 143
Hillcrest tract, 39, 56–57
Hoagland, Kenneth, 92, 97
Holloway-Gonzales Library, 133–134
horticulturalist ideology, 4, 5, 217, 229n17, 229n19
hospitals, 37, 38, 106
housing: and neighborhood annexation, 15–16, 52, 74, 97; and poor living conditions, 33, 37, 49–50; public, 51–52; and racial covenants, 38–39, 59, 60, 181, 200, 204; and residential segregation, 38–41, 56–57, 199, 219, 221. *See also* fair housing movement
Hudson, Lynn M., 33, 35
Huerta, Dolores, 6, 71, 77–78, 80, *116*, 216–217

Igler, David, 4, 19, 37
immigrant rights movement, 6, 217

immigration, 17, 53–55, 168, 180, 206, 213, 215, 218
Immigration and Naturalization Service (INS), 53, 54
Indianapolis (IN), 155, 162
Intergroup Relations Board (IRB), 48, 57–59, 60, 61, 91
International Longshore and Warehouse Union, 72, 85
Irene Peña v. Delano Union School District, 193–194
Italians, 17, 37, 42, 219

Jefferson School, 181, 193
Jensen, Grant, 203–204
Jewish Americans, 7, 48, 50–51
Jim Crow laws, 26, 36, 45, 51, 157, 179, 181, 200
Jiménez, José, 156–157, 160
Johnson, Georgia, 109, 112, 159
Johnson, Lyndon B., 68, 70, 74, 80
Johnson, Wayne, 148, 149, 150
Jordan, Ralph, 92, 95–96, 187

KCCU. *See* Kern Council for Civic Unity
Kelly, Edward, 39
Kennedy, John F., 258n103
Kennedy, Robert, 91
Kern Community College District (KCCD), 103, 116, 119
Kern Council for Civic Unity (KCCU): and antipoverty movement, 68, 91, 94; and Chicana/o movement, 65; and fair housing movement, 2, 48, 59–60; and fair media movement, 155, 156, 157, 158, 159–162, 163, 164–167; and Ray Gonzales, 128, 134, 141; and NFWA poverty grant, 86–87; and school desegregation movement, 183–185, 186, 188, 190; and White Citizens' Council, 61–62
Kern County (CA): and antipoverty movement, 71–75, 78, 86–87, 89, 90, 97, 242n17; and anti-unionism, 5, 6, 32, 125, 163; and Chicana/o movement, 65, 101–102, 103, 118–119, 122; conservative politics in, 4, 68–69, 84,

INDEX | 275

107, 133, 142, 173, 221; and election of Ray Gonzales, 103, 124, 127–132, 135–139, 144; and horticulturalist ideology, 4–5; housing segregation in, 4, 39, 40, 41, 49–50; and multiracial coalitions, 2–3, 48, 49, 50, 68, 142, 156; poverty in, 49–50, 68, 69, 70–72, 73; and racist policing, 42, 117, 148, 150, 151; and rural health care, 38, 168–169; school segregation in, 39, 181, 190, 191, 193–194, 210, 211, 221; and settlement in unincorporated areas, 24–25, 29, 33–38, 39, 40, 49–50; white supremacy in, 18, 26–28, 37–38, 40–42, 61, 107, 213, 221; and Williamson Act, 132–133
Kern County Board of Supervisors: and antipoverty movement, 68, 83–84; and discriminatory signs, 45, 51; and farmworker movement, 125, 126, 214–215; and Klan, 28; and racial gerrymandering, 216, 217; and tax reform, 133
Kern County CAP Committee, 73, 75, 78, 79, 83–84, 92–95, 97–98
Kern County Farm Bureau, 84–85, 88, 138–139
Kern County Liberation Movement (KCLM), 169, 170, 171, 172, 173
Kern County Medical Society (KCMS), 170, 171–173
KERO-TV, 156, 162, 163, 165, 166
Ketchum, William, 169–170, 173, 201–203
KGEE radio, 159–160
King, Martin Luther, Jr., 51, 231n40
KJTV, 164
Korean War, 106
Kramer, Al, 161, 162, 163, 164, 165, 166, 175
Kuchel, Thomas H., 78–79, 85
Ku Klux Klan, 26–28, 32, 44, 61, 159
KWAC radio, 163–164

La Cronica Mexicana, 23
LaFollette Commission, 32
Lamont (Kern County, CA), 49, 130, 170, 171, 232n3

Lange, Dorothea, 29, *30*, *31*, 32, *34*, *35*, 49
La Raza, 108–109, 118
La Raza Unida Party, 128, 161
Larkin, Terry, 148, 149, 150
Latinas/os, 213, 215, 216–217, 219, 220–221. *See also* Chicana/os; Mexican Americans; Mexicans, ethnic
Lau v. Nichols, 199
law enforcement. *See* policing
League for Innovation in the Community College, 119, 120
Lewis, Gaylen, 112, 248n40
libraries, 94, 133–134
Lincoln School, 21, 43, 44, 181, 182–183, 199, 201, 205
Loader, Clifford F., 78, 82
Los Angeles (CA), 33, 39, 53, 55, 57, 64, 133, 135–136
Los Folkloristas, 118–119
Love-Holloway, Ruth B., 133–134
Lowe, Ernest, 235n82
LULAC, 112, 248n40
Luna, Diego, 214
Luna v. County of Kern, 26
Lux, Charles, 4, 19
lynching, 27, 34

MacLean, Nancy, 12
magnet programs, 180, 207–211, 221
MALDEF. *See* Mexican American Legal Defense and Educational Fund
Martinez, Lupe, 192
Mathias, Bob, 76, 90, 93
McCarthy, Kevin, 144, 214, 215
McClanahan, Brent, 37–38
McClanahan, Christina, 37, 38, 43
McDaniel, Ivan G., 79
McGraw-Hill media concessions, 155, 157, 158, 159–160, 161–163, 164–168, 175, 176
McKinley School, 43, 181, 188
McWilliams, Carey, 29, 69, 229n17
MEChA, 109–110, *111*, 113, *121*
media reform. *See* fair media movement
methamphetamine, 218, 267n22
Mexican American Legal Defense and

Educational Fund (MALDEF): and fair media movement, 156, 160, 162, 166, 167; and racial gerrymandering, 26, 216–217; and school segregation, 191–197
Mexican American Political Association (MAPA), 72, 83, 110, 183, 186
Mexican Americans: and antipoverty movement, 68, 69, 71, 72–74, 83, 92, 93, 97; and Black-Brown unity, 8, 47, 48, 50, 57–58, 126, 133, 134; and term Chicano, 198, 227n6, 263n95; and CSO, 8, 52–55, 72–73; and election of Ray Gonzales, 127, 130, 135, 137; and fair media movement, 155, 156–157, 160, 161, 166, 168; and health care, 168–169, 170, 171, 174; and multiracial coalitions, 2, 8, 47, 48, 55, 57–58, 124; and NFWA poverty grant, 76, 78, 82, 83, 84–85, 89; and school segregation, 180, 181, 186, 190, 191–195, 198, 204, 211; and tensions with African American activists, 99, 142, 169, 170, 174, 182; and White Citizens' Council, 61, 62, 63, 64. *See also* Chicana/os; Mexicans, ethnic
Mexican Revolution, 24, 30, 42
Mexicans, ethnic: and 1930s strikes, *30*, 30–31; and housing segregation, 16, 29, 39, 40, 41, 49; and La Raza, 108–109; as racialized labor force, 19, 24, 28, 37, 38; and settlement in greater Bakersfield, 18–25, 38, 40, 42–43, 68, 232n3; and white supremacy, 27, 42, 234n51. *See also* Chicana/os; Mexican Americans
migration, 1–2, 4, 15, 16, 19–20, 28, 37, 70
military service, 104, 106, 107, 109, 160
Miller Lux Company, 4, 19, 37
Miller, Henry, 4, 19
ministerial alliances, 50, 51, 68
minority advisory councils (MACs), 167–168
Minority Coalition of Kern County, 117–118
Mitchell, John, 133, 134
Molina, Natalia, 17

Mondale, Walter, 171
Moore, Earl K., 158, 162, 163, 175
Moorpark College, 110, 112
Mosley, Robert, 174
Moss, Randolph D., 208
Mount Vernon School, 181, 190, 193, 199
multiracial coalitions: and antipoverty movement, 49–50, 68, 71, 72; and election of Ray Gonzales, 124, 127, 130, 134–135, 142, 143–144; and fair employment, 55–56; and fair media, 160, 161, 164, 166, 167; and farmworker movement, 3–4, 6–7, 126, 213; legacy of, 218, 221; and local government collaboration, 48, 55–56, 57–59, 63–64, 65; and school desegregation, 180, 186–187, 188; and strikes of 1930s, 28, 29–30, *30*; and urban civil rights movements, 2–3, 9, 10, 47–49; and White Citizens' Council, 61–64. *See also specific movements*

NAACP: Allensworth branch of, 35; and antipoverty movement, 68, 72, 93, 96, 97; and discriminatory signs, 45, 51; and fair employment, 55; and fair housing movement, 182; and fair media movement, 158; and farmworker living conditions, 49–50; and farmworker movement, 6, 8, 126, 231n40; and health care, 174; and local government collaboration, 58–59; and multiracial coalitions, 47, 59; and police brutality, 147, 150, 151, 152, 153–154; and school desegregation movement, 181–183, 185, 186, 188, 189, 190, 191, 200–201, 205; and youth recreation programs, 148–149
Nash, Linda, 17, 227n7
National Council of Negro Women, 72
National Farm Labor Union (NFLU), 5–6, 49
National Farm Workers Association (NFWA), 8, 59, 60, 69, 75, 76–90, 227n2. *See also* United Farm Workers
National Labor Relations Act (NLRA), 135, 137, 139
National League of Cities, 124–125

National Mexican-American Anti-Defamation Committee (NMAADC), 156, 160, 162, 164, 166
National Organization for Women, 167
National Urban League, 8
Nation of Islam, 62
Native Americans, 1, 17, 19, 108, 232n5, 247n20
Nava, Jesus Cruz (J. C.), 24
Nava, Julian, 119, 120, 121
Newsom, Gavin, 217
NFWA. *See* National Farm Workers Association
Nichols-Allen, Roberta, 37
Nichols-Brothers, Susie Bell, 36–37
Nieto, Jesus "Jess" Gilberto, 103, 104–108, 109, 110–118, *116*, 119–122, *120*, 249n65
Nixon, Richard, 131, 175–176, 248n47
Noriega, Al, 119, *120*
Noticias de la Raza, 114
Nunez, Max, 23

Oakland (CA), 33, 34, 55, 64, 153
Obama, Barack, 216
Obledo, Mario, 156, 168
O'Brien, Conan, 228n13
Office for Civil Rights (OCR), 189–190, 198–199
Office of Economic Opportunity (OEO): and antipoverty movement, 70, 73, 74, 93, 96, 97–98; and health care, 174; and NFWA grant, 71, 76–77, 78–80, 81, 85, 87, 88, 89–90
Ohanian, John, 202, 204–207, 209
oil industry, 26, 27
Oildale (Kern County, CA), 26, 40, 51, 205
Okies: conservative legacy of, 1–2, 4, 220; and horticulturalist ideology, 5; and migration to Bakersfield, 32, 40, 50, 73, 75; and multiracial coalitions, 49; and white supremacy, 26, 42, 43
Oropeza, Lorena, 101–102, 160
Oro Vista Housing Project, 52
Owens, Buck, 1, 228n14
Owens, Geraldine, 182–183
Owens School, 199

Park, Bill, 63, 93, 95
Parker, Everett, 157–158
Parker, Johnie Mae, 33, 70
Pasadena (CA), 34, 57
Pavich, Stephen, 84
Pawel, Miriam, 7, 75, 135, 230nn31–32
pensions, 8, 54–55
Pérez Ponce, Jorge, 115, 118
Phillips, William G., 87, 88
Pittman, Tarea Hall, 27, 58
Plessy v. Ferguson, 42
policing: and farmworker movement, 81, 91, 243n31; and harassment, 42, 116–118, 149–150; and racial brutality, 124, 147–148, 149–153, 175
poverty, 21, 49–50, 68, 69–71, 221. *See also* antipoverty movement
Powell, Adam Clayton, 85–86
Powers, Robert, 149–150
Powers, Steve, 149, 150, 153
Prasad, Anand, 71, 94, 95, 98
Price, Juanita, 41–42
Project MEChICA, 115–116
Proposition 14, 59, 60, 182
Proposition 21, 194
Proposition 22, 135
Pruett, Donald, 195–196

Quevado, Eduardo, 83

racism, 26–28, 37–38, 40–45, 56–57
radio, 109, 112, 157, 159–160, 163–164, 165, 166, 217
railroads, 2, 20–21, *23*, 24, 36, 41, 42
Ramos, Irene, 38
Reagan, Ronald, 67, 88, 98, 121, 209, 256n54
recreation programs, 148–149, 153
Republican Party: and agribusiness, 4, 133, 214–215; and antipoverty opposition, 69, 73, 75–76, 91, 93, 94, 97, 99; and ethnic Mexican constituents, 23, 218; and Ray Gonzales campaigns, 124, 127–128, 129–130, 131, 135, 140–143
Resolution 47–63, 57, 58, 63, 64
Reyes, Domingo "Nick," 156, 157, 164
Rivera, Debbie, *121*

Rivera, Willie, 215
Rodriguez, Alicia E., 27
Roland, Howard, 92, 93, 95
Romero, Ignacia "Nancy," 25, 234n48
Rosales, Arturo, 21–22, *23*, 25
Rosales, Donald, 22, 25
Rosales, Hermenegildo, 22
Rose, Margaret, 6
Rosen, Sanford, 48, 50–51
Ross, Fred, 8, 32, 53
Rubin, Mel, 1, 136–137
Rucker, Del, 62–63, 152
Rumford Fair Housing Act, 59, 60, 182

Salas, Rudy, 215, 217
Salazar, Ruben, 157
San Diego (CA), 34, 155, 160, 161–162, 165, 187
San Francisco (CA), 19, 38–39, 200, 201–202, 203
sanitation, public, 15, 33, 37, 49–50, 92
San Joaquin Valley (CA): African American settlement in, 33–38; ethnic Mexican settlement in, 18–25; expansion of railroads into, 20–21; importance of Bakersfield in, 232n3; Klan presence in, 26–28; and methamphetamine, 218, 267n22; and racialized labor force, 19–20, 28–32; and political conservatism, 1–2, 4–5, 67, 217–218; poverty in, 49–50, 71, 87; residential segregation in, 16, 28–29, 40–41, 43–44; white settlement in, 16–17, 26
school desegregation movement, 8, 179–211
schools. *See* education
segregation: and antipoverty movement, 64, 67, 68, 73, 74, 88; and Chicana/o movement, 103, 111; and farm labor, 28–30, 49; and multiracial coalitions, 2–3, 8, 45, 47, 50–52, 64; present-day, 221; public school, 39, 42–44, 62, 179–211; and racial covenants, 38–39, 59, 181, 200, 204; residential, 16, 33–42, 50–52, 56–57, 59, 219, 228n10, 233n15; and white southern migrants, 17, 26, 28

Selma (AL), 51, 60
Semana de la Raza, 113, 114, 130–131
Shafter (CA), *30*, *31*, 43, 232n3
Shaw, Art: and antipoverty movement, 72, 93, 94, 95, 96, 97, 98–99; and BPD, 153; and KCCU, 59; and White Citizens' Council, 62
Shaw, Marguerite, 188–189
Shell, Mary K., 138, 144
Shriver, Robert Sargent, 77, 78, 79–80, 83, 84, 89
Singleton, Benjamin "Pap," 34
Singleton, Joshua, 34
Siplin, Charles, 153, 159, 165, 166
Smith, Wallace, 20
Soldatenko, Michael, 102–103
Solomon, Gabriel, 58, 134, 165
sources and methods, 8–9
Southern California, 34, 38, 57, 135–136, 218, 228n7
Southern Christian Leadership Conference (SCLC), 8, 231n40
southern migrants, 26–28, 33, 34, 41–42, 213–214, 251n27
Southern Pacific Railroad, 20, 21, 22, *23*, 41
Stacey, Kent, 130, 131
Stanford University, 39, 106, 162
State Attorney General (SAG) office, California, 185–186, 187, 188, 189, 191, 195
State Board of Education, California, 183, 184, 185, 205
Steinbeck, John, 29, 32
Stevens, G. E., 58–59
Stewart, Jimmy, 151
Stiern, Richard, 62, 91, 92, 96, 131, 152, 153–154
Stiern, Walter, 1, 91, 142
strikes, 6, 28, 30–32, *30*, 49, 139. *See also* Delano grape strike/boycott
Strong, Vernon, 15, 40
Student Nonviolent Coordinating Committee (SNCC), 8, 60, 61, 64, 86, 87
sundown towns, 41, 51
Sunset-Mayflower tract, 15–16, 33, *34*, 50, 52, 72, 73–74

Taft (Kern County, CA), 26–27, 41, 51, 129
Tallman, John, 95, 97–98
Target Area Poverty (TAP), 71–73, 87, 94, 95, 96–98, 99, 181, 242n17
tax reform, 132–133
Taylor, William, 209
Teamsters, International Brotherhood of, 109, 136, 139, 231n40
television, 155, 157, 158, 160–161, 162–163, 166, 167, 168
Thomas, Bill, 124, 140–143, 144
Tintle, Ray, 117
Title I (Elementary and Secondary Education Act of 1965), 190, 191–193
Title VI (Civil Rights Act of 1964), 189, 191, 198, 199, 205, 208
Title VII (Civil Rights Act of 1964), 190, 193
Tomlin, Harold, 189, 201
Torres, Art, 137
traqueros, 20, 22
Triplett, Josephine, 35–36
Tulare (Tulare County, CA), 18, 28, 31, 36, 204
Tulare County (CA), 31, 36, 71, 76, 81, 85, 232n3

UFW. *See* United Farm Workers
Union Avenue (Bakersfield), 15, 20, 40
unions, labor: and anti-immigrant politics, 53–54, 139, 217; and antipoverty movement, 75, 79; and boycotts, 109–110, 135, 136–137; and early farmworker organizing, 28, 29–32, *30*, 49; grower antipathy toward, 4, 5–6; and health care, 176–177. *See also* United Farm Workers
United Auto Workers, 139
United Cannery, Agricultural, Packing, and Allied Workers of America (UCAPAWA), *30*, 32
United Church of Christ (UCC), 155, 157–159, 162, 165, 176
United Farm Workers (UFW): African American support for, 126, 231n40; and fair media movement, 163–164; and farm labor legislation, 135–140, 143, 144; and gender, 6, 7; and grape strike/boycott, 101, 107, 113, 124–126; and health care, 169, 170–171, 176–177, 258n103; legacy of, 1, 3–4, 5–8, 9, 166n19, 214, 215–216, 218; and lettuce boycott, 109, 110, 111; and multiracial coalitions, 3, 6, 7, 8, 30, 32; and Jess Nieto, 116, 116, 119; origins of, 227n2; and Miriam Pawel's work, 7, 230nn31–32; and undocumented workers, 54, 217. *See also* National Farm Workers Association
United Food and Commercial Workers Union (UFCW), 1
United Mexican Students (UMS), 106, 108
Universal Negro Improvement Association (UNIA), 35
University of California (UC), 104
Uranday, Esther, 176–177
urban civil rights movements: and farmworker movement, 3, 9, 102, 124, 213, 220; legacy of, 2–3, 14, 213–214, 219, 221; and multiracial coalitions, 2, 10–11, 48, 59, 65, 213. *See also specific movements*

vaqueros, 19–20
Vargas, Zaragosa, 24, 56
Vaught, David, 5, 229n17, 229n19
Vietnam War, 74, 103, 106, 109, 129, 131, 157
Vigil, Pete, 175
violence, racial, 18, 26–27, 27, 41–42, 74, 110, 149, 151–152
Visalia (Tulare County, CA), 28, 214
voter registration, 5, 53, 80, 87, 129, 131
Voting Rights Act of 1965, 216–217

Wade, Dan, 152
War on Poverty: conservative opposition to, 64, 74–75, 91–99, 170, 220, 257n100; and Economic Opportunity Act, 70, 90–91; limits of, 241n5; and multiracial coalitions, 2, 59, 65, 68; and NFWA grant, 69, 76, 82, 87, 88–89;

and recreation programs, 148–149, 153; and tensions within coalitions, 174, 220
Warren, Earl, 55, 219
Wasco (Kern County, CA), 29, 33, 44, 172, 232n3
Wattron, Frank, 111, 113
Webb, Vance A., 83–84
Weber, Devra, 28, 30, 125, 235n72
Weedpatch (Kern County, CA), 49, 172
Wellock, Thomas R., 2, 4, 69
White Citizens' Council, 61–64, 73, 159, 187
white liberals: and antipoverty movement, 68, 71; and election of Ray Gonzales, 124, 127, 129–130, 135; and ethnic power movements, 65; and fair media movement, 161, 164; and farmworker movement, 7, 30; and multiracial coalitions, 2, 47, 48, 50–51, 61, 102, 219; and police reform, 148, 150, 175
white migrants, 1–2, 15, 16–17, 26–28, 38–39, 41–42
Whittemore, Bob, 130
Wilkins, Roy, 231n40
Williams, Franklin, 6, 49–50
Williams, Robert, 37
Williamson Act of 1965, 132–133
Willis, Stanley E., 88
women, 6, 35, 130, 161, 167, 236n94
World War II, 2, 75, 104, 135